# The Irish Novel
## 1800–1910

# The Irish Novel

## 1800–1910

GEORGE O'BRIEN

CORK UNIVERSITY PRESS

First published in 2015 by
Cork University Press
Youngline Industrial Estate
Pouladuff Road, Togher
Cork, Ireland T12 HT6V

**British Library Cataloguing in Publication Data**
A CIP catalogue record for this book is available from the British Library.


ISBN-978-1-78205-125-1

Printed in Malta by Gutenberg Press
Typeset by Tower Books, Ballincollig, Co. Cork
www.corkuniversitypress.com

# Contents

# Acknowledgements

My interest in the nineteenth-century Irish novel was originally stimulated more years ago than I care to remember, when I was a PhD candidate at the University of Warwick. A long-overdue debt of thanks is owed to my supervisors at that time, Mr Ioan Williams and Professor Michael Bell, for their forbearance, encouragement and friendship.

Grateful thanks to Jonathan Williams for once again providing crucial advice and assistance.

Mr Brian P. Burns generously and genially gave permission to reproduce the cover image. Many thanks to him and to Dr Gregory W. Gromadzki, curator of the remarkable Brian P. Burns Collection. Thanks also, in this regard, to John McCourt of the McMullen Museum of Art, Boston College, for his prompt and courteous help.

My friends John Evans, Eamon Grennan, Vincent Hurley, Margaret Kelleher, Máire Kennedy, Tim Meagher, Denis Sampson and Terry Winch were again on hand with support, interest and good cheer. Very many thanks to them all.

Special thanks to my colleague and neighbour Professor Patricia O'Connor, who in her many acts of kindness was a friend indeed.

The staff and resources of the Joseph Mark Lauinger Memorial Library at Georgetown University helped smooth the scholarly path.

And to all at Cork University Press – thank you.

By no means least, to my family – Pam, Ben and Nick – love and thanks for everything, as ever.

# Introduction

As a means of highlighting and assessing the main themes and narrative strategies of the Irish novel in the nineteenth century, this book examines thirty representative titles ranging from Maria Edgeworth's *Castle Rackrent* (1800) to W.P. Ryan's *The Plough and the Cross* (1910). Both the choice of texts and nature of the critical discussion reflect the rise in interest in the novel in nineteenth-century Ireland that began to gather momentum among scholars and critics in Ireland and elsewhere in the closing decades of the twentieth century and has, since then, continued apace. Critical engagement with the full complement of conceptual and aesthetic challenges presented by the nineteenth-century Irish novel has produced a more comprehensive sense of the canon of the form,[1] resulting in a more diversified awareness of thematic concerns, artistic challenges and formal properties. This work of rediscovery and revaluation has also produced much more sophisticated analyses of the novel's significance to literary and cultural history, its standing as a commodity in a burgeoning literary marketplace, its critical reception, its sociological significance in relation to such matters as nineteenth-century readership and tastes, and its role in the development of the institutions of authorship and publishing.[2]

An important outcome of such inquiry is that the considerable body of literature constituting the nineteenth-century Irish novel no longer just 'takes on significance chiefly as a remaking of Irish life, which, by virtue of such artistic qualities as it possesses, does what history proper can hardly do – creates the illusion of the life of the past'.[3] On the contrary, the relation between literature and history, and between imaginative constructs and factual data, in nineteenth-century Ireland has come to be seen as a much more complicated nexus of effects and projections (indeed, in the discussions that follow, the novel suggests itself as an alternative or counter to historical actuality). 'There can scarcely be anything more lost than the Irish novel in the nineteenth century'[4] is now far from being the case, and the hopes for the form's rehabilitation with which that statement opened have in many ways been met. The significance of this extensive reclamation for

Irish literary history and culture remains to be determined, but, in view of the nineteenth-century novel's fate at the hands of earlier generations of Irish critics, this renewal of interest represents changes in the conception and critique of Irish literature.

The scope of attempts to silence and erase, and the degree of cultural estrangement that it conveys, is all the more noteworthy in view of the novel's pre-eminence in nineteenth-century Ireland.[5] Notwithstanding the influence and appeal of Thomas Moore's *Irish Melodies*, the visionary aura of James Clarence Mangan's poems, the ambition of Sir Samuel Ferguson's antiquarian verse sagas and the popularity of Dion Boucicault's melodramas – to name only some of the best-known accomplishments of nineteenth-century Irish writing – the novel was the expressive outlet to which Irish authors typically resorted. Maria Edgeworth's oft-quoted 1834 view that '[i]t is impossible to draw Ireland as she now is in a book of fiction . . . . The people would only break the glass, and curse the fool who held the mirror up to nature – distorted nature in a fever',[6] for all its revealing language, does not seem to have markedly diminished the production of novels on Irish themes by Irish authors. And though there may have been times when, as Anthony Trollope reports, Irish novels became 'a drug on the market',[7] whatever the resultant falling off, it did not affect the launch of his own career with three novels set in Ireland – even if he later regarded those works in a poor light.[8]

The slump that the Irish novel underwent came at the end of the nineteenth century, and was cultural as well as critical in character, occasioned in large degree by the revision of ideas of literary and cultural value created by the lyric turn of the Irish Literary Revival.[9] But the novel did not quite disappear from the cultural landscape being mapped out by Revivalists. W.B. Yeats, in his commitment to constructing a national literature, wished to fold fiction into his vision and to associate his own emerging aesthetic views and cultural politics with novelistic father figures, claiming that 'it was from the novelists and the poets that I learned in part my symbols of expression'.[10] Yeats's enterprise in helping to restore the work and name of William Carleton is undoubtedly noteworthy,[11] and his enthusiasm for the 'square built power'[12] of Carleton and John Banim was certainly genuine. Taken as a whole, however, Yeats' response to the Irish novel was fitful, particularly with regard to works of his own day.[13] As to James Joyce, his interest in his Irish novelistic predecessors was almost non-existent.

His request for 'any old editions of Kickham, Griffin, Carleton, H.J. Smyth &c, Banim'[14] produced no discernible effect on his artistic development. (The only nineteenth-century novelist who features to any degree in his work is Joseph Sheridan Le Fanu,[15] although Joyce's critical sense of George Moore as an avatar should also be noted.)

Beginning in the mid-1920s, and partly in reaction to Yeats, the criteria for national literature, and national cultural well-being generally, became more ideologically combative. This *Kulturkampf* held that the nineteenth-century novel was basically worthless, a repository of unacceptable depictions of Irish people and representations of Irish realities made in bad faith.[16] And though these views met with opposition, their widespread acceptance may be inferred from the virtual exile imposed on Maria Edgeworth for lacking the required ideological posture: 'as for entering into the national aspirations of Ireland, or realising that Ireland had a significant history of its own out of which a new history should develop, she would have been incapable of such flights'.[17] The critical consensus of the post-Revival period seems to have been that 'Irish prose literature has hardly yet as much as begun'.[18] Nationalist exceptionalism, whether that of the enthusiastic young Yeats or the defensive Daniel Corkery, left the nineteenth-century Irish novel to mark time in the outer reaches of literary history, more a bibliographical than an imaginative phenomenon.[19] Critical silence (preliminary as the foregoing sketch of it is) effectively removed the basis or the need to explore or explain what Irish nineteenth-century novelists were attempting to express and how they were trying to do so. As a result, these works were not only excluded from the complexity of the Irish literary tradition, but a sense of their connections to the novel in its English and European contexts was also denied.

Yet, to allocate the nineteenth-century Irish novel a place in literary tradition, however configured, is also to realise how distinctive – as well as, in ways that are important to understand, reactionary and belated – the form is. Such a realisation is all the more striking given the novel's auspicious nineteenth-century debut in 'the triumphs of Miss Edgeworth'.[20] The innovations of Sir Walter Scott – 'the broad delineation of manners and circumstances attendant upon events, the dramatic character of action and, in close connexion with this, the new and important role of dialogue in the novel'[21] – were to a significant extent developed from what he found in Edgeworth. And these effects are also eminently evident in Edgeworth's Irish successors. Yet similar resources do not produce similar narrative consequences, not even in John Gamble's *Charlton* (1823) and John Banim's *The Boyne Water* (1826), both historical novels.[22] Scott's novels depict a world that has been made. These are not merely stories with successful outcomes but testaments to order and legitimacy. And while the resources in question lend Scott's works a certain glamour and picturesqueness, they also assist in understanding how and what had been attained and established.

In the nineteenth-century Irish novel, however, the tasks of securing, stabilising and delimiting norms is constantly in jeopardy. The material on which the novelist draws seems intractable and recalcitrant, and there is an insistent uncertainty regarding the remedial processes that might make something less inchoate from it. Such reassurances of inheritance, possession and tenure are not readily available, as though the land itself is somehow elusive or unbiddable, characteristics that manifest themselves in eviction, mass emigration and famine. Manners often overcompensate for other deficiencies and uncertainties, so that they become occasions of burlesque rather than signs of confidence and *savoir faire*. Action is difficult to initiate and sustain; the threat of undoing seems greater than the promise of doing. Speech is typically reproduced with its sound rather than its dramatic or narrative import in mind. In a word, a comprehensive sense of exigency and disproportion prevails, as though the subject matter can be seen only in problematic terms, and the end in view is less comprehension or demonstrable progress than safety and relief. Particularly in works published before the onset of the Home Rule movement in the 1870s, history seems a manifestation of unmaking which the leading characters are obliged to witness but which it is difficult for them to handle. The desire for a remedy is keenly felt; the material, social and political wherewithal necessary to reverse the unmaking are not as readily to hand as the consciousness of being in difficulty. And although such security-seeking narratives become less typical of novels appearing towards the end of the century, the extent to which this is the case is limited. In these later works, new configurations of problematically regarded materials, and of responses to them, reproduce already established patterns of experience and sublimation. Identifying this pattern helps to form a sense of continuing concern and discursive response within the nineteenth-century Irish novel. The sense suggested below is not at all intended to be exhaustive, but its recurrence across genres, periods and authorial perspectives does suggest that at least it is possible to construct one account of the novel in Ireland between 1800 and 1910 that is less disparate than the contents of the novels themselves.

## A Mingled Yarn

Conditions that are 'at variance' (Le Fanu, *The House by the Churchyard* (1863), p. 258)[23] or that embody 'the general contrariety of things' (Somerville and Ross, *The Real Charlotte* (1894), p. 271) constitute the problematic, and these are pervasive throughout the nineteenth-century Irish novel. They are to be seen in the ruins that bedeck its landscapes as well as in less arresting but more insidious evocations of the past; they are to be found in the inadequacies of institutional life and the disproportionate character of the Big House's reputation and the peasant cottage's poverty. 'From the start . . . the Union was an unstable and incomplete moment',[24] and this state is reflected not only in the national tale itself, but in all the nineteenth-century Irish novel's genres, from the 'Irish Anglican response to historical conditions'[25] to the flirtations with social incoherence of William Hamilton Maxwell's and Charles Lever's military novels, and including 'the Irish land novel . . . the political novel and Fenian novel'.[26] It is because of how they characterise, articulate and confront their acknowledgement of the problematic dimension – how they paradoxically impart form to the experiences of uncertainty and the imminence of undoing – that the novels selected for discussion in *The Irish Novel 1800–1910* may be regarded as representative. And while each novel has its own conception of troubling subject matter, it can also be seen that these conceptions echo, reflect, contrast and are otherwise in dialogue with each other, suggesting as they do so the type of discursive intertwining that constitutes a literary tradition.

Something of these interconnections may be demonstrated by noting points of both thematic contact and points of contrast between paired texts. Problems of economic inheritance in *Castle Rackrent*, for instance, throw a light on difficulties of family heritage in Lady Morgan's *The O'Briens and O'Flahertys* (1827); situating contemporary concerns within scenarios depicting a socially and historically conflicted past preoccupy *The Boyne Water* and Gerald Griffin's *The Collegians* (1829); the fissures in Lever's well-lit social scenes find their psychological opposites in Sheridan Le Fanu's penumbral interiors;

W.P. Ryan's heterodox *The Plough and the Cross* challenges the ortho-doxy of Canon Sheehan's *Luke Delmege* (1901); the primitive feminine that is unhappily larger than typical Inishmaan life in Emily Lawless's *Grania* (1892) reappears as a modern disturbance in the Catholic bour-geois Waterford of Katherine Cecil Thurston's *The Fly on the Wheel* (1908); difficulties arising from the emerging demands of independ-ence and individuality enable Charlotte Riddell's *A Struggle for Fame* (1883) to be read as a critique of the eponymous careerist of May Laffan Hartley's *Hogan, M.P.* (1876). Whatever its social contexts and personal occasions, the present – its aggravations, contrivances, incompleteness and insecurities – remains socially friable, emotionally isolating and morally exacting.

The challenge of writing about the present is not confined to the Irish novel, but is generally applicable. 'The domain appropriate to the novelist is the history of remoter periods', claims a reviewer of *Charlton*;[27] and the sense of the problematic extends beyond the works of Irish novelists into those of English novelists writing about Ireland. The inclusion here of novels by Harriet Martineau, W.M. Thackeray and Anthony Trollope helps to refine distinctions between English and Irish fictional perspectives on interests common to both. Concepts of race, gender and class are in some senses shared by English and Irish novelists, but in other senses are at odds. The moral landscape may be Christian, but that does not entail a uniform application of Christian values. (Martineau, in particular, seems to have a merely perfunctory interest in values in this sense.) And while Irish novelists tend to be immersed in manifestations of the problematic, the three English nov-elists' emphasis is on solutions, with Thackeray and Trollope, especially, invoking the law as the instrument of regulation and appeasement.[28] In *Castle Richmond* (1860), the law is effectively the word of the father, and the dependence of the child on it is explicit. But typically characters – sons, especially – wish to be grown-up, as recurring attestations to manliness indicate; and, unlike its English counterpart, the Irish novel does not feature dependent children, as though to ensure that it is not on those without power or choices that it wishes to focus but on those who – though quite capable and responsible – must contend with the problematical restriction of their capacities and entitlements.

The outlook of these English novelists stands in direct contrast to that of works by Irish writers usually thought of as contributors to the

English literary canon. Rather than endorsing paternalism, such authors as George Moore, George Bernard Shaw and Oscar Wilde repudiate it. If Trollope is arguably the *echt* Victorian novelist, *A Mummer's Wife* (1885), *An Unsocial Socialist* (1887) and *The Picture of Dorian Gray* (1891) venture beyond Victorian limits into the free speech of disclosure, provocation and unmasking, particularly with respect to their exploration of differences, tensions and potential for change within such socially well-disciplined spheres as gender and class.[29] Moreover, the possibility that London's culture, society and manners are sources of problematic experience that Moore, Shaw and Wilde indicate is also present, though from different standpoints, in both Bram Stoker's *Dracula* (1897) and Riddell's *A Struggle for Fame*. The latter work is notable as an early, if largely rudimentary, instance of the critique of metropolitan systems and assumptions that its author's more illustrious successors were to develop,[30] while *Dracula*'s sensational scenario depends on the idea that the imperial capital is susceptible to corruption and breakdown. Clearly, aesthetic and ideological interests of the day shaped the sense of alternatives that *A Mummer's Wife*, *An Unsocial Socialist* and *The Picture of Dorian Gray* pursue, and in this they are related to shifts in emphasis in the turn-of-the-century novel generally. Yet the zest of their pursuit, and the subversive lengths to which it carries their narratives, their relocation of the site of problematic challenges and their typically satirical presuppositions regarding the English national character link them with such concerns in earlier nineteenth-century Irish novels as the grounds of identity, the constituents of social legitimacy, and the conception of a life of purpose. In earlier works, those matters are negotiated under the looming threats of dislocation and disunion. After 1870 or thereabouts, such threats tend to be much more freely acknowledged and articulated. Thus, the group of works discussed in *The Irish Novel 1800–1910* can be regarded as consisting of two phases – for descriptive and broadly contextual purposes, the O'Connell and the Parnell phases – that are in certain fundamental respects connected and in other significant respects remote from each other.[31] Even in relation to each other, the texts carry implications of both union and disunion, an expression of the duality that typifies their narrative structures' grasp of problematic materials.

Its publication date and that date's larger historical context establish *Castle Rackrent*'s 'foundational'[32] status *vis-à-vis* the nineteenth-century

Irish novel, but that status is not merely a matter of historical coincidence, nor indeed is it indebted to the encomia of Sir Walter Scott (with respect to the latter, '[c]ontrary to general modern opinion, it was not *Castle Rackrent* that prompted *Waverley*, but *The Absentee*')[33]. Nor is its significance limited to its inauguration of the Big House subgenre, even if it does contain 'the central characteristics of a literary tradition that survives to this day'.[34] Just as significantly, its use of voice, the editorial materials that both frame and provide interpretative assistance for what the voice conveys, and its comparative temporality (by which a previous period is used to illuminate a present issue) crop up in various ways throughout the works that follow. These range from Thomas Moore's 'pseudo-novel of agrarian rebellion'[35] to the tone of *The Real Charlotte*. The claim that *Castle Rackrent* is 'a transcript direct from life, unaltered in the telling, unshackled by any theory, unhampered by moralising',[36] may say more about its author's critical standards than about Edgeworth's novel, but it is a typical statement of the work's exemplary standing.

As *Castle Rackrent* in effect states, the year 1800 marks the end of an era. The same may be said of the year 1910, even if in literary terms evidence of terminus is less clearly delineated. Nevertheless, the intensification of parliamentary and extra-parliamentary political activity in the years immediately following the reign of Edward VII makes the year of his death not quite as arbitrary a cut-off point as it might initially appear. The year not only sees the end of the Edwardian period but is also a vantage-point from which to view the withering away of the Victorian frame of mind. This cultural change is not only relevant in an Irish context. Virginia Woolf's noted remark that 'on or about 1910 human character changed',[37] speculative though it is, acknowledges the sense of a turning point – a turning towards the modern – in the post-Edwardian period (a change that Irish novelists anticipated and helped to consolidate). As such, 1910 resembles 1800, but within an Irish context this resemblance is also just one face of a duality, since both years are also significant for historically opposite reasons. In 1800 the Act of Union was passed, whereas 1910 presages a period when major modifications of the Union seemed ever more likely with the anticipated passage of Home Rule legislation. The fact that these two dawns proved false further complicates both years' significance. What both years anticipated did not turn out to be the case. The dream of parity inspired by the integrative implications of Union did not materialise, and the succession of challenges throughout the century to its political and administrative implementation – mainly under the leadership of Daniel O'Connell, but also including Rockite disturbances, the tithe war, the Great Famine and others, land clearance, the Land War, the Home Rule movement – lent the constitutional arrangement the dual character of being a fact and a failure (or counterfactual). This duality is also a salient aspect of Irish nineteenth-century novelists' subject matter, imaginative awareness and strength of authorial purpose.

By 1910, the cultural temper, social anxieties and political tensions commonly associated with the modern era had been set in place. Extending the nineteenth century by ten years facilitates an outline of Irish novelists' engagement with these developments. On the one hand, the sense of disturbance and breakdown expressed in various ways by George Moore's naturalism, George Bernard Shaw's socialism and Oscar Wilde's aestheticism is echoed, though typically not in their essentially metropolitan terms (an exception is the critique of gender roles that Katherine Cecil Thurston's *The Fly on the Wheel* shares with *An Unsocial Socialist*). On the other hand, there is a marked inclination to see the modern as a hostile incursion, a contaminator of moral and spiritual values, and a propagator of the materialism that realism draws on and attempts to account for. Furthermore, this reaction effectively rejects those Irish novelists who shocked London, as though no common cause exists between their works and those of authors writing in Ireland. Nothing seems to have been learned from the possibility that the overlordship assumed by Lord Henry Wootton in relationship to Dorian Gray is a form of psychological landlordism, or that Count Dracula's dark deeds may be shades of Fenianism's invasive, alarming presence – although the connection between Fenianism and nocturnal, clandestine blood-letting is fundamental to the plot of Rosa Mulholland's *Marcella Grace* (1886).[38]

Instead, a strong sense emerges that a modern point of view is a threat to typical Irish ways and outlooks, a sense that in its implicit defence of tradition at all costs seems to make what is being defended both in need of great care and attention and also exceptional; and there is the additional implication that the protective role is in the authors' keeping, if not uniquely, then significantly so. The character of this reaction may seem to convey the contemporary zeal of cultural nationalism, but this is not necessarily so. In Shan F. Bullock's *Dan the Dollar* (1905), pastoral continuity, impoverished though it is, finds value in withstanding the eponymous protagonist's American-sourced wealth, the potential impact of which is more insidious than that of a supposed 'financial speculator'.[39] Cultural tradition in the forms of music and legend features in the rural County Fermanagh life of the novel, but it is at best merely a minor colourful accessory to a generally unprepossessing and unchangeable way of life. And while Canon Sheehan's *Luke Delmege* invokes a different conception of pastoral, it too is concerned with the damage to intellectual and spiritual well-being that may be caused by his young priest protagonist's exposure to clerical modernism. (Even though this manifestation of modernising has a strictly Catholic focus, it may also be taken as an unwelcome sign of the hastiness and freedom of thought typical of the times, as the view of Canon Sheehan as an 'unlikely, and no doubt unconscious agent of the *Zeitgeist*'[40] implies.)

An alternative treatment to this novel's concern with ideas, consciousness, ego and spirit is provided in W.P. Ryan's *The Plough and the Cross*. Yet in this novel too, despite its severe criticism of the Catholic hierarchy, spiritual values and their bearing on cultural and communal vitality remain of primary importance, though here the theosophical basis for those values seems to argue for a compromise between tradition and modernity. At the same time, in its endorsement of intellectual and institutional rebelliousness, the novel takes the temperature of an emerging generation, and its narrative of how best to invest that generation's energy in both urban remediation and rural resettlement is yet another manifestation of the novel as a vocal interruption in complacent public discourse. Moreover, in their opposing ways, *Luke Delmege* and *The Plough and the Cross* provide a context, and have path-clearing consequences for the new generation of post-1910 Irish novelists who formed part of that intelligentsia, while the lineage of Ryan's and Sheehan's protagonists has its origins in much earlier narratives of striving and idealism. It is fitting that the culmination of the nineteenth-century Irish novel that 1910 can be said to mark is less a terminus than a pivotal point, informed by conflicts of conscience and consciousness, concerns with legitimation, and hopes of less fractured and fractious times ahead. From the perspective of these concerns, it is possible to look back as well as forward at the Irish novel, and to reflect that – despite its frequently obtuse construction, the excesses of its modes of action and characterisation, and the convolutions of process and thought that it shares with the nineteenth-century novel generally – what the form undertook was critical to the formation of Irish literary culture. 'The Irish novelist, like any writer, was quarreling with himself and with his culture'[41] throughout the nineteenth century. This is a quarrel that could only be waged, not won. Yet it is the novelist's attempts to be victorious, to subdue his subject matter to biddable ends and to show that the problematical character of his materials will not succeed in overwhelming the world that gave rise to it, that lend the nineteenth-century Irish novel its interest. From the imagination under pressure comes the hope of wholeness.

## Representation and Containment

Although grouping the works examined in *The Irish Novel 1800–1910* according to chronology or genre or viewing them comparatively reveals unexpected continuities and associations, it can also give the impression that these novels are just coincidentally related, and that they merely constitute a mingled yarn, rather than substantiate a claim for representative status. And that claim is not quite supported by these novels' collective awareness of the problematic qualities of their subject matter. It is not only the nature of the material that is important but how it is structured to produce a communicative artefact, a narrative trajectory, a particularised account of duration, and a sense of an ending that give these novels their literary significance. The manner in which they typically achieve those expressive goals is to place their protagonists in a state of crisis. In this way, the problematic conditions are not only documented, they are given unique embodiment by the principal personage designated to suffer their consequences, to fashion a fitting response to them, and to exhibit both the necessity and the possibility of reform and remediation. Doing so will restore bonds of affection, will reunite place and person and will affirm the desirability of equilibrium and union, in contrast to the imbalance and alienation of the problematic.

The protagonist – generally male, although Lever's Kate O'Hara in *Luttrell of Arran* (1865), Charlotte Riddell's Glenavy Westley in *A Struggle for Fame* and Rosa Mulholland's eponymous Marcella Grace are three noteworthy exceptions – not only embodies the sense of crisis, he also exemplifies what is required to solve it. This dual character status sees him both embroiled in conditions and at the same time distinct from them, within and above, subjected and superior. How he negotiates between these outer and inner versions of himself – that is, how he attains a firm, viable form of self-representation – is the basis of his story. Securing this attainment answers the question of how to feel at home in the world of nineteenth-century Ireland that the crisis presents. The challenge of self-representation, thus, is mediated through instabilities with respect to origin, belonging, heritage and affiliation and these are imbricated with difficulties arising from pre-scribed identities like native, heir, citizen, subject and proprietor.

Much of the action dictated by both the disintegrative experience of crisis and by the recuperative efforts it enjoins concerns the protago-nist knowing the whole story. Indeed, without a reliable grasp of the requisite knowledge and the quality of consciousness that it nurtures, it is difficult to be a protagonist, as Maturin's *Melmoth the Wanderer* (1820) elaborately makes plain. Making good discrepancies between action and consciousness, also evident to a lesser degree in *The House by the Churchyard* and *Dracula* (in both of which a protagonist is also difficult to discern), is of considerable relevance to securing the grounds necessary for convincing self-representation. An analogy may be suggested between access to information and understanding and the reclamation of bogland in William Allingham's *Laurence Bloomfield in Ireland* (1864) and Kickham's *Knocknagow* (1873), the physical prac-ticality of which serves the same objective of augmentation and completion as the recovery of missing data. Both activities have con-notations of stability, renewal and productivity, of the sense of starting over that is both a corrective and a promise to the prevailing lie of the land. These twin landscapes of deficient consciousness and impover-ished property stretch beyond the handful of works mentioned to constitute the terrain covered by the thirty chosen novels.

It is how he negotiates between these spheres which establishes the protagonist's capacity for self-representation, although while that nego-tiation is being carried out, he occupies the insecure and uncertain position of being between spheres, deprived of authority by his incom-plete awareness, as well as by his lack of material substance. This *between* position typically reflects breaks in traditional lines of legacy and succession. Such failures are often the legacy of weak, unmanned fathers – Morrogh O'Brien in Lady Morgan's *The O'Briens and the O'Flahertys*, Harry Luttrell in *Luttrell of Arran* and Mervyn Mordaunt in *The House by the Churchyard* are cases in point. The effect of these inadequate, socially and politically agnostic household figureheads is underlined by a typical absence of mothers. (Even when mothers still exist, they tend to be secondary, one-dimensional personages of the handmaiden variety.) This lack influences the supply of sentiment and sympathy available to the protagonist. A depleted patrimony and metonymical fatherland is reinforced by a missing maternal endowment and metonymical motherland. These deficiencies can also lead to an imbalance between nature and nurture, whereby the world of the father's failings weighs more heavily on the protagonist than the mother's spirit of attachment and protection (although when a strong mother appears, as in *The Collegians*, these pre-Freudian complications become even more entangled). The economy of sentiment proposed by these stress factors is one more facet of problematic conditions that the protagonist must regulate.

Gaps in the protagonist's awareness are typically due to the concealment of relevant family history or the denial of that history's implications; and the critical condition in which the protagonist's family finds itself – the uncertain bases on which its name and status now rest – provides an intimate dimension to the general sense of crisis, emphasising the extent of the rent in the fabric of affairs and structures. The disunited family brings home, as it were, the menace of disunion generally; discontinuity in inheritance divorces past from present; the weak father is unable to provide leadership. These difficulties alienate the past, trouble the present and overshadow the future. The claim that *Castle Rackrent* has 'no sense of the impending future in it'[42] may be arguable in the light of Jason Quirke's succession, but as the century goes on the sense also adds to the protagonist's state of crisis by seeming to strand him historically in an unavailing present.

Other features detailing the environments of want in which the protagonist must make his way include ruins, remote locations and the peasantry's typically wretched habitat. Ruins evoke structures that have undergone not merely architectural damage. They also connote time's ghostly historical signatures and, as such, are paradoxically proleptic hauntings of what may befall should the problematic present not receive the healing it needs. The use of ruins as meeting places for such spectral agents of subversion and discontinuity as Rockites, Ribbonmen and Fenians gives lurid force to those presentiments, and also shows how the gothic mode can infiltrate narratives that have other imaginative agendas in mind. (This generic instability affects works as disparate as *The Whiteboy* (1845), *Laurence Bloomfield in Ireland* and William O'Brien's *When We Were Boys* (1890).) The remoter the setting, the more urgent those needs appear. The west of Ireland becomes the *locus classicus* of isolation from power and authority and thereby of extreme conditions, although its strange and derelict state can be sublimated in rapturous appreciations of its spectacular scenery. Heightened reactions are common to the look of the place and to its plight. The uplifting and the downcast offset each other. Natural attractions give perspective to scenarios that are otherwise depressing breakdowns in nurture, manifested in the tenantry's pitiable condition and the feckless ways of landlords.

The challenges to the protagonist are certainly formidable – arguably, like much else in the works concerned, excessively so, but that excess is a necessary authorial calculation, designed to convey the enormity of the crisis with which the protagonist has to contend and the difficulty of containing it. This strategy, in turn, requires exceptional gifts of courage, self-possession, persistence and good faith on the protagonist's part as he proves himself fit to discharge his duty, obey his finest moral instincts and surmount the many other barriers to attaining the validity and vindication of self-representation. The values and qualities of which the protagonist is a representative, and in terms of which he represents himself, are not only themselves ennobling, restorative and indicative of a natural aristocracy – an aristocracy of the heart – they are also correctives to the contexts in which he attempts to secure his position. As such, they are in conflict with a loose but comprehensive web of false representations, the multiple sources and manifestations of which contrast with the protagonist's integrity, morality and singularity of purpose. Turbulent historical conditions, such as those in *Charlton* and *The Boyne Water*, are especially likely to waylay the protagonist on his path of righteousness by accentuating, exploiting and intensifying already-existing uncertainties and differences, and by assailing his fidelity – or even his right – to what he aspires to call his own, whether material or sentimental. In those works, historical events overdetermine and streamline the common vicissitudes of fortune, calling into question not only such inherited structures as political allegiance and religious affiliation but his conscience and his life of feeling. Steadfastness, loyalty and a capacity to endure are the targets of war's peremptoriness and unpredictability; and these characteristics of conflict are reproduced in Gamble's *Charles*

Charlton and Banim's Robert Evelyn, being continually both on the move and in danger of misrepresentation. The latter danger also surfaces in the scaled-down version of history-haunted disturbance in *Marcella Grace*. Conversely, self-representation by means of such disturbance is successfully pursued by the protagonist of *When We Were Boys*, even though the form of self-representation attained is the effacement of a jail sentence, a fate that Rosa Mulholland's novel spares no effort in redressing.[43]

Occasions of falsification are not confined, however, to epoch-making historical episodes. On the contrary, they are very much part of the fabric of any scheme of action, and may indeed be the inspiration of agency, or attempting to subvert or appropriate what, in the right hands, would constitute a properly proportioned moral ecology. As a result, crisis tends to be mediated through such offences as embezzlement, forgery, perjury, subornation of witnesses, abduction, rackrenting, conspiracy, informing and related acts that are not only illegal, which is bad enough, but are also manifestations of greed, selfishness, poor judgement, which is worse, because they are acts of moral betrayal. In all these activities, the bond that is supposedly one's word is in a state of crisis, the honour that is the gentleman's escutcheon is ineffaceably tarnished. As forms of moral violation, they threaten the equilibrium whose most potent expression is in the unity, harmony and completeness that the protagonist seeks. The 'oddly sinister'[44] air attributed to nineteenth-century Irish fiction generally derives in large part from such wrong-doing, and when added to other narrative stand-bys, such as lost letters, family secrets, clandestine rendezvous and other types of concealment, they produce a hydra-headed despoiler of moral capital that the protagonist must extirpate. 'Identity games and characters who create counterfeit identities, either playfully or with malicious intent, or out of grim necessity, are prominent in Lever's fiction',[45] and that is certainly the case, but Lever is hardly exceptional in this regard, as *The Collegians*, *The Black Prophet* (1847), *The House by the Churchyard*, *Knocknagow*, *Hogan, M.P.* and *The Real Charlotte* show by their quite varied plots' dependence on malfeasance, while at either end of this spectrum of works lie *Melmoth the Wanderer* and *Dracula*, each mirroring the other's fascination with the insidiousness of the malign.

Although these novels deploy what might be paradoxically termed the reality of falseness in different narrative tonalities – moralistic, satiric, minatory – the various deceptive practices themselves are

structurally necessary as a means of justifying the protagonist. It is possible to read the triumph over falsity that the protagonist embodies as
exemplary not only from a moral but also from a political standpoint,
an attempt perhaps to lay the ghost of the corrupt methods used to
pass the Act of Union. 'The bargain of our parliamentary Judases is, at
least, intelligible and tangible and the "thirty pieces of silver" on the
palm acquits them of being romantic in their treason' (*Memoirs of
Captain Rock* (1824), p. 192), the practices in question being one more
exhibition of false representation. Be that as it may, one of the signatures of how the protagonist righteously prevails is a union that is
untrammelled, disinterested and ideal. It is not implausible to suggest
that the roots of such a conception, imaginative though it is, lie in the
problematic bequest of certain historical events.

Falseness is necessary as a source of drama, but it also stands
opposed to the deployment of fact, which is the other fundamental
structure of the nineteenth-century Irish novel. Indeed, the malevolence of false representation resides in its distortion of the ostensibly
reliable world of surfaces that constitutes novels' elaborate expository
activity. Novelists are at great pains to represent the look of things:
details of dress, domestic interiors, physiognomies, scenery, speech
and other empirical data with sensory impact are subjects of 'thick'
description. Moreover, the anthropological overtones of such an
approach make themselves known through novelists' interest in tax-
onomies, codifications and typifications with respect to the mentalities
and practices of folklore, superstitions, festivals, legends and suchlike
materials. William Carleton's presentation of *The Black Prophet* as a
source of 'authentic information' (p. v) in the letter to Lord John
Russell, prime minister of the day, which is the novel's foreword indicates the sense of authority that accrues to an author using a
documentary method. 'The "matter of fact" resonates across the Irish
writing of the period'[46] – and beyond, as the documentary aspects of
*Knocknagow*, *Marcella Grace*, *When We Were Boys* and even *The Plough
and the Cross* attest. 'Many novels claimed to be based on fact, though
this was rarely meant or taken seriously'[47] – perhaps (the basis of *The
Collegians* comes to mind); but in any case, the claim's rhetorical implications are of some significance.

The approach also represents the class strata of nineteenth-century
Irish society, carefully distinguishing one social level from another and
thereby depicting the social hierarchy that is implicit in the term

Ascendancy. Separated from each other materially, these strata are implicated with each other in other terms, a duality of subjection and dependence that also reinforces the problematic conditions. Aggregations of facts also generate representative types – the stoic peasant, the ebullient squire, the lord of the manor, the damsel in distress; all stock figures as familiar as the subjects of folk-song. The protagonist is the pre-eminent type, a variation on the story of the young man and his growth in worldliness beloved of nineteenth-century novelists everywhere.[48] Supplying the data that substantiates these types also has aesthetic effects. The most direct of these relates to the use of non-fictional expository models, primarily the essay (in *Memoirs of Captain Rock*, for instance, but also evident in Shaw's fiction as well as in the expatiations on the state of the country that throughout often replace action as a means of plot development). In *Melmoth the Wanderer* the parable and the sermon suggest themselves (and the latter is also significant in a variety of ways in both *Dracula* and *Luke Delmege*), while the oration is another adapted form, though it frequently masquerades as a monologue, as in, for instance, *The O'Briens and the O'Flahertys*. For the most part oral in origin and performative in nature, these models accentuate the importance of voice as an expressive device (even what has been called the 'conversable'[49] category of the essay has an oral component). Such forms hark back to those that the eighteenth century in particular favoured.[50] Their nineteenth-century usage risks creating degrees of imbalance between form and content, between knowledge and action, and between exposition and dramatisation, indicating that the *between* state also affects the novel itself; like its protagonists, it is by its nature in the making.

At the same time, however, Wilde's integration of some of these forms in *The Picture of Dorian Gray* is a noteworthy instance of not only his adaptation for novelistic purposes of his own essays and dialogues but also of what might be accomplished through an interactive mimesis of vocal forms. This example stands out among the mere statement of argument and counterargument in, for instance, *When We Were Boys*, *Luke Delmege* and *The Plough and the Cross*, though here too, as elsewhere, the resources of the voice, its undeniability as an instrument of self-representation, speak for itself (and in the case of Wilde, at least, it is clear that James Joyce was listening). Concern with formal aesthetic choices is also evident in the frequent use of intertextuality – allusions, classical tags, lines from Shakespeare, sometimes in profusion, as with the 'glossolalia'[51] of *The O'Briens and the O'Flahertys*, are commonplace. Such citations are also factual data, and while they are suggestive of cultural insecurity, they may also express a desire that Irish materials find their place in a wider discursive context, as though to allay the English connection (linguistic and otherwise) or to counteract Morrogh O'Brien's assertion that 'Ireland has no literary existence' (Lady Morgan, *The O'Briens and the O'Flahertys*, p. 302).

Supplementing the use of discursive intertextuality, and illuminating the larger implications of the nineteenth-century Irish novel's factual dimension – 'what may be termed "factual fictions"'[52] – is a pictorial intertextuality. Whether or not it is the case that 'a strong pictorial faculty . . . comes from an out-of-door life' (Emily Lawless, *Grania*, p. 109), the works under discussion do bear out the conclusion that '[t]here are aspects of the narrative literature of the nineteenth century that are less satisfactorily accounted for by a scrutiny of literary tradition than by reference to . . . *genre* painting – the Dutch, especially'.[53] In addition to their factuality, these pictorial references also serve more than descriptive or culturally enhancing purposes.[54] They also resonate with certain objectives and interest found at other levels and in other registers of the novels that refer to them by the very act of bringing their subjects to light, by requiring candid inspection, by communicating the importance of a revealing standpoint. Moreover, in addition to depicting faithfully, they also preserve their subject matter from contingency, change and false representation. Their surfaces are reliable. Thus they suggest an ideal of stability and permanence, a union between the world as found and a mode of representing it. Not surprisingly, when the picture of John Melmoth moves, it portends further abnormalities of time and space. And a sense of the representational that relies fundamentally on surfaces is central to Lever's fiction, which is not quite the same as thinking of his work as superficial.

In all, there is a clear, if not necessarily consistent or uniform, sense that 'the persistence of the representational or allegorical dimension to Irish fiction . . . [is] a legacy of the work of Lady Morgan and Maria Edgeworth'.[55] In addition to rendering surfaces legible, so to speak, pictorialising conveys an air of figuration, their presence suggestive of static, or posed, presences in a landscape. These are creatures of the gesture, the posture, the meaning look, the striking exterior. Such features add to their stock character, which is further underlined by a way of life organised around the rituals of the arranged visit, the dinner party, the morning ride, events that tend to be represented less as activities than as elaborately detailed *tableaux*. Further, the framing that is synonymous with picturing is also a pointer to the broader status the factual occupies. Accounts and descriptions and the various other methods of making known that are fundamental features of the Irish novel in the nineteenth century are in effect acts of translation, and identify the novelist as a mediator between presumptively unfamiliar material and an unknowing reader. These data are not there for their own sakes, but must be framed in certain fitting ways to be accommodated within the narrative enterprise as a whole. Facts stabilise as they delineate, regulated by purpose while being projected as truths. They are not permitted to retain their dispersed, heterogeneous character, but rely for relevance and credibility on compliance with a discursive regime. Superficially, ba fact is itself a discrete empirical entity, but it is also another thing, an integer contributing to the set of expositions, strategies, exchanges and preponderances that constitute the artifice of form.

This double character of facts, their documentary uniqueness and their morphological valences, prevents them from speaking for themselves, which is the imaginative power that realism gives them.[56] On the contrary, in every phase of the works selected for *The Irish Novel 1800–1910*, the mimetic is of much less consequence than the didactic, the moralistic, the monitory. These novels' factual dimension, in its various representational aspects, ultimately amounts to a rhetoric of containment, a means of delimiting the terrain in which crisis manifests and exhausts itself, with – as at the conclusion of *Dracula* – 'boundaries restored and traditional masculinity renewed'.[57] Realism typically allows facts greater mimetic dynamism through making them the basis of choice, action and change. The moralistic and other objectives of the nineteenth-century Irish novel, however, tend to inhibit action by considering it vulgar – when it is not a source of misrepresentation and disturbance, that is. Expression of action in melodramatic terms – the dark-and-stormy-night effect – is a means of pointing out its enormity and its unbalancing potential. Many instances, beginning with the Rackrents and including Thackeray's Barry Lyndon, link action with excess and failed fortune by means of the familiar rituals of duelling and gambling, but the cases of Griffin's Hardress Cregan and Somerville and Ross's Charlotte Mullen also depict action's grotesque face. Were the protagonist as unique as he is portrayed, he would be a man of action – a rebel, conceivably, a type that does develop in late nineteenth-century novels only to demonstrate futility. These later protagonists' failure, even in such a case as Dorian Gray's, repeats the fate of their fictional avatars by depicting them as those to whom things happen and for whom, by and large, obedience is a far greater virtue than initiative. Instead of taking action, the protagonist, as though to confirm a crisis-inducing impotence or paralysis, appeals to sentiment, to 'sympathy . . . considered as a sort of substitution, by which we are put into the place of another man, and affected in a good measure as he is affected'.[58]

The protagonist's appeal is central to a larger rhetorical gesture that his crisis-laden story and its problematical contexts wishes to make. And the appealing image (in various senses) that he represents is supplemented by other prompts to feeling such as abject peasantry, declassé patricians and helpless women. The cumulative effect of these embodiments of poverty, hardship and abandonment is to show that place and people are in a state of need, cut off from the forms and amenities through which social life attains a measure of concord, morally vulnerable, economically frail and generally in a painful state of inferiority. The documentary and implicitly instructive value of facts attempts to offset the country's status as a '*terra incognita*, at least to English statesmen'.[59] The affective value of the appeal – for wholeness, attachment, harmony; for a recognition of narratives that seem compulsively to repeat stories of fractured unions – is more difficult to determine. It has long been a critical commonplace that 'the Irish novel, in one of its aspects, can be termed a kind of advocacy before the bar of English public opinion'.[60] English familiarity with Irish novelists may be taken for granted on the grounds set out by Trollope and the frequent appearance of Irish fiction in London's leading periodicals and publishing houses, but appearing under the auspices of a Big House of the trade does not necessarily mean that Irish novels were received in the spirit in which they were intended.[61] If 'Mr Gladstone quoted *L. Bloomfield* last night in the House of Commons, describing it, according to the *Times* report, as an "extremely clever work"'[62], this hardly testifies to the appeal's effectiveness. There were indeed many words directed by English commentators towards Irish conditions, but for the most part tone-deafness seemed to obtain when the speech came in the other direction: '[t]he English public . . . will speak to Ireland; they will speak for Ireland; but they will not hear Ireland speak'.[63]

It is also conceivable that the note of appeal, its sympathetic character and its various resonances of support and connection may have been aimed at a local readership. Many of the writers in question had their works serialised in the *Dublin University Magazine*, 'the supreme archive of Irish Victorian experience'.[64] Both Lever and Le Fanu edited this publication, and its readers would presumably have been more alert and sensitive than English ones to not only the issues novelists presented but to formal objectives, such as their treatment of action, their sense of an ending and their assertion of moral propriety and responsibility. The distinction between an appeal *to* a receptive listener and *on behalf* of a worthy appellant seems useful to maintain here. It was not necessary that English readers be converted to the cause of Ireland, as the Irish novel states it, but that the cause be represented as not lost and that it could readily be articulated in the highest terms that the conventional gentlemanly, moral, hierarchical, union-forming codes of the day afforded. It is not that Irish readers necessarily relied on the novel to inform them of facts and sentiments that they frequently encountered in other modes. In the case of both readerships, the Irish novels that were most popular were those that amused, not those that raised consciousness. Rather, the appeal might best be regarded as a statement sufficient to its own occasion, declining to solicit the equalising agency of sympathy but making it available – again with a view to union. As such, it is a species of event analogous to a courtroom submission, a sermon or some such public pronouncement, an act that combines mediation with leadership that acknowledges troublesome worldliness, and that also has faith in those higher authorities, such as religion or the law, that resound with the righteous and unimpeachable judgement of the father. (In this regard, novels' frequent invocation of Providence is suggestive.) As a combination of surfaces and lacunae, the representative works under discussion perhaps resemble parables more than any other prose form, accounts of typical events whose meaning is ultimately to be grasped in the light of an ideal. From this perspective, however, the works may be more closely related to the romance than to the novel. Thus, from the standpoint of genre also, the interaction between problematical material and self-representing protagonist produces a dual focus, an uncertainty that seems less a matter of the perceived failings of nineteenth-century Irish fiction than of the structural demands of attempting to function simultaneously at the level of documentation and desire.

## The Reality of Romance

As is evident from his and her roles in *Charlton*, *The Boyne Water*, *Luttrell of Arran* and *Marcella Grace* – to name just four illustrative instances – the protagonist embodies the principle and character of the appeal, and it is in its terms that he seeks to represent himself. But this quest is rife with dangers, delays and deceptions, demonstrating that, from the protagonist's standpoint, his goal must be earned. To appreciate its value, it is necessary to undergo an ordeal of attainment. The difficulty of this rite of passage is consistent with, or is a means of verifying, the oppressive conditions with which the protagonist has to contend. As a vindication of his capacity for courage and persistence, he is ultimately rewarded. He returns to his own place and takes possession of it, which establishes his claim to social, material or, so to speak, 'factual' vindication. He also joins hands with his beloved, thereby authenticating his sentimental claims. Both forms of return are not only restorative and promise continuity, but are also both expressions of union and legitimacy. In addition, by lending themselves to a vocabulary of quest, ordeal, return and fair lady, the protagonist's experiences can be seen to use some of the basic archetypes of the quest dimension of romance.[65] That narrative form's repertoire of monstrous, hostile and exacting scenarios has been to a certain extent domesticated, or localised, in the cases in question. The chivalrous male finds his external and internal desires conjoined, which may not be an exact confirmation that '[t]he world of romance is a frightful nightmare enclosed in a beautiful dream'[66] but is at least a consummation expressing the triumph of the ideal in a reality that attempts to subvert it. This idea – both a return and a departure, a reconciliation of past and present – thus becomes the purportedly new, integrated and renovated reality that supplants, rather than diagnoses, problematical actuality. Indeed, there is no perceived need for diagnosis, since the new is a reversion to a perfected past.

Other features of the romance are also illuminating, such as its practice of locating its narratives 'in times, places and societies that represent an "otherness"'[67] *vis-à-vis* those of its own day. Such relocations constitute an important strategy for Irish novelists, and its recurring presence in not only historical novels but in such diverse works as *Castle Rackrent*, *The Collegians*, *The House by the Churchyard*, *Knocknagow* and *Grania* draws attention to previously untenable social codes and regimes and to the necessity of both a new start and an upright personi-fication of it. This temporal removal has a spatial counterpart in the depiction of Ireland as a foreign and remote place whose strangeness is a necessary precondition for restorative potential. Further, the marriage plot, which is also fundamentally important to the projection of renewal, is not merely redolent of a basic structure of romance but is that form's most obvious cultural and literary legacy, as seems to be acknowledged in the marriage of Mordaunt and Toody that concludes *The House by the Churchyard* and exhibits '[t]he rude and hospitable feu-dalism of old times' (p. 422). Arguably the narrative archetypes and venerable literary lineage that the romance enshrines offered a more familiar home than the newfangled novel to authors focusing on the social importance and personal value of continuity, and who in any case were in two minds about modernity and its legitimation of doubt. A survey of the whole corpus of nineteenth-century Irish fiction shows how frequently the term 'romance' was used in subtitles, a usage that probably reflects the literary market but which, even in that regard, sug-gests that Irish imaginative prose had a particular claim to the genre.

The marriage plot's significance is due in large measure to the virtues that the lady in question embodies, which are not only good in themselves and which she seems to possess *ab ovo*, but which also reciprocate the hope, fidelity and steadfastness that the protagonist exhibits in the face of adversity. Perhaps the nature and nurture dynamic is also at play in the display of mutual compatibility that the narrative arrives at, but what is more immediately evident is the assumption that the feminine is synonymous with the ideal. As Trollope's *Castle Richmond* (1860) shows, this is by no means an assumption exclusive to nineteenth-century Irish novelists. In an Irish context, however, it has a number of long-standing cultural and political reverberations and associations. That those of a traditional nationalist stripe are being eclipsed by the prospect of renewal that the successful outcome of the marriage plot connotes is perhaps a remote possibility. At the same time, however, the failure of the marriage plot in such novels as *Hogan, M.P.*, *A Struggle for Fame*, *A Mummer's Wife*, *Grania* and *The Real Charlotte* (and in certain respects *An Unsocial Socialist* and *The Fly on the Wheel* also) is a symptom of the troubles with union with which those novels are concerned on other levels, including that of a critique of romance. The failure is particularly noteworthy in *The Real Charlotte*, not only apropos of the eponymous protagonist but also of

Francie Fitzpatrick, the novel's juvenile lead and a version of a wild Irish girl suitably modified along class lines, futile pursuit of whom by the callow Lieutenant Hawkins is central to the work's interest as a cautionary tale.

Although Francie and Charlotte are counter-examples, the feminine – from Lady Morgan's Beavoin O'Flaherty to W.P. Ryan's Alice Lefanu – is typically represented idealistically. Emily Lawless's Grania O'Malley, with her seemingly larger-than-life physical prowess and energy, is essentially one version of an ideal native type, animal in all but sexuality, where, in common with Irish women of her class (it is alleged), she is an innocent. Similarly, passionate as Marcella Grace is on behalf of her tenants and in the cause of exonerating her husband, in the combination of which she 'proposes an alternative to social inequalities in Ireland by reversing gender roles',[68] there is little indication that her emotional range extends beyond the sympathy she compulsively exhibits (and thereby elicits). As Mary in *Dan the Dollar* demonstrates, the satisfaction of sexual hunger is not to be enjoyed at the cost of compromising the more enduring sustenance provided by her Catholic religion. With respect to Grania O'Malley, although disembodiment is not a term that seems to apply to her, when it comes to her sexual being, the term does point to the disconcerting emotional immaturity beneath her physically superior racial profile. She seems a rough-hewn, native edition of the daughter, the helpmeet, the handmaiden, the companion, the governess, which are the roles in which female characters typically appear, particularly the female who in her youth and high-mindedness matches the male protagonist. That Grania is denied marriage, these roles' ultimate reward, reflects the general untenability of island life. Although here too there are notable exceptions (both Alice Lefanu and Elsie O'Kennedy in *The Plough and the Cross* take plot-turning initiatives, and the plot of *The Fly on the Wheel* revolves around the unrepressed Isabel Costello), the tendency is to see women as virginal counterparts to male chivalry. 'Bovarysme' seems to be essentially an aspect of the twentieth-century Irish novel;[69] before that, the feminine graces of sentiment and sympathy, fidelity and trustworthiness, not only complement but ratify and enrich the protagonist's principle, uprightness and good faith.

The marriage plot's outcome upholds an act of union as the culmination and resolution of the protagonist's ordeal. In its demonstration that he is worthy of union, it validates the virtues that he has exhibited in the course of his ordeal, and it signifies his readiness to inhabit a phase of life whose harmonious promise is the required antidote to exacting experiences. In these ways, marriage stands as the resolution of crisis, and since what the protagonist has been through is typically a crisis of legitimacy and entitlement, the social and legal authentication that marriage represents makes it a symbolically persuasive corrective mechanism. Being wed is a form of attachment, belonging and home-making crucial to his self-representation, and proof of his fitness for life. With its promise of order and futurity, such a phase has particular resonance in an Irish context that has otherwise been represented as a place distinguished by such threats to a settled way of life as violence, hauntings and the various manifestations of false representation already noted. Another aspect of the Irish context, of course, is the Union, and it is possible to read the marriage plot, or the ideal of oneness that it enshrines, as an allegory (or parable, perhaps) of that larger political relationship. Such a reading may emerge from 'the gendered idiom of marriage and family, which operates in the nineteenth century as a mode of constructing difference and likeness in the relationship between England and Ireland'.[70] Plainly, Empire is the most compelling ideal of oneness available, a secular creed complete with a church-resembling hierarchy promoting and requiring not only uplifting modes of self-surrender, duty, responsibility and pride which constitute the white man's burden (with its chivalric, or even quixotic, connotations) but also other idealised embodiments of moral, social and institutional authority. It is not difficult to see in the imagined community of the imperium a magnified replica of the type of affiliation – selfless, voluntary, dedicated, integrative, lofty – that the marriage plot suggests. It may well be that 'you can't put women, or even novelists, into a theory' (*The Plough and the Cross*, p. 23), but in a sense the romance attempts to in imagining that the ideal is best thought of as a reality.

The possibility that such an ideal of union and the power of its image, in either its lower-case iteration of marriage or upper-case manifestation as Empire, may also be a false representation never arises. If the protagonist ultimately succeeds in standing for putting matters to rights, the moral economy articulated by his success trickles down to those beneath him in the hierarchy whose apex he represents. Yet it is clear too that the romance of return and renewal also comes under a good deal of stress. This apparent turn can be dated from around 1870. The novel of union is an appeal for the ideal of social cohesion (organised along conservative and traditional lines that, it was implicitly hoped, still held good). In complicated ways, this is the novel of the Daniel O'Connell era in Irish public life. Such statements did not lose their currency at a precise date, for instance following the publication of *Laurence Bloomfield in Ireland*. Adjustments in novelistic perspectives such as those that entitle *Hogan, M.P.* to 'seminal'[71] status do, however, become increasingly discernible after the appearance of Allingham's work. This development coincides with the second great political movement in nineteenth-century Ireland, which under the leadership of Charles Stewart Parnell, saw a return to and renovation of constitutional activity to revise the Union's terms. It would not be entirely accurate to maintain that in this context the novel's earlier appeal is transformed into an assertion. As *Hogan, M.P.* mockingly points out, the nature and quality of parliamentary representation is extremely dubious, and the novel also regards the emergence of a Catholic Dublin bourgeoisie in a jaundiced light. Yet, such scepticism is a noteworthy change in emphasis, and it prefigures other fissures in the ideal of oneness; while, tonally, works are more candid, more urgent and more critical.

In addition to the breakdown of the conventional marriage plot already noted, and also to the marriage interruption in *Marcella Grace* and the grotesque distortion to which it is subjected in *Dracula*, other departures signify attempts to move away from the romance. The notes of feminine dissidence struck in their differing ways by George Moore's Kate Ede, Charlotte Riddell's Glenavy Westley, Shaw's Agatha Wylie and others are, regardless of their ultimate viability and outcome, indications of an independent-mindedness inconceivable in the female characters of *The Collegians*, *The House by the Churchyard*, *Laurence Bloomfield in Ireland* or *Knocknagow*. This note is also sounded on the cultural and political front in *When We Were Boys*, *Luke Delmege* and *The Plough and the Cross* – indeed, 'O'Brien's novel is . . . the voice of the emergent Catholic intelligentsia',[72] a decisive turn of cultural events. Many of these works also introduce middle-class characters, to some extent in order to satirise the mimicry of manners that denotes both their *arriviste* status and their social ambition, but also to reflect the emergence of a new constituency with an interest in the kind of jurisdictional uncoupling that is Home Rule's aim.

This cluster of shifts in focus and emphasis, unevenly distributed across a range of texts as they inevitably are, suggests at least an incipient movement towards a greater – and different – degree of realism in the Irish novel. However belatedly, the passage from romance to realism seems to be taking place. Such a transition is one of the major phenomena of nineteenth-century literature as a whole, and its significance for the novel's formal evolution, both in general and within specific national contexts, is a commonplace of literary history. The relationship between the romance and the novel, and in particular the question of how the latter may be regarded as a critique of the former, is as complicated as it is crucial, and debated by many major critics and novelists over a considerable period of time.[73] One conclusion to which considerations have led is that the romance 'lies outside the main tradition of the novel', largely on the grounds that it 'expresses rather than criticizes the desires of the mind'.[74] Whether or not it is necessary to be so definitive, the romance's utility as an artistic and discursive benchmark should be noted. The tensions discernible in the novel's attempts to establish more fluent alternatives to the romance's gestural and typifying strategies are more revealing than its supposed formal independence. The nature of these tensions is suggested by ascribing to the novel a 'very minute fidelity' and identifying the romance's interest in 'the truth of the human heart',[75] negotiating both of which were seen to be germane to emerging national literatures – and the romance has continued to maintain a complicated and fertile presence in American and other New World fiction.

Nevertheless, it is difficult to say that any nineteenth-century Irish novelist possessed the 'inestimable merit of a complete appreciation of reality'.[76] There may be a greater impetus to attest to current realities, to respond to contemporary cultural pressures, to assert more explicitly the spirit of critique, to anatomise both English social structures and national character, to speak more loudly in an Irish or even in a national voice, but for the most part the same discursive strategies are used to carry out these objectives as were used in the past. The breakthrough in handling and subject matter made by George Moore – evident in the censorious reception with which his early works, including *A Mummer's Wife*, received – is certainly important. But though in *A Mummer's Wife* Moore can be seen to adapt for unexpected purposes certain tropes and structures familiar from earlier Irish novels, such as the revelation, staginess and the desiring consciousness, no school of Moore ensued. In a similar vein, *The Real Charlotte* may indeed be a 'masterpiece of Lukácsian realism',[77] and the quality of its characterisation, its knowing social observations, its mimicry of verbal and non-verbal vernaculars, the fluidity with which it treats its set-pieces, and its brusque way with its own class and cultural origins are not only sharp and fresh, but they also seem to provide a lead for *The Fly on the Wheel*, though there they are present to perhaps a less polished degree. Yet even works as socially alert and as replete with plausible surfaces as these are also greatly indebted to romance, for, while they certainly perceive romance's abortive trajectory, their narratives are also prompted by inner strivings for recognition (or self-representation) that constitute a version of Freud's family romance *avant la lettre*.

The latter perception is apparent from the persistence of crisis and remedy as the enabling dialectic in all three novels. Their protagonists are not required to earn self-representation; they already possess it, as their capacity for action amply demonstrates. But their self-representation is not the synonym for self-possession that earlier, more responsible but less free protagonists attain. There is a subjective performativity about Kate Ede, Charlotte Mullen and Isabel Costello which leads to a loss of control and which also points to a problematic sense of command in their social contexts. The terms of crisis (individuality) and its unsettling spheres (sexuality) may be new, but the structuring of the narrative discourse seems more like a rearrangement than a development – for example, the need for nurturing fathers and the presence of failed natural fathers is as much in evidence as ever. The ordeal that these three convention-defying protagonists go through is one of their own making, and it thus entails disaster for them. The observation that 'though sympathy can't alter facts, it can help to make them more bearable' (*Dracula*, p. 104) does not apply to them, since no reader would wish to be in their places. The freedom with which they behave keeps them distant and different from the reader, and the gap is a measure of how their self-generated and self-seeking reality is at odds with community-conserving norms. Here, too, the novel asks to be regarded as a test case of morals and manners, as a gauge of flawed personalities and worthy personae, as an exemplary means of revealing wrong and exposing sinners, and as a site of judgement. There seems to be an implicit connection between freedom of action, together with the self-seeking by which it is articulated, and the unavailability of the ideal (or of the properly uplifting culmination of earlier protagonists' romantic quests). As other novels of this Parnellite phase show, freedom is dangerous, and this perspective reproduces the

spirit and, perhaps more surprisingly, the letter of an already established narrative model.

In the verisimilitude of their textures and tonalities, in their sense of
social structure and behavioural nuance and in their acknowledgement
of challenges to male power, the three novels in question are exceptional. They also suggest a renovated form of factual fiction, or at least
more closely exemplify works of 'the fact school' category than  those
of 'the thought school'.[78] But the latter emphasis is also pronounced.
Works including *An Unsocial Socialist*, *When We Were Boys*, *Luke
Delmege* and *The Plough and the Cross* demonstrate the use of thought
and ideas as new framing devices (and without wishing to privilege the
dubious authority of taxonomy, *The Picture of Dorian Gray* and *Dracula*
may also be considered 'thought' novels). In these novels, romance and
the quest for an ideal not only remain but become more elaborate and
more explicit, sophisticated, critically minded and impassioned than
before. This state of discursive affairs reflects the greater ideological
self-consciousness of the late Victorian period, and a recognition of the
populist dimension of socialism, naturalism and Irish nationalism
created wider public interest in ideological debate and intellectual
engagement. The works in question suggest that thought now becomes
the basis for the appeal as a significant structure of the Irish novel, thus
serving the same purpose as sentiment previously did – although, as
before, the sentiment tended to reinforce thought rather than act as its
opposite.

Shaw is a particularly noticeable case in point, and indeed for him
romance becomes something of a windmill at which he continually
tilts. His claim that '[p]eople are seduced by romance because they are
ignorant of reality'[79] acknowledges both romance's presence and its
inadequacy. This duality is partly indebted to Lever's novel *A Day's
Ride, A Life's Romance* (1863),[80] but it is a duality that Shaw wishes to
sublimate in ideologically secured revelations and exposures. It is not
merely that in *An Unsocial Socialist* '[t]he marriage to Henrietta was a
horrible mistake because it was supported only by romance; the marriage to Agatha has a better chance because it is grounded in reality'.[81]
It is also significant that the reality in question is a theoretical construct
of Trefusis, the protagonist – a world to come, the power of his
sermonising projection of which very much seems like an appeal to an
ideal. The success of the marriage plot is also noteworthy in this
regard, so that this work also suggests a redeployment of familiar

narrative resources and objectives, rather than the radical break with traditional forms and outlooks that Trefusis ostensibly advocates.

Clearly Trefusis is interested in promoting radical ideas, but his ideological errantry is not a matter of merely altering conditions and persuading the citizenry to behave more sensibly, which will enable them to see through traditional but misleading outlooks and representations. Behind such worthy objectives is an ideal of greater social cohesion and a more equitably regulated moral economy. The vocabulary has become more conceptualised, the tone more combative and the scenarios more metropolitan; but the dynamic of problematic subject matter and ideal outcome has not greatly altered. The same somewhat unresolved interplay between Trefusis's speech acts and their sublimation in the most desirable outcome possible – between critical ideas and an ideal – is also evident in *When We Were Boys*, *Luke Delmege* and *The Plough and the Cross*. These works, too, are novels of striving and attainment, of ordeal and reward, self-representation and its exemplary virtues. In their depiction of conflicting ideas and the intensification of an ideal, they are also noteworthy cultural documents, particularly since the ideal they share is that of the nation. Yet the oneness in which they conceive of the dream of nationhood seems structured in the same terms as that of Union. Youth enshrines and validates the energy and ardour with which the singularity of the ideal is pursued. As *When We Were Boys* makes clear, the nation requires an ethic of service, of duty, self-sacrifice, endurance and many of the other values familiar from earlier novels. The embodiment of these qualities by the protagonist Ken Rohan leads to the social occlusion of a prison sentence, but in view of the sympathy he generates from a combination of Irish and English supporters (the latter being the most significant) this outcome consolidates rather than dispels the power of what he has affirmed. Ken's defeat is in effect a false representation. What he truly represents – and safeguards with the quixotism of youth – is the unassailable integrity of the ideal.

Regarded in another light, Ken Rohan also represents a triumph of consciousness over the institutional realities of the law, an attainment that may be read as a parable of the superiority of Irish spirit over dull English policy. Consciousness, high-mindedness, purity of heart, and the national ideal also feature prominently in both *Luke Delmege* and *The Plough and the Cross*, where they are articulated not in the political circumstances of backward-looking *When We Were Boys* but in a contemporary spiritual and clerical environment. Nationalistic consid-erations are by no means irrelevant to this context, however; indeed, it is from these works' emphasis on the national as, above all, a spiritual sphere that their dialectical energy derives. And though the ideal is prominent in these protagonists' thinking, so also is the experience of crisis, resulting from the problematical status of their ideals in the social contexts where they attempt to realise them. The most significant of those contexts is the Catholic Church, which in both cases is not only a powerfully unifying institution but a bastion of continuity, tradition, eternal verities and unvarying values. This institution is the residence of the fathers, ever-vigilant custodians of faith and rightness, whose authority has been strengthened throughout the nineteenth century by the failure of the forces of sectarian reaction to prevail against it. To deviate from its moral and doctrinal leadership is to be misled by false ideals, as Luke Delmege eventually comes to realise in a particularly comprehensive enactment of the motif of return. The modernistic inclination of his thought has been essentially a temporary turn resulting from his service on the English mission. The critique that this inclination implies is replaced by acceptance of Irish Catholicism, a plainer, less intellectual and more populist outlook, marked by sympathy, duty and the pastoral virtues proper to its spiritual estate that in non-material ways appears similar in structure to the ideal of landlord–tenant relations advanced in, for instance, *Marcella Grace, Laurence Bloomfield in Ireland, The Black Prophet* and *The Whiteboy.*

The alternative to Luke Delmege's return is Fergus O'Hagan's depar-ture, which resolves the crisis he experiences in challenging the Church, or its hierarchy, to change. His ideal of a more vital, liberal clergy is impossible given the episcopal powers that be, whose tradi-tional mentality stands less for the imperishable rock of Peter than a stumbling block to enhancement of the national spirit. In this narrative also, the challenge is to bring an ideal into reality, to set an example, to find suitable frameworks and support systems to harness and transmit its energy, to bring about forms of stability which may preserve and sustain high-minded perspectives and the lofty mien. In addition, an Ireland imagined as the contemporary world's unique upholder of the resources of the spirit – a view that distinguishes all three of these novels – reinforces the exceptionalist dimension of nationalist thought. And yet the reality that unites daily life with noble, or grandiose, aspi-rations; that highlights individual consciousness as a means of representing a collective desire; that envisages a rejuvenated oneness arising in response to a Union that cannot serve its purpose – all remain for the coming times. The reality of the day is represented in terms of a reformulated ideal, not in terms of how reality itself might accommodate the reformulation, much less be changed as a result. The novels in question contain ample instances of objection, argument and other types of cerebration. As such, they may be considered prototypical expressions of independence, but as prototypes they are unable to evolve. Like their predecessors, these works are imaginatively confined to positing rather than enacting. Theirs is also more a rhetoric of wishing and hoping than of choosing and doing. Mirroring the society in which they originate, they are unable to secure a form in which the relation between what is desired and what may be accomplished might reflect an integration of what the reader is invited to assent to and what the reader knows from experience. Hence, 'Irish fiction . . . is marked by a hiatus between the experience it has to record, and the conventions available for articulating it'.[82] The *between* state, the state of becoming and of possibility, exists in this hiatus.

The male excitability of Luke Delmege and his fictional contemporaries, the dissident initiatives of Kate Ede and her various female followers, the onset of national spirit and the emphasis on thought and consciousness collectively represent a literature of union-breaking, of conventions falling apart and social hierarchies being challenged. Yet there is also a sense that this is insufficient, that it is not enough to reject realities as actually constituted; an alternative, superior, uplifting reality must also be represented, or at least personages capable of conceiving of such a heightened sphere must represent themselves in such terms. Whether the present is inadequate, historically speaking, or timeless, religiously speaking, it is difficult to see it as it is. For that reason, a form that might frame and substantiate it, or the protagonist who is its representative, proves extraordinarily challenging to construct. A review of *Knocknagow* sees it as both 'very unconventional' and as 'another proof that our writers of fiction can find ample material for the exercise of their handicraft in the real "realities of Irish life" and character' while still concluding with the tedious but evidently relevant question, 'Shall any romance writer ever arise, to do for Ireland some part of the grand work that Sir Walter Scott did for Scotland?'[83] And the question retains its relevance, up to a rather demoralising point: 'We desire a Walter Scott that he may glorify our annals, popularise our legends, describe our scenery, and give an attractive view of the national character . . . but as for desiring to possess a great novelist simply for the distinction of the thing, probably no civilized people on earth is more indifferent to the matter.'[84]

The rest is silence, according to this statement. Not only is the Literary Revival disregarded but it also appears that even the most accomplished Irish novelists have no critical reception and no readership in Ireland. This standpoint's accuracy is a matter for the sociology of literature, but one implication seems to be that a work such as *The Picture of Dorian Gray*, for instance, is beyond the pale of Irish literary culture, not wholly because of Wilde's notoriety but also because there is no real interest in such a novel's methods or concerns. Yet the quality of Wilde's engagement with representation, with the fictive or artificial nature of the ideal and social actuality's problematic relationship with it, contains much that sheds light, formally and otherwise, on what preoccupies and in a sense confounds the nineteenth-century Irish novel. Wilde shows that the author can control dualities of polished dialogue and melodramatic action, metropolitan manners and adventures in decadence, aesthetic appreciation and spilled blood because of an awareness that his protagonist cannot. This awareness is no mere commonplace omniscience; rather, it informs a critique by creating a dialectic between representational categories rather than sublimating one category into another. The urgency with which the nineteenth-century Irish novel continually desires to make an 'ought' from an 'is' inhibits the spirit of critique, defers rather than acknowledges the reality of crisis, evokes sentiment in place of thought, and as a result limits – in that spirit of duty, obedience and devotion that is so crucial to its engagement with its subject matter and its appeal to the reader – its imaginative potential and cultural authority.

This introductory essay and the essays that follow are attempts to consider the novels selected in the terms that they themselves propose. The intention is to arrive at readings of the novels in question by identifying and analysing their main structural motifs and thematic preoccupations, and to indicate what the recurrence of these elements signifies. But the argument for the persistence of romance that is the main outcome of these readings is not intended to overlook the works'

compositional disproportion, the 'absurdities of plot',[85] or other perceived failings. On the contrary, quite apart from being signs of the
novel's growing pains regardless of its national context, these features are
regarded as cognitively and formally expressive rather than errors or
lapses, and it is important not to evaluate them on the basis of their
mimetic adequacy or other code of verisimilitude, but rather with a view
to what it is they help to convey – even, or particularly, when their contributions seem fake or forced. Acknowledging the indications of excess
or the imminence of being overwhelmed that such features create is particularly relevant in view of the emphasis placed by nineteenth-century
Irish novelists on states of mind – not only such affective states as fear,
doubt, misgiving, abandonment and desire in various forms but also
realisation, recognition, revelation and other fundamental prompts to
the presumptive security of knowing and possessing. For the protagonist not only to discover who he is when he is at home (and who he is
when he is not) but to identify with that discovery as a means of access
to other moral and material modes of representation is a crucial aspect
of the broader story that the works discussed here tell. And something
analogous to a faith in finally knowing seems to sustain the protagonist
through his various fields of crisis, however heuristic that faith may
seem as he makes his way.

Those remarks, however, should not be taken as another manifestation of 'the compulsion to identify an overarching narrative of the
development of fiction'.[86] As suggested above, and in a great deal of
what follows, development is a somewhat questionable concept, inhib-
ited by not only the delay that is an intrinsic component to the romance
of the quest, but also to problems of action presented by the *between*
condition, and by other interstitial and 'anomalous' factors pertaining
not only to '[t]he crisis of representation which seems to have afflicted
the early nineteenth-century novel',[87] but to its continuing iteration
throughout the century and beyond. The temptation to unify is difficult to resist, but the obviously selective nature of the textual basis for
discussion ensures that anything even remotely approximating a total
picture of the nineteenth-century Irish novel is out of the question. This
book suggests just one set of considerations in a field where 'sheer
variety and diversity'[88] are essential critical watchwords. Thus, what is
identified in terms of quest, romance and the ideal here also points
towards adventure as a recurring trope, as well as towards the
*Bildungsroman* and the salience of the young man as protagonist.

Omnipresent dualities of world and self, fact and falsity, trial and vindication also pertain to or perhaps derive from conceptions of the novel as either 'largely a Protestant form'[89] or as an expression of Catholic concerns regarded from 'primarily sociological and political sense rather than a denominational' perspective.[90] Determining relations between such standpoints and the novel's compositional strategies and narrative poetics brings into focus such matters as the significance of the Christian ethos for the construction of maleness, the connection between charity and the law, the force of the phrase 'made in God's likeness', ideas of both rights and sin, all regarded in confessional contexts which, while they claimed the immutability of their moral foundations, were at the same time experiencing serious doctrinal upheaval. The relation of feelings of sympathy to religious belief, and the further connection of those feelings to the implementation of justice and reform, are implicit in the nature and orientation of the novel's appeal. And unevenness in the rate of appeal's change from sentiment to ideas also reflects shifts in the denominational landscape.

The unavoidable presence of the English cultural and linguistic imperium influences the careers of nineteenth-century Irish authors but also, because 'the society which these writers confronted was alarmingly resistant to the conventional forms of the English novel',[91] the forms and purpose of their work had un-English textures and themes. Genres and modes, such as comedy, gothic, melodrama and the novel of manners in the hands of Irish authors, attest to the inevitable independence of their perceptions, even despite these authors' efforts to attempt, by means of their works' appeals, to offset or sublimate the separatist implications of such perceptions. The representation of difference with a view to erasing it is one of the most fundamental dynamics of the body of work examined here, and this dynamic is reinforced by the manner in which English authors – also inevitably – subsume Irish material under English concerns. This latter practice also makes it difficult to see beyond Anglo-Irish literary interchange to the larger context of the European novel, connections with whose contemporary developments are, like much else, rather belated. Typically and familiarly, Irish novels both depart from and connect with European works and genres, historically through biographical associations (that suggested between Maria Edgeworth and Ivan Turgenev is the best-known instance), formally through the uneven and significantly differentiated standing of the novel in the national literatures of nineteenth-century Spain, Germany and Italy, and aesthetically through such modalities as naturalism and melodrama.

This book is neither the first word nor the last in critical surveys of the nineteenth-century novel. In writing it, however, I have become conscious that there is something more at stake than an attempt to carry out a critical reading of a set of texts from, as it were, the inside – that is, with regard to how they are organised, what their structures suggest, and how repetition of those structures indicates larger patterns of expressiveness and inquiry. Acknowledging, formulating and articulating nineteenth-century Irish subjectivities, in addition to lending them existential validity and authority, seem to have been a task prompted by authors' sense of urgency, coupled with an awareness that there was both a great deal to talk about and a great difficulty in doing so. These pressures produced narrative forms in which establishing and maintaining a sense of proportion proved extremely troublesome, both with regard to such matter and to artistic method. Not surprisingly, scenarios that threatened to submerge, stifle and otherwise overpower are frequent, and equally unsurprisingly, the need to allay such threats at all costs is also almost overwhelmingly strong. Every situation is dramatically testing; every situation enjoins escape.

The need to find matches, to complement, to conjoin and ultimately to unite may exemplify the statement that '[i]n Irish experience, art does not exploit reality; it completes, perhaps concludes it'.[92] The native soil of this need consists of constraint and uncertainty, isolation and estrangement; the artifice of responses to these states of mind understandably reflects aspiration and desire, balance and integration. It is by virtue of being artifices that the works in question are human documents, animated by an impetus to shed worldliness in favour of simplicity, naïveté, innocence or purity. One way of acknowledging the various levels of interplay between duress and relief is to think of them as constituting a stereotype: 'This dreamy spirit, this seeking after illusions, this thirst for the supernatural, and impatience of mere facts and realities, is certainly a characteristic of the Irish of today.'[93] Another way is to find a sufficiently cogent means of comprehending and evaluating why such a culturally significant and imaginatively diverse means of access to conditions as the novel is not content to abide by the resources of the mimetic, a reluctance suggesting a belief that reality must not and should not be represented as imperfect and unconsummated. The nineteenth-century Irish novel is evidently not interested solely in literal representation. In addition, the realities of judgement and righteousness require witness – and perhaps it is in their anxiety to ensure such ancillary but overdetermining rhetorics hold sway that these works dwell to such an extent on attempts to transcend the status of being subject. In any event, it is clear that the nineteenth-century Irish novel is not Stendhal's celebrated mirror in the roadway.[94] If realism is nothing but 'the rage of Caliban seeing his own face in a glass' (*The Picture of Dorian Gray*, p. xxiii), then it is not good enough. Nor will the Irish novel permit itself to be considered Stephen Dedalus's 'cracked lookingglass of a servant'.[95] Rather than employing the stability, neutrality and ostensible reliability of those representational devices, the nineteenth-century Irish novel may be seen as continually adjusting its bifocals in order not just to see its material but to see through it, to face hauntings and presentiments and to face them down, to unveil the past and clarify the future, and to discern if indeed it is in dreams that responsibilities begin.

# Notes

1  See James H. Murphy, 'Canonicity: the literature of nineteenth-century Ireland', *New Hibernia Review*, vol. 7, no. 2 (Summer 2003), pp. 45–54.

2  Many of these matters are considered in Jacqueline Belanger (ed.), *The Irish Novel in the Nineteenth Century: Facts and Fictions* (Dublin: Four Courts Press, 2005).

3  Horatio Sheafe Krans, *Irish Life in Irish Fiction* (New York: Columbia University Press, 1903), p. v.

4  Rüdiger Imhof, 'The Nineteenth-Century Irish Novel and the Necessity of Putting It Back on the Map', *Linenhall Review*, vol. 10, no. 2 (Autumn 1993), pp. 6–7 (6).

5  The extraordinary scholarship of Rolf Loeber and Magda Loeber, with Anne Mullin Burnham, *A Guide to Irish Fiction, 1650–1900* (Dublin: Four Courts Press, 2006) bears out this point. This invaluable resource is also available online: www.lgif.ie. See also Stephen J. Brown, SJ, *Ireland in Fiction*, vol. 1 ([1916]; Shannon: Irish University Press, 1969).

6  Cited in Marilyn Butler, *Maria Edgeworth: A Literary Biography* (Oxford: Clarendon Press, 1972), p. 452.

7  Anthony Trollope, *Castle Richmond* ([1860]; Oxford: Oxford University Press/World's Classics, 1989), p. 1.

8  Anthony Trollope, *An Autobiography* ([1883]; Oxford: Oxford University Press/World's Classics, 1998), pp. 80, 156.

9  Though not only by this development. The novel's occlusion is also implicit in the view that 'Anglo-Irish literature . . . first caught the breath of national life in the vivid and inspiring pages of [Standish] O'Grady's bardic histories and romances', Ernest A. Boyd, *Appreciations and Depreciations* (New York: John Lane, 1918), p. 3.

10 W.B. Yeats, *Explorations* ([1962]; New York: Collier Books, 1973), p. 235. Attempts to reproduce these elements apparently inform Yeats' novel *John Sherman* (1891), which he claimed omitted 'the ordinary stuff of novels'; John Kelly and Eric Domville (eds), *The Collected Letters of W.B. Yeats, vol. 1, 1865–1895* (Oxford: Clarendon Press, 1986), p. 257.

11 For Yeats and Carleton, see his articles, 'William Carleton', 'Carleton as an Irish Historian' and 'William Carleton', in John P. Frayne (ed.), *Collected Prose by W.B. Yeats I: First Reviews and Articles, 1886–1896* (New York: Columbia University Press, 1970), pp. 141–6, 166–9, 394–7. See also R.F. Foster, 'Square-built Power and Fiery Shorthand: Yeats, Carleton and the Irish Nineteenth Century', in *The Irish Story: Telling Tales and Making It Up in Ireland* (London: Allen Lane, 2001), pp. 113–26.

12 John Kelly and Eric Domville (eds), op. cit., p. 199.

13 For further discussion of this subject, see Margaret Kelleher, '"Wanted an Irish Novelist": The Critical Decline of the Nineteenth-century Novel', in Belanger, op. cit., pp. 187–201.

14 Richard Ellmann (ed.), *Letters of James Joyce, vols. II and III* (New York: Viking, 1966), II, p. 186. Ellmann tentatively identifies Smyth as a member of Young Ireland, not an author. He is not included in Loeber and Loeber, op. cit. See also Emer Nolan, 'James Joyce and the Nineteenth-Century Irish Novel', in John Nash (ed.), *James Joyce in the Nineteenth Century* (Cambridge: Cambridge University Press, 2013), pp. 17–30.

15 Kevin Sullivan, 'The House by the Churchyard: James Joyce and Sheridan Le Fanu', in Raymond J. Porter and James D. Brophy (eds), *Modern Irish Literature: Essays in Honor of William York Tindall* (New Rochelle, NY: Iona College Press, 1973), pp. 315–34.

16 The best-known statement of this view and of the argument framing it is Daniel Corkery, *Synge and Anglo-Irish Literature* ([1931]; Cork: Mercier Press, 1968), pp. 10 ff.

17 Stephen Gwynn, *Irish Literature and Drama in the English Language: A Short History* (London: Nelson, 1936), p. 59. Unlike Corkery, Gwynn's literary formation was in *belles lettres*. His critical orientation here is not the same as that of 'Novels of Irish Life in the Nineteenth Century' in his *Irish Books and Irish People* (Dublin: Talbot Press, n.d. [1919]).

18 Seán O'Faoláin, 'The Emancipation of Irish Writers', *Yale Review*, vol. 23, no. 3 (Spring 1934), pp. 485–503 (488), cited in Paul Delaney, *Seán O'Faoláin: Literature, Inheritance and the 1930s* (Dublin: Irish Academic Press, 2014), p. 141. O'Faoláin maintained this view: 'there was nothing before George Moore in prose . . . except minor forerunners, who are now of no interest to anybody but historians', O'Faoláin, *Vive Moi!* (London: Hart-Davis, 1965, p. 243; London: Sinclair-Stevenson, 1993, p. 246). For O'Faoláin's opposition to Corkery, see his review of *Synge and Anglo-Irish Literature* in *The Criterion*, vol. 11, no. 42 (October 1931), pp. 140–2.

19 Although see Ernest A. Baker, *The History of the English Novel* ([1936]; New York: Barnes & Noble, 1950), 10 vols., VII, pp. 11–61.

20 Sir Walter Scott, 'General Preface to the 1829 Edition' of the Waverley Novels; *Waverley* (Oxford: Oxford University Press/World's Classics, 1986), p. 353.

21 Georg Lukács, *The Historical Novel* ([1947]; Harmondsworth: Peregrine, 1969), p. 30.

22 'I compare not myself with a great Scottish writer', Gamble writes, though goes on, in a revealing historical aside, to claim for his own work greater 'impartiality', the lack of which is 'a fault which has been attributed' to Scott; 'Preface', *Charlton*, pp. v–vi.

23 This and subsequent citations are from the editions of the works in question listed in the 'Bibliographical Note', pp. 211–12 below.

24 Ina Ferris, *The Romantic National Tale and the Question of Ireland* (Cambridge: Cambridge University Press, 2002), p. 6.

25 Jarlath Killeen, *The Emergence of Irish Gothic Fiction: History, Origins, Theories* (Edinburgh: Edinburgh University Press, 2014), p. 11.

26 James H. Murphy, *Irish Novelists and the Victorian Age* (Oxford: Oxford University Press, 2011), p. 262.

27 *Westminster Review*, vol. 1, no. 1 (January 1824), pp. 278–9.

28 For the significance of the law in *Castle Richmond* and the nineteenth-century novel generally, see Derek Hand, *A History of the Irish Novel* (Cambridge: Cambridge University Press, 2011), pp. 95 ff.

29 Both Charles J. Kickham's *Knocknagow* (1873) and William O'Brien's *When We Were Boys* (1890) also challenge the cultural remit that 'Victorian' covers, though in quite a different way.

30 For Riddell, see Margaret Kelleher, 'Charlotte Riddell's *A Struggle for Fame*: The Field of Women's Literary Production', *Colby Library Quarterly*, vol. 36, no. 2 (June 2000), pp. 116–31.

31 For example, both Anna-Maria Hall's *The Whiteboy* (1845) and *When We Were Boys* describe visits to the picturesque and sanctified ground of Gougane Barra. In the former novel, the occasion is a nocturnal muster of agrarian agitators; in the latter it is a pleasant and harmonious day out for Irish, English and American supporters of the national cause.

32 The term is borrowed from Seamus Deane, *Strange Country* (Oxford: Clarendon Press, 1997), p. 1, where Edgeworth is referred to as a 'foundational' author.

33 Marilyn Butler, *Maria Edgeworth: A Literary Biography* (Oxford: Clarendon Press, 1972), p. 394.

34 Vera Kreilkamp, *The Anglo-Irish Novel and the Big House* (Syracuse, NY: Syracuse University Press, 1998), p. 50.

35 Tom Dunne, 'Haunted by History: Irish Romantic Writing, 1800–1850', in Roy Porter and Mikuláš Teich (eds), *Romanticism in National Context* (Cambridge: Cambridge University Press, 1988), pp. 68–91 (86).

36 Emily Lawless, *Maria Edgeworth* (London: Macmillan, 1905), p. 92.

37 Virginia Woolf, 'Mr Bennett and Mrs Brown', *Collected Essays, Volume 1* (New York: Harcourt, Brace & World, 1967), pp. 319–37 (320).

38 Even when George Moore directed his attention to the Irish scene in *A Drama in Muslin* (1886) and *The Lake* (1905), the influence of his technique and thought on Irish novelists at the time seems to have been negligible, except in the case of the young and dismissive James Joyce.

39 Patrick Maume, 'The Margins of Subsistence: The Novels of Shan Bullock',

*New Hibernia Review*, vol. 2, no. 4 (Winter 1998), pp. 133–46 (143).

40  F.S.L. Lyons, *Culture and Anarchy in Ireland, 1890–1939* (Oxford: Clarendon Press, 1979), p. 91. There is much evidence indicating that Canon Sheehan was not 'unconscious'.

41  Thomas Flanagan, *The Irish Novelists, 1800–1850* (New York: Columbia University Press, 1959), p. 36.

42  Butler, op. cit., p. 357.

43  Fenianism is also a phenomenon to be belittled. 'I don't give that the name of rebellion which will never call for even one charge of cavalry to put it down' is how Fenianism is denied a historical character by Maurice Tyrone, MP, protagonist of Justin M'Carthy's *A Fair Saxon*, 3 vols. (London: Tinsley, 1873), II, p. 12.

44  Colm Tóibín, 'Foreword', to *The Real Charlotte* (London: Capuchin Classics, 2011), p. 7.

45  Julian Moynahan, *Anglo-Irish: The Literary Imagination in a Hyphenated Culture* (Princeton, NJ: Princeton University Press, 1995), p. 89.

46  Claire Connolly, *A Cultural History of the Irish Novel, 1790–1829* (Cambridge: Cambridge University Press, 2012), pp. 14–15.

47  Murphy, *Irish Novelists and the Victorian Age*, p. 14.

48  See Franco Moretti, *The Way of the World: The* Bildungsroman *in European Culture* (London: Verso, 1987). The limitations of this figure in the nineteenth-century Irish context is suggested by the final image of Morrogh O'Brien in *The O'Briens and the O'Flahertys*, who, despite attaining prominent military rank in France, has little about him of such contemporary protagonists as Julian Sorel in Stendhal's *Le Rouge et le Noir* (1830) or Eugène de Rastignac in Balzac's *Père Goriot* (1835). An advance in rank is not necessarily what *Bildung* signifies.

49  David Hume, 'Of Essay Writing', in Stephen Copley and Andrew Edgar (eds), *David Hume: Selected Essays* (Oxford: Oxford University Press/World's Classics, 1996), p. 1.

50  For *Memoirs of Captain Rock*'s echoes of Swift, see Vivian Mercier, *The Irish Comic Tradition* ([1962]; Oxford: Oxford University Press, 1969), p. 198.

51  Joep Leerssen, *Remembrance and Imagination* (Cork: Cork University Press/Field Day, 1996), p. 55.

52  Margaret Kelleher, 'Prose Writing and Drama in English, 1830–1890: from Catholic Emancipation to the fall of Parnell', in Margaret Kelleher and Philip O'Leary (eds), *The Cambridge History of Irish Literature*, 2 vols. (Cambridge: Cambridge University Press, 2006), II, p. 450.

53  Mario Praz, *The Hero in Eclipse in Victorian Fiction* (Oxford: Oxford University Press, 1969), p. 1. In her later years, Maria Edgeworth revealed 'a suspicion that my manner was too Dutch'; see Augustus J.C. Hare, *The Life and Letters of Maria Edgeworth*, 2 vols. (London: Arnold, 1894), II, p. 249.

54  Among cases in point are *Melmoth the Wanderer*'s comparison of the elder Walbergs to figures by 'Teniers or Wouverman' (p. 529), Lady Morgan's taste for 'Salvator Rosa's strong, but careless figures' (*The O'Briens and the O'Flahertys*, p. 233) and one of Le Fanu's characters describing another as 'a living Watteau' (*The House by the Churchyard*, p. 109).

55  Murphy, *Irish Novelists and the Victorian Age*, p. 262.

56  For one noted treatment of the thorny issues pertaining to realism in the nineteenth-century Irish novel, see Terry Eagleton, 'Form and Ideology in the

Anglo-Irish Novel', in *Heathcliff and the Great Hunger* (London: Verso, 1995), pp. 145–225.

57 Murphy, *Irish Novelists and the Victorian Age*, p. 223.

58 Edmund Burke, *A Philosophical Inquiry into the Origin of Our Ideas of the Sublime and Beautiful* ([1757]; James T. Boulton (ed.), London: Routledge & Kegan Paul, 1958), p. 44.

59 Thomas Moore, 'To-day in Ireland', *Edinburgh Review*, vol. 43, no. 86 (February 1826), pp. 356–72 (358).

60 Flanagan, op. cit., p. 38.

61 Some of the issues in question are treated in Charlotte Riddell's *A Struggle for Fame*, a work that was ahead of its time, inasmuch as '[t]he whole range of the conditions of literary production was in the air by 1890'; John Goode, 'Introduction', in George Gissing, *New Grub Street* (Oxford: Oxford University Press, 1993), p. xv.

62 William Allingham, *A Diary, 1824–1889* ([1907]: Harmondsworth: Penguin, 1985), p. 99.

63 G.K. Chesterton, *George Bernard Shaw* ([1910]; New York: Hill & Wang, 1956), p. 11.

64 W.J. McCormack, 'Introduction: The Intellectual Revival (1830–50)', in Seamus Deane et al. (eds), *The Field Day Anthology of Irish Writing*, 3 vols. (Derry: Field Day, 1991), I, pp. 1173–7 (1176). See also Wayne E. Hall, *Dialogues in the Margin: A Study of the* Dublin University Magazine (Washington, DC: Catholic University of America Press, 1999).

65 For romance generally, see Northrop Frye, *Anatomy of Criticism: Four Essays* ([1957]; NJ: Princeton University Press, 1973), especially pp. 304 ff. See also Gillian Beer, *The Romance* (London: Methuen, 1970).

66 Alberto Varvaro, 'Medieval French Romance', in Franco Moretti (ed.), *The Novel*, 2 vols. (Princeton, NJ: Princeton University Press, 2006), I, pp. 156–80 (174).

67 Varvaro, op. cit., p. 166.

68 Tina O'Toole, *The Irish New Woman* (Basingstoke: Palgrave Macmillan, 2013), p. 82. For New Woman fiction, see also John Wilson Foster, *Irish Novels, 1890–1940: New Bearings in Culture and Fiction* (Oxford: Oxford University Press, 2008), pp. 276–333.

69 Patrick Rafroidi, 'Bovarysm and the Irish Novel', *Irish University Review*, vol. 7, no. 2 (Autumn 1977), pp. 237–43. The exception noted is *A Mummer's Wife*.

70 Mary Jean Corbett, *Allegories of Union in Irish and English Writing, 1790–1870* (Cambridge: Cambridge University Press, 2000), p. 3.

71 Murphy, *Irish Novelists and the Victorian Age*, p. 164.

72 James H. Murphy, 'William O'Brien's *When We Were Boys*: A New Voice from Old Conventions', *Irish University Review*, vol. 22, no. 2 (Autumn–Winter 1992), pp. 198–304 (299).

73 A sense of how the issue was initiated and sustained is given in Ioan Williams (ed.), *Novel and Romance, 1700–1800: A Documentary Record* (London: Routledge & Kegan Paul, 1970); also relevant here is Sharon Murphy, *Maria Edgeworth and Romance* (Dublin: Four Courts Press, 2004).

74 Alexander Welsh, *The Hero of the Waverley Novels* (New Haven, Connecticut: Yale University Press, 1963), pp. 8, 9.

75 Nathaniel Hawthorne, 'Preface', in *The House of Seven Gables* ([1851]; Oxford: Oxford University Press/World's Classics, 2009), p. 1. For a discussion of

romance in the literature of the New World, see Doris Sommer, 'Irresistible Romance: The Foundational Fictions of Latin America', in Homi K. Bhabha (ed.), *Nation and Narration* (London: Routledge, 1990), pp. 71–98.

76 Henry James, 'Anthony Trollope', *Century Magazine*, vol. 26, no. 3 (July 1883), pp. 384–94 (385).

77 Eagleton, op. cit., p. 214. How this novel, given its narrative of breakdown, or this brand of realism, also exemplifies the realist novel as 'the form *par excellence* of settlement and stability, gathering individual lives into an integrated whole' (op. cit., p. 147) is not clear, and perhaps is thought irrelevant, since 'social conditions in Ireland hardly lent themselves to any such sanguine reconciliation' (ibid.).

78 George Moore, 'Turgueneff', in *Impressions and Opinions* ([1891]; London: T. Werner Laurie, 1914), p. 46.

79 George Bernard Shaw, *Cashel Byron's Profession* ([1886; revised eds, 1889, 1901]; Harmondsworth: Penguin, 1979), p. 13.

80 George Bernard Shaw, 'Preface', in *Major Barbara* ([staged 1905; published 1907]); Harmondsworth: Penguin, 1964), p. 9.

81 Richard Farr Dietrich, *Bernard Shaw's Novels* (Gainesville, FL: University Press of Florida, 1996), p. 159. Shaw considered that 'it was a fall for Trefusis when he married Agatha . . . but it was inevitable': Dan H. Laurence (ed.), *Bernard Shaw: Collected Letters, 1874–1897* (New York: Dodd, Mead, 1965), p. 189.

82 Eagleton, op. cit., p. 224.

83 Anon, Review of *Knocknagow*, *Irish Monthly*, vol. 7 (1879), pp. 554–5. An alternative view is to dismiss the question of form entirely: 'Frankly, I don't trouble whether this book is Art or not. Neither am I concerned whether the bibliophile will class this as a novel, a treatise, a pamphlet, or a work of travel', D.P. Moran, *Tom O'Kelly* (Dublin: Cahill, 1905), p. 232. The critic is evidently irrelevant.

84 Stephen Gwynn, *Irish Books and Irish People* (Dublin: Talbot Press, n.d. [1919]), p. 7.

85 Robert Tracy, *The Unappeasable Host: Studies in Irish Identities* (Dublin: University College Dublin Press, 1998), p. 46.

86 Murphy, *Irish Novelists and the Victorian Age*, p. 5.

87 David Lloyd, *Anomalous States: Irish Writing and the Post-colonial Moment* (Durham, NC: Duke University Press, 1993), p. 6.

88 Jacqueline Belanger, 'Introduction', in Belanger (ed.), *The Irish Novel in the Nineteenth-Century: Facts and Fictions*, p. 13. The observation is made with a view to broadening critical concern with the Irish nineteenth century beyond a preoccupation with realism.

89 Connolly, *A Cultural History of the Irish Novel, 1790–1829*, p. 124.

90 Emer Nolan, *Catholic Emancipations: Irish Fiction from Thomas Moore to James Joyce* (Syracuse, NY: Syracuse University Press, 2007), p. xii. See also James H. Murphy, *Catholic Fiction and Social Reality in Ireland, 1873–1922* (Westport, Connecticut: Greenwood, 1977).

91 John Cronin, *The Anglo-Irish Novel: Volume I. The Nineteenth Century* (Belfast: Appletree Press, 1980), p. 11.

92 W.J. McCormack, *Ascendancy and Tradition in Anglo-Irish Literary History from 1789 to 1939* (Oxford: Clarendon Press, 1985), revised and enlarged as *From*

*Burke to Beckett: Ascendancy, Tradition and Betrayal in Literary History* (Cork: Cork University Press, 1994), p. 4.

93 P.A. Sheehan, *The Intellectuals: An Experiment in Irish Club-life* (London: Longmans, Green, 1911), p. 174.

94 '. . . un roman est un miroir qui se promène sur une grande route', Stendhal, *Le Rouge et le Noir*, edited by Henri Martineau (Paris: Garnier, n.d.), p. 357.

95 James Joyce, *Ulysses* ([1922]; New York: Viking, 1986), p. 6.

# 1800

## Maria Edgeworth, *Castle Rackrent*

*Born in Black Bourton, Oxfordshire, Maria Edgeworth (1767–1849) lived from her youth on the family estate at Edgeworthstown, County Longford. Her early writings made significant contributions to both children's literature and educational theory and were produced, like many of her subsequent works, under the dominant influence of her father, Richard Lovell Edgeworth. The ideas in* The Parents' Assistant *(1796) and* Practical Education *(1798) shape the rest of her oeuvre, and their didactic intent remained a hallmark of Edgeworth's tone and point of view. Not even the uniquely ludic* Castle Rackrent *is entirely free of didacticism, while Edgeworth's later Irish novels –* Ennui *(1809),* The Absentee *(1812) and* Ormond *(1817) – are more explicit lessons in fiction's moral and social utility. This belief in the novel as a source of knowledge and instruction is one of Edgeworth's most notable bequests to nineteenth-century Irish writing. Her expression of the precept in plots that crucially concern discoveries and solutions is a template that later novelists of nineteenth-century Ireland revert to time and again.*

*Both* Ennui *and* The Absentee *were published in the first and second series, respectively, of the author's* Tales of Fashionable Life *(1st series, 1809; 2nd series, 1812). As their collective title suggests, the series contains metropolitan settings and subject matter, and the manner in which these are shown to coexist with and to have a bearing on Irish conditions is an important demonstration of how Anglo and Irish literary, cultural and social differences may be represented. In addition, Edgeworth's fascination as an outsider with English high society forms a substantial part of her output. Dating from* Belinda *(1801) – arguably her most accomplished work in the 'silver fork' sub-genre – her other novels of the English élite include* Patronage *(1813),* Harrington *(1817) and* Helen *(1834). Drawing on a well-travelled familiarity with London and European salons of her day, these works highlight Edgeworth's acute and frequently impish eye for domestic detail and social nuance, as well as the sharp wit in penetrating the pretensions and illusions of such settings which she initially honed in the satirical scenarios of* Castle Rackrent.

*Her Irish works, however, remain Edgeworth's most substantial achievement. As her friend Sir Walter Scott was the first to acknowledge, these novels were the first to undertake representations of local and regional realities, and to perceive in them the expressive and interpretative* value of remote settings and idiosyncratic social customs. And while the moralistic and ideological content of her approach are the ultimate grounds of its significance, in developing a sense of local colour Edgeworth valuably particularises and differentiates both material phenomena, such as dress, habitation and economic activity, and intangibles like colloquial speech, folk life and lore, and collective memory. The 'Glossary' accompanying Castle Rackrent is one instance of her innovations, as is her basing Thady Quirk's language on the speech of John Langan, an Edgeworthstown steward. And her An Essay on Irish Bulls (1802) is a more elaborate treatment of the foreignness and difference in Irish adaptations of vernacular English.

Edgeworth's highly cultivated awareness and acknowledgement of difference, and her imaginative attempts to create a discursive space for it, can on occasion make her tone sound condescending and her critical standpoint somewhat diagrammatic. Inhabiting her own difference as a daughter of the manor, with the complex of emigrée origins, social advantages and feminine disenfranchisements that came with such a position, prompted originality perhaps but not independence. And her output as a whole testifies to the importance of fidelity to family, name and inherited duty. Yet her keen social observations, her corrective disposition, her pathbreaking use of marginal settings and neglected landscapes lend her a cultural standing unique among the landlord class in the Ireland of her day. And in addition to the part it played in the development of the Irish novel, Edgeworth's fiction also made a significant contribution to expanding the thematic scope and the representational range of nineteenth-century English and European literature.

'That's the secret of Castle Rackrent,' replies Nick Carraway in F. Scott Fitzgerald's *The Great Gatsby* when asked if he is in love, evidently assuming that the name of the house is a gothic credential. But while Castle Rackrent's ruination may point distantly towards one of the gothic's typical sites, Maria Edgeworth is not a romantic writer, and Castle Rackrent has nothing to hide. Far from concealing anything, this house's condition and the reasons for it are entirely apparent to all but its owners, none of whom is particularly mysterious or is haunted by family history as the proprietors of gothic households are. Castle Rackrent's dilapidation is less architectural than economic, the direct result of misconceived attempts to maintain its way of life, what the novel's subtitle refers to as 'manners'. Its structural problems are inbuilt and systemic and have their origin not in the malevolence and misfortune that are the gothic's stock-in-trade but in a name that is grounded in contradiction. In this name, the social eminence and historical noteworthiness that a castle usually connotes is undercut by a term synonymous with excess, exploitation and an incorrigible ignorance of landlordism's *noblesse oblige*. Rackrenting is hardly unknown to castle-owners. Here, however, the activity is also a family name, giving it an intimate ancestry and destiny, as though the family in question were bred to the practice, its birthright generated by extortion, oppression and related forms of social instability. And the congruence between family name and family lifestyle becomes increasingly evident from the unintentionally incongruous efforts of the narrator, Thady Quirk, to show his masters in a flattering light.

One source of Thady's pride in the family is that it is 'one of the most ancient in the kingdom' (8). But venerability is no hedge against improvidence. The Rackrents seem related to each other merely by the shared trait of economic overreaching. Instead of exhibiting a history, tradition or even a secure lineage (no Rackrent produces a direct heir) that might justify Thady's oft-repeated profession of 'friendship for the family' (7), Sir Patrick, Sir Murtagh, Sir Kit and Sir Condy are connected through excess and extravagance. And the roots of this behaviour are in the land, or rather in the manner in which they manage it. Sir Murtagh's leases have 'strict clauses with heavy penalties, which Sir Murtagh knew well how to enforce' (15), and are noteworthy for the amount of free labour the tenantry must donate. Sir Murtagh's wife (*née* Skinflint) – 'as . . . great an economist as you could see' (17) – offers free schooling in return for the pupils 'spinning gratis for my lady' (13). Sir Kit Rackrent's regime arbitrarily sees 'all the old tenants turned out, when they had spent their substance in the hope and trust of a renewal from the landlord' (21). And the genial passivity of Sir Condy, last of the line, proves as undermining as his predecessors' high-handedness. While his wife mindlessly indulges in lavish interior decoration, the property passes to Thady's son Jason, a legalistic and social usurpation that leaves Thady 'crying like a child' (78).

Yet *Castle Rackrent's* economic concerns are not the whole story, as the novel's subtitle – 'An Hibernian Tale Taken from Facts, and from the Manners of the Irish Squires, Before the Year 1782' – indicates. And by encompassing personal behaviour, treatment of others and associated aspects of 'manners', Thady's narrative discloses counterproductive and abusive patterns of relations that parallel the Rackrents' economic activity. The excesses of Rackrent land management are as much a matter of temperament as of unreasonable management. Sir Patrick's self-destructive drinking, Sir Murtagh's obsessive recourse to the law, Sir Kit's compulsive gambling – or, as Thady puts it in one of his gems of understatement, 'he was a little too fond of play' (23) – show each head of the family to be at the mercy of his impulses and appetites.

The recurring wilfulness of Sir Condy's predecessors contrasts with his own diffidence and complacency. But he displays these characteristics to such excess that he unquestioningly cedes property and position to 'my son Jason', as Thady, with rather distancing formality, always refers to him. This transition, and the opportunities afforded Jason to connive at it, are unwelcome developments, and how they come about is a cautionary lesson to the landlord class on the ultimate costs of a mismanaged system and self-inflicted weaknesses; that is, of a misalignment of public and private interests. 'Aye, Sir Condy has been a fool all his days' (96) are his last words. Just as telling is the way Sir Condy's death confirms his deathbed confession. Not only does he expire in a bout of drunken flamboyance, but in doing so he replicates the death of Sir Patrick, the avatar of Thady's narrative, whom Sir Condy has memorialised in the misguided belief that Sir Patrick is worth remembering. Thus the Rackrent family history comes full circle, an *ancien régime* doomed by the very liberties it has thoughtlessly mistaken for its rights.

These liberties differ from one Rackrent to another, but there is a family resemblance in how the liberties are asserted. Overelaborate gestures, overcompensatory actions, unreasonable demands and unjustifiable expectations represent family behaviour throughout the generations, amounting to what might be termed moral rackrenting, a taxing of the world at large with needs and impositions that it cannot possibly meet. Thady's extraordinary loyalty is the primary instance of how reductive and infantilising the family can be, and his unusual position in the household is an outsider's inside view of the Rackrent world of manners. Perspectives change over the course of Thady's history, initially revealing the more public character of Rackrent manners before focusing on domestic life under Sir Kit and Sir Condy. Yet the two standpoints are basically complementary, there being little difference between Rackrent activity in either the public or private spheres. This congruence underlines Edgeworth's sense of the identity of interest existing between upholding the social contract and maintaining soundly structured private commitments. Both forms of engagement require those elements of propriety and good order that manners connote. These the Rackrents lack.

In all cases, Rackrent activity derives from an exhibitionistic conception of the landlord's role. Sir Patrick, who contributes to public well-being by inventing raspberry whiskey, makes a show of himself by his hospitality. Confusing Castle Rackrent with Liberty Hall, Sir Patrick becomes a by-word for over-indulgence, a way of life marked by insensibility, loss of control, and disregard for duty. In ensuring that 'he gave the finest entertainment ever was heard of in the country' (9), Sir Patrick renders sociability a spectacle of disproportion, thereby overriding manners' regulatory influence. In contrast, Sir Murtagh is noteworthy for the excessive assertions of control expressed through his resorting whenever possible to the law. He behaves as though justice's rational discourse and institutional soundness will substantiate whatever argument he makes, regardless of its merits and of the fact that '[o]ut of forty-nine suits which he had, he never lost one but seventeen' (15). In keeping with his 'great regard for the family' (16), Thady claims that Sir Murtagh 'was a very learned man in the law' (ibid.), and Sir Murtagh himself holds that 'learning is better than house or land' (15). But neither house nor land can prosper from the poor judgement that Sir Murtagh shows in continually trying to prove himself. It seems no more than justice when he expires while preventing his wife from having the last word 'in a dispute about an abatement' (18).

The 'jarring and sparring' (17) of Sir Murtagh's marriage, little though Thady makes of it, anticipates the much more serious conjugal discord of Sir Kit and Sir Condy. Sir Kit may be 'quite another sort from Sir Murtagh' (19), but his compulsive gambling means that he too is '[b]ad news still for the poor tenants' (20), and it also provides Jason with the quasi-legal openings that lead to his takeover of Castle Rackrent. Gambling also leads to Sir Kit marrying 'the grandest heiress in England' (23) – Thackeray's Barry Lyndon, a Rackrent contemporary, follows Sir Kit's example. Here, too, however, he is a failure; his marriage is an unthinking union of alien elements. To Thady, her ladyship initially appears to be 'little better than a blackamoor' (25), a view that is not improved by the discovery that she is Jewish. Utterly insensitive to the fact that his wife is 'a foreigner in a strange country' (ibid.), Sir Kit insults her difference. First, he 'made it a principle' (29) to serve sausages. When she refuses him her diamond cross, he confines her to her room, violating their marriage vows and reducing her status in the relationship to that of a piece of property. And like his forebears, Sir Kit essentially succumbs to repetition, dying in a duel – an extreme form of gambling – while in pursuit of a second wife.

As for Sir Condy, his marriage is more literally a lottery: he chooses Isabella Moneygawl on the toss of a coin. But Bella's dramatic temperament and expensive taste – 'a mad woman for certain' (47) – are an impossible match for a man whose ambition is 'to live in peace and quietness, and have his bottle or his whiskey punch at night to himself' (49). Inertia becomes his intimate, not Bella. Homeless, loveless, landless, unfit for his successive roles of student, lawyer, parliamentarian, landlord and husband, Sir Condy is the last word in Rackrent ineptitude. His indifference recapitulates the imbalance and futility of his forebears so comprehensively that a new dispensation is inevitable, although it is also clear that Jason Quirke's sly gombeenism, unlike his predecessors' administration, is no laughing matter.

The fissures that permeate Castle Rackrent's economic, social and interpersonal structures, that abort each family member's ambition to maintain a cogent and plausible representation of himself, and that reveal the nothingness of the Rackrent name, not only constitute the subject matter of Thady's narrative. They also inform its conception, including the conception of Thady himself. The Rackrent inability to tell the family's own story in its own way leads to Thady occupying the dual role of family retainer and family memorialist. The latter role gives him unprecedented authority, but it also leaves his servant's status intact. He speaks in his own voice and idiom, and has 'voluntarily undertaken to publish the Memoirs of the Rackrent Family' (7), a generous and unusual tribute. Yet the upshot of his enterprise is paradoxically nullifying. His many iterations of his 'regard for the family' (21) are counteracted by equally numerous instances of the family being unworthy of such devotion. The reputation for 'honesty' that Thady never fails to mention seems like the one consistent feature of a continually deteriorating landscape. But its consistency relies on a willingness to silence himself whenever a critical judgement seems called for, on knowing his place and the subservient manners deemed appropriate to it, and on dismissing anything coming between himself and the family.

This pattern of response complements Rackrent forms of excess in its exorbitant deference, self-effacement and dependence. Thady belongs to the family because he too is a prisoner of his own practices; he too is reduced to a tissue of untenable claims even as he seeks credibility. Unlike Jason, who uses knowledge as power, and who therefore can represent himself on his own terms, all Thady knows is to cling to his masters. Sir Condy, the most impotent Rackrent, is 'ever my great favourite' (37). He and Thady seem more like father and son than Thady and Jason. Yet the metonymic force of *Castle Rackrent's* principal name indicates that there is also more to the name Quirk than there appears to be. Thady's conclusion that his chronicle has 'nothing but truth in it from beginning to end' (96) cannot support the finality with which he imparts it. And he shows no signs that his expression of loyalty and honesty betray a more many-sided reality than that to which these singular virtues of his attest. There is an underside to the memorial he raises, a counter-narrative that he, like his masters, must avoid or repress in order to maintain their positions. Thady's subjective, self-preserving approach renders his material one-dimensional. That in turn makes him an unreliable narrator, and his unreliability contains the seeds of subversive potential, whether or not he is aware of them. He is a Quirk – an oddity – who is not quite the conventional representation of his servile role, who attempts to reside with the reader on the same 'rent free' (7) terms as he did in Castle Rackrent, and who asserts his claims to deference so consistently that the fact that he is Jason's father can appear peripheral – Jason, who fleeces the allegedly revered Rackrents and introduces an entirely new, ungenial order of things.

The view that Thady's perspective is limited is substantiated in the first instance by the editorial apparatus framing his narrative. These materials in effect reorient 'the plain round tale of faithful Thady' (96) by placing it in a historical context and by eliciting a moral from it. The resultant gap between the narrative and the editorial points of view locates Thady between the Rackrent era and the period after 1782. This gap also alerts the reader to the telling significance of discursive imbalance in *Castle Rackrent* as a whole, in doing so adding to the interplay of disproportion from which the novel's satirical piquancy derives. But this satire is no Swiftian *saeva indignatio*. Rather, 'when Ireland loses her identity by an [sic] union with Great Britain, she will look back with a smile of good-humoured complacency on the Sir Kits and Sir Condys of her former existence' (5). Yet this projection is as suspect in its completeness as Thady's testimonial. The thought that '[n]ations as well as individuals gradually lose attachment to their identity' (ibid.) has its own one-dimensionality. Besides, how to represent the Union's fissiparous actuality while also maintaining an ideal of integrative promise is now the challenge with which the cultural commitment and artistic energy of nineteenth-century Irish novelists had to contend.

# 1820

## Charles Maturin, *Melmoth the Wanderer*

*Charles Robert Maturin (1782–1824) was born in Dublin and educated at Trinity College. In 1803, following family tradition, he was ordained as a minister of the Church of Ireland and took up his first appointment at Loughrea, County Galway. He returned to Dublin in 1805, where for his remaining years he ministered at St Peter's, Aungier Street.*

*During his lifetime, Maturin's literary reputation and success was based in large part on his play* Bertram, *produced on Lord Byron's enthusiastic recommendation at Drury Lane in 1816. Its successful run received added momentum from publication of the text, which became a bestseller; and a hostile review by Coleridge made it a footnote in the history of poetics (the review is reprinted in Chapter Twenty-Three of* Biographia Literaria). *Despite various efforts to achieve it, further stage success eluded Maturin. His* Sermons *(1819) were well-received, as were his* Five Sermons on the Errors of the Roman Catholic Church *(1824). The preacher's delivery and exegetical inventiveness may well have influenced his dramaturgical aspirations, and are readily detectable in his imaginative prose.*

*The title of Maturin's first novel,* The Fatal Revenge; or, The Family of Montorio. A Romance *(1807) – published under the pseudonym Dennis Jasper Murphy – points to the author's attraction to intense conflict, foreign locales and the most extravagant fictional genre of the day. Maturin's next novel,* The Wild Irish Boy *(1808), does not follow this initial gothic trend; rather, as a national tale, it is indebted to Lady Morgan's celebrated* Wild Irish Girl *(1806) in its attempt to discover quite what such a tale requires. The assistance of the gothic imagination to this discovery is a feature of* The Milesian Chief *(1812), while* Women; or, Pour et Contre *(1818) focuses on Maturin's preoccupation with sectarian matters. This concern is also central to* The Albigensians *(1824), the only Maturin work in the genre of the historical novel developed by his mentor and benefactor Sir Walter Scott, with whom he began an influential correspondence in 1812.*

*None of these novels approaches the narrative elaborateness or thematic breadth of* Melmoth the Wanderer, *nor did they enjoy the international acclaim that helped to give this novel a distinctive place in the canon of nineteenth-century European fiction (Balzac and Baudelaire were among its admirers). The work's Faustian element also contributes to its European reputation. But a more immediate impact on contemporary readers was created by its powerful atmosphere, stylistic excess and sensational scenarios. Repeated and somewhat unnervingly sustained representations of torture, sequestration, abandonment and other physical and psychological abuses made it the most accomplished tale of terror of its day. And the vogue for this sub-genre indicates a more general attraction among Anglophone and European readers for the extreme, the clandestine, the eclipse of the powers that be by powers of a more exotic and subversive character, and the emergence of more impassioned, if also more embattled, states of consciousness. The prominence of such features place Melmoth the Wanderer among those pioneering works featuring Romanticism's experimental psychic landscapes. Yet the novel is less a carnival of Romantic exorbitance than it is a critique of it. Frequent monitory interpolations throughout the novel are reminders of this critique, as is its overarching concern with Christian witness and sectarian division that have distinctive Irish resonances. This critique also haunts the nineteenth-century Irish novel, as the recurrence of its dynamics of purity and danger, and menace and survival in the works of Sheridan Le Fanu, Bram Stoker and Oscar Wilde (who in his post-prison life took the name Sebastian Melmoth) confirms.*

'The Lord said to Satan, "Where have you come from?" Satan answered the Lord, "From roaming throughout the earth, going back and forth on it"' (Job 1:7). This is one of the many biblical texts that could serve as an epigraph to the story of 150-year-old John Melmoth, a native of Wicklow, who spectrally wanders at will from Ireland to the Spain of the Inquisition, from Restoration London to an island paradise in the Bay of Bengal, with 'a power to pass over space without disturbance or delay' (696) and without being restricted to the common lifespan. Such command over time and space seems supernatural. But Melmoth's powers are malign contraventions of the natural order, the reverse of the transfiguring enhancement that the supernatural commissions. A full complement of threatening conditions – dark and stormy nights, shipwrecks, roaring winds, raging seas – mark Melmoth's presence. Such phenomena reflect the abnormal meteorological and environmental horrors of 1816, the year in which the novel is nominally set. But, imaginatively speaking, these disturbances heighten and darken particular narrative moments in generic gothic fashion and also contribute to the atmosphere of destruction and crisis that a creature '"[s]eeking whom he might devour"' (649, quoting the

First Epistle of Peter) generates. The gothic effects help to convey 'the fearful power of his unnatural existence' (481); but they also contribute to a sense of the moral climate that surrounds Melmoth's behaviour as a dangerously unsettled, unpredictable, hostile and disruptive force. Excess is the signature of the destructiveness that actuates him. And though Melmoth argues for a difference between 'personages . . . so nearly allied, and yet so perfectly distinct as the devil and his agent, or agents' (568), such a distinction is a mere nicety in view of his activities and their repercussions.

Getting to know such a figure, seeing beyond the surface of his portrait likeness and finding the meaning of the forbidden manuscript relating to him – engaging in a right-minded inquisition, as it were – is what Melmoth's namesake and descendant undertakes. Doing so makes up *Melmoth the Wanderer*. But it presents a temptation and a difficulty for young John Melmoth. '[T]he wild and awful pursuit of an indefinite object' (59) that grips the young man, and the allure and repulsion that his ancestor exerts, bring home the antinomies on which the narrative elaborates. As a student, John is understandably drawn to inquiry, even if in this case it means disobeying the 'adjuration' (58) of the dying uncle who is his only relative. Reading, instead of, as commanded, burning the manuscript, is a localised, familial version of defying authority for the sake of forbidden knowledge – a primal sin, that is not unlike his ancestor's exchange of his soul for power. Yet, the manuscript leaves its inheritor 'perplexed and unsatisfied' (80), partly because of the 'agony of consciousness' (101) that Stanton, its author, suffers (largely by being confined to a lunatic asylum through Melmoth's machinations), and also because it is incomplete and inconclusive. Melmoth becomes Stanton's 'ruling passion' (98), despite the 'crisis of . . . identity' (86) the former causes. John burns the portrait, but the 'stupid horror' (56) of his initial reaction to its subject's evil eye is only one of the many, deeper, marks he must continue to live with. To overcome that legacy of disquiet requires much more information, knowledge that exemplifies greater thematic universality, possesses more social and institutional diversity, and that is broader in argument and intellectual consequence.

John apparently does not know how to find the forms of knowledge that can supplement Stanton's manuscript. His inexperience requires him to be the recipient of them. He must learn from one who has overcome. Such an instructor providentially appears in the person of Alonzo Monçada, lone survivor of a shipwreck off the Wicklow coast. It is his 'Tale of the Spaniard', and its tributary narratives, that reveal what Melmoth truly represents. As an escaper from misrepresentation and the oppression it has entailed, Alonzo has the authority to impart these narratives, and in the note of deliverance that they consistently strike they become parables that enlighten the auditor. Moreover, distinctive as the protagonists and contexts of the different tales are, they are all interrelated, 'a union of dissident sounds' (155) that, despite their diffuseness and extent, are 'beads strung on the same string' (398). Alonzo's own story, 'Tale of the Spaniard', set in the corrupt dystopia of the Spanish Inquisition, has its complement in the prelapsarian utopia of 'Tale of the Indians'. And the long-suffering Protestant Walbergs in 'The Tale of Guzman's Family', whose righteousness eventually secures their inheritance and maintains their unity, are counterparts of the Mortimers in 'The Lovers' Tale', who exchange the Church of England for Presbyterianism and so are entitled only to the pain and suffering of disinheritance and estrangement.

Other contrasts abound: Spain – '[a]ll Spain is but one great monastery' (257) – with England; the 'fear, falsehood and misrepresentation' (146) of Spanish Catholicism with the staunchness of Sir Roger Mortimer, the *paterfamilias*, whose primary virtue seems to be that he 'held the Catholics in utter abomination' (589); the 'impregnable innocence' (381) of Immalee on her Indian island with the tormented Isidora, whom she becomes on her repatriation to Spain. And such contrasts are also intrinsic to *Melmoth the Wanderer*'s intellectual superstructure, where they signify not only very broad concerns with struggles between good and evil, truth and falsity, free will and determinism, but more nuanced conflicts regarding knowledge and feeling, desire and repression, and 'the opposing claims of our artificial and our natural existence' (548). The tensions between opposites are experienced by characters not only in relation to their circumstances but within their own weakened and divided natures. If, as Alonzo attests, '[w]e have not strength to contemplate the whole of our calamity' (207), his interdependent narratives provide an overview leading to a proper contemplative perspective.

From such a standpoint, Melmoth can finally be faced. Seeing him for what he is, acknowledging him as a distinctive, discernible reality, is a precondition for coming to terms with him. But such awareness is the product of wholeness; it is not only a matter of consciousness but of physical endurance. Melmoth's aim is to detach the soul from the body, and it is the body that he initially terrorises. Thus Alonzo, Immalee/Isidora, the Walbergs and the Mortimers are all subjected to physical abjection with a view to weakening their will and rendering them dependent. Falsely representing himself as an ally who can save his victims from the perilous circumstances in which he discovers them, Melmoth preys on their vulnerability and on the fact that they are now in crisis as a result of being themselves either falsely represented, like Alonzo and the Walbergs, or because by their pure natures they are irresistible to 'the Cain of the moral world' (399). An opportunism that Melmoth's wandering facilitates enables him to manifest 'the demon of his superhuman misanthropy' (404) when the merely human is usually at its nadir. (Immalee is the exception, at least while on her island; on becoming Isidora, she, more intensely than any of Melmoth's other quarry, undergoes a 'terrible crisis of her fate' (505) at his hands.) And 'the rich, varied and copious stores' (397) of his mind, his capacity for argument, the guile, subtlety and confidence that are customarily associated with his ilk, his compelling physical presence, and the aura of 'the fearful powers of his "charmed life"' (418) that he exudes, all constitute Melmoth's compelling self-representation. His impressive manner is consistent with his inner drive to impose himself, so that it seems he can hardly fail to secure dominion over those whose sovereignty has been abrogated, who have been denied self-representation and who have been forced to forego their place in the world.

Yet fail he does. Starving, confined, disgraced and embodiments of 'patient misery' (642) though they may be, all to whom Melmoth proposes his devil's bargain reject him. Perhaps their experience of subjection enables them to see his offer of escape in exchange for their souls as the ultimate form of enslavement. Perhaps they intuit that, since they have already suffered in the name of freedom – freedom of choice, freedom of conscience – what Melmoth proposes can mean only tyranny. And since freedom is already theirs naturally, to accept that it is in another's gift, that they should settle for an alternative to what they already possess, compromises their rights to self-representation and diminishes the power of their own agency. The case for those rights being in-born is suggested by the 'community of nature' (279) shared by Alonzo's natural birth, untainted Immalee's home in 'the lovely independence of nature' (402), the Walbergs' 'domestic felicity' (528) and the unity that it exemplifies, and the steadfastness of the true Mortimer family heritage. No one 'exchanged destinies' (697) with Melmoth, and his realisation of this failure is the death of him. If, as he says, '[m]ine was the great angelic sin – pride and intellectual glorying' (647) – both watchwords for excess and disproportion, and both facets of false representation – his inability to be recompensed for his subversive peregrinations is a fatal blow to his overreaching efforts. And in the nightmare of his final descent into perdition, as terrifying a mental event as anything his would-be victims have undergone, he sees those intended subjects ascend, each eluding his desperate grasp. In this vision, the repercussions of Melmoth's assertion that 'I hate all things that live' (422) have their final expression. '[O]ne who had traversed life from Dan to Bersheba, and found all barren, or – made it so' (666) is sent down. This end comes, fittingly, at the spot where Alonzo has found landfall and safety.

The vision of ascension discloses the various narratives' exemplary, sermonising component, showing not only how salvation rebukes terror but that, for Alonzo and the others, good comes out of evil. But such conclusions are not only a broad vindication of virtue confronted by moral monstrosity. They also, rather more narrowly, privilege the Church of England as the conduit of the grace that nature requires to reveal its essential spiritual core. This assertion is based on contrasts between other claims to the true and the good and those of the Established Church. Thus, Spain, a redoubt of '[o]nly Catholics' (454), is an iniquitous place of confinement and oppression, where the Inquisition enacts a consummately gothic repertoire of sequestration, subjugation and torture. Such extremes are pursued in the service of the 'national drama' (232) that Catholicism is said to be. As such, it is the opposite of the 'mild, benevolent, and tolerant' (395) Christianity whose rectitude is further enhanced by Melmoth describing it with 'acrid and searing irony' (410). The false representation attributed to Rome's 'stupendous system' (300) is also evident in its hypocrisy, external spectacle, and the comprehensive array of 'constraint, falsehood, and dissimulation' (662) which Immalee/Isidora and Alonzo experience at its hands. Such a spiritual imperium must be resisted. Alonzo never surrenders the legitimacy of his freedom of choice and moral agency, his bastardy notwithstanding. And Isidora transcends her clerical oppressors by proving herself more Christian than they, as her affirmation that 'I must love my destroyer' (689) testifies.

If not Protestants as such, the two young people's hearts are in the right place, between the devil and the Holy See. And as though to confirm the material value of resistance, the meek Walbergs eventually inherit through the 'true will' (564) of their Catholic relation the property that is rightfully theirs, while Mortimer Castle and its holdings remain intact, despite internal and external assault. The Mortimer way of life is further consolidated by its association with the national ethos of a Protestant England utterly different from that of 'Spain, where the abominations of Antichrist prevailed' (558). Together, all those for whom Alonzo speaks make up a union of 'the people of God' (558), and they transcend the barriers to faith and freedom. Seen in an English setting, such barriers cast an ominous historical shadow. Melmoth's abnormal lifespan indicates that his birth coincided with the Restoration. And Elinor Mortimer's Puritanism menaces family fortune and tradition with that outlook's radical politics. What is viewed as Elinor's apostasy is in part the result of false representation. But the combination of 'republicanism and the Presbytery' (594) that she espouses also represents falsely what the novel conceives to be the Christian spirit. Puritanism is an extreme, and the psychological desolation it occasions Elinor is the counterpart of the physical cruelty Catholicism inflicts on Alonzo and Isidora.

It is by virtue of the novel's combination of sectarian critique and the United Kingdom's history that the relevance of Melmoth's Irishness emerges. Both these structural components underlie the recurring spectacle of frightening insecurity that the work's surface represents in such exhaustive detail. Ireland is a confessional terrain whose seventeenth-century formation is still contested. A middle ground, the necessity for which is depicted both in Catholicism's extremes of medieval reaction and Presbyterianism's extremes of hierarchical usurpation, has still not been secured. The temptation to wander, either from loyalty to the spiritual aristocracy of the Established Church or from the state and its institutions which protect and endorse the official religion, remains an undeniable and nightmarish departure. The thought of such deviations might well strike terror in those who remember the 1790s, and who perhaps are *Melmoth the Wanderer's* primary Irish readers. The temptations can take a variety of forms, and can be difficult to find words for; the novel uses pictorial and musical allusions to suggest their irresistibility. But their intellectual resourcefulness, psychological predation, and capacity for guerrilla-like speed of action ultimately constitute what Alonzo calls a 'theology of utter hostility' (307) – an architecture of false representations. Misleading pathways to supremacy are the *raison d'être* of those who would lead us astray. Fidelity to prescribed embodiments of lordship, together with support for the new dispensation of political union, is a necessary prophylaxis against the soul-destroying terror of the alternative, particularly if 'the failure of tenants and the fall of the value of lands' (43) on the Melmoth estate becomes more general. At this critical juncture, threats to integration and consolidation must be extirpated – and indeed they providentially are, designating the coming generation (Alonzo and John Melmoth) as not only the appalled witnesses to the end of the wanderer and his code but also, because of what they have learned, the residents of a less crisis-haunted representation of 'home' (703).

# 1823

## John Gamble, *Charlton; or, Scenes in the North of Ireland. A Tale*

*John Gamble (1770–1831) was born in Strabane, County Tyrone, and graduated with a medical degree from Edinburgh University in 1793. In 1799 he became an army surgeon and served in Holland in the War of the Second Coalition against revolutionary France. He saw action at the battle of Alkmaar and was on the staff of the military hospital at Henesden; but little of Gamble's service, or of his life generally, is known. Sight impairment, however, was one result of his military experience.*

*Gamble seems to have returned to Ireland around 1810, and for the next ten years or so produced a series of fictional and non-fictional works focusing on the land, people and recent historical events of northern Ireland. Of his non-fictional works, the best known are two travel books,* Sketches of History: politics and manners taken in Dublin and the north of Ireland in the autumn of 1810 *(1811) and* A View of Society and Manners in the North of Ireland in the Summer and Autumn of 1812 *(1813). Northern Ireland is also the setting of Gamble's fiction, including the novels* Sarsfield *(1814) and* Howard *(1815). He also published* Northern Irish Tales *(1818).*

*These novels show that Sir Walter Scott's influence, though Gamble, here as elsewhere, is by no means uncritical of his best-selling contemporary. In particular, Gamble takes a keen interest in class, and advocates on various occasions on behalf of the middle class. And he is also concerned lest Ulster Presbyterians, whom he sees as making up this class, become that region's forgotten people. In literary taste and tone, Gamble reveals a classical temper. His works show little interest in either the politics or psychology of Romanticism. This intellectual orientation reinforces his loyalty towards the idea of a middle ground, and is also one of the bases for his plain style, the field work that supplies his subject matter, and the wry wit that typically informs his depiction of a part of the country that,* pace *William Carleton, is under-represented in the nineteenth-century Irish novel.*

This novel undertakes the seemingly straightforward task of conveying the youthful protagonist's experience of the 1798 rebellion in Ulster. But the project is more complicated than it first appears, partly because of the originality of Charles Charlton's character, but partly also because – owing to being represented through the collective and typifying views constructed by historiography and cultural memory – the events in question have already been too prejudicially parsed to sustain an inclusive narrative. Rather than dwell on the events themselves, *Charlton* presents their antecedents and aftermaths by means of a series of encounters between the protagonist and the rebellion's contending parties. Charlton's reactions to these largely verbal exchanges lead him to one exceptional and problematic circumstance after another, but these difficulties highlight such concerns as choice, agency and self-possession. The upshot is a work that reflects on the mortal lot – on man's cupidity, vanity and presumptuousness; on 'chance, which is nothing more than the course of events' (III, 221), as social and political upheaval particularly demonstrate – while wearing the uniform, as it were, of a military adventure.

Even the historical engagements *Charlton* includes – actions at Antrim town and Saintfield, County Down, as well as the 'indescribable' (II, 224) Battle of Ballinahinch, where Charlton inadvertently 'commanded [a] handful of horsemen' (II, 226) – are offset by others of a more dubious historical provenance, such as the chaotic rebel victory in the 'mock battle' (II, 66) of Dennyclough. All these actions receive fragmentary and inconclusive treatment. The protagonist's most substantial military encounters are requirements of the novel's narrative arc, when he is a prisoner of 'ignorant and prejudicial' (III, 185) fencibles. The materials of cultural memory, particularly ballads, receive greater attention. Rebels give 'Paddy's Resource' and 'The Boyne Water' (that 'gazette in rhyme' (III, 29)) a full airing in the course of bacchanals that occur so frequently as to suggest that the uprising is an unthinking, delirious expression of high spirits. Throughout, dining and drinking are indispensable to *Charlton's* sense of social occasion, revealing Ulster to be a land of plenty. And though loyalists exhibit 'none of the glee of the opposite party' (I, 212) – that is, the Presbyterian side – the picture of them sinking drunkenly to their knees to protest allegiance to the Crown unites them in discomposure. Charlton does not join in the sing-alongs, nor does he kneel. He does not identify with any faction, party, outlook or inclination. He only represents himself, a choice – or form of resistance – that is all the more significant in a context where taking sides is all-important. Charlton's insistent, and at times abject, individuality is the source of the interplay between encounter and escape that structures his story.

Each scene of *Charlton* shows the young surgeon's resistance to or rejection of the rebellion's brief, intense and various forms of disordered and disruptive speech, thought and action. The conditions he experiences convert troop movements into escape routes, mountains into hideouts, barns into recruiting centres, and meadows into battlefields. A co-opted environment is created, replacing natural settings where each component has its own standing. In the course of Charlton's travels, nature's integrity and pastoral coherence – exemplified by his native Bourne – give way to conflict and division, to social change, as opposed to nature's reliable cycle. Man's self-glorifying pursuit of his rights deface and denature home and the pieties it connotes. It also furnishes the region with a set of associations quite contrary to those local habitations and those names from which it derives its primary, unsocialised character and which denote the bond between man and his natural surroundings. Rebellion violates a contract that pre-dates the social one.

An additional difficulty, however, is that of retaining one's human nature, or rather to accept that rebellion is within its spectrum. Charlton's hair is styled 'à la Republicaine' (I, 28) – he looks like a croppy. But that is not how he wishes to represent himself, repeatedly claiming, 'I am no republican, not even in theory' (I, 198). Although he is for the most part physically in the rebel camp, he resists their ideology, dwelling instead on such imponderables as the transience of all man's schemes and the inutility of the heart at a time of hatred. Such thoughts accord with those of Charlton's putative patron, Lord Eglamour, who sees the rebellion as the 'revulsion of all generous feeling; a dislocation, as it were, of the present and the past' (I, 129).

The young man's concern is consistent with his profession; as he remarks, 'let others make wounds, I mend them' (I, 31). But his views also draw attention to the novel's emphasis on consciousness. Charlton represents an intellectual and emotional counterweight to inter-communal physical assertions and attacks. The virtue of his position is borne out not only by his survival but by the unexpected, indeed the revolutionary, manner in which he ultimately attains safekeeping. This outcome is ratified in love and marriage, ensuring not only a conventional ending but also placing union above division. Such a culmination is a tribute to continuity and tradition – to what is natural. And the reclamation of the natural, even in the stylised bower of bliss where Charlton and Eglantine Eglamour are last seen (his bride's unfortunate name seems tailored to the surroundings) indicates another noteworthy aspect of his anti-rebellion stance. The rebel's reward for his usurping energies is unnaturally premature and violent death, physically on the battlefield or the gallows, and psychologically through the defeat and alienation represented by dispossession, prison and exile. In contrast, Charlton is a man of feeling whose formation is perhaps in the pre-revolutionary eighteenth century and in whom personal sentiment transcends public tumult.

Charlton's rejection of collective action, and the self-consciousness in which it is rooted, makes him politically neutered and philosophically melancholic. His representation of himself in such terms is expressed both in his aversion to the democratic temper of the company in which he spends much of his time and in his apparent infatuation with Lord Eglamour. When the latter abandons him, Charlton is in the problematical position of objecting to events that he is powerless to resist. His recognition that 'circumstances might make him a democrat, but in his heart he was an aristocrat' (I, 106) merely locates him between those two political options. His story is of somebody who is helpless, who must escape, who must rely on others to be saved. These others are all loyalists, from the Orange milkmaid, in whose clothes Charlton avoids capture, to the self-sacrificing Newman, his rival for Eglantine Eglamour's hand. All this support is vindicated, as is Charlton's position, in his eventual acquittal for alleged rebel activities in 'a real court of justice' (III, 212) – that is, one administering civil law, not the rather impromptu court-martial that earlier sentenced him to death. The presence of a string of individual loyalist abettors also helps the novel to conclude by receding into a saccharine haze, having found coherence at a point when 'the reign of law was restored' (III, 218). That restoration further substantiates the critique of rebellious, or indeed revolutionary, ardour that Charlton articulates.

Yet, the young man's singular outlook is only one manifestation of consciousness. The rebel mindset is also much in evidence, so much so that it is as if consciousness is rebellion's true signature, and that its actions are indefensible because so is its thought. Charlton has hardly left home when he meets Cowper, a printer and 'a great friend of freedom, or of the people rather, for that was the great phrase of the day' (I, 5), who prides himself for having set various texts for the times, including the *Rights of Man* and numerous ballads. Silenced by the law, Cowper is now a member of what is called the Union (Catholics and Presbyterians united by common interests) and is determined to express in action what he can no longer advocate in print. And Cowper leads Charlton to the latter's old preceptor, Reverend Dimond, currently a United Irishman militant. The minister has a habit of interlarding his ideological harangues with classical tags, thereby adding to his asseverations subtexts of heroic action and tragic defeat which both uplift and pass judgement on what Charlton perceives to be a hasty and ill-considered 'insubstantial pageant' (I, 266). And Dimond's intertextuality also indicates a conflict within him between his formative classical training and the romantic sensibility of his newly acquired secular faith. This conflict resembles the tension in Charlton between doctoring and soldiering; but as a 'Union' leader, Dimond cannot afford to acknowledge the possibility of a divided self, unlike Charlton, who attains significance because he cannot deny how conflicted his position is.

In speaking up for their cause and its principles, Cowper and Dimond also make room for the novel's tacit criticism of recent Franco-American theory and practice. The rebellion's intellectual origins facilitate an argument for its coherence and correctness based on textual grounds (a form of argument familiar to Presbyterians). Argument gives consciousness agency, and it also demonstrates that the commonality of interests between classes and confessional communities denotes a form of understanding out of which other forms can arise, such as those that could generate economic cooperation, shared cultural activities, and mutual political objectives. Yet, despite the verbal, conceptual, scriptoral and lexical structures of the rebels' position – their acceptance of

how their campaign is premised on logomachy and a spirit of critique –
these modern aspects of the United Irishmen are largely downplayed.
Though 'the United Irishmen (those of the North at least) more at home
in arts than in arms, thought that the battle was almost to be won by
much writing and speaking' (I, 235), this orientation is in fact an aspect
of their performativity, or false representation. Unlike their Catholic
comrades, the Presbyterian 'only *appeared*' (II, 185) ablaze with revolutionary energy; 'when the Rubicon was to be passed . . . moral sense
resumed its influence' (ibid.) and, swayed also by reports of bloodier
events in the South, 'sick of politics, sick of innovation and change . . .
laid down his unnatural weapon, the pike, resumed his natural imple-
ment, the shuttle' (II, 186). In this retreat, the weaponry of the book,
both as 'a sign of disaffection' (II, 5) and perhaps as a source of it as
well, is surrendered, 'for to say of any one, particularly if he was a
Presbyterian, or wore his hair short, that he was a reading man, was
little better than saying, that he was one of the wicked' (II, 5–6).

As Charlton observes, 'the Catholic played for life, for dearer than
life . . . he played with a zeal, a fidelity, a devotedness, equal to the
greatness of the stake' (II, 183). But such excess is at the problematic
heart of the rebel ethos. It reflects, instead of intellect, the unreason of
sensation, passion and enthusiasm, mental states that falsely represent
principle and argument. So it is that insurgents appear 'as if they were
about to rehearse a show, rather than a rebellion' (I, 233). Charlton is
reproved by a 'fair enthusiast' (I, 184) for his deficiency of sentiment:
'you reason, but a Republican . . . *feels* for his bleeding country' (I,
183). To rebels, their enterprise is 'an affair of sentiment' (I, 82), to
which song, drink and general exuberance lend an evanescent air of
freedom. The carnivalesque atmosphere is perhaps to be expected
among freelancers, just as brutality and pillage are characteristic of
their mercenary opposition. Nevertheless, such an enactment of liberty
is a heedless and possibly self-deceiving prologue to the 'bloody drama'
(I, 252) of actual fighting.

Yet, if rebel consciousness places the insurgents between progress
and dislocation, Charlton's position is also wayward and unformed,
floundering until his fortuitous deliverance between radical change
and conservative rigidity. Despite 'relying on my innocence' (II, 24)
and on a belief in the harmlessness of his attempted detachment, 'he
must immediately, *nolens* or *volens*, become a United Irishman' (I, 244).
His hairstyle may suggest that affiliation, but his lack of worldliness

belies it. He can 'pass for a girl' (I, 6) and later does so; and in homoso-
cial rebel circles his atypical maleness stands out. He has not yet
managed to 'throw away your Cecilias and Evelinas' (I, 15), and does
not read the *Northern Star*. Cowper calls Charlton 'my man of wax' (I,
18). Yet, soft and impressionable though he is – shown in his adulation
of Lord Eglamour – he is also reserved and vigilant, as any vulnerable
young man might well be when setting forth in 'a troublesome world'
(I, 3). In a sense, Charlton is the protagonist of a *Bildungsroman*. But
*Bildung* is not available. Thus he must find a guide. Dimond could
occupy the role, but his guidance leads Charlton away from himself, as
the minister concedes when Charlton falls foul of the law: '[i]t was I
who brought you to this' (III, 195). The novel's other clerics, soldiers
and politicians are not credible father figures either. And even if Lord
Eglamour did not reject Charlton because of political differences, their
connection would have been contaminated by his lordship's mistress,
Miss O'Regan ('that dragoon in woman's clothes' (III, 97) who is
Charlton's *bête noir*).

Before guidance arrives, Charlton can take no side: 'I hang between
heaven and earth, and am likely to get support for neither' (I, 99). All
he can do is go on experiencing. But it is noticeable how little he learns
from his experience and how nothing of moral consequence results
from his interrogation of his uncertainty and insecurity. He accom-
plishes nothing either on his own behalf or on anybody else's. The
designation 'citizen brother' (I, 248) has no appeal for him, nor has a
specific course of action; rather, 'to stretch himself on the great ocean
of events, to be borne backwards or forwards, as fate should decide'
(II, 137) is the destiny that attracts him. He seems an archetype of
indeterminacy, misrepresented by purposes not his own and purpose-
less in his efforts at self-representation. It is not surprising to learn that
'during the whole of my narrative I have not represented him as a hero'
(III, 192).

Yet, in accordance with *Charlton*'s general contrariness, its foolish
and desperate protagonist is not allowed to be an anti-hero or to throw
his life away. Faced with either the gallows or the social oblivion of
American exile, he is 'no longer himself' (III, 101). But a *deus ex
machina* appears in the shape of his rival in love, Newman. A loyalist,
Newman affirms the novel's disinclination to foreclose on rescue and
renewal. He twice assists Charlton to escape from jail, defends him at
his civil trial and leaves Charlton in possession of Eglantine Eglamour's

love and property. This revolutionary sequence of events – comprising a peace offering prompted by nightmarish guilt (elaborated in *Melmoth*-like detail and intensity) for past misdeeds and betrayals – makes a new man of Charlton. He is saved and safe. He has been given freedom, and all by chance, as it at first appears. Remorse of conscience is allayed by life-changing acts of restitution; both parties benefit from altered dispositions; Newman reforms his past, Charlton becomes entitled to a future. Such outcomes contain distinct echoes of social and political amelioration and reconnection. Moreover, the 'ideal perfection' (I, 88) of the Eglamour property is 'more akin than at first would appear to political innovation' (ibid.), a kinship that perhaps Charlton's transformed world with Eglantine ratifies. Such a reading both individualises the experiences of rebellion and gives them the symbolic value of unity and peace of mind. 'I found the Northern Irish character . . . unknown; I leave it known' (I, xi), Gamble says in his preface. But by structuring his knowledge as a middle ground, he has also, even if in rudimentary form and stoically prosaic style, arrived at an interpretation of his findings.

# 1824

## Thomas Moore, *Memoirs of Captain Rock*

*Thomas Moore (1779–1852) was born in Dublin and, on graduating from Trinity College, went to London to read law. He spent the greater part of his not always uncontroversial or remunerative career in England. Aided by aristocratic patrons, he made rapid social progress and, although his poetic facility became evident in his early* Odes of Ancreon *(1800), a book of translations, his reputation was initially based on his composition and performance of songs. Other volumes of verse followed his anacreontics, some of which were condemned for their no more than lukewarm erotic insinuations. A commission to write lyrics to music by Sir John Stevenson led to the appearance in 1808 of the first volume of Moore's celebrated* Irish Melodies *(the series, in ten volumes, ran until 1834). These songs, which he performed to acclaim, made Moore's name, and their continuing popularity throughout the nineteenth century and afterwards, as well as being notable contributions to the sociology of taste and to the development of Irish cultural self-consciousness, have also tended until recently to overshadow Moore's other work in verse and prose.*

*As soon as the* Irish Melodies *consolidated Moore's position as a salon-pleasing performer, a role from which it is not difficult to infer elements of a complaisant stage-Irishness, he turned his talents to satirical verse. This departure reverses the effects of the* Melodies, *replacing sentiment with wit and pathos with a degree of attack, as shown in the first volume of such work,* Corruption *and* Intolerance: Two Poems *(1808).* Moore developed this vein in Intercepted Letters; or, The Twopenny Post Bag *(1813) and* The Fudge Family in Paris *(1818), the latter being perhaps his most accomplished satirical work; its tone and setting are part of the comedy of manners developed during the nineteenth century by Irish writers from Edgeworth to Wilde. Further collections of satirical verse include* Odes upon Cash, Corn, Catholics, and Other Matters *(1828). Moore's other notable verse production is the lengthy and vastly popular* Lalla Rookh: An Oriental Romance *(1817), modelled to a certain degree on the early successes of his friend Lord Byron and showing, amidst much else, the versatility of his grasp of contemporary tastes.*

*Moore's substantial prose output includes the biographies* Memoirs of the Life of the Right Honourable Richard Brinsley Sheridan *(1825),* The Life and Death of Lord Edward Fitzgerald *(1831) and* The Letters and Journals of Lord Byron *(1830). In addition to their choice of controversial subjects, these works are notable additions to the form, although complications arising from his handling of the manuscript of Byron's memoirs have perhaps discredited Moore's reputation as a biographer. Lord John Russell's eight-volume edition of Moore's* Memoirs, Journals, and Correspondence *(1853–56) contributes to Irish literary history by documenting what it was to be the most widely read and socially best-placed Irish writer of the immediately post-Union years. Among Moore's other prose works are* The Epicurean *(1828), a romance; and both* Travels of an Irish Gentleman in Search of Religion *(1833) and* History of Ireland *(1835–46) are further expressions of his national sentiment.*

*Largely owinng to his songs' permanent place in the repertoire, Moore has had an afterlife enjoyed by very few Irish writers, and he has attracted more biographical attention than many other members of the Irish literary canon. At the same time, he has also been the subject of a considerable amount of critical misgiving, much of it directed towards the cultural politics his works exemplify. He conveys an image of being neither devotedly Anglo nor committedly Irish. Yet, despite – or perhaps because of – its ideological deficiencies, Moore's output also represents the challenges of finding new formal and imaginative resources in a greatly changed cultural landscape. The shifts within his oeuvre between lyric and satire, the romantic and the documentary, ancient glory and present exigency, give some sense of these challenges and of the difficulty many other Irish writers in the early nineteenth century experienced in determining exactly how their audiences and their literary interests coincided.*

As its title announces, the *Memoirs of Captain Rock, the Celebrated Irish Chieftain, With Some Account of His Ancestors, Written by Himself* is a work of self-assertion. Whoever the Captain might be, he is evidently a person of consequence, rank, notoriety and lineage. The memoir form in which he represents himself is a further claim to distinction and singularity; its two-part structure accentuates his standing. The opening section underlines the significance of his antecedents and their legacy; in the second part, the account of his own life and times shows him to be a worthy heir to the name and its inheritance. The family's history of outlawry – all groups engaged in agrarian agitation are 'ROCK associations' (72) – gives it an unimpeachable legitimacy (a view typical of the text's *Rackrent*-like narrative strategy of satirical inversion). And that legitimacy is represented by steadfast opposition to the acts of conquest, appropriation and erasure characteristic of England's unchanging rule in Ireland. As in *Castle Rackrent*, much ironic interplay derives from matters of authenticity and legality. The *Memoir* is confessional only inasmuch as it unapologetically inveighs against the Rocks' unbreakable resistance to those political interests and administrative manoeuvres that foment and feed on 'the eternal division and disunion of the people' (70). And just as the family identifies subversion with public service, the Captain has adapted the memoir form to construct a personal interpretation of the historical record.

Although described as merely 'a faint and rapid sketch of the chief measures taken by our English masters, from the time of Henry II to the accession of his late Majesty, to civilize and attach the Irish people' (75), the *Memoir* also outlines the Captain's discursive terrain. Historical events demarcate this territory, but '[a]s I am not writing a History of the English power in Ireland' (35), events are selected not only to document the chronological span but to present what the Rocks made of them. Reactions include 'no less than forty rebellions' (38) undertaken by one chieftain in Elizabeth's reign, 'a Corporal ROCK of the brave Sarsfield's regiment' (65), and the origins of the Captain's father in the 'Levellers' (82). And as 'an amateur of rebellions' (48), the Captain follows his predecessors' example. But noteworthy as such responses may be as historical episodes, as testaments to difference, as expressions of fidelity to faith and fatherland, and as manifestations of continuity, they show that the Captain does not represent himself in historical terms alone. To the statement of values that he sees even the crudest manifestations of obduracy making, the Captain adds his own unique type of resistance, which he finds in reading and writing. His focus on historiography highlights knowledge, analysis and style, and differentiates this member of the Rock family from his action-oriented forefathers (though perhaps his father's oral arguments bequeathed a taste for critique). By reading, the Captain demonstrates his ability to see through the false representations by which the English interest sustains itself. By writing, the Captain finds a permanent form in which he can preserve and defend Rockite subversion. The Captain represents himself as capable of action, but also, more crucially, of understanding.

Consciousness is command. Through it, the Captain earns his rank and his entitlement to leadership. He is not merely the worthy embodiment of a tradition but the archetype of the alternative for which that tradition, culturally and ideologically, stands. Family history ensures that 'it has always been my pride and ambition to uphold the glory of the name of ROCK' (85), but it is his own perceptions that point out Cromwell's 'perversion of religion' (57), that anticipate a time when 'the exclusiveness of the sectarian is lost in the fellowship of man' (89), and that view the Act of Union as having 'demoralized and denationalized our upper classes' (146). And it is the satirical tone, analytical acumen and alertness to context of the Captain's verbal sallies, rather than the success of one or other violent skirmish, that confirm which these are indeed his 'authentic memoirs' (6). The lexical and writerly qualities of authorship articulate as persuasive a sense of the Captain's authority as his vaunted militancy, and his consciousness remains his freest theatre of operations. The relish and attention to detail with which he attacks historians' and legislators' misrepresentations are much more in evidence than accounts of military actions.

As a result, *Memoirs of Captain Rock* is something of a palimpsest, a text that, if not exactly composed of other writings, relies on a wide variety of them – histories, translations, citations, extempore verses, statutes, speeches, a tithe-book and extracts from an ancestor's journal for 1641 that convey 'the concentrated essence of Irish history' (53). Such intertextuality offsets the repetitive nature of the Captain's claims and accusations, but it also indicates that his narrative represents a state of mind, an interior zone that is both shaped by and proof against others' constructions of those concepts – belief, truth, justice, rights – on which 'a humanized population' (91) might be sustained. This mindset is not only central to the Captain's identity, it also counteracts the racial stereotype of the Irish as ignorant and uncivilised. He may have been educated at a hedge-school, but such seats of learning, 'like the academies of the ancients, are in the open air' (98), an ostensibly fine-spun comparison which, in a characteristic reversal, the Captain's command of Greek and Latin substantiates. His education shows how little his outlook owes to English; as such, it is a resource to draw on in his onslaught against English educational methods – an attack that may be usefully considered alongside Maria Edgeworth's pedagogical interests.

The Captain's intellectual prowess enables him to see through the rationalisations and ideological apologetics used to justify domination, whether those revealed in the 'false light' (47) of the philosopher David Hume's interpretation of history or through the means 'whereby divine laws as well as human are reversed' (152) in Ireland. By characterising what the conqueror believes to be his rights and duties as an amalgamation of contradictions, category errors and incoherent prescriptions, Captain Rock asserts his independence, separateness and autonomy of thought and action. And, having 'to myself satisfactorily exposed' (110) the political and administrative bases of Irish social dysfunction, he attains representative significance as the voice of an alternative to the 'odium, ill-blood, and discord' (144) that prevail. When he asks rhetorically '[w]ill our rulers *never* read history?' (32), he not only reproves the powers that be for having no thought for their misdeeds but also elevates his own hermeneutical endeavours. While rejoicing in his identity as a lord of misrule, and addressing his audience with something of the impishness, performativity and iconoclasm of such a figure, the Captain at the same time indites a critique possessing intellectual cohesion and formal integrity, whereas those who exert righteous dominion seem capable of doing so only by means that are conceptually specious and structurally coercive.

The ostensible order of the day that the Captain spells out – incoherent, baseless and unjust – is essentially the creation of an elaborate and sustained tissue of misrepresentation, falsehood, 'forced hypocrisy' (88), 'monstrous anomalies' (137), and related practices and positions. Singularly and cumulatively these constitute the signature of those votaries of 'the Temple of the Anglo-Irish Janus' (35) whose words and acts presume to delineate Irish reality and Irish destiny. This false god is the tutelary spirit of the law-maker, the law-enforcer, the land-holder, the cleric, the educator and the official. And foremost among these agents, all of whom are united in 'preferring victims to subjects' (20), are members of the Orange Order. To the Captain, they exhibit the clearest case of false representation. Though Irish, they identify themselves as surrogates, or middlemen, for a regime based on discrimination. Though Christians, they support policies and accept entitlements that are antithetical to the christian commandment to love one's neighbour; and – again emphasising the importance of texts – they cite scripture for their oppressive purposes. In sum, the Order's sectarianism both maintains that 'inexhaustible fund of Discord' (61) synonymous with Irish conditions and perpetuates Rockite opposition.

This polarisation has been aggravated in the Captain's own time, most notably by the 'crisis' (149) of the 1798 rebellion and the Act of Union – 'Frankenstein's ghastly patchwork' (161) – that ensued. In these events, Orangeism behaves as an archetypal 'small privileged *caste*' (124), a self-serving oligarchy whose activities lord it over 'a race of victims' (69). As such, this group is structurally at one with both the Established Church, the tithe-levying rapacity and proselytising educational policies of which reveal it as a well-armed social engineering task force, and with a parliament whose 'deliberations and decisions, except for purposes of corruption, were mere acting and child's play' (112) – the stuff of false representation, that is. When unchristian practices are reproduced in a secular culture whose 'consummation' (146) is a masquerade of subordination and bad faith, order is not to be expected; and as the Captain never tires of pointing out, every new official exaction will only fortify 'the Faction of the ROCKS, whom centuries of defeat has not discouraged' (177). This defiance holds good even when reforms are enacted by the Patriot Parliament, a development that the Captain initially views with trepidation. But, as his father calmly foresees, any change can only ultimately be for the worse. The Act of Union confirms that prediction, and the Captain reinforces it through his belief that 'a Union will put Emancipation further off than ever' (182).

The satirical animus with which the Captain unmasks the establishment's two-faced character, his copious use of relevant source materials and his narrative's paucity of action may suggest that the *Memoirs* are more like a pamphlet or essay than a novel, but evoking such eighteenth-century forms places the Captain in his own times. It is also a reminder of a potential line of development for nineteenth-century Irish imaginative prose. Yet, not even the *Memoir* fully avails of this line. The inclusion of an editorial framework adds a further, exclusively fictional, dimension. (The framework is essentially the outcome of a chance meeting with a stranger, the type of fortunate happenstance the fabricated nature of which requires suspension of disbelief.) The Captain permits a kind of literary abduction by relying on an English editor to present his material to the public. The alignment of interests indicated by entrusting the manuscript of the *Memoir* to somebody engaged in 'the honourable, but appalling task of missionary to the South of Ireland' (2) reveals the Captain's didactic purpose. On reading the *Memoir*, the editor draws the intended lesson: 'it is the Rulers, not the People of Ireland, who require to be instructed and converted' (5). This conclusion bears out the Captain's view of history as 'philosophy teaching by examples' (45) – yet one more illustration of his constant faith in texts' shaping power.

Texts are not merely significant in their own right, although their archival authority and moral compass (regardless of the direction in which it points) are vital to substantiating the Captain's standing as a figure equal to anything that affronts or attempts to deny him, as well as one with the wit and acuity to defend himself. Texts operate at a variety of levels, and as such exemplify multiplicity. Their ability to be intermediaries between writer and reader is perhaps a model of the means to combat '[t]hat principle of exclusion . . . upon which all sects are more or less founded' (130) – including, presumably, the Rockite one. Texts exemplify continuity and connectivity. What the Captain has to say and the Editor's acceptance of it establish a third location, independent of but also relevant to them both. This space is perhaps a middle ground. The complementary events of the *Memoir* consist of the Captain giving his word, and of the Editor taking him at his word. Doing so may show the latter to be naïve – his view of the Captain as 'rather of a romantic disposition' (184) shows that he does not appreciate what a Captain outdoors by moonlight connotes – but it is a gesture of the good faith that the Captain has found so lamentably lacking in transactions between classes, creeds and parties. If the Captain seeks to persuade, the Editor seems to have no objection to being persuaded. And even if the Editor is a dupe, the fact that the Captain uses him as a means to an audience suggests that the ears of the other side are available.

Yet, although such a text-affirming transaction is a significant gesture, it does seem to undermine the power of the deed in Rock family tradition. The one action in the *Memoir* to stand out – the rescue of the poor woman and her cow by the Captain's father – has strong emblematic value but nothing more. Granted, the *Memoir* is not a dramatic narrative, but the Captain's unvarying protestation against what he can neither forestall nor alter does represent him in rhetorical terms. It is not that the Captain is devoid of ideas, but, if calling for a 'community of feeling' (173) impresses, there are no signs that the idea has been thought through. In declaring that the Union and the Ascendancy are his 'joint prey' (178), ferocious phrasing overshadows pursuit of his quarry. Arrest and transportation testify less to resistance than to a surprising vulnerability and, assuming that his son and heir will be 'as tempestuous and troublesome' (186) as himself seems formulaic rather than political. Perhaps the limits of the Captain's approach are suggested in his dismissal of 'the seduction of . . . fair republican theories' (166) to which the United Irishmen succumb. 'I have two souls, a soul for right, and a soul for riot' (61): thus, too flippantly, the Captain pretends to a unity between thought and deed. But this declaration of unity is a rhetoric whereby *Memoirs of Captain Rock* sublimates the conflicts, tensions and difficulties that anybody representing himself in historical terms experiences.

# 1826

## John Banim, *The Boyne Water*

*John Banim (1798–1842) and his brother Michael (1796–1874) wrote under the pseudonym 'The O'Hara Family' (John 'Abel', Michael 'Barnes'), but it is widely accepted that, though they collaborated, John was the moving force in the literary partnership. He was the brother who actively pursued a literary career as a member of that generation of expatriate provincial Irish writers who sought in the London of the 1820s opportunities not offered by Irish cultural life. His London career benefited substantially from the friendship of Gerald Griffin.*

*Born in Kilkenny, John worked as a journalist for a number of provincial publications before emigrating. His first London success was a poem, The Celt's Paradise (1821), based on St Patrick's legendary encounter with Ossian; and in the same year his play Damon and Pythias was successfully produced at Covent Garden. The works that made the Banim brothers' names, however, were the Tales by the O'Hara Family, the first three-volume series of which was published in 1825 and contained such noted works as* Crohoore of the Bill-Hook *and* John Doe; or, The Peep o' Day. *A second three-volume series appeared the following year and includes arguably their best-known and most accomplished work,* The Nowlans. *Other joint works include* The Denounced *(1830; containing* The Last Baron of Crana *and* The Conformist*) and* The Bit o' Writin' and Other Tales *(1838). The novel* The Anglo-Irish of the Nineteenth Century *(1828), originally published anonymously, is the work of John alone, while* The Mayor of Windgap *(1835) is attributed solely to Michael. This work contains* Canvassing, *often considered an expression of the brothers' O'Connellite leanings, though written by Harriett Martin of Ballinahinch. After John's death, Michael's literary output virtually dried up, his one work of substance being* The Town of the Cascades *(1864), a temperance novel.*

*Formally and thematically, much of what the O'Hara Family wrote – including* The Croppy: A Tale of 1798 *(1828) – are works of historical fiction; John Banim was known in his day as 'the Irish Walter Scott'. Most O'Hara Family works, however, are arguably more notable for their social range than for their historical materials. Indeed, the works' concern with Anglo-Irish relations seems less significant than their alertness to the nuances of class, their graphic representation of rural violence and their intimate familiarity (largely deriving from the closeness of Michael's ear to their native ground) with the unsettled state of both local conditions and national prospects. In dealing with this material, The Banims also reveal the challenges faced by the first generation of post-Union Irish novelists in establishing the expressive terms in which an altered social and political landscape might be represented.*

In Gamble's *Charlton*, differences between the opposing parties are basically expressed through their military activities, with the conditions from which opposition arises kept at a distance. Although a novel entitled *The Boyne Water* can hardly avoid military events, in contrast to *Charlton* these are represented in relation to the interests and motives of the contending sides. Significant action is not confined to the field, but moves from palace to prison camp and from debating chamber to ruined domicile, thereby conveying a strong sense of the ideological and political factors influencing the course of events. And unlike *Charlton*, *The Boyne Water* draws on the historiographical record of the period, perhaps following the example of Moore's strategic intertextuality in *Memoirs of Captain Rock*. Banim's use of these contextualising materials can be so long-winded that *The Boyne Water* may seem too historical and insufficiently novelistic. And other elements of the narrative also contribute to the novel's unbalanced rendering of the letter and the spirit of historical fiction. Nevertheless, Banim's elaborations of context result in a notably comprehensive approach to the representational demands of his material.

One important implication of the novel's breadth and inclusiveness is the sense of historical totality that it suggests. Virtually nobody, whether agent or victim, can escape the pressure of events. The historical moment's confrontations and retaliations, together with the self-representations deriving from them, equally affect *The Boyne Water's* twin protagonists, Robert Evelyn and Edmund M'Donnell, as they do the leaders of the day – Patrick Sarsfield, Reverend George Walker, General Schaumberg, King James II and William of Orange – all of whom are besieged by the conditions that they have created. Separated by rank, military expertise, confessional ardour and political resources as the protagonists are from the historical actors of record, their shared experience of the problematical demands of changing times illustrates the novel's totalising perspective and ambition. To represent oneself in terms other than those unsettling a country that had 'enjoyed more peace, or at all events rest, than could be recollected in her previous history' (I, 19) seems an imponderable challenge. Much more likely is the death or exile that many of the most powerful personages suffer.

The nature of the challenge may be appreciated in the changes in time and space that result from the disruptive materialisation of historical conflict. Time loses diurnal repetitiveness and becomes the medium of a different quality of presentness, consisting of rumour, report and an unwonted degree of vigilance. Robert Evelyn and Edmund M'Donnell cede the tempo of their home-bound activities to the arbitrariness of a historical schedule. And historical action is such that increasing areas of space are required to contain it. The novel's geographical range makes this development particularly prominent. In addition to the eponymous site, Derry, Ballyneety (or 'Ballyneedy' (III, 343)) and much territory in between are detailed. This topographical and otherwise diverse range of locations includes the typical landscapes of the nineteenth-century Irish novel – the demarcated estate and the unbounded picturesque vista – but is not limited to them. Cities provide some of this territory's coordinates, and Derry, Dublin and Limerick also represent where preponderant interests reside and thus become interpretative markers, as do such non-urban emplacements as bivouacs, prisons, command posts and walls within which the protagonists' dramas are enacted.

Robert Evelyn and Edmund M'Donnell are both Irish, but their identity is not signified by the opposing religious affiliations and contrasting political outlooks that historical circumstances have abruptly made more consequential than ever, but by their both being settled, longstanding landowners. Events originating in England dispossess each of them, break the integration of place and person that their homes and heritage represent, and threaten to disconnect the knowledge of homeland from the idea of country. The two young men suffer not only loss of property and the abrogation of its ethos of settlement, but also the dispersal of family affections and attachments. Amidst a cacophonous combination of political clamour, sectarian speechifying and clash of arms, the prospect of a future becomes increasingly troubled. Neither Evelyn (as he is called throughout) nor M'Donnell stands much of a chance of asserting his own distinctiveness – cultural in Edmund's case, politically liberal in Evelyn's. Their basis of self-representation has been undermined by the historical requirement to identify with the collective and exclusive positions of either the Catholic and Jacobite camp or the Protestant and Williamite one, positions that are inflexible and overdetermined. And the extremes created by the crisis into which the English crown and constitution have fallen are reproduced not only in sectarian antagonisms but in the narrative's structural interplay between loss and restoration, terminus and deliverance, erasure and triumphalism.

This interplay is present from the outset, as is its formation in response to public events. The homeward-bound Evelyn family – orphans Robert and Esther, their aunt Jane and her husband, and a veteran of the 1641 rebellion named Oliver Whittle – have their journey effectively and almost permanently redirected at Carrickfergus by a crowd celebrating the accession to the throne of James II. This demonstration is greeted with sectarian vituperation by Jane and Whittle – 'the benighted personages of our story' (I, 146). But this reaction does not allay other omens of upheaval and distress, such as a tornado ('then not unknown in Ireland' (1, 55)), and an encounter with the spectral Onagh, whose wild Irishness previews the derangement that dispossession may entail. But those disturbances are counteracted by the timely appearance of Edmund and Eva M'Donnell, siblings the same age as Robert and Esther, and the Evelyns gladly accept the hospitality of the M'Donnell home in nearby Glenarriff. Not only Catholic but Gaelic as well – the composer Carolan, a recurring presence in the novel, is another house guest (he and Onagh comprise something of a Gaelic chorus, impotent though watchful witnesses to the main events) – the household is a revelation to Evelyn. This is an enclave different from everything he has seen in his own native place beside Lough Neagh. The existence of 'the English ascendancy among us' (I, 121) notwithstanding, Glenarriff has retained 'its own customs, its own language, and its own race' (I, 128), as though immune from historical change. Here the four young people coexist in 'the rare peace of sectarian toleration' (I, 168); indeed, 'they all loved' (ibid.). In due course, Evelyn pledges himself to Eva, as does Edmund to Esther, and not even Edmund's departure for the West Indies, where he must attend to what is coyly termed 'the state of certain properties' (I, 205), seriously impinges on the idyllic spirit of union that is Glenarriff's exceptional dispensation.

Evelyn sees Edmund off from Dublin. They find the city simmering with anti-Jacobite sentiment, an arresting contrast to Glenarriff's amity and affection. And when Edmund lands at Carrickfergus after a two-year hiatus, the turmoil that had previously threatened the Evelyns now menaces him. Reforms by James II aim to belie the seemingly predominant view that 'Papists have proved that they are unfit for civil rights' (I, 271). Social representation of Protestants and Catholics is about to change, inciting the former's opposition, the uncompromising divisiveness of which supplies *The Boyne Water* with its narrative momentum. This prospective change also reflects both the power of regal authority and the King's moral worth as a ruler whose aim is to 'settle all liberty of conscience by a law' (III, 269). The opposition leader is the Reverend George Walker, a friend of Evelyn's late father, 'a heretic minister' (I, 244) whose fire-breathing harangues are countered by an equally vociferous and extreme Dominican preacher, O'Haggerty. In such a tempestuous environment, the prospect of unity represented by the lovers of Glenarriff has little chance of holding. Walker advises the independent-minded Evelyn that '[w]e must swim with the current of the times' (I, 300). And although Evelyn regards the clergyman's outlook as essentially unchristian, arguing that 'difference does not imply inferiority' (I, 306), he finds himself bound to keep faith with his co-religionists, and obeys orders to defend the 'little colonial city' (II, 50), Derry. Loyalty to one's own standpoint must surrender to Walker's quasi-tribal exceptionalism. And since personal loyalty is an implicit critique of the communal kind, it must remain internalised, a matter of unswerving conscience rather than of history's adventitious energies and the politics that attempts to structure them. The immunity from criticism of one's own culture and community reinforces the rigidity of its postures, gestures and rhetoric while effectively nullifying not only the basis but the necessity of self-representation. And the power of *la force des choses* to short-circuit the connection between uncritical thought and reflexive action also affects Edmund's case. He joins the Earl of Tyrconnell's pro-Jacobite forces and finds himself on manoeuvres on his own home ground, where in the recent past he and Evelyn played together.

The two young men are both friends and enemies, and the resulting conflicts and contradictions are played out through jails and escapes, alarming mistakes and fortunate falls. An air of crisis supervenes, nowhere more so than during the siege of Derry, in which hubris contends with expiation, and conditions veer from the Apprentice Boys' 'important frolic' (II, 53) of closing the city gates to the imminent surrender of the besieged, than whom, in Walker's words, '[t]he poor Israelites at the Red Sea stood not in sorer trouble' (II, 294). With the lifting of the siege, however, Evelyn and Edmund part ways, and this separation also changes the novel's emphasis. Esther Evelyn has died during the siege, and Edmund, having 'lately been dismissed, with a severe and degrading sentence, from his regiment' (II, 393), disappears into the ranks of the Rapparees, whom he had previously condemned as 'these scoundrels' (II, 147). He adopts the persona of the 'formidable freebooter' (III, 324) Yemen-ac-knuck, a self-representation that is consistent with the general falseness of the Rapparees as a body. Led by 'General' (II, 146) Galloping Hogan, these guerrillas are portrayed in a manner comparable to depictions of Whiteboys, as historical deviants who exploit without the rationale of cause or principle the turbulence of conflicting orthodoxies. In enlisting with them, Edmund identifies with the most egregious aspects of historical reality, revealing thereby the depth of his own loss and displacement and his lack of faith in recuperation. The Rapparees are no proper basis for self-representation, as is suggested by the culmination of Edmund's outlaw phase in a career of European 'wanderings' (III, 427) as a member of the Wild Geese.

In contrast, Evelyn pursues the hopeful path of a quest for Eva, from whom sectarian differences have estranged him. His objective promises restoration and reconciliation. And the quest also prioritises romantic possibility over historical actuality, which in turn occasions a discursive departure. The resulting hybrid form of historical romance makes contingency and dislocation necessary preludes to reintegration and return. Eva's belief that she and Evelyn must 'live as strangers to each other – except in the heart – until . . . we can meet in undivided love' (II, 214) acknowledges the sectarian status quo, but Evelyn's goal is contrary to sectarian discrimination. His service in the Jacobite army – 'the right side [and] assuredly the gallanter one' (III, 154) – bears out his singularity. And being granted permission not to take arms against his Williamite brethren further suggests his exceptional standing. The dominating influence of denominational politics has been relaxed in his case, showing that personal fidelity is not incompatible with communal loyalty. In establishing that standpoint, Evelyn is shown to have won through to representing himself, the state of his heart, and those related elements that constitute his own steadfast person. His faith in what matters to him derives its credibility from his occupation of a position between the unavoidability of military involvement and detachment from the excesses that provoke and inflame it. He neither goes to the extremes of the Rapparees nor to those which drive Walker and O'Heggarty to carry out 'the consummation of their bigotry' (III, 246) at the Battle of the Boyne. '[T]he sympathy of a man's heart for man' (III, 154), in Sarsfield's words, is the basis for Evelyn's self-representation. And the virtues of his unique stand are substantiated not only in his survival and reunification with Eva but also in his return to his homestead, whose values of settlement and continuity are embodied by a new generation of Evelyns.

The chivalric character of Evelyn's accomplishment – its sense of ordeal, search, honour and repatriation – finesses historical contingency and is a triumph of human sentiment over party affiliation, but that triumph does not overshadow the significance of the vicissitudes, dangers and dislocations that Evelyn has had to endure. His testing experiences of upheaval and displacement replicate those that define Catholic historical destiny, represented by *The Boyne Water*'s labyrinthine subplots, featuring female characters and their travails, journeyings and misguided false representations (the rather gothic story of Onagh is emblematic of the others). Moreover, the novel's marriage plot as well as the marriage partners' homophonic names provide a basis for considering other types of closeness. These subsidiary stories help to emphasise the relevance of race, sexuality and class to the ostensibly private sense of union that Eva and Evelyn represent. But it is the exceptional character of marital success that provides a bulwark against the disappointments, political and otherwise, of the peace, and that enable Evelyn to retain the good faith that motivated his pursuit of union. This extrapolation is conveyed in a letter from Evelyn to exiled Edmund: '[m]an cannot always be unjust to man; even for his own relative character and happiness he will love and do all befitting and meriting honour to his brother' (III, 435).

The note of harmonious and exemplary unity on which *The Boyne Water* concludes will perhaps have had a contemporary resonance for the novel's readers. And so too will the manner in which Evelyn's actions and their outcome focus on the possibility of redress. Here is a story of somebody sorely tested, hounded and endangered by circumstances obviously not of his own choosing, who yet is able to turn his experiences to exemplary account, retaining his sense of an alternative in the heat of battle and notwithstanding the apparent obligations of his birthright. In his case, change is not entirely destructive, principle can be upheld, continuity may be resumed, and denominational affiliation does not have to be alienating or coercive. It may not be quite the case that Banim is anachronistically ascribing to Evelyn the values of liberty, equality and fraternity, although the values he does represent are worth comparing with those of Murrogh O'Brien in *The O'Briens and the O'Flahertys*, in view of both works' political contexts. But Evelyn does not need to be a proto-republican to appeal to a nineteenth-century readership. As an upright, disinterested Protestant gentleman, a seeker of fruitful union and denominational amity, his openness and integrity, and his refusal to be subjected to the imperious onrush of history, Evelyn appeals in his own terms. And he quite appreciates the implications of those terms, as is indicated in the hopes he expresses for a union that will be 'a recantation of old slanders, and a concession of old rights' (III, 435). Representing such an outlook in the 1820s, when sectarian overkill was such a prominent feature of public discourse and when sharp reminders still lingered of antinomies between the Crown's imperatives and the prerogatives of home, is unlikely to be entirely coincidental.

# 1827

# Lady Morgan, *The O'Briens and the O'Flahertys*

*Lady Morgan (1783–1859) was born, according to a legend she herself propagated, on a boat sailing from England to Ireland. Her father, Robert Owenson, was a noted actor who had settled in Dublin in the mid-1770s. Initially tutored by the poet Thomas Dermody, Lady Morgan subsequently attended a number of Dublin schools. With Dermody's encouragement she wrote a number of poems, a volume of which was published in 1801, by which time she had spent some years working as a governess. It was during those years that she first made the acquaintance of Thomas Moore, to whose career her own has some revealing parallels. Owenson was a member of the Abercorn household when in 1812 she married Sir Thomas Morgan, that family's physician. For the next twenty-five years the couple maintained a house in Dublin, a stay that, punctuated by many lengthy sojourns in France, Italy and elsewhere in Europe, ended in their moving to London, where Lady Morgan spent the rest of her life.*

*Largely on the basis of her best-known novel* The Wild Irish Girl *(1806), Lady Morgan was already a celebrated author and socialite when she joined the Abercorn household, and her fame as the latter during her lifetime equalled if not outstripped her reputation as a writer. Her career as a novelist began with the epistolary romance* St. Clair *(1803). A historical romance,* The Novice of St. Dominick *(1805), followed.* The Missionary *(1811) draws on other contemporary literary trends such as gothic and orientalism, while* Woman; or, Ida of Athens *(1809) is perhaps the strongest representation of the feminism that is an important aspect of all her fiction. In addition to novels, Lady Morgan also wrote travel books –* France *(1817),* Italy *(1821) and* France in 1829–30 *(1830) – as well as works of a more speculative nature, among them* The Book of the Boudoir *(1829) and* Woman and Her Master *(1840). A number of her other non-fiction writings are of specifically Irish interest, the most substantial being* Patriotic Sketches of Ireland *(1807). This work supplements the perspective of her national tales, just as her* Life and Times of Salvator Rosa *(1824) usefully illuminates one of the sources of not only her own aesthetic sense but that of many Irish nineteenth-century novelists.*

*Lady Morgan's most important contribution to the literature of her day, however, consists of a series of national tales, a sub-genre that she did much to expand and complicate. Beginning with* The Wild Irish Girl, *the series also includes* O'Donnel *(1814) and* Florence Macarthy

(1818). These novels feature a somewhat uneasy mix of the materials of Sir Walter Scott and the methods of Ann Radcliffe. Their historical concerns, patriotic in hue and polemical in exposition, are further animated by settings that rely on such stock items of gothic as darkness, detention and dilapidation. Contrasting with such conditions, however, are characters whose undaunted natures and faithful spirits represent them as instances of a certain conception of indomitable Irishry. These frequently opinionated works drew the critical condemnation of many leading critics of the day on the grounds of Jacobinism, though it might equally be argued that Lady Morgan's literary excesses derive from her performative heritage and inclinations, the latter exemplified in her impersonation of the harp-playing Glorvina, The Wild Irish Girl's protagonist. Yet, despite her artistic shortcomings, Lady Morgan's works have a number of features that contributed to Irish literature's emerging repertoire of tropes. Among these are a sensitivity not merely to cultural heritage and indigenous traditions in themselves but to how these are sources of discursive authority; a preoccupation with the rebel and the type of political righteousness his ordeals endow; the feminine embodiment of national sentiment and national aspiration; an engagement with the spatial and visual components of narrative; and above all, perhaps, a critical perception, however melodramatically articulated, that the conversion of aims into action results in crisis.

'What an abridgement of the history of the land . . . is the story of the O'Briens and the O'Flahertys' (428) declares Beavoin O'Flaherty, succinctly but perhaps a little forlornly acknowledging the significance of the two eponymous families as not only structures supporting a sense of personal value and social utility but also acting as custodians of cultural heritage and historical tradition. No other institution in the late eighteenth-century world of this narrative can approach the special standing, complicated lineage and personal attainments of the O'Briens and the O'Flahertys. This emphasis echoes Captain Rock's preoccupation with name and status, and like the Memoirs of Captain Rock the narrative is buttressed with a good deal of intertextual precedent and learned references, although, rather than satiric, the tone in this case is somewhat hectoring. The presence of élite personages – a general, an abbé, a lord – represents a sense of social elevation and power, and this is replicated in the author's high-flown, ambitious style. The combination of worldly and writerly authority is perhaps an intentional contrast to upstart squireens such as the Rackrents and their demotic amanuensis. The well-placed members of the old Irish noble families represent the temporal continuity often associated with aristocracy.

This temporal authentication is all the more necessary because of their spatial displacement. But although the personages in question are all exiles, their lineage and status are spatially certified by their complicated but enduring affiliation with the Abbey of St Grellan, at Moycullen, 'Barony of Iar Connaught' (45). This building is part of both families' history and the differences that have occurred between them regarding it is one of the ways in which the narrative's concern with larger divisions is rehearsed. Just as the breach between the O'Briens and the O'Flahertys is related to the significance of a structure, the attainment of 'a national union' (303) must also be on the basis of structures, whether these are the Irish Volunteers, the United Irishmen, the renovated male and female confraternities of Cong and the Abbey respectively, or some amalgamation of all three, the potential for which *The O'Briens and the O'Flahertys* acknowledges but declines to develop.

The Abbess of St Grellan's is Beavoin O'Flaherty, namesake of the Abbey's founder, Beavoin O'Flaherty ny Brian, 'mother of Brian, great monarch of all Ireland, called Brian Borru' (48). That foundational mixture of royal blood and religious profession represents a loftiness the very chronology of which lifts it out of the sphere of English influence. Her embodiment of inner zeal and external grandeur lends the founding abbess something of a mythic status. By combining those properties, she represents an ideal of integration and unity that is clearly on a loftier plane than the conception of union that the merger of Irish and English parliaments presumes to exemplify. The latter version of union is effectively the culminating event of *The O'Briens and the O'Flahertys*, a point of terminus and dereliction rather than one of origin and uplift. Unlike her noted avatar, however, the latter-day Beavoin is only temporarily an abbess of what is the restored structure, not only because military action ruins the Abbey again but because she has the additional duty of shadowing the novel's protagonist Murrogh O'Brien. Dating from her initial sight of him in Rome's Villa Borghese (both characters' personal backgrounds have a strong European colouring), Beavoin continues to be present, though unrecognised, wherever the young man's ardent ways take him. Already having served as a 'soldier of fortune' (221) and now an undergraduate at Trinity College, Dublin, Murrogh embodies a new generation's aspirations infused with an illustrious, embattled heritage. Such a personage also shows the ease with which the author slips from the individual to the representative; indeed, she conveys the sense that the two categories' coexistence is the desired consummation of her protagonist's activities.

Joining the role of *doppelgänger* to that of guardian angel, Beavoin stands by Murrogh as he makes his way through contemporary Dublin's social and political arenas, a refined, subtle, harp-playing reminder and representation of the spirit of her illustrious O'Flaherty predecessor. Her presence is such that even the impulsive Murrogh eventually concedes that '[w]herever woman presides . . . there must be placed the focus of all power and influence' (427). Applied to Beavoin, this view identifies her as not only the narrative's presiding spirit but as the embodiment of a feminine ethos of rescue and retrieval that is necessary to counterbalance Murrogh's adventurous and potentially self-destructive maleness. As though to reinforce Murrogh's male style, he is also visited periodically by Shane, the foster brother with whom he spent his earliest years on the Aran Islands. A physical giant, Shane seems to be for the most part a moral midget, a murderer whose miraculous escape from hanging proves short-lived. He is 'the very genius of the wild and solitary' (391) Connemara landscape that is his native place and he also exhibits 'the picturesque savagery of which his form so well assorted' (ibid.). Beavoin describes herself as having been in childhood 'the "delicate Ariel" of this Irish Caliban' (501), and though she seems an essential monitor of Murrogh's plans and attitudes, Shane is indispensable in his own way and saves Murrogh from himself in many a scrape. Shane is a raw and disproportioned prototype of Murrogh's attraction to risk and physical confrontation, acknowledgement of which eventually leads him to conclude that '[t]he army was his true vocation' (536).

There was a time, however, when Murrogh could fierily proclaim 'Ireland is my vocation' (295), and indeed such seems to be the case from his first appearance in the novel. At that point he is an Irish Volunteer, and his appearance is on the occasion of a triumphalist spectacle, a field day in which the false representation of exhibitionism overshadows other less superficial aspects of what is on display. Murrogh's membership of the Volunteers implies an identification with the organisation's democratic character. Not only have the Volunteers brought about physical transformation – '[a] race, which had ever been deemed comely, became improved by military discipline' (100) – but social change. This is '[a] military institution, so singular in its nature as to include the several gradations of nobles and commons, merchants, yeomen, and mechanics' (101), a preview, presumably, of the society to come. And when Murrogh takes his place alongside Lord Charlemont, the two 'exhibited the splendid representation of the men of Ireland's best days' (121). But the Phoenix Park field day in which Murrogh takes part is merely a mock battle, and rather than leading 'the youthful soldier' (ibid.) to productive military or political action, or even to an acknowledgement of such matters, its only outcome is that he impresses Lady Abina Knocklofty (*neé* O'Blarney), who sees him as 'a regular hero of romance' (133).

The vanity expressed in Murrogh's boast that '[t]o feel and to act, had been the habit of his life' (490) is somewhat disturbed by Lady Knocklofty's allure and her appetite for having 'my frolic' (456). He finds it difficult to resist her high-toned society and the self-indulgent *soirées* that host 'political vampires' (209) and reveal her guests' transparent performativity. Such occasions are reactionary contrasts to Volunteer pageantry. And Murrogh is also vulnerable as a result of alienation from his father, the apostate Lord Arranmore, from whom Murrogh stands to inherit no more than his title following the collapse of his Dublin townhouse – another instance of the novel's interplay between structure and instability. Further, Murrogh is expelled from Trinity for being a leading figure amongst 'those young incendiaries, who are known agents of the jacobinical societies' (218). And he hardly secures his standing by being sworn into the United Irishmen, committing himself to the ideal of 'national redemption' (303) and accepting a position in the Connaught command of that organisation. This appointment places him in the ranks of the 'Jesuits of the Union' (308), even though, in keeping with his labile enthusiasm, Murrogh declares, 'I distrust, I dislike secrecy' (304). These vulnerabilities and susceptibilities to romantic masquerade and political clandestinity are the twin foci of power in a Dublin that 'exhibited the appearance of a town besieged' (158). In this restless and tense environment, Murrogh cannot feel at home. No doubt his egotism and rebelliousness are expressions of 'Rousseau-ish feelings' (308), and these get in the way of his commitment. In any event, the brightly lit drawing room where feminine intrigue holds sway, the dank backstreets in which the United Irishmen meet, and the wild, open spaces of his Connemara homeland all fail to provide him with a satisfactory means of representing himself. Murrogh evidently requires a broader sphere of action, a more established public forum, a more powerful form of self-validating maleness, and a valorisation of his temperament than embattled Irish conditions afford. His joint allegiance to Lady Knocklofty and republicanism is certainly not conducive to 'that independence which is the sole base of the best and noblest pride' (229).

The apparent unavailability of the Volunteers as a context also tacitly contributes to Murrogh's self-representational difficulties. Their flags and uniforms obviously have a more than representational value, but that value in itself is a call to the virtuous action that Murrogh desires and that Knocklofty superficiality and United Irish secrecy frustrate. And a measure of the representational's significance is indicated by *The Annals of the Isles of Arran and Moycullen, or the Green Book of St. Grellan* that Murrogh discovers in O'Brien House. Dealing with each family's home ground, this volume has been translated by an O'Flaherty and annotated by Murrogh's father. A precious object in appearance as well as in content, what particularly strikes Murrogh are its illustrations of both upstanding ancestors and their subject dependants, the emotional appeal of which to what he attempts to dismiss as 'his womanish sensibility' (243) is impossible to deny. Here depicted is a lineage in whose terms he could represent himself. Murrogh may be 'an epitome of the regenerated age to which he belonged, going with its views, and animated by its spirit, a worshipper of La Fayette, a disciple of Mirabeau' (231), but now he can also align rebellious modernity with an illustrious patrimony. This heritage is authorised by, secures and denotes the cultural capital of both O'Briens and O'Flahertys. Beavoin's later claim that 'arguments are words, but images are facts' (503) underlines not only the impact the pictures have on Murrogh but their general testamentary prestige as forms of historical undeniability. And it may also be that Murrogh finds in them compensation for the conviction that he has been '[f]rom my birth, a victim of false impressions' (306).

Acting on a productive relationship between his Irish inheritance and his political modernity appears to be a legitimate objective for Murrogh, and his journey westward seems to promise such a significant step forward. A rough prototype of such a relationship appears in his succession on his father's death to the Arranmore title, which is not only 'his right . . . [but] by raising him above the mass . . . would increase the utility of those efforts, which he was more than ever determined to make for the civil and religious liberties of his countrymen' (400). In his Connaught fatherland he can replace Dublin's temptations and affiliations with Beavoin's disinterested concern and Shane's run of the country. And yet both these would-be protectors of his, representatives of essential components of his birthright, also occasion conflicted allegiances and are covert in their activities and confusing in their appeal. Both seem a distraction from the kind of activity that is so prominent and pressing in Murrogh's thoughts. Neither can provide the type of structure that might be expected of a homeland or a homecoming; and the wish of the backward-looking Mac Taff sisters, Murrogh's closest kin, to make him one of them seems a dead end. All that recommends his native ground, evidently, are its 'sublime' (382) views. But spectacular countryside is not necessarily hospitable, and Murrogh is lost for a good deal of his Connemara sojourn. Remoteness seems a synonym for lack of community, and, in addition to being 'destitute of all human industry' (383), Murrough finds that if one local befriends him another betrays him to the authorities. Moreover, further complications arise from his inability either to take control of or to abandon his Dublin attachments. Lady Knocklofty appears – she has a western home – to prolong Murrogh's emotional confusion; and his authorship of a 'political *brochure*' (503) leads to his arrest. Murrogh conveys the futility of his return in referring to it as 'this adventure' (374).

Politically speaking, Connaught proves infertile ground, leaving Murrogh between options, the position that most accurately represents him. And even the resolution of O'Brien–O'Flaherty family differences is largely Beavoin's doing, while she and Shane secure Murrogh's eventual escape from Kilmainham and the gallows. His Irish career is a series of increasingly marked oscillations from one source of pressure to another, such that, like the architectural style of his father's ill-fated town house, he resembles 'an amalgamation of incompatibles' (228). His experiences may exemplify the trials of a young man in turbulent times, but his unchecked inclination towards gesture and assertion result in a self-representation that signifies being at the mercy of events, not commissioning or even learning from them. The novel's lack of a *Bildung* dimension seems to reinforce Beavoin's view that '[t]o be born an Irishman is a dark destiny' (494–5). But the brightly lit Paris *salon* in which the two are last seen presumably compensates for the penumbra of Irishness. There, a mute, rather statuesque Murrogh, in the uniform of an officer in the *Grande Armée*, represents the apotheosis of his energies. In his exile he is following in O'Flaherty family footsteps, as Beavoin's presence alongside him confirms. Their union suggests that an inflated family romance has abridged the national one.

Or perhaps those two narratives have been ideally 'engrafted' (247) in the image of a couple who have sublimated their personal histories in their political affiliations.

# 1829

## Gerald Griffin, *The Collegians*

*Gerald Griffin (1803–40) was born in Limerick, and, as was the case for many Catholics at the time, received an irregular education at a variety of local hedge schools. At the age of nineteen he left Ireland for London, attracted to the literary life there, having met John Banim and noted that writer's success with* Damon and Pythias *(1821). Griffin's early ambition to emulate Banim's stage success was not realised, and he spent the next three years as a Grub Street nobody, producing (often pseudonymously) much journalism and reportage and living in poverty, despite Banim's offers of assistance. Again following Banim's example, however, Griffin took up prose fiction, publishing* Holland-Tide, *a collection of stories, in 1827. A second collection,* Tales of the Munster Festivals, *followed in the same year. With the publication of* The Collegians, *Griffin's literary stock reached its height. This novel was both a notable success in its own day and in a prolonged afterlife. It was adapted for the stage by Dion Boucicault as* The Colleen Bawn *(1860) – not to be confused with William Carleton's novel* Willy Reilly and His Dear Colleen Bawn *(1855). In addition to being the basis of an opera by Jules Benedict entitled* The Lily of Killarney *(1862), it has been considered the inspiration of Theodore Dreiser's* An American Tragedy *(1925). In the early twentieth century it was filmed twice;* The Colleen Bawn *was the title on both occasions. And* The Collegians *also supplied Brian O'Nolan with the nom-de-plume under which his celebrated* Irish Times *columns appeared, Myles na gCopaleen (Myles-na-Coppulleen, as Griffin has it).*

*With the exception of his song 'Aileen Aroon', a perennial in the Irish sentimental song repertoire, Griffin's remaining works are rather overshadowed not only by the success of* The Collegians *but by its social portraiture and thematic daring. Two shorter works,* The Rivals *and* Tracy's Ambition, *were also published in 1829, and Griffin attempted a variety of different genres thereafter –* The Christian Physiologist *(1830), a collection of* contes moraux; The Invasion *(1832) and* The Duke of Monmouth *(1836), historical novels; and* Tales of My Neighbourhood *(1835), a miscellany of prose and verse. With the possible exception of the first two mentioned, none can remotely compare with* The Collegians. *These later works suggest Griffin's uncertainty regarding form and content, and a lack of direction as to where his talent might take him, and these problems were compounded during the 1830s by increasingly grave misgivings about the literary life and his own contributions to it. These doubts culminated in his renunciation of writing in 1838, when he destroyed most of his papers and entered the Christian Brothers. A volume of stories,* Talis Qualis; or, Tales of the Jury Room, *appeared in 1842, and the same year a play,* Gissipus, *received a successful London production.*

*The setting of* The Collegians *has ensured that Griffin remains closely associated with the city of Limerick and the nearby Shannon estuary. As a result, he risks being classified as a regional writer, but that designation is an underestimation. His works undoubtedly evoke a strong sense of place, accentuated perhaps by the exile's gaze, but they convey more than mere picturesqueness. Their treatment of light and shade, for instance, shows an alertness to atmospheric nuance and psychological climate. And, as in the Banims,* Tales of the O'Hara Family, *Griffin's depictions of provincial life sharply observe subtle shadings of class difference. Moreover, the fascination in his most notable works with the protagonist as over-reacher shows a depth of moral engagement and psychological originality that makes Griffin's career the most intriguing of pre-Famine Irish nineteenth-century novelists, as well as, in its ultimate failure, one of the most revealing.*

One morning in the summer of 1819, the body of sixteen-year-old Ellen Hanly was washed up on the coast of County Clare. She had been missing for over a month. Foul play was suspected in her death, and two men were subsequently arrested in connection with it. One was John Scanlan, a member of a well-to-do local family, who was emotionally involved with the victim; the other was Stephen Sullivan, a boatman employed by Scanlan. Both men were put on trial (Scanlan was defended by Daniel O'Connell), found guilty and hanged. Suggestions that Griffin covered the trials are implausible, but the case was a *cause célèbre* of the day, and its sensational facts provided the basis for *The Collegians*. Famously exemplified by Stendhal in *Le Rouge et le Noir* (1830) and later by Flaubert in *Madame Bovary* (1857), the adaptation of newspaper material for fictional purposes clearly broadens the artistic and thematic range of the nineteenth-century Irish novel, giving *The Collegians* an originality that the focus of its narrative on drama and excess tends to disguise.

But then this is a novel of disguises. Not only are Hardress Cregan's attempts to cover up his fatal clandestine marriage to Eily O'Connor at the heart of the plot, his efforts are intensified by his ultimately self-destructive wish to suppress the marriage's consequences. Even the novel's very title – a term that hardly occurs in the text – is in the nature of a mask, its connotations providing the protagonist with a false front and suppressing the fact of his double life. A collegian is a university-educated young man, one who has been exposed to the putatively beneficial intellectual and cultural influences of study and college life and who, as a result of being acculturated to the forms of disciplined judgement those influences promote, is now qualified to take his rightful place in the world. Such orthodoxies are exemplified by Cregan's friend, neighbour and fellow-student Kyrle Daly, whose entry into the law profession confirms that he is prepared to represent himself as being in possession of the wherewithal to discharge his duties in society. Kyrle will do so by representing others. In his case, it may be said that he has reached the conclusion of his formative period; his *Bildung* – that is, the growth of his consciousness and self-realisation – has attained that optimum level of consciousness displayed by the youthful characters of many a nineteenth-century European novel. This level is the necessary platform for agency and action. But Kyrle Daly, important as he is as a moral counterweight to Hardress Cregan, is not *The Collegians'* central concern. Indeed, his occupation of the high ground, as opposed to his friend's frequenting of estuarial slob-land, removes him from the novel's drama. And rather than meeting the generic requirements of the *Bildungsroman*, Griffin's work, more interestingly, runs counter to that genre, resulting in a novel that is anti-*Bildung*, or perhaps dark *Bildung*, detailing Hardress's growing enmeshment by selfishness and evil rather than the rise in the world that might be expected of a collegian. This reversal is another aspect of Griffin's originality, and his portrait of what might be called Hardress's oppositeness is substantiated by a narrative texture made up of journeys in darkness, erosions of intimacy, manhood represented as malevolence and action shown only as destruction.

Priggish, upright Kyrle is a useful, though not particularly animated, antithesis to libidinous, fallen Hardress. But telling as the contrast between the collegians is, the novel pivots on the relationship between Hardress and Eily O'Connor, the girl he covets and who, as a result, is sacrificed to his mistake. Daughter of Mihil, a rope-maker, Eily lives in Garryowen – Owen's garden, 'almost a synonime for Ireland' (2) – and there is no doubt that she is its flower, and that her naturalness is a total contrast to what has nurtured the collegian. But already Garryowen's edenic air has been tainted. And it is because the place is vulnerable to hooliganism that Hardress establishes contact with the O'Connors by, in one of the novel's many cutting ironies, offering Eily and her father his protection. Soon Hardress's attention turns Eily's head, to the extent that she leaves behind her beau, that 'perfect Ulysses' (56) Myles-na-Coppulleen, and 'like criminals in prison' (93) she and Hardress contract a secret marriage before a defrocked priest. Eily's abandonment of both Myles and her doting father are serious betrayals, uncharacteristic not only on personal grounds but also because they offend against the close communal ties of her class. And it is class, to issues of which *The Collegians* is particularly alert throughout, that makes Eily's marriage even more untenable than any such arrangement would ordinarily be, since Hardress is also involved with Eily's social opposite, Anne Chute of Castle Chute.

Obviously in the dark regarding Eily, Hardress's mother encourages his attachment to Anne. Mrs Cregan tells her son that 'I had rather see you in your coffin than matched below your rank' (135). Anne has breeding and tradition. Her home is where 'a council of the Munster chieftains, in the days of Elizabeth' (48) met. The attachment is reinforced by the fact that Anne and Hardress are related (their mothers are stepsisters). She has rejected Kyrle Daly in favour of Hardress; and she has come for an extended stay at Cregans'. Poised, polished and glacial, Anne's femininity is also the reverse of Eily's; and, as Hardress confesses to Kyrle, 'I love the wild hedge-flower simplicity before the cold and sapless exotic fashion' (80). But his marriage, more a formal *fait accompli* than a lived experience, does not allow him to inhabit fully 'the wild orchard of nature' (83) that is his heart's desire. Nor does the more cultivated Anne prove especially responsive to his somewhat flamboyant male style. Not only is Hardress divided as to where his loyalty should lie, the objects of his loyalty themselves represent opposed and irreconcilable characters, temperaments, social training and family background. This division seems to have oedipal origins; Hardress is the son of a weak father and dominating mother. Mrs Cregan's power is evident in matchmaking, although she relies on a tissue of false representations to determine the kind of union her intended couple should embody. (The same type of prescriptive falsification emerges in Hardresss's treatment of Eily, an amalgamation of impulsiveness, wilfulness, pride and self-deceiving idealisation.) But

Hardress, confessing both his incipient bigamy and the fact that 'I am a murderer' (232), reverses how his mother sees him.

As is the case of so much regarding Hardress, what he accuses his mother of seems excessive – '[t]his whole love-scheme, that has begun in trick and ended in blood, was all your work!' (235). And even if this were true, it would not be the whole story. Another undeniable influence on his character, and a powerful contributing factor to his divided state of mind, is the male culture represented by many local older men, who perhaps cut their teeth as trouble-making rakes in Garryowen. Griffin disguises *The Collegians'* origins in his own day by setting it in the late eighteenth century, but there are also other advantages to the change in chronology. One of these, as the reference to 'the famous Catholic concession of 1773' (3) suggests, is to indicate that families like the Cregans and the Dalys were then beginning to attain higher social standing and fuller political recognition, an aspect of the novel that would not be lost on its first readers. And, as though to reinforce the point, Kyrle Daly's man, Lowry Looby – '[t]he Mercury of the cabins' (28) – ends up 'upon the poll-books for the late memorable election' (294) in Clare, when Daniel O'Connell was elected. As a collegian, Hardress ostensibly seems to be removed from patterns of behaviour established by the district's ancient fire-eaters. Yet he has the same initials as two of the most notorious of these predecessors, Hepton Connolly and Hyland 'Fireball' Creagh. And Hardress's capacity for wrongdoing, like theirs, arises out of self-indulgent and irresponsible liberty-taking. Hardress might not stoop to the repellent 'pinking' (166) to which his deformed henchman Danny Mann is subjected, but his abusive and exploitative treatment of Eily throughout their marriage does, in its arbitrary hounding of the defenceless, suggest itself as pinking's psychological equivalent.

It is not that Hardress has knowingly embraced the older generation's cavalier male exhibitionism and excess. Indeed, there are occasions when he seems to represent a covert reversal of such manners. Once, during a hunt – an event synonymous with the squirearchy's breakneck style – the sight of blood causes Hardress to faint; and if 'no one ventured openly to impute any effeminacy of character to the young gentleman' (242), the thought evidently crosses the huntsmen's minds. (This is not the only occasion on which there are allusions to effeminacy with regard to Hardress.) At the same time, he seems incapable of Kyrle's denunciation of Creagh 'and your mean and murderous class' (204). Hardress appears to have internalised a certain form of social heritage without quite realising it, much less accepting it as a responsibility. As a result, he is caught between two eras, neither the son of an earlier, unselfconscious time nor of a more judicious present. And a similar type of antithesis characterises his parental endowment. He may have inherited his mother's 'national warmth of temperament and liveliness of feeling' (115), but he has his father's inner weakness. Thus, he is not only trapped between Eily and Anne, or between 'two modes of evil' (177) – murder and bigamy – in which his involvement with them seems destined to culminate; in addition, his sexual identity, his parents' psychological legacy, the collegian's veneer over a consciousness devoid of self-discipline, further complicate his capacity to represent himself.

In short, Hardress Cregan cannot help being his own worst enemy. Representing anything over and above the narcissism of his 'philosophical vanity' (95) – the principal witness to which is Eily, who must remain undisclosed and unavowed – is clearly beyond his capacity, and the fact that 'the flow of generosity in Hardress Cregan was never checked or governed by motives of prudence or of justice' (38) indicates that what seems to be a continuity between his inner life and his impact on others is actually a tension. In time, his consciousness, which his collegiate experience might have made an instrument of moral reckoning and an aid to self-possession, becomes a medium of torture. As perhaps is fitting for one 'just as proud . . . as Lucifer himself' (113), Hardress's self-representation is based on negativity – exorbitant desire, breach of faith, self-deception and moral collapse. In mistaking how to represent himself, he can only be a representative of what not to be for others. His arrest at his wedding to Anne – a moment of witness, a moment intended to counteract division and promising union – is the public enactment of his protracted inner fall from grace.

Marriage to Eily is where this fall begins. Early in their acquaintance, the girl seems like 'a lay nun' (5), a phrase anticipating the cloistered condition of her marriage. Confinement in remote, untamed locations as, effectively, a ward of Danny Mann, Hardress's foster-brother, boatman and 'my *fidus Achates*' (168), violates marriage's mutuality, trust, intimacy, and prospect of a future. What Hardress has perpetrated is more like an abduction (like the duelling that Kyrle Daly condemns, another outmoded eighteenth-century practice) than anything more honourable or conscientious. It is not clear what Eily thought awaited her; she too, if rather more understandably (she is no collegian, after all), allowed her immaturity and vanity to lead her on. Yet if she proves to be one-dimensional and 'unelastic' (183), she does make various efforts to redress her abjection, indicating a better sense of what is fitting than her educated husband. It is less her helpless tie to Hardress that constitutes her marriage bond than her being held by Danny. His fierce fidelity – another reversal; he is faithful to a falsity – means that not only is Eily in his keeping, so too in a sense is Hardress; he is not accidentally nicknamed Danny the Lord. And by thought and deed, the servant is the master of the situation, including Eily's fate. But, in one of the novel's most unexpected instances of the return of the repressed, the connection between master and man breaks down. And here too Hardress is the author of his own destruction. His brief assault on Danny duplicates the attack that caused the latter's deformation. It also shows that in the interim Hardress has learned nothing. Right and wrong are still not fixed poles for him. Danny, already complicit in a betrayal that leads to a death, does not shirk from incriminating his supposed master. Eily's death has made them equals, morally speaking and before the law, Kyrle Daly's domain.

With Hardress's demise, the way is clear for Kyrle to renew successfully his interest in Anne Chute. Their marriage marks a new beginning, a different dispensation, a union that represents virtue and good faith in the plain light of day. The dark days of Hardress, and the penumbra of historical benightedness that lies behind them, fade away. Such a conclusion is no doubt worthy of the heightened seriousness of the novel's tone and style and its melodramatically articulated anatomy of conscience. And it is also a conclusion that suggests a view of *The Collegians* as a more earnest, but also more daring, treatment of themes advanced in *Castle Rackrent*. For both Hardress Cregan and Sir Condy Rackrent, education, family, social status, a personable manner are all very well, but they come to nothing if there are no broader cultural and social frameworks to ratify them. Hardress and Sir Condy endure self-inflicted waste, but they are also casualties of a way of life that seems excessively and gratuitously *laissez-faire*. The prevailing structures – economic in Edgeworth's emphasis, moral in Griffin's – must fall. And Griffin goes further than his predecessor, not only by producing what might be termed a novel of manners with a vengeance but also by suggesting a different landscape, one that can be improved only by the enfranchisement of those unrepresented by the old exclusions.

# 1832

# Harriet Martineau, *Ireland: A Tale*

*Harriet Martineau (1802–76) was born in Norwich to a family whose Unitarianism was arguably the most decisive influence on not only her intellectual formation but her career-long engagement with ideas and public policy, which made her the pre-eminent woman of letters in mid-nineteenth-century England. Her earliest writings appeared in the* Monthly Repository, *a local Unitarian periodical. An 1832 decision to live by her pen led Martineau to London, where her views on political economy soon attracted favourable attention.*

*Rapid changes in English industries, cities and demography provided Martineau with the raw material of some of her early books, and how she handles this subject matter is the basis for her reputation as a pioneer of sociology. Of these early works,* Illustrations of Political Economy *– stories illustrating her social views – is the most notable. Launched in 1831, the series consists of twenty-three issues in all, of which* Ireland: A Tale *is the ninth. In their instructional and reformist intentions, these narratives are related to the works of Maria Edgeworth, though sadly lacking Edgeworth's wit. And their didactic and programmatic character is also a feature of Martineau's novels, among which* Deerbrook *(1839) and* The Hour and the Man *(1841) are the best known (the latter is a treatment of Toussaint l'Ouverture and the Haitian rebellion). Broadly speaking, the imagination was not a faculty in which Martineau showed a great deal of interest.*

*The wide variety of her non-fiction works, however, testifies both to her observational skills and to her reformist politics;* Letters from Ireland *(1853), based on her 1852 tour of the country, is a case in point. So also are her travel writings, particularly* Society in America *(1837) and* Eastern Life: Present and Past *(1848). Among her other noteworthy publications are a discourse on method entitled* How to Observe Morals and Manners *(1838); a narrative of her own times,* History of the Thirty Years' Peace *(1849); and an* Autobiography *(1877). Martineau was a voluminous journalist, a committed feminist, and a supporter of Darwinism; and she also introduced the philosophy of Auguste Comte to English readers. Ireland does not occupy a very prominent place among her intellectual concerns, but her visits to and writings on the country are not only indicative of her public-mindedness but also represent how Irish conditions lent themselves as a proving ground for Victorian intellectuals.*

The novel opens in '[t]he Glen of Echoes . . . one of the most obscure districts of a remote country' (7), an area of the County Mayo coast where neither individuals nor community are particularly in evidence. This paucity is all the more noteworthy in a work that uses numbers to telling effect in support of its prescriptive standpoint, the intellectual roots of which are in a Malthusian concern with Irish overpopulation and its effects on the efficient management of the land. In view of this concern, *Ireland's* dearth of characters, particularly of those in the most populous group, the peasantry, seems paradoxical. But Martineau justifies it in her 'Preface' to the work by explaining that 'my personages are few because it is my object to show, in a confined space, how long a series of evils may befall individuals in a society conducted like that of Ireland, and by what a repetition of grievances its members are driven into disaffection and violence [i]'. This argument may not seem particularly watertight, but it does emphasise an approach to character based on utility. The shift between 'personages', 'individuals' and 'members' is an indication of the uncertain grounds for self-representation that Martineau considers available to her characters, and tacitly previews the pattern of disruption and displacement that gives the narrative what little momentum it possesses.

Representing conditions that seem barely tenable is not the only purpose grievance-stricken entities serve. They also carry out what the author sees as the more useful service of opening the eyes of those who are in charge – landlords, legislators and their ilk; 'those whom it most concerns' [i], as the 'Preface' puts it. The lower orders do not just represent themselves; indeed, the manner in which they might do so – the aforementioned 'disaffection and violence' – seem likely to eliminate any standing to which they might aspire. Rather, they are representatives of a complex of deficiencies – neglect, insecurity, impoverishment, dependence – that only their overlords can eradicate. Yet, reform when it eventually arrives consists of mass emigration, conclusively confirming that the peasantry most successfully represent themselves and their social reality in terms that negate them. The emigration scheme is considered a boon by landlord and peasant alike, and the fate of those who cannot benefit from it underlines that general view. The exceptions are the remaining members of the Mahony and Sullivan families, on whose social destiny the novel is focused. Each of them exemplifies an alternative and more unfortunate form of negation, or disappearance, than that offered by the emigrant ship. Dora is sentenced to transportation for life. Her husband, Dan Mahony, opts for Whiteboyism and a fugitive's life. Their infant son is entrusted to

Dora's father, who turns his back on an offer of assistance from the union of interests consisting of the reforming landlord Tracey and the local priest, Father Glenny. Prototypes of silence, exile and cunning, respectively, Sullivan, Dora and Dan are fitting emblems of what has become of their native place.

Over the course of the novel, the Glen of Echoes becomes an intentionally fabricated hollowness in which resound the keynotes of what the author sees as rational and enlightened policy based on a metric derived from the collusion of statistics with the balance sheet, the unimpeachable scriptures of political economy. By extension, the novel's title denotes a place of evacuation, devoid of home-grown affections, attachments or entitlements, a landscape secured and methodised in the name of administrative efficiency, a property nurtured by uniformity and devoid of difference and the natural, though not necessarily intractable, friction it generates. And the shadow of such a landscape, together with the outlook that formed it, is detectable in the rural settings of later Irish nineteenth-century novels such as *Laurence Bloomfield in Ireland*, *Knocknagow* and *Marcella Grace*.

The paradoxical interdependence in *Ireland: A Tale* between themes of removal and improvement is largely enacted through episodes of representation and misrepresentation. Such occasions feature not only the Sullivans and the Mahonys; the upper classes, too – Tracey, the returned absentee landlord, and his 'resident proprietor' (9) neighbour Rosso – maintain their presence by staking a claim to one or other position along the narrow spectrum of their ameliorative interests. The peasantry relies for public standing on written material such as leases and letters; their social superiors converse among themselves about what concerns them. What is written is a signature of impermanence – leases are untenable; letters prove incriminating. The statements shared by landlords and clergymen, in contrast, have the lapidary character of the law – arguments possess the force of policy; social structures readily issue from what are no more than opinions. In the case of leases, for instance, formalised language can be deprived of its binding power, whereas informal drawing-room exchanges have an authoritative finality. Supposedly trustworthy modes of discourse and transaction misrepresent the peasantry, culminating in Dora's trial for perjury, while at the same time ideas are pursued at leisure as to how best Dora and her kind will 'understand the law . . . respect the government [and] . . . act upon the belief that men of various creeds and offices may dwell together without enmity' (170). Who such men may be and how their benign command would function is beyond *Ireland's* scope. And since there is no common, dependable language, and thus no reliable or consistent method of representing what the Sullivans and Mahonys are as they stand, there can be no common ground. Instead, there can only be what Rosso terms 'the education of circumstances' (73), arbitrary and unending instruction in adaptation and compliance dictated as the landlord sees fit.

The force of such circumstances, and familiarity with its strangely erasing body of knowledge, are underlined when contrasted with how education in the more usual scholastic sense features in the narrative. Rosso has also provided the local school, and he and Tracey agree that book-learning is most important; as the latter proclaims, 'let education be abundantly given, so as to afford us hope that the people may in time understand that their interests are cared for' (137). Literate Dora is the school's brightest pupil, but, under duress from her father, she unwittingly signs away the family holding by putting his name to a flawed lease. Subsequently, under pressure from Dan, she writes a threatening letter, the upshot of which is her surrender to the authorities literally by her own hand. Her written plea for time to make arrangements for her infant son while she is in jail goes unanswered, adding to and intensifying the impossibility that Dora's word be taken as her bond, as landlords say theirs must be. In complying with Dan's epistolary demand, she experiences an overwhelming passiveness 'that arose from a sense of the uselessness of opposition' (105), and during her incarceration she remains haunted by crushing marginalisation and depression. These feelings are exacerbated by the constant wailing of her child, an expression of the helplessness of being without an alternative. It seems as though her literacy has cost Dora all that would give her purchase on a place in life – home, capacity to mother, mental faculties, husband. The prospect of her trial produces 'utter indifference' (161); as she anticipates the event, 'she didn't remember that she had a part to perform' (ibid.), so that the opportunity for self-representation is lost. The actual hearing is the occasion of 'a full and deep consciousness of her misery' (164), although Dora shows so little sign of it that it is difficult to know if her demeanour conveys composure or inertia. And the virtually complete silence she maintains 'from first to last' (ibid.) suggests that her transportation has already begun.

The comprehensiveness of this portrait of nullity is momentarily offset as Dora leaves the courthouse after sentencing. Overhearing the adverse comments of some bystanders regarding what her literacy had led her to, she reveals something of how she might have performed had she defended herself. After interestingly rebutting the notion that literacy as such is necessary to threatening letters by referring to the repertoire of menacing hieroglyphics also used in such documents, Dora points out that 'the school in which my husband and I learned rebellion was the bleak rock, where famine came to be our teacher' (166). This defence, noteworthy not only for its sentiments but for its grammatical precision and brogue-free tenor, is a testament to self-representation. And indeed it may also represent the case of those to whom it is addressed, though this possibility cannot be confirmed, since Dora's escort interrupts and removes her before any of her listeners respond. Her arraignment of the environment, rather than the planned system, as the principal agent of her ultimate dislocation may also seem like an opportunity lost. Dora's perspective may not amount to a reasoned critique, perhaps, but its power to signify emotional meaning should not be discounted. From that point of view, her words are a valuable reminder that not only has the feminine never had much visibility in the Glen of Echoes – a casualty perhaps of Martineau's limited cast of characters – but also that the life-making capacities, the ways of thought, the types of action, the qualities of feeling typically embodied by nineteenth-century female characters, have no place in 'a desert like this' (113). Interiors, whether domestic or psychological, must be foregone in an environment where the material and the managerial have pre-eminence and where male leadership, whether of a rebellious or reformist stamp, determines the order of the day. This absence is acknowledged by Dora almost from the beginning, when '[t]o have Dan to lean upon was everything' (38). And as a further instance of how unused to representing herself Dora is, she pines for the guidance of Father Glenny: 'he would tell me how much I may venture as a woman' (119). Of all the removals, disruptions and erasures of *Ireland*'s story, the most complete and exhaustive are those that bear on Dora's destiny.

The downward trajectory of her experiences are marked to a unique degree by abandonment, vulnerability and, above all, isolation. And her solitude is not only debilitating in itself, it contrasts starkly with the collective character of men's lives. Men are portrayed as not only acting together, but of acting in accord. Perhaps Rosso and Tracey do not initially share the same outlook, but once the latter justifies his approach, Rosso declares his readiness 'to live in fellowship' (138) with his assertive neighbour. As a pendant to this unity, Rosso frankly affirms the landlord pre-eminence for which *Ireland* consistently argues by bidding 'farewell to all Catholic oaths to wade knee-deep in Orange blood, and to all Protestant likenings of the pope and his flock to the devil and his crew' (ibid.). Economics creates its own politics, evidently, by obviating one of the period's major sources of political difference. A similar union is reached by an exchange of views between Father Glenny and Reverend Orme, the local Church of Ireland incumbent. This meeting ends in an agreement to suspend not only two important clerical income streams but two practices that give them significant social power: Orme will defer 'the useless endeavour to exact tithes' (156) and Glenny will no longer demand a two-guinea wedding fee. This compact abridges the churches' role as spiritual *rentiers*, and in doing so reinforces landlordism's secular leadership by seeming to coincide with the assertion of pastoral authority by Tracey's reformist schemes. Glenny has long anticipated this clerical partnership, and the allocation of power within it, referring before Tracey's return not only to the landlord's Catholicism but to how it establishes him as an 'ancient possessor of the soil, only kept at a distance by being deprived of . . . political rights, and as anxious as gentry should be for the prosperity of [the] people' (58). Again, the economic emphasis is paramount, as is the understanding that landlords represent themselves in this interest. (*Ireland* rejects the case for government as a partner in social administration, as its lengthy objections to Poor Law legislation makes clear.)

The local Whiteboy band emphasises male collaboration to a more obvious degree than any of the above alignments, so much so that Dan's participation in subversive activity elicits Dora's rather barbed accusation that 'you have plighted and pledged yourself to your band since you swore you would wed me only' (97). But shared Whiteboy interests and unity of purpose are devoid of the clear articulation and undisguised aims of the landowners' system. Indeed, Whiteboyism's failure to function as a system seems to be a corollary to its illegitimacy. In opposing the rule of law as it stands, the principles of land tenure as they presently operate, and without the institutional representation on which rules and regulations are established, Whiteboyism amounts to nothing more than an incoherent and sporadic Jacquerie, much more so than in Mrs Hall's *The Whiteboy*. Seen exclusively in terms of destructive or at best directionless action, the activists embody what Glenny describes as 'the law of this district . . . plunder or be plundered' (143), and his point is proven in the lengthy digression in which the band attempts to take advantage of a shipwreck. Wreckage indeed is what awaits them, as Rosso foresees: '[t]he noblest in their natures, the brave and high-spirited, will become white-boys, and die amidst acts of outrage, or on the gibbet' (69) – the latter another form of erasure. The attraction of the putatively safe emigrant passage speaks for itself; even the middle course between wreckage and land-fall suggested by transportation seems a benevolent option.

While union and amity appear possible among reasonable men, the Whiteboys, who deal in action rather than words, cannot be included among those who reason, a view dismantled in Moore's *Memoirs of Captain Rock*. They are the unreconcilable, occupying a no-man's-land beyond the remit of pastoral, whether manifested by improving landlord or safeguarding priest. In a sense, they represent the unreclaimed and profitless land itself, an entity that, as the military measures taken against them indicate, can only be conquered. By appearing to take the law into their own hands and breaking it, the Whiteboys may not exactly show how 'the interests of the people can be safely committed to their own guardianship' (80), but it is equally difficult to accept that the Traceys of that world, who presume to hold those interests in trust for the people, are any more legally minded. Dan Mahony's view that 'when there was an end of justice, there was an end of law' (85) seems quite as cogent as Tracey's rather choleric outburst: '[l]et all usurpers of unjust authority, all who make the law odious and justice a mockery, be displaced from office' (137). This remarkably unselfconscious declaration seems to regard the law as an extension of the rights of property.

Martineau's vision of an abuse-free hierarchy as a structure that will advance and protect a mutuality of interest between rulers and ruled does not inhibit her sympathy for 'the soul-sickness of pauperism' (75). If anything, her reformist attitude is strengthened by her piteous regard. But these sympathies do not impinge critically on her *roman à thèse*, the objectives of which are spelled out in the 'Summary of Principles Illustrated in This Volume' with which the narrative concludes. And Martineau is too imaginatively limited to elaborate on the unexpected homologies and provocative paradoxes that her material contains. Although her work does address the problems of the present, she prefers to solve rather than to represent these problems' essentially conflicted character. Instead of depicting the realities of Irish life, *Ireland: A Tale* demonstrates the continuing generic and expressive difficulties that rendering those realities in fictional form reveals.

# 1845

## Anna Maria Hall, *The Whiteboy*

*Anna Maria Fielding (1800–81) was born in Dublin and spent her early life in Bannow, County Wexford. In 1815 she went with her family to London, and spent the rest of her life there and in Surrey. In 1824 she married Samuel Carter Hall, whose background was also Irish; it is as Mrs Hall that she is known to literary history. As were so many Irish writers in the early nineteenth century, Samuel Carter Hall was very closely involved in the hectic publishing world of the metropolis, work in which his wife soon joined him. By S.C. Hall's count, they produced over five hundred books together. In addition to her own published work, Mrs Hall also edited a number of periodicals, most notably, during the 1860s, the* St James' Magazine.

*Mrs Hall's extensive output contains plays, short stories, children's literature, travel writing, temperance tracts, a voluminous quantity of journalism, and a number of novels, including* The Buccaneer *(1832),* Marian *(1840) and* The Outlaw *(1847). As might be expected of this vast amount of material, quantity trumps quality, and much of her writing is submerged in the great mass of commentary and colour pieces required to fill the innumerable pages of contemporary periodicals. In that regard, her career is an interesting illustration both of the professionalisation of writing and of the rapid expansion of print culture in Victorian England.*

*Fiction was not Mrs Hall's strength, but such works as* Sketches of Irish Character *(1829),* Lights and Shadows of Irish Life *(1838),* Stories of the Irish Peasantry *(1840), and in particular the three-volume* Ireland: Its Scenery and Character *(1841–3), written with her husband, are noteworthy instances of the cultural impetus to view the country as a source of knowledge requiring description, codification and publication. This impetus was shared variously by taxonomists, collectors and statisticians, and appears in the writings of antiquarians, in government Blue Books, and in the work of the Ordnance Survey, as well*

*as in the publications of literary travellers, among whom Mrs Hall is the
most industrious.*

The year is 1822, and Edward Spencer, a landlord in Berkshire, is travelling by steamer from England to Ireland to take over Spencer Court,
an estate on the Cork–Kerry border left to him by his late uncle (he
has also inherited land in the north of Ireland, but apparently conditions there do not require his attention). Among those also on board
are the recently widowed Lady Mary O'Brien, with whom Spencer has
long been enamoured from a distance, and a number of passengers
with Spencer Court connections. These include Dean Graves, a clergyman who gives Spencer lengthy lessons on what awaits him, and
Abel Richards, a turncoat, proselytiser and middleman whose nefar-
ious activities are the counterpart of Whiteboy clandestiness and
unrest. As a 'deep-minded, thoughtful, refined Englishman' (I, 20),
Spencer is an exception to the passion that Irish issues generate. He
believes that his moderating presence will bring sweetness and light,
particularly since 'he felt a deep and earnest sympathy for the Irish
peasant' (I, 52). As evidence of his good faith, he begins his Irish
sojourn by replacing his English servants with Irish ones, whom he
dresses in green livery, dines at Blarney with the local priest, attends
politely to the talk of Master Mat, a schoolmaster turned prospector for
antiquities, and affects a high-minded disregard for the party antagonisms of class and creed that vitiate life on the land.

It might be expected that in introducing the inexperienced Spencer
as its opening gambit, *The Whiteboy* will proceed to demonstrate how
his presence is not the end in itself that he believes it to be but, following lines established by earlier nineteenth-century Irish novelists, is
modified by an education in Irish ways. And in certain respects this
novel does draw on elements of Maria Edgeworth's moral enlightenment and Lady Morgan's romantic typification of national character, in
addition to following rather lamely in the footsteps of *Memoirs of
Captain Rock*. But once arrived in Ireland, Spencer maintains such a
state of non-alignment that he neither influences nor is influenced by
the incendiary events that take place. He makes very slow progress to
Spencer Court; his claim that 'I *am* an emancipator' (I, 67) seems more
like a rhetorical assertion of self-representation than an indication of
engagement or ideological awareness. Spencer is neither challenged
nor changed by anything he experiences, whether it be his failed
pursuit of Lady Mary or being on hand at the ambush that constitutes

the story's decisive set piece. Being held captive by the Whiteboys simply gives him the opportunity finally to meet Ellen Macdonnel, his sole equal in rectitude and self-control. He may be 'young "hot-and-cold"' (II, 149) to his fellow landlords, but that criticism only signifies that he neither shares their vindictive and exploitative ways nor does anything to oppose them. Rather than a protagonist who earns his place in the scheme of things through the demands of being a stranger in a strange land, Spencer is a success story *avant la lettre*, representing merely by virtue of his detached presence and unexamined principles the only imaginable alternative to all the various uncertainties of his environment. He has to wait only ten years for Whiteboy disturbances to subside, at which point his goodwill and sweet reasonableness come into their own. Set up as a *Bildungsroman*, the novel generically and in other respects reveals a failure of nerve.

Evidently having nothing to learn and no good reason to develop, the Englishman is relegated to a static subsidiary role, observing, commenting and reacting as circumstances suggest; and the author's endorsement of his upright mien only enhances the woodenness of his integrity. As a result of representing a foregone conclusion, the work's prospective protagonist emerges as its least interesting character, a personage whose colourless personality and stainless moral nature comprise an unwittingly ironic representation of the designation 'white'. Owing to Spencer's neutrality, *The Whiteboy*'s principal interest is as a catalogue of the violence, vengeance, bigotry, bullying and the many related actions and positions from which he stands aside. Such symptoms of the plainly recalcitrant state of the civic realm indicate that conditions have not been improved by Ireland's recent accession to the United Kingdom, a change of which Spencer's arrival is ostensibly an expression. But whether the English interest is absent or resident, the polity is broken. Its signature occasions are deception, secrecy, betrayal, self-delusion and related manifestations of false representation. These are underwritten by a shared propensity for exorbitance on the part of those two social mainstays, the economy and the judiciary. In keeping with this panorama of social inadequacy, the scene of the action – which stretches from Macroom west to the Kerry border and also includes the south-west coastline around 'what is now the ruinous village of Skull' (II, 205) – is a landscape of dispossession, a milieu without manners, a domain whose inhabitants are represented either in terms of their poverty or their greed, where social relations typically consist of landlords 'exacting a serf's homage, without giving a baron's protection' (I, 116). This region is not too distant from the three-thousand-acre estate of Edmund Spenser at Kilcolman, established during the Plantation of Munster, an event the novel perhaps unintentionally brings to mind in its allusive account of the Macarthy family's dispossession, or perhaps pallidly hopes to redress in the person of the modern Spencer.

Even the various localities' striking picturesqueness ultimately fails to be a redeeming feature. The recognition of '[w]hat a sad contrast was there in the natural and moral beauty of this scene' (II, 13) is yet one more acknowledgement of fractured conditions. Not only is there a gulf between imposing landscape and belittled people, one also exists between men of property and men of no property, between the Catholic underclass and its Protestant overlords, as well as extending to the racial divide between Celt and Saxon. 'We are two nations' (I, 8), Lady Mary O'Brien informs Spencer, and it is imperative to represent oneself in terms of one or the other. And just as Spencer is fixed in his passivity, both sides – or 'parties', as they are called, a formal denomination that confers on them a political character that in all other respects the narrative denies them – are equally locked into theirs.

Each contending interest seems capable of returning only ill for the Englishman's putative good. One form of ill is represented by Abel Richards, and his gouging, self-aggrandising ways. As Spencer's 'half bailiff, half steward, which he himself called "agent"' (I, 81). He falsely represents the landlord's outlook and intentions and he reinforces this distorting influence through sectarianism, expressing his pretensions to piety both in mealy-mouthed religious clichés and in the distribution of 'bitterly-worded tracts' (I, 126) supplied by Dublin-based sectarians. The other manifestation of ill is represented by the Whiteboys. Foremost among these is young Lawrence Macarthy, the last of the line, and son of a misalliance between a would-be 'patriot' (I, 105) and Annie Cumming, sister-in-law of Edward Spencer's uncle. Lawrence, 'a wild, high-spirited, unlettered boy' (1, 115), is the one who is not only denominated 'the Whiteboy' (II, 36) but denounced by Abel Richards as '*the* one, the invisible, Captain Rock, the unseen, unknown agent, principal mover – everything, in fact' (I, 255).

This accusation's excessiveness merely typifies Richards' disproportionate representational style. Yet it also does draw attention to how difficult it is to identify accurately who the Whiteboys are. Lawrence plays a prominent, though not decisive, role in the disturbances depicted, but it also seems that he is as much a victim of a conspiracy as he is a representative of his people. It might be argued that it is Louis O'Brien, Lady Mary's brother, a British Army deserter, who has the political self-consciousness and Francophile leanings to give the Whiteboys the quality of leadership required. Moreover, he is in command at the climactic ambush. But ultimately he does not have a conspirator's commitment, and in any case does not seem to share his followers' localised populism. The latter outlook is embodied by the firebrand Byrne of Inchageela (sic), but his precipitate action during the ambush 'destroyed not only himself, but his project' (II, 189). Or it may be that the ur-Whiteboy is Lawrence's foster-brother Murtogh of the Strong Hand, particularly since he 'was a few removes, perhaps, from a savage' (I, 306) and thus familiar from the popular iconography of Irish agrarian agitation. The Whiteboys are all these – and the many others who, having been sworn in, 'bent his knee over the tomb of Arthur O'Leary' (I, 316) – and none. More problematic than any particular Whiteboy is the vague but pervasive 'wild, uncertain, unorganised cause' (1, 293) that the movement represents, as though it is a type of weather or some such presence, inscrutable as to structure or intent. Its origins, admittedly, are said to be a reaction to the system of land management controlled by, as Lawrence Macarthy has it, 'those bastards of the soil' (II, 31). But the violence of that reaction depersonalises its practitioners and nullifies their claims, partly due to the heavy-handed forces of so-called law and order but also because violence is shown as an abstract entity that manifests itself by blindly confusing right and wrong – a pernicious form of false representation. And its consequences lead irresistibly to defeat, exile and death, permanent cancellations of all types of representation. These consequences are the inevitable pendants to the false representation – notably secrecy, disguise and 'false swearing' (I, 206) – on which Whiteboyism relies and which confounds its objectives; as the action intensifies, 'there were . . . abundant misrepresentations afloat among them' (II, 50).

The response to Whiteboyism – martial law, militarism, the quasi-judicial 'depositions' (I, 249) taken at Macroom Castle under an authority figure known only as the Master of Macroom – identifies the movement as a crisis – 'this fever, this terrible turmoil' (I, 230), as the Master puts it. And from one point of view it is a crisis in 'the great purpose of Irish life – action' (II, 162). An equally significant aspect of

Whiteboyism, however, is that it is said to reflect the state of mind of a peasantry 'with but limited knowledge of the influence of moral power' (I, 106). The people do not know what they are doing. They are essentialised as 'incapable, as unwilling, to reason' (II, 52), even as they are fondly regarded (by Dean Graves, for instance) for their capacity to feel. But this capacity is also the wellspring of that impulsiveness that makes Lawrence 'the agitator of the present without attempting to be the legislator of the future' (II, 55) and Louis too easily seduced by 'the romance and daring' (II, 141) of leadership.

Such deficiencies of temperament are not necessarily inevitable, however, as Ellen Macdonnel shows. Born in the north of Ireland but reared at Spencer Court, she is, through her mother, Lawrence's stepsister. Initially she seems to share his rebellious outlook. '[I]f I could but see a chance of the independence of my country . . . I would die to achieve it – die, to render it a country instead of a province' (I, 154), she claims (anachronistically echoing 'A Nation Once Again', published in 1844), but she exhibits a different side of her heritage when a desperate Abel Richards turns up outside her bedroom window seeking shelter after his house has been burned. Reluctant as Ellen is to accommodate him, she believes herself bound by the unwritten laws governing proper conduct 'beneath an Irish roof' (I, 183). While she conceals Richards, Lawrence Macarthy comes looking for help, which Ellen also provides, accepting for safe-keeping from him certain Whiteboy documents, as the spying Richards observes.

Ellen thus occupies a middle ground between Richards and Lawrence, displaced into a more fraught and exposed version of Edward Spencer's separateness. She risks either succumbing to Richards' power, which will result in betraying Lawrence, or lying about Lawrence's visit and betraying herself. Crucially, however, 'her self-possession did not desert her' (I, 192) and she finds a spatial representation of the middle ground in a remote retreat. Here, too, is where Spencer is confined after his futile interruption of the Whiteboys' pre-ambush midnight muster, and it is here that the two finally meet, although in view of their mutual concern for the future of Spencer Court, a connection between them has already been established. To support her, Edward 'offered her the affection and protection of a brother' (II, 113), but Ellen's concern for Lawrence prevents that degree of relatedness. The debacle of the ambush leaves Lawrence and Louis 'with the only chance of preserving their existence . . . to quit Ireland' (II, 213), and they take refuge in a sea cave near Schull until a boat chartered by Lady Mary O'Brien arrives. Ellen, dressed as 'a Kerry peasant girl' (II, 226), appears, to discover that Lawrence has been encouraging Louis' militancy by promising that it would earn him Ellen's hand. Nor is this the end of false representation: the boat that duly arrives has Abel Richards on board and he takes Ellen, Lawrence and the faithful Murtogh prisoner (Louis escapes to America). At sea, Lawrence is wounded in a bid for freedom, and Murtogh perishes in his successful attempt to drown Richards. Lawrence and Ellen are held at the local coastguard station, and the former expires of his wound, his final request being that Ellen sing 'The Minstrel Boy', which in the circumstances is a not very euphonious echo of 'the poetry of war' (II, 7), the supposedly uplifting measures of which militancy created.

By opening and closing its narrative at sea, *The Whiteboy* might seem to suggest that all concerned are not only in the same boat, but that the best available boat is one of the new steamers plying between England and Ireland (this service was inaugurated in 1816). This is the vessel that Dean Graves believes 'will draw the countries close together, induce an influx of English capital' (I, 24) and generally act as aptly mechanistic counterpart to Spencer's outlook. With that outlook in mind, the novel ends not in the Whiteboys' defeat but, a decade later, when Spencer Court strikes visitors as being 'exactly like England' (II, 285), although '[t]o have said that the spirit of insubordination was altogether overcome . . . would be absurd' (ibid.). It is in the successful securing of his property that the virtues of Spencer's non-party stance and his adherence to 'medium thoughts' (I, 227) are rewarded.

Not only does Spencer have no wish to go further than Spencer Court, he believes that any additional developments in the public sphere are ill-advised. 'Give employment and remuneration for it, and you effectually strangle rebellion' (II, 289) may express the acme of the landlord's enlightenment; just as his statement that 'I consider . . . Catholic Emancipation as only the first of a series of boons, or rather, the earliest demonstration of justice – wisely given' (II, 299) may well be the position of a liberal Unionist. But his objection to 'men who unfortunately consider that now emancipation is obtained, they must spend the other half of their lives on a project which they themselves cannot, with all their enthusiasm, consider feasible' (II, 300) shows that perhaps it is time that he replaced 'my dreams, Utopian as they were' (II, 305) with a more cogent appreciation of political aspirations.

Such a change in outlook would recognise freedom, justice, equity and similar provisions for social concord as natural rights, not gifts to nurture a status quo. But the representation of such a view is outside the scope of a temporising romance like *The Whiteboy*, a work whose significance has less to do with the originality and perception of its representations than with its attempted mimicry of the national tale, a genre that at the middle of the nineteenth century the Irish novel was looking forward to superseding.

# 1847

## William Carleton, *The Black Prophet*

*William Carleton (1794–1869) was born in the townland of Prillisk in the Clogher Valley of County Tyrone. Educated in local hedge schools, he left home in his teens with the intention of entering the priesthood. When this intention was not realised, Carleton spent much of his youth and early manhood participating in and absorbing the mentalités and cultural life of his native place. These he memorialised to arresting effect in his fiction. Eventually departing for Dublin, he initially worked in the city as a teacher, though he was unable to secure the educational opportunities that were one of the primary reasons for leaving home.*

*Carleton's earliest work was published in* The Christian Examiner, *edited by the evangelical proselytiser Caesar Otway. Elaborating on these early pieces and modifying somewhat their point of view, Carleton went on to produce his landmark collections,* Traits and Stories of the Irish Peasantry *(First Series, 1830; Second Series, 1833). Abandoning the novella form of the most impressive* Traits and Stories, *Carleton subsequently devoted himself to the novel, beginning with* Fardorougha the Miser *(1839), which like many of his novels first appeared serially in the* Dublin University Magazine. *He also contributed to* The Nation, *a temporary change of affiliation. Among his many novels are* Valentine M'Clutchy, the Irish Agent *(1845),* The Emigrants of Ahadarra *(1848) and* The Castles of Castle Squander *(1852). These works tend to be dioramas representing generic problems of life on the land and the inimitable local personalities that enliven the* Traits and Stories. *Carleton's post-Famine novels, written in discouragement, show a marked diminution of the energy that W.B. Yeats termed 'fiery shorthand'.*

*Of Carleton's background, the poet Patrick Kavanagh has written, 'He was no more a peasant than is your obedient servant.' Nevertheless, it is on the lives of pre-Famine Ireland's rural population that Carleton drew throughout his career. His complicated attitudes towards cottiers' and small holders' way of life, his distance from it and the impossibility of forgetting it, his criticisms of its numerous imposed and self-inflicted limitations, his fond appreciation of its cultural vitality and physical immediacy, are the basis of works which, whatever their technical imperfections, are unique. This is not because of their subject matter alone, but because the author's linguistic exuberance, melodramatic propensities and oleographic scene-painting infuse his material with a spirited abundance that almost seems a type of freedom. Carleton gave a world to literature; his peers and successors unhappily declined to develop it. And his appearance in Seamus Heaney's 'Station Island' is a reminder that Carleton is a figure whose cultural significance and artistic identity continue to haunt the Irish imagination.*

The year is 1817, and Irish conditions seem to be the same as the previous year – 'The Year Without a Summer' – when climatic and demographic disasters beset most of Europe, and in the remote rural pocket in which *The Black Prophet* is set, land and people are on the brink of catastrophe. Everything that can go wrong has gone wrong; '[t]he whole land, in fact, mourned' (330). Famine is rampant, its effects represented in scenes that horrify not only by their graphic physical detail but by a sense of the sufferers' own awareness of their weakness and abjection. Typhoid is epidemic. Rioters, led either by mentally disturbed locals or by outsiders condemned by Carleton as 'politicians' (328), attack wagons laden with food for export, incidents symptomatic of a more general social deterioration marked by an abandonment of 'the decencies and restraints of ordinary life . . . all of which constitute the moral safety of society' (222). In a pairing of antithetical adjectives that is typical of the novel's rhetorical and imaginative complications, 'the whole country was in a state of dull but frantic tumult' (221).

As an extension of that sense of doubleness and antithesis, to do conditions justice requires two conflicting but interrelated stories. Clearly the forces of darkness cannot be overcome without a struggle, and to indicate that this is true not only for the characters in question but also for the author, Carleton frequently calls attention to the challenge of his undertaking in phrases like 'it is extremely difficult to describe Sarah's appearance and state of mind' (281), and 'the sufferings . . . are such that no human pen could at all describe' (330). What is an obvious rhetorical tactic also speaks to the challenges that must be met to represent material whose vivifying qualities are missing – challenges of witnessing, of language and of imaginative redemption.

The struggle within and between the stories is elemental for both the author and his characters – life against death, good against evil, light against darkness.

One story focuses on the eponymous protagonist, Donnel Dhu M'Gowan, whose temperament, outlook and activities – dark looks, murky past and nocturnal exploits – identify him as an embodiment of the prevailing blackness. The Prophet is somebody who, in going from bad to worse, has reached the moral nadir of attempting to get away with murder – an objective that resonates bitterly with the conse-quences of the authorities' seeming indifference. (Carleton directly appeals against governmental inaction, most forthrightly in the letter dedicating the novel to Lord John Russell, the Prime Minister of the day, which prefaces the text.) His daughter Sarah's description of herself as 'a divil's limb' (9) confirms Donnel Dhu's place in the novel's moral economy, and it is a resounding judgement rather than a con-trived irony that, prophet or not, he has no future. As events reveal, his past catches up with him. This outcome is deemed only right and proper in the novel's scale of values, and is the principal means of rep-resenting the resolution of the struggle between the two stories. This resolution conveys the hope that the bad old days are over.

Carleton also tacitly advances this hope in his factual observation that the 'prophecy-man' is 'a character . . . that has nearly, if not alto-gether, disappeared' (15) from rural Ireland. The existence of such characters, with their millenarian cast of mind and arcane prov-enances, is an indication of contemporary peasant susceptibilities and anxieties. But the prophet is also an exceptional figure, as is indicated by the remoteness of his cabin from the community at large, the rest-lessness and vigilance that mark him even in a setting significantly affected by both, and the relentless consistency with which he applies himself to suborning all around him. Carleton suggests that the Prophet's black-heartedness originated many years earlier, when he was 'making United Irishmen' (369), but M'Gowan's treachery seems less the product of ideological or political engagements than of the more primal pathologies represented by his satanic persona.

This persona shows Donnel Dhu in the same context as those other characters in the novel who hold life cheap and act accordingly. Of these, Darby Skinadre – 'the very Genius of Famine' (59) – is the most repellent. A merchant, usurer and early representation of the gombeen man, he uses his resources to exploit the hungry and hopeless, even while, as in one pathetic instance, a victim drops dead of want at his unyielding feet. Skinadre also covets the farm where the unfortunate Dalton family live, and his bribery to secure the lease uses money for his own self-aggrandisement that might assist his suffering neighbours. Blackening his character still further is his outrageous hypocrisy; he never loses an opportunity to represent falsely his charitable disposition, making these claims at the very same time as his business methods create further travail. In acting as an agent of an economic system that evidently permits freedom without responsibility, he is 'a libel upon the laws by which the rights of civil society are protected' (393).

The prevailing system of landholding represents inequities and amorality that are analogous to Skinadre's personal behaviour. Here, the Hendersons, father and son, are the irresponsible parties, middlemen who hold leases granted by the landlord's agent and profit from them regardless of human cost. Carleton's treatment of these characters is not quite so palpably damning as that of Skinadre, but there is no doubt that they also are self-serving to the point of corruption. Their "'big house'" (365) – a term Carleton places in quotation marks with a view, perhaps, to distancing it or registering it as an alien structure or an entity whose standing is outside the common lexicon of place and home – has 'a rude and riotous character' (89); the ejection of the now homeless Daltons is a pitiless act; and young Dick Henderson's abduction plot is a measure of his moral inadequacy. And in the case of both Skinadre and the Hendersons, what goes under the guise of a system is the reverse of that concept, supplanting organisation with unpredictability, regularity with insecurity, and productivity with deprivation.

Corruption is the link between the Prophet and the pillars of local society, and Carleton shows that the connection is more than thematic by giving M'Gowan a hand in Dick Henderson's abduction plans. Like Skinadre and the Hendersons, M'Gowan must defraud the world as he finds it, adapting its properties for his own protection and well-being, and obviously misrepresenting himself as a result. M'Gowan is not even his correct name; those who suspect him of murder have no means of acting on their suspicions, and he is also a false prophet, one 'foretellin' . . . as it sarves his purpose' (11) and who 'laughs in his sleeve at the people for believin' (ibid.), as Nelly, his common-law wife, remarks. As with the usurer and the middlemen, the Prophet's corruption comes not only from his activities but from the 'two-fold character'

(12) that such activities create. But whereas persons of wealth and property can get away with what they do, and are blind to the conflict between their methods' ostensible legitimacy and their harmful consequences, the same is not true of M'Gowan. His claims to legitimacy are much thinner, and his world is a tissue of signs and portents indicating the constant threat of unmasking that he is under. As the upshot discloses, inability to keep in the dark the fact that he is indeed a murderer will prove fatal.

The novel's other story also deals with darkness and false representation, but in this case, the focus is on the victims, the hunger-ravaged, fever-ridden, expropriated Dalton family, whose suffering from famine has been gratuitously compounded by intentional iniquities. Ultimately, the Prophet has no hope of saving himself, or of anybody saving him; his presumption of power foreshadows his doom. In contrast, the helpless Daltons must be saved; to leave its members to their fate would be to endorse the moral and physical blackness threatening to destroy them. Condy, the paterfamilias, is particularly in need of help, for along with all his other troubles, he is falsely accused of a murder supposedly committed twenty-two years earlier (another instance of the past's unfortunately enduring influence, a point relevant to the novel's representing the events of 1817 in the context of 1847). This murder never did take place; the widespread belief that it did is one reason why the Prophet's crime continues to go undetected. The Daltons' miserable circumstances show the combined impact of the novel's three malign, dehumanising agents. Condy has nothing to hide, is a victim of the economic system, and his means of self-representation, hunger and homelessness signify only emptiness.

Not surprisingly, the family spends much of their time lying down, a position contrary to their innate uprightness. And, in a further illustration of how misrepresentation can morally degrade, innocent Condy declares himself a murderer, unconsciously assuming thereby a version of his corrupt victimisers' 'two-fold' identity. The extent of his physical and psychological deterioration demands Condy's exoneration. With respect to the murder charge, an unexpected array of *dei ex machina* ensure his acquittal, while at the same time uncovering the Prophet's perfidy and guilt. Yet, important as it is that justice be seen to be done, that there is an official public forum where wrongs may be righted and that the words of others bear witness to the merits of the degraded, Condy's release also seems like an official, depthless exercise in the power of mercy and charity that the accused and his family have already been shown on a more heartfelt plane. These saving graces have been administered by Mave Sullivan, niece of Condy's alleged victim.

In her selflessness, courage, tenderness and sympathy, Mave is the Prophet's equal and opposite. The name by which she is familiarly known, *Gra gal* (*grá geal,* 'bright love'), is a rebuke to darkness, just as her physical beauty and composed demeanour evince a sweetness and light that repudiate the Prophet's shady presence. Her corporal works of mercy (in a work that is inevitably very conscious of the body) are a counterweight to the covert and exploitative activities in which the novel's worldly males engage. And, as though proposing not only formal representation of her angelic presence but imparting to it a structural significance, her devotion is said to be such 'as would have won her a statue in the times of old Greece, when self-sacrifice for human good was appreciated and rewarded' (279).

Moreover, in going to the Daltons' assistance Mave risks broadening the rift with her family that her romantic involvement with one of the Dalton sons, also named Condy, has opened, but she convinces her parents that 'her sublime mission' (272) is a statement of value transcending both family ties and inherited hostilities. Through her moral imagination, Mave rises above the difficulties afflicting not only her own people but those with whom they differ. Her healing actions constitute a type of leadership as she returns good for evil and solidarity for estrangement. Her qualities are also an expression of the author's faith in not only the virtues but the possibility of steadfastness and application, qualities in which the peasantry are frequently deficient in other Carleton works, including the impatient and repetitive *Paddy Go Easy* (1845). Mave's daily existence consists of facing down dangers. Her singularity, with its recuperative and reconciliatory effects, is an antidote to doubleness. To underline further the dangers she confronts, she is the target of young Dick Henderson's abduction intrigue. Unlike the Prophet's disregard of his neighbours – 'to all this . . . he paid little or no attention' (170) – in immersing herself in others' suffering Mave acquires immunity to every threat to her well-being, self-possession and integrity. She not only survives, but her disinterested good works assert the spirit of survival. Animated by 'hereditary . . . decent pride and independence' (73), this spirit also possesses, in its compassionate and redemptive powers, a fundamentally Christian character, the novel's endorsement of which is all the more noteworthy in view of the almost total absence from it of pastoral presences of every ecclesiastical stripe. The one exception is the priest who discovers in passing a grotesque *pietà*, 'sunk to the mere condition of animal life' (346) – a scene adapted for the tutelage of the protagonist's conscience in Trollope's *Castle Richmond*. Mother and child are entrusted to the care of the Sullivans.

As though to affirm definitively her exemplary benevolence, Mave also takes under her wing the Prophet's daughter Sarah. Mave's counterpart in looks and 'symmetry' (4), Sarah is her opposite in temperament – when first encountered she looks like 'some beautiful vampire' (7), her teeth having drawn blood in a fight with her stepmother. In time, Sarah rejects home and her father's influence, and entrusts her 'generous but unregulated heart' (195) to Mave's goodness, a change that is as great a psychological boon to the lonely, motherless girl as being physically nursed. Not just charity is at issue here. Mave's treatment of Sarah suggests that even as untamed a nature as the latter's is worthy of inclusiveness and humane regard. Mave's kindness profiles social rehabilitation and restitution, therapies as essential as those her more diurnal forms of care-giving offer. In an illustration of *The Black Prophet's* melodramatic emotional economy, Sarah replaces Mave as Dick Henderson's abductee, infecting him with the typhoid that eventually kills him, thereby ending the Henderson regime. The disease also ostensibly kills Sarah, though her spirit is mortally wounded by an abortive reunion with her natural mother and the knowledge that it is on the latter's evidence that her father is to be hanged.

Such extraordinary concatenations of characters and events are typical of *The Black Prophet*, but, if these excesses, and the exaggerations of plot, characterisation and rhetoric that facilitate them, appear to force the novel's issues to the point of imbalance or even incoherence, that is a reflection of the extremes that Carleton wishes to represent. His objective is not drama, but truth. His 'Author's Preface' to *The Black Prophet* declares his intention 'to record in the following pages such an authentic history of those deadly periods of famine . . . as could be relied upon with confidence by all' (viii). To this end he occasionally interrupts the narrative to provide documentary evidence and anthropological observations in support of the record. These digressions are intended to confirm Carleton's assertion that 'the strongest imagery of Fiction is frequently transcended by the terrible realities of Truth' (viii). He speaks with authority, thereby substantiating his work's appeal to those remote from its contexts and conditions, an audience believed to include 'our Landlord readers' (238) and other, moral, absentees as well.

Yet *The Black Prophet* is not confined to didactic purposes. Notwithstanding the novel's Goyaesque palette depicting dreadful scenes of destitution and inanition, and its bleak perspective on the body politic's inadequacies, Carleton claims in his preface that the work's 'principal interest' is 'the workings of those passions and feelings which usually agitate human life' (viii). A rather generalised interest, perhaps. Yet it could hardly be more apropos. Its pre-eminence even suggests a certain pressure to retrieve something of value from a landscape of deprivation and want, to make good, however clumsily and using however conventional a set of pieties, in the hope that dark times can not only be illuminated but eliminated.

# 1856

## W.M. Thackeray, *The Memoirs of Barry Lyndon*

*William Makepeace Thackeray (1811–63) was born in Calcutta and reared in England. At Cambridge he contributed to undergraduate publications, but left the university without a degree. A period of uncertainty followed which included a good deal of travelling – Thackeray spent some time in Germany – and a certain amount of dissipation, including gambling. Two early journalistic ventures were unsuccessful, and he also failed in his artistic ambitions. Like many of his contemporaries, Thackeray turned to periodical writing, and in the course of the 1840s became a leading contributor to* Fraser's Magazine *(edited by William Maginn) and to the* Morning Chronicle *and, especially, to* Punch. *Many of these contributions appeared under such pseudonyms as Michael Angelo Titmarsh, Charles James Yellowplush and George Savage Fitz-Boodle. These pieces were eventually published in book form and show Thackeray's versatility – as a satirical social commentator in* The Book of Snobs *(1848) and as a literary critic in* The English Humorists of the Eighteenth Century *(1853). His early writings also included travel books, most notably* The Irish Sketch Book *(1843). Periodical writing continued to be an important part of Thackeray's output throughout his career; in 1860, when his name as a novelist was well established, he became the founding editor of the* Cornhill Magazine.

*Although Thackeray's extensive apprenticeship also features a certain amount of fiction, his reputation as a novelist of stature dates from the appearance of* Vanity Fair *(1848) and was consolidated by* The History of Pendennis *(1849–50),* The History of Henry Esmond *(1852), and* The Newcomes *(1854–55). Unlike* Barry Lyndon, *these works use an omniscient point of view, though in ways that sometimes can suggest the puppeteer's detachment from his puppets. Thackeray's novels also rely to a considerable degree on their female characters, and his representation of them is not only artistically accomplished and culturally significant but is also noteworthy from a conceptual standpoint. His perception of the strengths of the supposedly weaker sex and his alertness to their place in society make his women intriguing diagnostic probes into the body politic of private life, its hierarchies, bids for power, marital inequities and thwarted desires. The status of women as central to social structures that evidently intend to render them marginal is a revealing development of Thackeray's early pseudonymous narrators, figures whose apparent social superfluity masks their revealing viewpoints. All such characters exhibit belonging and restlessness, status and insecurity, authority and vulnerability; and the influence of class in both representing and effacing the legitimacy of the self is also significant.*

*Many of these features of Thackeray's fiction make their initial, rudimentary or at least overstated appearance in* The Memoirs of Barry Lyndon, Esq. *Entitled* The Luck of Barry Lyndon, *'edited by G.S. Fitz-Boodle', the novel was first published as a serial in* Fraser's Magazine *between January and December 1844, and later substantially revised and retitled. The novel can also be seen to mix the author's literary awareness with his literary milieu. With respect to the former, as has long been recognised,* Barry Lyndon *is indebted to Henry Fielding's* Jonathan Wild *(1743) – itself a blend of the satirical and the picaresque. Additionally, Thackeray parodies popular genres of his own day such as the Newgate novel and the military novels of Charles Lever. Also readily detectable are the spirits of Sheridan's Sir Lucius O'Trigger, Sir Jonah Barrington's* Personal Sketches of His Own Times *(1830), and the much-cited* Adventures of Captain Freeny *(possibly referring to* A Genuine History of the Lives and Actions of the Most Notorious Irish Highwaymen . . . *(1795 et seq.)). Moreover, his London-based Irish friends, such as William Maginn and Sylvester Mahony ('Father Prout'), would have contributed to Thackeray's fascination with misfits, over-reachers, pretenders and liars, figures essential to his novels without a hero.* Barry Lyndon *is such a figure, as was his prototype, Andrew Robinson Stoney (1747–1810), of Borrisokane, County Tipperary.*

The novel's full title reads *The Memoirs of Barry Lyndon, Esq., Of the Kingdom of Ireland, Containing An Account of His Extraordinary Adventures; Misfortunes; His Suffering In The Service Of His Late Prussian Majesty; His*

*Visits To Many of The Courts of Europe; His Marriage and Splendid Establishments in England and Ireland; And The Many Cruel Persecutions, Conspiracies, And Slanders Of Which He Has Been A Victim.* This summary of the novel's contents not only parodies by its length the eighteenth-century style of titling, it also alerts the reader – through the use of such terms as 'extraordinary', 'suffering', 'splendid', and so on – to the narrator's need to gloss the experiences he is about to present. Even before the story begins, a way of viewing it has been proposed, as though to forestall the reader reaching an independent assessment of the memoirist's ups and downs. Such an approach implies that there can be no discrepancy between what the narrator says and what the reader understands, but it is the novel's very many instances of such a discrepancy that are the principal sources of its satirical effect. Such a narrative strategy – one that relies on appearances being seen through and exaggerations and self-justifications being debunked – not only exposes the adventurer, it also reveals his story's extravagances as a misfit's overcompensations, a ruffian's deceptions, and a braggart's distortions. The more the narrator tries to make of himself, the easier it is to belittle him. The greater his claims to be a person of consequence, the more readily his inferiority and unworthiness emerge. Instead of being the vindication the narrator seeks, these confessions are a crisis in self-representation, in which, as the title indicates, race and class have noteworthy parts to play.

The falseness that defines the narrator's make-up begins with his name, Redmond Barry (his forename perhaps an allusion to the noted rapparee, Count Redmond O'Hanlon). The Lyndons have been the Barrys' enemies from Elizabethan times, and it is through marriage that Redmond becomes a Lyndon. His adoption of that name modifies his Barry origins and gives him the guise of an Anglo-Irishman, an elevation in standing substantiated by marriage, but by little else. This change of name and status is consistent with the many name changes that preceded it: 'I was of the Redmonds of Waterford country' (49); Barry of Barryogue, Redmond de Balibari, are some of the others used as circumstances require, which is only to be expected from such an adventurer and opportunist, a character who must continually improvise a presence for himself. Regardless of truth or principle, he has to keep going at all costs. One reason for Barry's extemporaneous way of life – one well suited to his two avocations, soldiering and gambling, and that is also reflected in his hair-trigger readiness to fight a duel – is that he was born into a history of loss. Even if 'truth compels me to assert that my family was the noblest of the island, and, perhaps of the universal world; while their possessions, now insignificant, and torn from us by war, by treachery, by the loss of time, by ancestral extravagance, by adhesion to the old faith and monarch, were formerly prodigious' (3), all he has now, following the excesses of his father, Roaring Harry Barry, is the name. And what is in that name except hot air, meant to inflate the notions of a glorious past and of present eminence? Barry's idiolect compensates for the absence of economic and moral substance that is his inheritance.

Roaring Harry's early death leads to Barry being fostered by his mother's people, the Bradys. His youthful experiences are prototypes of the adventures in love and war – or rather in love *as* war – that constitute his adult career. He falls in love with his cousin Nora (who was 'christened by Dr. Swift' (19), a boast that like all Barry's claims has nothing to back it up), but Nora is obliged by the state of Brady family finances to pursue Captain Redmond Quin. Barry challenges his rival to a duel, and, mistakenly believing that he has killed his man, sees no alternative but to run away, or, as he says, 'it was my fate to be a wanderer' (43). Justification of his flight is difficult to reconcile with his version of how he reacted at the sight of the supposedly slain Quin: 'I did not feel any horror or fear . . . seeing my enemy prostrate before me; for I knew that I had met and conquered him honourably in the field, as became a man of my name and blood' (47). This statement encapsulates the codes of maleness and of manners that serve as Barry's false fronts throughout. Moreover, part of not taking this narrator at his word entails allowing for retrospective attempts to improve his standing.

His representation of himself as a nobleman to a pair of confidence tricksters encountered on his arrival in Dublin results in a decision to enlist, and almost immediately he is fighting Prussians in the Seven Years' War. 'I loathed the horrid company into which I had fallen' (68), however, and his experience of service in the field appals him to the extent that 'I am not going to give my romantic narrative' (101) of them, a comment revealing, among other things, Thackeray's reaction against tales of military adventure then in vogue. At the same time, though he never rises above the rank of corporal, Barry answers to being called Captain, and also points out that the soldier's life 'is a frightful one to any but men of iron courage and endurance' (101). It is in the ranks that Barry also acquires the doctrine of '[a]ttacking' (191) that guides, if that is the word, his subsequent forays. Although he indicates that such undertakings are the result of deep-laid stratagems, in the event they represent impetuosity and exhibitionism rather than that sense of action that affirms its origins in forethought and self-possession. Barry does not have a self to possess; hence his life of predation on others. Such a career suggests that the object of action is to foment crisis. Barry is effectively a revolutionary, a breaker of unions. All his actions and adventures are manifestations of infidelity. In this, Thackeray may be reflecting Repeal tensions. Or he may be counteracting *Memoirs of Captain Rock*.

In one of his many acts of passing, Barry disguises himself in the uniform of the well-named Lieutenant Fakenham, and deserts, only to resume soldiering in the Prussian Army. A meeting with his exiled Uncle Cornelius, now styling himself the Chevalier de Balibari (so called because the family home, from which, being a Catholic, he has been disinherited, is Ballybarry), puts the protagonist on the road to fame and fortune. They make a formidable pair of card sharps, and 'held our own, aye, and more than our own' (136) at faro during a sojourn in the cut-throat society of the Duchy of X –. This way of life Barry defends by pointing out the unwarranted slurs 'cast upon the character of men of honour engaged in the profession of play . . . . The broker of the Exchange who bulls and bears . . . what is he but a gamester?' (128). As one of the 'knights of the dice-box' (134), Barry is merely changing the venue of his military exploits, for isn't gambling 'something like boldness? does *this* profession not require skill, and perseverance and bravery?' (130), not that he showed any of these in arms. Against the odds, Barry also bids for the attentions of the beautiful young Countess Ida. Just as in his other pursuits, he is brazenly candid about his methods and objectives: 'Who can say that I had not a right to use *any* stratagem in the matter of love? Or, why say love? I wanted the wealth of the lady' (143). But his unselfconscious sense of entitlement is thwarted. A hasty exit from the Duchy of X – ensues, and he returns to England, that 'silly constitutional country' (151).

No sooner does he land in London than he lays siege to Honoria, the wife of the ailing Sir Charles Lyndon, who has befriended him. Her ladyship may have 'nothing divine about her' (188), but she is also the enamoured of the 'very young and green' (214) Sir George Poynings (Barry is too busy putting this swain in his place to dwell on his historically resonant surname). Before long Honoria is widowed. Marriage to Barry ensues, and he 'procured his Majesty's gracious permission to add the name of my lovely lady to my own' (233), thereby literally becoming an Anglo-Irishman, which in this case seems an officially sanctioned form of false representation. Lady Lyndon has property in both England and Ireland, though because the latter country is being 'ravaged by various parties of banditti . . . Whiteboys, Oakboys, Steelboys' (222), the newlyweds settle in Devon. His altered status finds Barry reflecting 'how the possession of wealth brings out the virtues of a man' (243), while at the same time he goes through his wife's fortune and treats her cruelly even as he protests 'I was only a severe and careful guardian over a silly, bad-tempered, and weak-minded lady' (244). He also has the hostility of Lord Bullingdon, Lady Lyndon's son by Sir Charles, to contend with. Barry sees off this young man by sending him to fight the rebels in America (historical events supply the novel's few temporal markers). A false report of Bullingdon's death leaves the way clear for Bryan, Lady Lyndon's son by Barry, to inherit.

Yet, 'now that I was arrived at the height of my ambition, both my skill and my luck seemed to be deserting me' (247). A series of losses ensues, not merely at the card table but at home, with young Bryan's needless death, and in Barry's failure to be an effective representative when elected to parliament and the subsequent loss of his seat. With the assistance of Sir George Poynings, Lady Lyndon is finally able to secure her interests, while further help is provided by Redmond Quin, 'son of my old flame Nora' (294), regarding her ladyship's Irish holdings, indicating that Barry's first duel was not the success he imagined. Lord Bullingdon also returns, alive and well (even death can be falsely represented in these memoirs). This coalition is a reminder that Barry continually breaks from whomever he becomes attached to, and that his destructiveness is a function of his loner desperation, disguised as arrogance. The opposition party's collective efforts see him confined to the Fleet Prison, where he spends his declining years penning his apologia, attended on by his doting crone of a mother.

Much has been made of the narrative vigour and tonal mastery of the work that launched Thackeray's career as a novelist. In addition, it is not difficult to see Barry Lyndon as the prototype of the author's more complicated – or more emotionally engaged – protagonists who also pursue the illusory attractions of Vanity Fair. The somewhat puritan comedy of Barry's story is a prominent vein running through the Thackeray *oeuvre*. But Barry is also an Irish protagonist, and it is on the representation of that identity that his memoirs fundamentally rely. Since his memoirs are a record of emptiness, malevolence, exaggeration, cheating and self-promotion, this identity appears to be void of any redeeming feature. It may be argued that Barry is no more than a literary construct, and his talent for fabrication, particularly when attempting to justify his choices and his actions, indicates perhaps his 'uncommon taste for reading plays and novels' (14). Moreover, he belongs to a vanished eighteenth-century world, although somebody who reports the Dublin of 1771 to be 'as savage as Warsaw almost, without the regal grandeur of the latter city' (199) seems to exceed even his powers of false representation. In short, wherever Barry goes he fails to belong, and his outsider status – which places him beyond the social, marital, legal and every other institutional pale – is nowhere more evident than when, through marriage, he acquires an Anglo-Irish dimension, or façade. This acquisition is the ultimate confirmation of his alien nature, the equivalent in culture and manners to his 'very dark and swarthy . . . complexion' (103). As untamed as he is overstated, as duplicitous as he is reckless, as purblind as he is brazen, Barry seems to be one of those cartoon monsters who appeared through the nineteenth century representing Irish unfitness, and it is not too difficult to detect the influence of 'Mr. Gillray's own pencil' (96) on how he is portrayed. Such a figure, who consists of nothing but surface, only belongs when weak and insipid continental society accommodates him. Nearer home, the concerted application of the law puts him in his proper place.

Thackeray makes it plain that ultimately Barry Lyndon as a character is no more than an exercise in self-cancellation, a prisoner of the way of life that he claims to be his deliverance. With respect to literary history, he is literally the last word in picaresque effrontery, and it is that genre that feels the brunt of Thackeray's satire. Although the narrative method of *Castle Rackrent* and *Memoirs of Captain Rock* come to mind in *Memoirs of Barry Lyndon*, in those two instances the satirical target is clearly in public view. Barry Lyndon, however, seems something of an Aunt Sally, a character whose reminiscences are not worth remembering. Such a creation may be the product of Thackeray's snobbery. The novel's distancing, distorting, separatist and abortively subversive elements, together with their cultural and historical implications, seem of little interest to Thackeray, nor does the ease with which the déclassé and the deracinated empower ridicule. Nevertheless, mocking Irishness in terms of its self-representational failures does throw a revealing light on the formal and thematic challenges with which the development of the nineteenth-century Irish novel had to contend.

# 1860

# Anthony Trollope, *Castle Richmond*

*In many ways, Anthony Trollope (1815–82) is the Victorian novelist* par
excellence. *His mother, Frances, was a noted writer in her day, but that
did not smooth her son's path to authorship, although it was evidently
from her example that he became so prodigiously productive that he is at
least as celebrated in literary history for non-stop industry as for literary
artistry. From the West Indies to New Zealand, there is hardly a corner of
the British Empire that escaped his attention, while on the home front he
devoted many of his most substantial works to the relationship between
individuals and major institutions, notably the Church of England, in the
six novels comprising the Chronicles of Barsetshire, and parliament in the
Palliser novels, another six-novel sequence. Throughout Trollope's output,
the interplay of manners and morality, between personal rectitude and
public decorum, is an abiding preoccupation.*

*Trollope was born in London and, following an abortive public school
education, eventually became a clerk in the postal service. Here too he
failed to thrive, but his 1841 appointment as Deputy Postal Surveyor at
Banagher, County Offaly, was a decisive turning-point in his development. In Ireland, he began his writing career, developed a passion for
hunting, married, and advanced in the ranks of the post office. Trollope
spent two periods in Ireland, amounting to fifteen years in all. The first
period included postings to Clonmel and, after promotion to Surveyor,
Mallow. This period lasted until 1851. Returning to Ireland in 1854, he
was Surveyor of northern Ireland, although he was based in Dublin. He
went back to England in 1859. Trollope's professional duties required
extensive travel throughout Ireland, and he is certainly the nineteenth-
century English novelist most closely acquainted with the country. This
familiarity with townlands, baronies and demesnes may be seen not only
in such early novels as* The Macdermotts of Ballycloran *(1847) and*
The Kellys and the O'Kellys *(1848) but informs some of his most noted
works, in particular* Phineas Finn, the Irish Member *(1869) and*
Phineas Redux *(1873). Those two works also are significant for their
representations of Irish characters in the heart of the imperial metropolis.
Other Trollope novels with an Irish setting are* An Eye for an Eye *(1879)
and* The Land Leaguers *(1883), the latter unfinished at his death.*

*In all, Trollope published forty-seven novels, and wrote half as much
again in various other forms, including short fiction, biography and,
especially, travel books. The influence of his Irish years on his development as a writer still awaits systematic examination, though it seems
reasonable to suppose that the experience of organisational responsibility
and attainment of authority during that formative time influenced both*

*the narrative control and the focus on hierarchical social arrangements*
*that are his fiction's stock in trade. Although many nineteenth-century*
*Irish novelists share such essentially integrative concerns, Trollope's per-*
*spective on them further illustrates the differences that remain between*
*the Anglo and the Irish outlook.*

As its title indicates, *Castle Richmond* is a Big House novel; or rather, reflecting Trollope's familiarity with Irish conditions, it is a novel about three country houses of different sizes, each with its distinctive status. This recognition of social gradation has its own cultural significance, but more to Trollope's point is that each house also represents the distinctive character of its owner's manners – the moral style of how each maintains his or her position in the world outside the home. This emphasis on living up to one's responsibilities shows that *Castle Richmond* is working in a vein that, in its fundamental concerns with possession and proper order, is not all that far removed from that of *Castle Rackrent*, despite the clear differences in tone and context between the two novels.

Of the three houses, the eponymous castle is obviously the most important, but that importance to a considerable extent derives from the ways in which its neighbours, Hap House and Desmond Court, impinge upon it. These properties are located in an area that Trollope knew well, 'that Kanturk region through which the Mallow and Killarney railway now passes' (2). The modernity of rail travel has not entirely dimmed the setting's historical associations, though here too the author takes care to differentiate. Castle Richmond, to all appearances, is so innocent of history that it might be 'in Hampshire or in Essex' (3), and its owner, Sir Thomas Fitzgerald, 'might have been a Leicestershire baronet' (ibid.). In contrast, according to local legend, the gloomy pile of Desmond Court has had its cement 'thickened with human blood' (ibid.). This is the domain of the widowed Lady Mary Desmond and her teenage daughter Clara, 'the heroine of this story' (5). The least noteworthy dwelling is Hap House, home of young Owen Fitzgerald, a relation of the Castle Richmond family but sharply distinguished from Sir Thomas and family by being in temperament a 'Laertes' (340) and in manners resembling one of the old-fashioned squirearchy. 'It is impossible that these volumes should be graced by any hero', but if there were to be one, 'Herbert Fitzgerald would be the man' (45). He is Sir Thomas's stepson and presumptive heir.

The story of Castle Richmond is one of a house under stress. The sense of structure and stability that the castle connotes, its economic fate as a property and its social destiny as a symbol of eminence, are threatened by a number of undermining occurrences. These threats are all marked by subtle forms of violence. 'Sedition . . . in Ireland, in late years . . . has not been deep-seated' (66); that is not what menaces Sir Thomas and his holdings. What disturbs him is more insidious and less easy to identify and counteract. Some of the pressures are generated by how relations develop within the three-house triangle, through the changing affiliations between Clara, Owen and Herbert, but, although the marriage plot that seeks both to explore and contain these interpersonal tensions takes up a large amount of the narrative, there are also influences from outside the triangle which compound the uncertainties besetting Castle Richmond and which make it appear as if the property is in danger of passing from Fitzgerald hands. Such an event is as alarming an affront to landlord hegemony and the presumptive rights of property as an unsatisfactory resolution of the marriage plot, as is suggested by the fact that both the internal and external pressures are primarily directed at Herbert Fitzgerald.

Malign external forces take two distinct forms. One of these is the Famine (*Castle Richmond* opens in 1847), an event that clearly has the power to disrupt relations between landlord and tenant unless prompt action is taken. As such, it provides a template for the more intimate, more culpable and less providential difficulties in which the main characters become embroiled. Moreover, Herbert's public-spirited participation in local famine relief not only rehearses his eventual triumph over personal adversity but suggests that this triumph is to be expected of a landlord of his moral calibre. It is as though by doing the right thing by his tenants he is entitled to be rewarded with both Clara and Castle Richmond. As to the Famine itself, there is nothing in *Castle Richmond* to compare with the scenes of suffering depicted in *The Black Prophet*. Suffering is not denied but it is seen as a necessary precondition for amelioration. Relief efforts 'brought people together who would hardly have met but for such necessity' (70) – Herbert and Father McCarthy are cases in point. The narrator asserts that 'in my opinion the measures of the government were prompt, wise, and beneficent' (69); and, for all his privations, 'the poor cotter . . . as a class, has risen from the bed of suffering a better man' (68).

These rather Panglossian statements are rendered tenable because '[t]he destruction of the potato was the work of God' (65). Therefore, although the disaster's origins and motives must remain inscrutable, they should not be thought malevolent. As a result, the Famine is not to be placed within the moral landscape that the concerns of man and his choices occupy, and thus has no direct plot implications, but it can provide a backdrop of good and evil against which the good and evil that the characters are exposed to can play out. Given how calamitous acts of God are, it behoves all concerned to ensure that their interests are secure, that these are represented in the light of righteousness and propriety and that the inherited order of things is protected. A disaster like the Famine makes social coherence all the more necessary, and all social classes should behave accordingly. And if a misfortune like the Famine can be endured and survived, then overcoming man-made trouble – also created by a seemingly perplexing, exacting and demor-alising intervention – becomes much more likely.

This trouble comes in the persons of Matthew Mollett and his son Abraham. Mollett senior, then calling himself Talbot, was once married to Lady Fitzgerald, plain Mary Wainwright at the time. Wrongly presumed dead, Mollett now resorts to blackmailing Sir Thomas with a view, also held very strongly by Abraham, of making Castle Richmond theirs. Among the most serious consequences of the moral blight and economic threat that this pair visits on the Fitzgeralds is that if his mother's history is revealed – which here seems to be a synonym for believed – she will be seen as a sinner who has been falsely representing herself, Herbert will no longer be heir and Owen will inherit the property. The plausible falsities that the Molletts represent will, unless countered, lead to further falsities and disruption. In addition to the moral questions that will arise, the established order will give way to displacement, alienation and the manipulation of lawful entitlement. The legal dimension is as indis-pensable a structure as Castle Richmond itself, although the novel's perspective makes it clear that both moral and civil law combined are necessary to achieve justice. Private life may be contaminated, but it also may be redeemed, by events beyond its control, an outlook that Trollope also seems to suggest applies to the famine-ravaged peasant.

The Mollett incursion has a sentimental counterpart in the *idée fixe* that Owen Fitzgerald has developed about Clara Desmond. Although Owen is no criminal, his brash and forceful male manner has an insis-tence to it, a type of emotional extremism, which is capable of unbalancing relations in ways that may be as damaging as the Mollett conspiracy. And the susceptibility of the most private and closest connections to upheaval is further revealed when Lady Desmond comes between Owen and her daughter. Here, too, false representation is the armature of disruption. Lady Desmond claims that Owen is unsuitable for Clara because he is *déclassé*, but this social pretext masks her desire to have Owen for herself, a match that he considers an unthinkable act of egotistical over-reaching. The sibling-like affection that Herbert and Clara show for each other represents emotional balance and orderliness, and their eventual union is a fit expression of this balance. Moreover, their staunchness in the face of adversity, their withstanding what they cannot fully comprehend – the prospective loss of his patrimony in Herbert's case, and alienation from her mother in Clara's – earn them the right to a just and morally unexceptional outcome. Submission and endurance to the worst the world can do has an ultimately redemptive effect. Yet, while Herbert and Clara represent a correct disposition, one that is neither grasping nor conniving, that is neither infected by financial opportunism nor sexual taboo, success is not attained by that alone. On the one hand, the experience of an ordeal is required. Herbert has to go through the actuality of losing Castle Richmond, together with the concomitant experience of being 'a nobody' (216), and, on the other hand, help from the proper quarter must be available to make smooth the painful rite of passage. Appropriate support is essential. Owen's morally dubious offer to defer his inheritance of Castle Richmond in exchange for Clara is exactly the wrong idea.

The reciprocal relation between the necessities of being tested and being aided emerges once Herbert leaves for London to become a lawyer's clerk. Sinking to the level of employee denotes the difficulty in representing himself that, shorn of property and family, he has to face. A further sign of this problem is given by the walk he takes through Westminster, ending at the Houses of Parliament. Not long before, 'he had thought himself almost too good for Castle Richmond, and had regarded a seat in Parliament as the only place which he could fitly fill without violation to his nature' (461). Now, unable to represent himself, hopes of representing his class or interests are vain. At arguably his lowest point, however, Herbert realises that recuperation will not be accomplished in a palace of laws, but through a return to Ireland, where 'he might teach himself . . . to endure the eyes and voices of men around him' (465). Home is where his crisis of self-representation is best confronted. His return to Castle Richmond is a gesture of reunion, as his tenants' welcome indicates. Herbert's display of proper spirit – a combination of courage, humility and patience – represents him as virtuous in himself and morally commendable by the world at large.

The corrective supplied by uncovering some salient facts bears out the rightness of Herbert's behaviour. Earlier, Sir Thomas, on the point of dying of 'a mind diseased' (324) – his inability to resist the blackmailing Molletts corrodes his consciousness – has summoned his London solicitor, Prendergast, to consider the allegations against Lady Fitzgerald, but, after a protracted investigation at Castle Richmond, Prendergast was convinced that the Molletts were correct: Sir Thomas' children were illegitimate. A semi-literate letter from a greed-besotted Abraham Mollett, however, directs Prendergast, accompanied by heavy-handed hunting imagery, to Matthew Mollett's east London lair, a domicile that contrasts utterly with the Irish one he coveted. The ailing miscreant confesses all, including his extensive career as a bigamist (Prendergast discovers him in the care of yet another former spouse). This confrontation reveals that Mollett had represented himself falsely to Mary Wainwright. He was married when he wed her; therefore their marriage was illegal. The civil law and the moral code collaborate in re-establishing the equilibrium on which freedom relies. Fitzgerald integrity is restored, and with it the hegemony and continuity for which Castle Richmond stands. The family are no longer the 'strangers there' (344) that they had temporarily felt themselves to be. And Trollope ensures that the moral account is also fully rendered with respect to Matthew Mollett. He too must live with himself, which in his case means that he has to endure '[t]he cold, hungry, friendless, solitary doom of unconvicted rascaldom' that is 'the most wretched phase of human existence' (473).

Solitude is also the fate of Lady Desmond, whose endeavours as an emotional conspirator could have had calamitous, house-toppling, results. Her final effort to possess Owen merely confirms his undying fixation on Clara. Unlike her ladyship, '[h]is heart was to him a reality' (485), and representing himself in those terms 'he would still be manly' (481), but, unlike Herbert, he is unfit to retain his place on his native ground. He sets off to hunt in Africa, accompanied by young Patrick Desmond, whose hero is Owen and who certainly needs a father figure, even if his departure raises questions about the future of Desmond Court. Perhaps that house's unhappy history has run its course. Such an inference would be consistent with the quiet triumph of Castle Richmond and the reserved, upright style that it enshrines. It is also fitting that Lady Desmond ends up alone. 'English to the backbone' (9) she may be, but she is also 'a woman of mercenary spirit' (479), and the demands of the latter identity ensure that she offends against the codes of behaviour that *Castle Richmond* endorses. She attempts to force the issues of her relationship both to Clara and to Owen, rather than observing the doctrine of *festina lente* ('make haste slowly') preached by the wise old London lawyer who is Prendergast's superior. Circumstances enjoin that same pace on Herbert and Clara, to their eventual advantage; and it is also tacitly approved of by the sedate pace of Trollope's narrative. And in her eventually isolating manners, Lady Desmond removes herself from that sphere of collaboration and retrieval so necessary to Herbert's receiving 'all the good things that Providence had showered upon him' (489). The sphere requires London for completeness, as Prendergast's activities demonstrate. There are moral concerns common to both rural Ireland and the metropolis. The commonality is projected in the cooperative effort between landlord, clergy and government in response to the providential onset of the Famine. This combination of interests has restorative effects that are paralleled by Herbert's personal success; among them is 'rents paid to the day' (489), an assurance of Castle Richmond's continuing good economic health. Such unions – local, domestic, administrative – are to be read as synonyms of justice. As Prendergast reflects, 'was not justice, immutable justice, better than law?' (412).

To map his moral position onto the landscape of Famine Ireland, Trollope uses an 'I', a narrative persona who rehearses, echoes and affirms the rights and wrongs of *Castle Richmond*'s most crucial actions. The sense of executive judgement that this narrator conveys confirms that the several strands of the story, all in some way or other indicative of disunions of various kinds, can be productively harmonised. The representation of such a *point d'appui* differentiates *Castle Richmond* from Irish novels' treatment of its themes of entitlement, succession, domestic harmony and public concord. Indeed, following *Castle Richmond*'s appearance, Irish novels begin to consider the possibility of an alternative to the type of fostering implied by the reliance for security of Irish property and position on the apparatus and resources of English law, a connection that this novel sees so benevolently and regards as the only available representation of equity and goodwill.

# 1863

# Joseph Sheridan Le Fanu, *The House by the Churchyard*

*Joseph Sheridan Le Fanu (1814–73) was born in Dublin and, after graduating from Trinity College and the King's Inns, established himself as a newspaper proprietor and author. Like much of his subsequent work, the short fiction that inaugurated Le Fanu's writing career – eventually published as* The Purcell Papers *(1880) – initially appeared in the* Dublin University Magazine, *then under the editorship of his college friend Isaac Butt. Le Fanu also published two novels during the 1840s. The first of these,* The Cock and Anchor *(1845), is set in the seventeenth century; its subtitle –* Being a Chronicle of Old Dublin City *– anticipates the sense of the capital conveyed in* The House by the Churchyard. *This historical interest is treated in a more conventional manner in* The Fortunes of Colonel Torlogh O'Brien *(1847), a work too indebted to Sir Walter Scott's influence.*

*Le Fanu continued to contribute short fiction to the* Dublin University Magazine *both under the editorship of Charles Lever and throughout the 1850s, although in that decade his productivity as a novelist went into temporary abeyance. In 1861, however, he bought the* Dublin University Magazine, *which he owned and edited until 1870, and here his major fiction was serialised, beginning with* The House by the Church-yard *[sic]. A brisk succession of novels followed, including* Wylder's Hand *(1864) and, most notably,* Uncle Silas *(1864). Other novels include* Guy Deverell *(1865),* The Wyvern Mystery *(1869) and* The Rose and the Key *(1871). Many of these works have English settings. This period also saw the appearance of his most substantial body of short fiction, much of it in such leading periodicals of the day as Dickens'* All the Year Round. *These works were collected in* In a Glass Darkly *(1872), which may be regarded as a companion to* Ghost Stories and Tales of Mystery *(1851).*

*Like many nineteenth-century Irish novels, Le Fanu's seem shapeless in form and plot. In his case, however, these perceived deficiencies are fundamental to the mysterious events and concealed histories of his subject matter. And his explorations of the unknown and unacknowledged owe their typically pedestrian pace and digressive development to a narrator who both needs to face the worst and understandably delays in doing so. The worst is that the world of appearances, the empirical present, may be subverted, bringing into question the ways in which an essentially hierarchical social order is maintained. In addition to its class system, its code of manners, its modes of vigilance and the legitimacy of its institutional and professional practices, the prevailing social scene can also disclose, quite unexpectedly, an alternative system of signs and portents, suggesting how thin-skinned the surface world is. Such symptoms of danger and impermanence may even go so far as to persuade individual psyches that what is seen in the light of common day is a figment, and that those phenomena thought of as figments – hauntings of various descriptions – constitute a more compelling reality.*

*In such scenarios, threats to house and lineage, to personal standing and integrity, to faith and other forms of affiliation, become the order of the day. The protagonist of these works typically proceeds in uncertainty and anxiety beyond the remit of the status quo. These conditions, together with Le Fanu's acute senses of atmosphere, unreadiness and misgiving, have led to his works being classified as sensation novels, a sub-genre of Victorian fiction that resonates with late twentieth-century concerns. In unveiling in their own day problems of provenance and difficulties of heritage, of the weight of the past and the frailty of the present, Le Fanu produced parables of the Anglo-Irish double world and its precariousness, even if it would unnecessarily limit his fiction's appeal and penetration to confine them to any one interpretation.*

The story opens at a remove, its relevant materials a legacy to the narrator Charles de Cresseron, but once he has introduced these materials, this figure withdraws, as perhaps 'your humble servant' (3) should, although there is also something ghostly about his doing so. This opening's play of presence and absence unobtrusively introduces the doubleness that affects almost every aspect of the narrative. Other binaries are also in evidence. The distance of the story's events in time and place is bridged by de Cresseron's courteous, civil tone. His seemingly digressive manner signals the significance of digressions to the revelations to come. 'Softened' (ibid.) by distance, events nevertheless retain a capacity to shock, and, as the narrative goes on, its bifocal character becomes increasingly prominent and relevant, indicating that full disclosure requires a structure of oppositions, antitheses, enmities and divisions.

The action proper opens with an unexpected nocturnal burial on a dark and stormy night and, although the subsequent narrative is basically concerned with unravelling that mysterious event, it is also at pains – too much so, perhaps – to contain it within a context of community and continuity. This context is most immediately conveyed by the setting, Chapelizod, which at the time of the action – the year is 1767 – 'was about the gayest and prettiest of the outpost villages in which old Dublin took a complacent pride' (1). The locals are neighbourly: bibulous Father Roach is on good terms with the rector, Doctor Walsingham, while the latter shares his antiquarian interests with 'young, queer, erudite, simple' (22) Dan Loftus; the military, garrisoned in the nearby Phoenix Park under the command of General Chattesworth, constitutes less a show of force than a source of spectacle, as a field day on Palmerston Green affirms. Such threatened lapses from amenability as there are amount to no more than harmless misunderstandings, though these both prefigure and, in their essential good nature, contrast with the wilful wrongs that emerge to shock and horrify. Chapelizod's tone and tempo – a far different place from, say, the 'fighting county' (42) of Galway, notwithstanding the unsettling impact of the peremptory and foreboding midnight interment – suggest themselves as correctives to the eighteenth-century Ireland represented in *Castle Rackrent* and *The Memoirs of Barry Lyndon*. Here, communal life is typified by those who serve. All the prominent – that is, male – residents possess professional expertise and appear to embody the sense of duty that is its ethical counterpart. It is with this Chapelizod that, a hundred years later, de Cresseron identifies.

But the scene is deceptive, its Fieldingesque amity a reminder perhaps that it is a necessary fiction (an 'open volume of *Tom Jones*' (90) is pointed to). Bitter tensions exist between Charles Nutter, agent of the local landlord Lord Castlemallard, and an army surgeon, Sturk, his rival for the agency (the latter lives in the house by the churchyard). And the burial brings to the area a Mr Mervyn, an outsider who excites local 'fascination' (14) long before it is known who he really is, much less that '[h]is whole life had been a flight and a pursuit – a vain endeavour to escape from the evil spirit that pursued him' (ibid.). Yet it is not immediately clear how matters will come to a head between the agent and his adversary. Mervyn's haunting by a severed hand may be a dreadful omen, but it takes place in his Ballyfermot house, beyond the tensions of Chapelizod. Moreover, Mervyn is neither so distant nor so doom-laden as to ignore the attractions of Gertrude 'Toody' Chattesworth, the General's niece. The General may detect 'a taint of blood' (60) in Mervyn, but this is the heritage he seeks to expunge, not a resource he desires to commission. Indeed, he is the marrying kind, and this eventual consummation, which concludes the novel, represents an emergence from darkness to light, an affirmation of continuity, and an instance of and also a contribution to the harmonious current that underlies and sustains the community's ways. Despite his family history, Mervyn is enabled to enter into union, that fundamental signature of belonging.

The current's central place and natural properties are represented by Chapelizod's river Liffey: 'it's sad and it's merry, musical and sparkling . . . . Always changing, yet still the same . . . . It tells everything, and yet nothing' (107). It reflects the life around it and in its continuous flow conveys the unassumingly persistent spirit of that life. These personifications of the river, made by Richard Devereux to his beloved, Lilias Walsingham, the rector's daughter, conclude with Devereux likening Lilias to a river nymph, wedding the feminine to the spiritual and so imagining a joint human and deific wellspring to feed the beneficent 'ever-running water, an emblem of the eternal change and monotony of life' (208). In this blend of sources there is perhaps the literary birth of Joyce's Anna Livia, not only in the babbling waters but in its communal counterpart, the 'throbbing murmur of our village – a wild chaos of sound' (343). Among the current's other tributaries are the eternal, the sensory, the playful and the light-filled. Whether or not these qualities are additional connotations of the feminine, they do seem antithetical, if not indeed naturally opposed, to the actions and epochs, the cunning and concealment, the darkness and destructiveness, that spring from the novel's other narrative point of origin, the vault containing 'the nameless coffin' (11). From there arises a surge of male power, of violence, lying, concealment and related activities nurturing false representation, all of which make for a shadowy backdrop that contrasts fundamentally with the river's lucent transparency.

Mervyn's fretful disposition and the fact that he 'had formed no very distinct plan of life' (59) – his form of service remains uncertain – are closely connected to the coffin that he has seen to its resting place, but this connection provides neither closure nor agency. As for the latter, the use of power, control, knowledge and planning comes from a different source, another outsider, who appears to be quite removed from whatever bedevils Mervyn, while being intimately connected with it. This character is Paul Dangerfield, Lord Castlemallard's English agent. He may share Mervyn's 'strange pallor' (81), but he seems the young man's superior by virtue of his air of 'intellectual mastery, and sarcastic decision' (ibid). During his Chapelizod sojourn, Dangerfield also attempts to win Toody Chattesworth. Initially, however, he makes his greatest impact on Sturk. Once more, as in all that relates to disruption and trouble, the impact is mental; it is within – in dreams, memories and complications of conscience; all invisible to and concealed from the communal world – that the disturbance occurs. The sight of Dangerfield stirs up thoughts and memories that Sturk has considered long buried, and these are so strong and of such a distressing nature that it is as though Dangerfield is their ghostly embodiment. The distress is two-fold; it derives from the violent content of what Sturk remembers and also from the quite real possibility that 'dreams may have an office and a meaning, and are perhaps more than a fortuitous concourse of symbols' (116). If the latter is the case, the sensational material must be interpreted, which in turn requires it to be brought out into the light of day.

What haunts Sturk is a night of roistering and gambling that he witnessed many years before in an English inn, a night that culminated in a murder that Sturk was unable to prevent. The central figure in these events was Dangerfield, known as Charles Archer at the time, and he had two henchmen with him, one of whom is Ezekiel Irons, now Doctor Walsingham's wraith-like parish clerk. But Dangerfield and his men escaped incrimination for the murder. Another member of the party, Lord Dunoran, was tried for the crime, found guilty and killed himself in his condemned cell. It emerges in the course of bringing these events to light and exposing Dangerfield that Mervyn is 'the only son of that disgraced and blood-stained nobleman' (263), heir both to the title and to the sins of the father. Oppressed by what is almost a definitive crisis of self-representation, Mervyn seeks release not only for himself but as an act of restitution, for, as he informs Dangerfield, 'the fame and fortune of a noble family depend on searching out the truth' (290). This search will rectify the past and eliminate the double-dealing and two-faced behaviour that do so much to make the present resemble 'a horrible masquerade, full of half-detected murderers, traitors, and miscreants' (389). Exposing the resourceful and formidable Dangerfield is no easy matter, however, particularly because the pace required to penetrate his stony exterior is not urgent or dramatic but erodent or riverine.

Le Fanu's representation of Dangerfield's icy demeanour, of the impression of impenetrability that his light-reflecting spectacles convey (as though signifying that nobody can see through him), and of the manipulative insincerity expressed through the 'burlesque and irony' (335) of his social manner, keeps him at a distance and sustains his enigmatic, alien character. His unmoving, impersonal demeanour disqualifies him from membership of the Chapelizod community, and his evident desire to be no part of it in itself shows that he is lacking in proper sentiment. As a result, the falseness of his self-representation should come as no surprise. As his name implies, Dangerfield has the power of a snake in the grass – or perhaps, bearing in mind the novel's imagery, he might be regarded as a stone in the living stream. Certainly he is obstructive enough to be thought of in that way. Locating a dead Charles Archer in whom to conceal himself is merely the most elaborate of his deceptive stratagems. This partial, though crucial, reliance on a dead stranger also counterpoints Mervyn's connection with the dead, yet another of the novel's doublings, reversals, contrasts and parallels. But Mervyn wishes to exonerate his dead. To protect himself, Dangerfield needs to exploit his. Part of the moral implications of his doing so are conveyed in Mervyn's remark that he is dealing with a 'half man, half corpse – vampire' (293); a middle-class Dracula.

If 'nowadays our whole social organization is subservient to detection' (223) – an observation that aligns *The House by the Churchyard* with the novels of Wilkie Collins and with Dickens' later works – that must be partly because there are greater chances of avoiding detection. This is a modern development, the result of a world where time and space have been contracted by speed. In its pedestrian pace, *The House by the Churchyard* implicitly rejects such advances. In the preferable conditions of the eighteenth century, discovery of evil-doing is a moral matter, a just reward for patience and a tacit faith that murder will out. The hermeneutics of surfaces, on which detection relies, extrapolating inner realities from outward appearances, evolves in Chapelizod in keeping with the essentially virtuous tenor of communal life. An alien to that life, a non-joining outsider, a self-made misfit, will almost necessarily hang himself. And in this case, not only the gathering of information, but the nature of the information itself – an amalgamation of repressed, half-remembered and concealed data – is a measure of what is at stake. In addition, the nature of the data is such that it takes an especially circuitous path to lead Mervyn out of what he calls 'the labyrinth in which I'm lost' (291). This circuitousness is represented by a number of seemingly tangential subplots. Yet these, almost inevitably it seems, become tributaries to the narrative's main drift, bearing valuable knowledge and helping to refresh the Chapelizod ethos that Dangerfield has defiled.

Thus, the relationship between Robert Devereux and Lilias Walsingham both replicates the novel's structure of opposites and illustrates how difficult it is that good should prevail, even when it is desired. Devereux is 'a fast man' (137), a debtor, attractive and reckless – 'so handsome, so impulsive, so unfathomable – with his gipsy tint, and great enthusiastic eyes, and strange melancholy' (234), a figure so 'at variance with himself' (258) that he suggests a blend of Dangerfield and Mervyn. 'The darker knowledge is mine' (241), he acknowledges, Marlowe's *Doctor Faustus* in hand, and such knowledge in part derives from his seduction and abandonment of a native girl, 'poor wild Nan' (237), as she calls herself. But deserting Nan for Lilias does not entitle Devereux to live in the light. Lilias dies, an event that, though quietly observed, is also sensational in its apparent arbitrariness, and sufficiently shocking for Devereux to reform himself.

This subplot's interplay of damage and belatedness foreshadows how Dangerfield ultimately comes to grief. Physical reasons contribute to his undoing, notably Sturk's confession after trepanning – in effect an operation on his consciousness – by Black Dillon, a Dublin surgeon who has 'the power of a demigod, and the lusts of a swine' (324). Yet it is his rivalrous and egotistical pursuit of Toody Chattesworth, Mervyn's beloved, that ensures Dangerfield's downfall. Emerging from his coma, the darkness Sturk has harboured comes forth in words that secure a case against Dangerfield. But it is his protracted pursuit of Toody that thwarts the miscreant; as he reflects, '[h]ad I married, I should have left the country' (413). But Dangerfield is not one from whom union should be expected and, though it would be unnecessarily reductive to think of him as an interfering Englishman who disturbs the smooth course of ordinary Irish life, his contemptuous view of his arrest as 'rather an Irish proceeding' (374) adds a further layer to his falseness. Further, it is the Irish House of Lords that eventually exonerates Lord Dunoran, whose prison suicide is Dangerfield's own expiatory fate. The preservation of an Irish form of Mervyn's name – Mordaunt, meaning dare death – is also part of the narrative's tribute to its period, a time that is seen as uniting the personal, communal and institutional in Ireland, just as *The House by the Churchyard*'s meandering, discursive streams eventually combine in righteous cleansing, an attainment valorising the indispensable currents of feeling and trustworthy representations conveyed by 'the honest prose of everyday life' (298).

# 1864

# William Allingham, *Laurence Bloomfield in Ireland*

*William Allingham (1824–89) was born in Ballyshannon, County Donegal. Arguably the best-known Irish poet of the mid-nineteenth century, his early verse was influenced by the ballads that he collected during his various postings as a customs officer (these include Coleraine, New Ross, Donegal town and his birthplace). As well as writing his own ballads, he published an anthology,* The Ballad Book *(1865). Allingham was also on close terms with the London literary scene, which he first experienced in 1843 and visited regularly thereafter, numbering among his friends such luminaries as Thomas Carlyle, Dante Gabriel Rossetti, and particularly the poet laureate, Tennyson. In 1870, Allingham resigned from the customs service to work as a sub-editor on* Fraser's Magazine, *where* Laurence Bloomfield in Ireland *originally appeared in serial form between November 1862 and November 1863. He succeeded to the editorship in 1874, and held that position for five years.*

*A prolific and resourceful lyric poet, a number of whose poems have been set to music, Allingham published regularly following* Poems *(1850). Other volumes include* Day and Night Songs *(1854),* Fifty Modern Poems *(1865),* Evil May-Day *(1883) and* Blackberries *(1884). A number of his books were illustrated by such artists as Rossetti and Millais, and in that respect are bibliographically significant. Certain features of Allingham's work – his sense of place, his treatment of colour and atmosphere, his eye for natural detail – struck a chord with the young Yeats and are echoed and reflected in the works of many Irish Literary Revival poets. Besides* Varieties in Prose *(1893), Allingham produced two other prose works,* Rambles by Patricius Walker *(1873), a collection of essays first published in* Fraser's *on English places, though also including pieces on the areas around Ballyshannon and Enniskillen. Allingham's other prose work is his* Diary *(1907), a record of his friendships with famous contemporaries, which contains a good deal of table-talk and sketches of people and places that are enlivened by vivid, impressionistic detail.*

*Nothing in Allingham's output rivals the ambition of* Laurence Bloomfield in Ireland. *As a verse-novel it reflects the mid-century vogue for the genre, exemplified by such well-known works as Christina Rossetti's* Aurora Leigh *(1856), Arthur Hugh Clough's* Amours de Voyage *(1858) and Robert Browning's* The Ring and the Book *(1868–9). These poems also highlight protagonists in foreign countries who to one degree or another are not at ease in their surroundings. This state of* uncertainty is also one with which Laurence Bloomfield has to deal, and perhaps it is for this reason that Allingham subtitled the work 'A Modern Poem'. Later subtitles – 'The New Landlord' in the 1869 edition, and 'Rich and Poor in Ireland' in the 1893 reissue – although not necessarily chosen by the poet, indicate the work's more homely interests. And while Laurence Bloomfield in Ireland has modernising tendencies, its largest artistic debt is to the more conventional pastoral affections that are fundamental to Allingham's imagination.

Twenty-six-year-old Laurence Bloomfield, an absentee landlord, 'Irish born and English bred' (6), returns to his birthplace after graduating from Cambridge University and extensive travel in Europe and America. During his absence he has held different attitudes to Ireland, from a romantic schoolboy's infatuation with the country, to identifying in his student days with the Empire and its representatives among Ireland's land-holding elite. As an orphan, the 'beardless Burke' (8), who took the latter position, seems to have found security and assurance in the thought that his name, too, would be '[w]ith names ancestral in the Lodge enroll'd' (9). But, Laurence outgrows this affiliation as well, possibly because he recalls that 'My rebel grandsire, sixty years ago/With Grattan gave his vote in College-green' (257), though this recollection occurs only when the young man has decided that he can represent himself as his own kind of landlord, one at odds with the self-seeking and cold-heartedness of neighbouring estate owners.

His path to that attainment forms the narrative of Allingham's verse-novel. But, initially, Laurence's motives for returning are difficult to assess. 'The pain of too much freedom Bloomfield knew' (52), yet he is also not equipped to settle down and commit himself to his social responsibilities, and the foreign character of land and people, together with his lack of experience in taking charge, produce a markedly detached attitude to his patrimony. Although he shows signs of possessing a social conscience, taking action in the light of it seems a challenge. Yet inaction is not necessarily weakness; rather it reflects the difficulty somebody like Laurence – 'A complex character and various mind,/Where all, like some rich landscape lies combined' (6) – must inevitably confront in focusing and choosing. This difficulty is compounded by the fact that his interior landscape has no objective correlative. 'Autumnal sunshine' (3) may beam on the young master as he makes his way back to Croghan Hall, but for the most part the prospect is not pleasing: the land is dismal and neglected, and the social atmosphere antagonistic and oppressive. Whether, and by what means, Laurence will establish a mode of representing himself in such an environment so that he may discharge his duties as he sees fit is problematic, particularly since '[p]ublic ambitions are not to his mind,/His nature's proper work seems hard to find' (11). A particularly steep learning curve awaits such a neophyte, and while his intellectual capacity may help him to come to terms with '[e]xperiences so multi-form and strange' (13) as those of the parish of Kilmoylan, it seems that it will be quite some time before such experiences can be har-nessed to productive purpose. The daughters of local landlords may 'quote *Evangeline, Traviata* play' (55), but such accomplishments are a far cry from creating a social ensemble in which 'rich and poor, har-moniously conjoint/Form'd alto, basso, in a counterpoint' (16).

One obvious barrier to this dream of concord and unity is the pre-vailing ethos of the local landlord oligarchy, a committed member of which is Laurence's uncle, Sir Ulick Harvey. Laurence makes the acquaintance of the oligarchy's members and learns of their outlook at a dinner given by his uncle, an event that seems intended to be the young man's induction into the rules and practices by which the land is lorded over. In their decadence and viciousness, all these dinner guests are equally offensive. The nature of their presence is asserted by misanthropic Lord Crashton's house, where '[a] stout and high enclo-sure girdles all,/Built up with stones from many a cottage wall' (25). And the state of Dysart's place brings Castle Rackrent to mind; while, rather more daringly, his son Tom is described as 'a staunch good Protestant by creed,/But half a Mormon, judged by act and deed;/A dozen wives, he has, but underhand' (30). The list of offences, defences and malpractices is lengthy, but the landlords are united in their concern to make the most of their property. Thus all share Sir Ulick's 'whim . . . /To 'square' the farms on all his wide estate' (24); that is, to amalgamate his tenants' smallholdings and make a land fit only for grazing. Such modernisation will result not only in mass evictions but in the dismantling of local culture and traditions. The extent of tenant vulnerability is conveyed in Sir Ulick's belief that '[t]he Laws were for the Higher Classes made' (23); the lower classes should keep their hands off an '[o]rder and grade as plann'd by Providence' (ibid.). The practical consequence of these views is a belief that 'tenant-right is robbery or worse' (46) – and that landlord expropriation is not. This outlook is ratified and implemented on pretty much a daily basis by

James Pigot, 'agent wise and great,/Rich man himself, grand juror, mag-istrate' (22), whose authority maintains Sir Ulick's will and gives no ground to Laurence's 'philanthropic dreams' (46).

Laurence hears out his uncle without asserting a position of his own, although what he is told causes him to wonder: 'Can we, by politics of coin or birth,/Own, like a house or hunter, God's round earth?' (51). This is a question that the tenantry may also have asked themselves. Unlike them, Laurence has a choice. The nature of that choice becomes clearer to him when he disagrees with Pigot's assertion that 'this country sorely needs/A quicker clearance of its human weeds' (45). Yet, he is still willing to give Pigot the benefit of the doubt, seeing the agent as 'business-like and bold, not base' (57), reminding himself that '[n]ovels and newspapers alone afford/Th' angelic peasant and his fiendish lord' (ibid.). And Laurence also perceives that his own level of culture – his attachment to 'all life's finer part' (59) – inhibits his devel-opment into somebody 'whom actual toils engage' (ibid.). The narrator's observation that '[m]an's life is double: hard its due to give/Within, without, and thus completely live' (60) seems especially applicable to Anglo-Irish Laurence, whose education and culture are English but whose material interests and practical responsibilities con-stitute his Irish home. This Irish dimension not only pertains to Laurence alone; it also crucially concerns his tenants. The 'crisis of his life' (59) – the challenge to be an improving landlord and an exception to both his uncle's sense of entitlement and to Pigot's exercise of the whip hand – is gradually eased by his translation of his feelings of *noblesse oblige* into various forms of remedial action benefiting the com-munity at large. These actions combine respect for the agricultural status quo by retaining tillage with a much-needed modernisation of the town of Lisnamoy – 'could anywhere be found/A Town more ugly, ev'n on Irish ground?' (181) – by improving schooling and the water supply, by building a town hall and by supplanting the 'dismal "Royal"' (242) with The Bloomfield Arms.

Such innovations help to redress the 'piteous lack of manly confi-dence' (201) typical of the tenantry, and at least tentatively bring into balance the 'two scales' (94) that historically have found the people to be outweighed by the law. The improvements also countermand the Ribbonism that is the peasants' sole form of agency. Their dwellings resemble 'the cavern of Despair' (88); '[t]he present seems a prison-house' (120); their future probably lies in 'the prairie . . . the Western wood/There, with your little purse and vigorous arm,/Be king (for so you may) of house and farm' (78). Not for the first time in the nineteenth-century Irish novel, tenants are represented as responding to their destructive conditions with destruction of their own. Pigot has received a death threat 'sined, Captin Starlite' (49), and Neal Doran, son and heir of Allingham's typical cottier family, sees no alternative to becoming a Ribbonman. The narrator feels obliged to point the moral: 'Mark the great evil of a low estate;/Not Poverty, but Slavery, – one man's fate/Too much at mercy of another's will' (77). The physical representation of this fate is conveyed spatially; by reclaiming land, the Dorans merely make their holding more attractive to the grasping grazier – 'wide-spread farms absorb the petty fields' (80); even the locals' sense of place is subject to expropriation. When the Ballytullagh eviction – *Laurence Bloomfield in Ireland*'s central and most celebrated scene – takes place, not only are the inhabitants dispersed and their homes levelled, but the place itself is erased, though '[s]ecluded Ballytullagh, small, unknown,/Had place and life and history of its own' (92).

Some of that local history provides the setting for Neal Doran's swearing in on the island of Innisree, with its ancient ruined church and a round tower that stands 'like a poem, scatheless and sublime' (124). Neal is no great subversive: 'To help "the patriot cause" with heart and hand;/So Neal aspired; and all was vague and grand' (122). The Ribbon leadership are darker figures, however: the Delegate, for one – with his '[h]uge fungoid ears, harsh skin befitting those' (160) – conforms to the image of the agrarian agitator propagated in English periodicals. But ugly as Ribbonism and its representatives might be, they persist as an alternative state of consciousness to the typical peasant state of mind, manifested in '[c]ontempt of prudence, anger, and despair,/And *vis inertiæ*' (139). And indeed the Ribbonmen make their mark: the threat to Pigot's life is carried out. By the time of that attack, Laurence has successfully challenged the agent's authority. His new duties, including that of justice of the peace, introduce a more humane administration. Neal Doran, who has been arrested for Ribbonism, is released when Laurence puts his legal knowledge to use. And this occasion of deliverance also features Laurence's physical embrace of Neal's father, who had collapsed under the burden of his son's trouble, a tableau whose resonances speak loudly and clearly for Laurence's success in representing himself in just and feeling terms.

With Pigot's assassination, sweetness and light obtain throughout the parish. This development, like many of the work's other significant junctures, is conveyed spatially. Cabins, Innisree's ruins, the architectural ugliness of Lisnamoy's churches, the grimy back room where Ribbonmen meet, these and other structures, together with their fates and usages, maintain a sense throughout of a here-and-now, of local habitations and their names. (They also include a 'Big House' (82). Allingham's orthography has the same distancing effect as Carleton's use of the term in The Black Prophet.) Contrasted with Laurence's Croghan Hall, Pigot's Newbridge reveals a complete deficiency in '[t]h' instinctive touch of strong yet tender skill/ . . . which we name artistic sense' (214), while in Laurence's home '[h]is own true touch alive on every part/Gave without cost the luxury of Art' (232). Spacious and gracious, the latter house is a fit setting for a colloquy between Laurence's enlightened friends – a house party that makes a vivid contrast with that initiating dinner at Sir Ulick Harvey's. The guests include noted politicians and officials, a member of the Pre-Raphaelite Brotherhood, and 'George Roe . . . /Our Irish antiquary' (256) – somebody, that is, who also finds value in the landscape without having to exploit it.

Although the colloquy does not pretend to envisage the future – 'What comes at last? Our grandsons, they may know' (261) – certain forward-looking views emerge, not least Laurence's endorsement of tenant rights, his declaration that '[s]mall nations to conglomerates I prefer' (260), and his frank avowal that '[h]e stood aloof from every stated creed' (263), a gesture towards the possibility that sectarianism will go the way of Ribbonism, 'that morbid sign, a proof of social schism' (271). The house party concludes with a Midsummer Eve's picnic on Innisree, followed by a bonfire, an age-old celebration whose ritualistic significance is further enhanced by the attendance of guests and tenants together. This togetherness extends to George Roe's vision of the entire country glowing with the 'mystic flame' (265) of bygone days, a rather more inspiring alternative to Pigot's vigorous snuffing out of what he fears to be an inheritance of 'Captain Rock's commands' (193). The 'earthly paradise' (213) that Pigot believes that he has built for himself is a mere material construct, and a monument to nouveau riche vulgarity at that. Once he has resolved to represent himself in terms of his refined nature and superior culture, Laurence soon eclipses the agent's false lustre. And not surprisingly, in view of

Allingham's attachment to the Pre-Raphaelites, *Laurence Bloomfield in Ireland* concludes in a sunlit panorama of the landscape, extending and irradiating the prospect of home and homeland.

It seems appropriate that a second-hand copy of *Laurence Bloomfield in Ireland* is on Leopold Bloom's bookshelves, for there is much that is second-hand in Allingham's work: rapacious landlords, unscrupulous agents, a peasantry that alternates between passivity and violence, and a hero thanks to whom '[m]aster and servant lived in mutual trust' (280), at last. These features of the work are so prominent that they almost overshadow the aspects of it that escape generic treatment, but, when the narrator reminds himself that 'what Horace says, how hard/It is to sing of every-day affairs' (199), he also reminds the reader of how down-to-earth his material often is. This level is reinforced by its localised geographical setting. The recognition of parish, hamlet, town-land and similar specific habitations eliciting unique attachment is thought worthwhile not because, in a manner that the nineteenth-century Irish novel has made familiar, they stand for the place mentioned in Allingham's title. They are also worthy of concern in their own right. In addition to its humanistic significance, this local focus anticipates the sense of place in *Knocknagow*, a work that also draws on such suggestive Allingham material as land reclamation, evic-tion, the changing post-famine landscape, and most especially a sensitivity to belonging and the psychological sustenance it provides. Further, use of the heroic couplet also represents the integrity of place by formally preventing the proceedings from falling apart. The verse form models the type of union and balance that Laurence's relation to his fellow-countrymen comes to represent.

This culmination is the product of the deliberateness with which Laurence accepts his responsibilities. His unselfish decision to remain where he is, the knowledge that he brings to his role, his respect for the soil and for the historical relics that make such respect appropriate, his analysis of the social make-up of the area such that he envisages 'a novel class' (259) of peasant proprietors, all represent an active consciousness – a thoughtfulness that productively redirects the reaction and back-wardness of his uncle's generation. The newcomer's singularity and independent-mindedness, drawn in broad strokes though it admittedly is, may not be sufficient to entitle *Laurence Bloomfield in Ireland* to be thought 'a modern poem'. Its interest in eliminating problems, rather than in probing them further, must also be considered in this regard.

Nevertheless, by mixing in a flexible but stable form the ideal of 'a manly life' (252) with the reality that 'daily life's material enough' (89), and the old-fashioned ambition 'to make some accord/Of wish and fact' (285) with forward-looking secularism, *Laurence Bloomfield in Ireland* is not only a revealing transitional text in the development of the nineteenth-century Irish novel, it also enacts the possibility of self-representation based on the resources of consciousness.

# 1865

## Charles Lever, *Luttrell of Arran*

*The reputation for slapstick, frivolity and a general condescension to Irish provincial life that Charles Lever (1806–72) acquired with his very popular early novels made his name a synonym for the artistic failings and cultural inadequacies of the novel in nineteenth-century Ireland. Only in recent times has his fluent pen and chequered career been subject to the kind of attentive readings that establish him as a novelist of some significance, less half of a stage-Irish double act with Samuel Lover, as had long been the conventional view, than a connoisseur of social surfaces and insincerities whose mature works counterpoint the interior fictional landscapes of his friend Sheridan Le Fanu (to whom* Luttrell of Arran *is dedicated).*

*Lever was born in Dublin, qualified as a doctor and became acquainted with rural Ireland while holding positions in County Clare, during the cholera epidemic of 1832, and in County Derry. He also travelled to Canada and on the Continent and practised medicine in Brussels, sojourns that are early expressions of the restlessness that beset his career and that typifies his fiction. Influenced by William Hamilton Maxwell's* Stories of Waterloo *(1829) and* Wild Sports of the West *(1832), Lever began his career with* The Adventures of Harry Lorrequer *(1839), less a novel than a skein of picaresque japes. Similar works on military themes followed, including* Jack Hinton the Guardsman *(1843), notable for its depictions of Irish garrison life. In 1842, Lever became editor of the* Dublin University Magazine, *a position he held until 1845. Rather than opposing that stern Tory organ to the militant energies of* The Nation, *he pursued an inclusive editorial policy, publishing, in addition to local authors such as William Carleton, contemporary European materials. During this period he also befriended W.M. Thackeray and Anthony Trollope; Lever is the dedicatee of the former's* Irish Sketch Book *(1842). A disinclination to engage in the cultural and ideological disputes of the day led to his resigning his position and his leaving Ireland, seldom to return.*

*His departure made Lever one of the notable nineteenth-century Irish writers in exile, and introduced a more sober and more socially alert dimension to his writing, beginning with* St Patrick's Eve *(1845). Though he retained his picaresque leanings, novels such as* The Martins of Cro' Martin *(1856), drawing on the Martin family of Ballinahinch, County Galway;* Davenport Dunn *(1855), on the ruined financier and politician John Sadlier (better known in literature as the model for Mr Merdle in Dickens'* Little Dorrit *(1857)), and* Lord Kilgobbin: A Tale of Ireland in Our Own Time *(1872) show a greater willingness than hitherto to regard problematically the standing of the Big House, the transience of social position and the vicissitudes of public life. To these works should be added his long-running Cornelius O'Dowd column for* Blackwood's Magazine, *in which he sounds off in characteristically unbuttoned fashion on the foibles and failures of the day, revealing well-informed criticisms of both Irish conditions and European politics and diplomacy, particularly those of Austria and Italy. These columns were published in three volumes as* Cornelius O'Dowd on Men, Women and Things in General *(1862–5) and reflect Lever's experience as British consul at Spezzia and subsequently at Trieste, where he died and is buried.*

On the map, Lever's Arran consists of 'three or four insignificant dots off the coast of Donegal' (I, 140), but their geographical character is not as anonymous as their remote location might suggest. Self-contained but dependent, a distance but not a departure from mainland concerns, abundant in antiquarian flotsam and jetsam 'of little intrinsic value' (I, 142) while at the same time – initially at least – appearing not to have a future, attractive to visit but demanding to live on, the place establishes a natural anchorage, as it were, for the types of duality Lever wishes to explore. His Arran – or rather, his Innishmore, the main island – is a home for racial, social and cultural bifurcations; a property presided over by John Luttrell, a landlord whose despairing presence amounts to a form of absenteeism; and a way of life that ekes out a marginal existence with a ruined chapel in the foreground and an unforgiving ocean as a backdrop. Fittingly, the Luttrell family colours appear on a 'half-black, half-white ensign' (I, 157) and its crest is 'a very strange crest – a heart rent in two, with the motto *La Lutte Réelle*, a heraldic version of the name' (I, 205). To engage *la lutte* at a level more *réelle* than that of an escutcheon is the challenge that the narrative maps out, a task that requires hitherto unexamined aspects of island life to be confronted, such as race, class and self-determination.

That confrontation is the destiny of the novel's younger generation, but it is also what John Luttrell has so signally failed to undertake. In ways that are rather too programmatic, Luttrell represents the family colours. His present status is an anomalous mix of landlord and chieftain, somebody who has gone native but as a result is unable to live with himself. And he seems to find the resemblance between his depressed outlook on life and the 'neglect and desolation' (I, 1) of his island domicile both inevitable and unbearable. Yet once he was 'the first man of his day at Christ Church, the great prizeman and medalist, "the double first"' (I, 23). A temperamental rather than ideological attraction to the United Irishmen, however, led to public exposure and allegations of treachery, as perhaps might have been expected from a member of a family that has been 'always half-way between two opinions' (I, 26). Failing to represent himself in terms of his intellect, politics and social status, Luttrell withdraws to his ancestral 'Barren Islands' (I, 199). There his youthful penchant for displaying irreconcilable facets of his character takes the form of marriage to a peasant woman, a misalliance ruinous to both partners. His wife's premature death pushes him further into depression, a condition whose consistency furnishes Luttrell with the morose, alienated and monolithic singularity of a man who is an island.

Luttrell has one son, Harry, a member of Lever's large fictional family of spirited young men, who, when a visitor likens him to Robinson Crusoe, responds 'I wish I was Robinson' (I, 33). Effectively orphaned by his father's neglect, Harry is more or less given away to Herodotus 'Hairy' Dodge, an American slaver and Civil War blockade-runner, and is absent from the narrative for prolonged periods engaged in feats of derring-do under a commander whose bearing evokes 'Lynch-law, or no law' (I, 67). As a father figure, Dodge seems as great a contrast as possible to the morally and physically marooned Luttrell, and Harry's setting sail with him represents how economically and emotionally impoverished his patrimony is. He must become a man out of his father's sight, and his years before Dodge's mast develop Harry's physical prowess and capacity to hold his own in a world of male enterprise and challenge, although such service does not represent the whole Harry. His reputation notwithstanding, Lever here is not primarily interested in swashbuckling action. The focus of *Luttrell of Arran* is on action of a different, though no less courageous, sort and features another kind of journeying.

This features the entry into English high society of Harry's first cousin Kate O'Hara. On a yachting trip that takes in Arran, Sir Gervais Vyner, an old, though estranged, friend of Luttrell's, changes his mind about building on a local beauty spot – 'Arcadia, with a little more rain, and a police force' (I, 103) – and instead decides on a different type of development by taking Kate into his north Wales home with a view to making a lady of her. Despite the oppressively correct standards of Vyner's way of life, Kate shows an impressive aptitude for poise, manners and fashion, while also exhibiting 'that intense thirst for knowledge, so marked a trait in the Irish peasant nature' (I, 228). Nurtured in this culture of appearances, she acquires a cultivated finish permitting her to pass in the drawing-room world, but her feats of passing and the vigilance required to be a convincing personification of *savoir faire* are sources of entrapment. Kate's surface accomplishments make her the prey of various unscrupulous and unappetising suitors, circumscribing still further the narrow, chilly round of her immediate circumstances. Moreover, Kate has not allowed her heritage to be suffocated, and she neither denies nor forgets the peasant past and O'Hara history in which her nature is rooted. 'Her father was in banishment, the commutation of a sentence of death. Of her two brothers, one had died on the scaffold, and another had escaped to America' (I, 8) – like Harry, Kate has been orphaned by an inheritance of absence. And to represent herself without falseness, she must determine what relationship to establish between where she is and where she has come from. This undertaking is complicated by her grandfather's legal travails and the machinations of the unsavoury, two-faced O'Rorke, a political malcontent who owns the 'the Vinegar Hill' (I, 96) public house.

These difficulties are compounded by the attentions of one of the Vyners' neighbours, ageing Sir Within Wardle, a former diplomat and the last word in worldliness – '[a]ll that he had ever known of life was passed among people of admirable manners and very lax morals' (I, 314). This ardent seeker of Kate's hand stands in something of the same relation to her as 'Hairy' Dodge does to Harry, though their dubious credentials as authority figures underline the imperative that both young people assert their autonomy and integrity, particularly when in both cases their bodies are at risk as well as their ready willingness to serve. 'There are changes of condition that seem to rend identity' (I, 286), Kate muses, reflecting on her vulnerability when Vyner family politics ensure that she does not accompany the household to Italy. This thought prompts a keener consciousness in her of the divided identity created by leaving Arran in the first place. Sir Within sees her as a showpiece – 'Greek art itself had nothing finer in form' (I, 259) – and his connoisseur's gaze has a petrifying, proprietorial effect that, for all her Vyner training, Kate must subject herself to; indeed, Sir Within's curatorial regard may represent the culmination of being put in one's place, as prescribed by her experience throughout *chez* Vyner. Between Sir Within's advances and her increasingly endangered grandfather, Kate represents the tensions of a *lutte réelle* of her own.

The struggle is to keep English body and native soul together, and in waging it Arran becomes an essential landfall and resource. Kate's return there, however, is to assume the Luttrell name (following a false report that Harry has drowned), rather than revert to her origins. Regarding the peasantry, she tells Luttrell, 'I know as little of them as you do' (II, 86), while, in giving her his name, she says, 'you fill the full measure of my ambition' (ibid.). That ambition has always been to become a person of consequence, neither a daughter of the people nor the artificial accessory that the Vyners and Sir Within consider her; her ambition is what initially led her to leave with Vyner. Now she asserts, 'I am going to try if I shall not like the real conflict better than the mock combat' (II, 103). Arran is the real, an emptiness that Kate in her zeal for self-representation can change. Her improving energies would be a credit to an Edgeworth protagonist; and an illustration of her remedial efforts is her importation of 'some glasses of vaccine to inoculate with' (II, 296). Her ameliorative, unLuttrellish exertions revive a landscape sunk in inertia, and her tenacity regarding her grandfather's legal problems – 'he was simply defending what was his own' (II, 173) – is a version of his wrongdoing that resonates with Kate's Arran endeavours – enlarging the range and implications of her commitments. In her leadership and loyalty, Kate weds Luttrell to Arran in a manner that is more pragmatic and more progressive than any previous Luttrell has achieved. They 'were all so half worldly, half romantic, and one never knew which side was uppermost' (II, 248). Not so Kate. She is more than name and position; she is also heart and spirit, and her enactment of unity is all the more impressive by being voluntary.

Yet, despite her tireless efforts, and even when, following John Luttrell's death, she is indeed 'Kate Luttrell of Arran' (II, 79), her self-representation is not entirely authentic. Authenticity is reserved for

Harry, the place's and the name's true heir, and the only one whom the peasantry gladly supports. His return to Innishmore – from the dead, as it were – takes place on Christmas Eve, and he is given a welcome fit for a saviour. As a result, Kate feels usurped: '[d]o you fancy that we poor creatures of the soil do not resent in our hearts the haughty contempt by which you separate your lot from ours?' (II, 305). Once again, her 'road in life' (II, 307) leads away from Arran, this time to Australia, where her grandfather is being transported. Harry, however, is not so easily rejected, and his attachment to Kate is not merely personal. He also sees her in representative terms, as landfall, domicile and home: '[w]here she is there shall be my country' (II, 332). Kate is his compensation for both dispossession through paternal neglect and life-threatening experiences under Dodge. And although the novel ends on a tentative note, rather than on a ringing affirmation of union, there is little doubt that the future belongs to Harry and Kate together. Such a prospect concludes their own time of individual trial, and envisions a wholeness in place of the divisions of race and class which have hitherto undermined both Luttrells and Arran. This prospect does not necessarily mean that *la lutte réelle* has ended, but together the young people do seem capable of bearing out John Luttrell's view that '[i]t is out of our own rough energies must come the cure for our own coarse maladies' (I, 60).

Luttrell states this view to Sir Gervais Vyner, but it applies not only to old friends or to the new generation. It is also a sharp pointer to the standing of Englishness in *Luttrell of Arran* – a surprising aspect of the work, perhaps, since Lever is probably the last nineteenth-century Irish novelist to be credited with such critical thinking. But a denouement that suggests union and restoration gains in emphasis when those two values are elsewhere in the novel subject to false representation. Such representations include not only Kate's life in the Vyners' and Sir Within's theatres of reification, but her treatment by the various villains who insinuate themselves into the high-toned and well-managed lives of those two knights of the realm. Whether high or low class, these Englishmen cannot give Kate anything she wants. Her experiences at the hands of opportunists like Grenfell and Ladarelle are essentially exploitative in character, and the perpetrators no better than O'Rorke, their eventual hireling. Meddling in Irish affairs – conveyed through attempts to abduct, seduce and otherwise deprive Kate of her natural dignity and freedom – is the work of unprincipled self-seekers, moral middlemen, so to speak (a type also prominent in Le Fanu's *The House by the Churchyard*).

Further, the style, taste and sense of social command typical of Kate's English fosterage also turns out to be based on falseness. Both Sir Gervais and Sir Within end up at a loss, their propriety and *politesse* eroded by the unexamined sense of entitlement that had appeared to sustain them. Sir Gervais proves as unable to manage his household as he is to protect his economic interests. Losing his investments, he becomes seriously ill, a double collapse that is the obverse of Harry and Kate's Anglo-Irish revival. Sir Within has nothing within. His falseness is reflected in his fetishistic acquisitiveness, a self-indulgence that masks its compulsive desire to appropriate. Sir Gervais's bloodlessness and Sir Within's decadence, and the unchecked malevolence of their social inferiors, may not add up to an indictment of English inadequacy, but together these failed males' various efforts to annex Kate merely provide her with the wherewithal to assert her own agency.

'Large, loose, baggy monsters' is how Henry James famously described three-volume novels, and *Luttrell of Arran*, with its tissue of subplots and the reproduction in its narrative digressions of 'the restless spirit of our race' (I, 189), is a textbook instance of what he had in mind. Yet, by wandering here, there and everywhere, Lever conveys the variety and persistence of the pitfalls and barriers that constitute and necessitate *la lutte*. And the novel's elaborations, however creakily they hang together, interestingly outline the extent of the former military novelist's rethinking of the ground of struggle and how best to map it. Equally, if not more, to the point is the final standing of Kate O'Hara. She is a female protagonist who all too readily could have become a victim. The fact that she does not, and the racial, class and gender bases on which she does not, are perhaps unusually empowering for an Irish novel of the day. It may be an overstatement to see in Kate yet one more iteration of the femininised nation, but at the very least her experiences represent the complex kinds of interaction that relationships between identity and community require. In a work that is essentially premised on orphanhood, impoverishment, displacement, and the inadequacies of paternalism (all resonant in famine's aftermath), Kate's integrity and resilience emerge as virtues indeed. Possessing nothing but her much put-upon self-reliance, she represents, if not a renovated image of independence, a new and arguably unexpected statement of those aspirations that animate the protracted

and seemingly inescapable struggles of so many of the nineteenth-
century Irish novel's leading characters.

# 1873

## Charles Kickham, *Knocknagow*

*A native of Mullinahone, County Tipperary, Charles Joseph Kickham
(1828–82) came to literature comparatively late in life, having previously devoted himself to political activity. Inspired initially by both the
Repeal movement and the cultural nationalism of The Nation, he witnessed the abortive 1848 Rising, and continued thereafter to be active in
local land politics. But his faith in constitutional methods waned, and in
1861 he became a member of the Fenians. Two years later he moved to
Dublin to become a contributor to the Fenian weekly The Irish People.
His arrest in 1865 led to a fourteen-year jail sentence which he served in
various prisons in England. He was released in the 1869 Fenian amnesty,
whereupon he became a man of letters. His novels include Sally
Kavanagh (1869) and the posthumous For the Old Land (1886); and
he also wrote several well-known lyrics, most notably 'Slievenamon'. But
Kickham also remained politically involved, serving as president of the
supreme council of the Irish Republican Brotherhood throughout the
1870s until his death and showing himself to be something of a diehard in
his opposition both to Home Rule and the land war.*

*Long-winded and sentimental, Knocknagow is far from being the
most artistically interesting nineteenth-century Irish novel. Its publication in countless editions, however, suggests that its pastoral hues and
tones greatly appealed to the public, as well as, in more complicated
ways, to the agendas of cultural taste-makers. A large number of these
editions appeared in the 1920s and '30s – at a greater remove from
Kickham's time than the author was from his raw material. The novel's
popularity is also reflected in the fact that it was filmed in 1918. While
the novel is not devoid of aesthetic or formal interest, it is as a phenomenon in the sociology of Irish literature that Knocknagow has earned its
enduring reputation.*

'But . . . KNOCKNAGOW IS GONE!' (620). These are the novel's final
words, but though they sound a lament for a community's dispersal, in
view of the narrative they conclude it is difficult not to hear also a
memorialising overtone of 'Long live Knocknagow!' in them. For the
novel dwells not only on those forces that have brought about the end
of the eponymous locality. It is also – indeed, much more so – concerned with the way of life of that insignificant 'hamlet' (42). The

forces in question are those at the landlords' disposal, and are used at their discretion with an arbitrariness that renders untenable continuity, inheritance, tenure and the various other related social norms and forms conducive to sustaining the life of a place. Eviction and emigration, which replace the native's connection to his birthplace with a distorted and abstract attachment to it, are the customary means whereby these forces manifest themselves. And what in other contexts might be considered positive aspects of landlord activity – their economic soundness, material reality, financial profitability and general worldliness – are here seen to constitute an imbalanced, over-determined and inhumane regime, an institutionalised set of practices the rationale for which produces an array of chronic social bereftness – poverty, illness, alienation, violence and demoralisation – through the removal of those for whom the land is their natural habitat.

The motive for the landlords' clearance policy is a change in land-use from tillage to 'the big grass farms that's the ruination uv the counthry' (268), as one of the locals puts it. And whatever economic and managerial sense this modernising move may make, morally speaking it seems no more than an expression of greed, especially given the peremptory fashion and underhanded machinations with which it is carried out – '[h]alf of Knocknagow is swept from the face of the earth' (515) in one day. It comes as no surprise when events reveal that the chief perpetrators of the land-grabbing, that 'bad pair' (33), Isaac Pender and his son Beresford, are also guilty of forgery, an effectively metonymic instance of false representation. Inasmuch as the Penders represent no interest but their own, they are false, manipulating both tenants and Sir Gerald Butler, the absentee landlord whose agent is Pender senior. In not being obligated to anybody, the Penders have a free hand. But such freedom is mere licence, and rather than being conducive to sustaining a sense of equity or adherence to a social contract, it only legitimates exploitation and injustice.

At the same time, however, there is nobody to call the Penders and their like to account. The novel opens with Henry Lowe, Sir Gerald Butler's nephew, coming to spend Christmas with the estate's principal tenant, Maurice Kearney, and his family. But *Knocknagow* does not conform to the Englishman-in-Ireland sub-genre. Lowe, 'a homeless wanderer at present' (9), may observe his new environment and listen to what he is told about it, but he can never be other than 'a strange gentleman from England' (41); and his exclusion from the marriage plots that are threaded throughout the novel is a noteworthy departure from the intimations of larger unions that these plots typically rehearse. Although *Knocknagow* does not have a point of view regarding the contemporary nuances of relations between Ireland and 'what is sometimes oddly enough called "the sister country"' (1), Lowe's redundancy tacitly rejects the thought that he and his host have common interests. Though Pender is not strictly correct when he notes that Lowe 'never went near any of the tenants' (288), more to the point is that Lowe remains unaware of the agent and his methods.

Leaving the Englishman unwed and unhoused – when last heard of he is soldiering in India – may be seen in a faintly separatist light. More obviously, however, it also underlines *Knocknagow's* focus on the subject of its subtitle, 'The Homes of Tipperary'. On the one hand, this emphasis takes into account those actions, policies and legal manoeuvres inimical to home's connotations of permanence, security and belonging, and on the other, the properties of home – its cultural practices, its neighbourliness, its household gods and pieties, its representation of a whole fabric of usages and interconnections that make homestead a prototype of community – sharply contrast with the uncertainties of the world the landlord made. These uncertainties are caused by changing times, and their unpredictability and discontinuity are signs of who is in control. For those not in control the spatial sphere of home, its domestic interior and the adjoining external landscape, appeases temporal erosion. Home is where the tests of time may be withstood, and attachment to home exhibits fidelity, commonalty, an acceptance of mutual interests and the security of sharing in a group identity. Pender believes that '[t]he great point is to divide' (290) the tenantry, but the great point about the natives of *Knocknagow* is that they are indivisible, uniquely staunch, loyal to each other and to their native place. And home is the signature of that steadfastness. To demolish the home, then, is to dismantle a whole human ecology that owes its presence not to economic demand or political domination but to the more elementary entitlements that arise from the primal kinship to blood and soil.

The novel represents that attachment in a series of *tableaux vivants*, a method that has less to do with narrative development than with maintaining figures in their place, complete with appropriate gestures and postures. This approach invokes an aesthetic of stasis by means of which *Knocknagow* shows its concern for what change will take away, and which is essential to the novel's reliance on memory and com-memoration, but it is not merely a device or an instance of technique. Stasis is also central to the most important aspect of tenant life, namely security. As Larry Clancy, father of one of the novel's many brides, declares, 'I gave my daughter to Ned Brophy, because he has a good lase . . . . Security is the only thing to give a man courage' (220). And security is crucial not only apropos of landlords and leases; it also informs occasions of holding one's own in the daily round. These occa-sions emerge in the course of the visits that continually take place between Knocknagow's householders. Usually just informal displays of neighbourliness – far from the pre-announced, full-dress set-pieces – the visits, by virtue of both their regularity and their disregard for class difference, convey the community's indivisibility. They are a form of contact that both monitors and supports the status quo; and, through repetition, the voluntary bonds of community life are maintained, most affirmatively when illness, misadventure or injustice threaten.

The diurnal is made all the more durable by the locals' subliminal awareness of how vulnerable they are. And their commonplace, or natural, socialising also shows the resources of generosity, kindness and sympathy – a communal inner life, as it were – that help to withstand the vicissitudes of a world they cannot own. These resources' refine-ment and disinterest transcend the moral ugliness of the 'serfdom' (479) that confines tenants to economic utility alone. 'The people are good if they only get fair play' (223) is the judgement of a local priest, implic-itly testifying to their being made of stuff as fine as a modern materialist. Thus the people are more authentic and legitimate, more true to their place in the world, and more truly governed through their interchange of affections than by those who would usurp that innate economy of sentiment. In wordly powerlessness lies inner strength.

The elaborate moral frieze in which *Knocknagow* preserves the native spirit is a memorial to the fact that '[t]he Irish peasant is a being of sentiment' (478), but his actual dwellings also contribute to the memorialising endeavour. A variety of these is presented: the cabin of saintly, crippled Norah Lahy, Mat 'the Thresher' Donovan's 'humble little Tipperary home' (160), and the farm from which foolhardy and unfortunate Tom Hogan is evicted. (The Kearneys' comfortable Ballinaclash Cottage is obviously not a peasant home, but that family's superior social standing does not mean that its heart is not with the people, and indeed a point comes when, after their temporary eviction,

Mary Kearney 'can now understand what the poor people suffer in being driven from their homes every day' (547).) In all cases, the homes are well maintained. Flowers in their gardens are tokens of domestic well-being within and, as though to rebuke earlier representations of native living, a general impression is conveyed of good order, cleanliness and competence. Here, daily life is not abject and contaminated, and, as well as an absence of squalor, idleness and demoralisation, there is little material want and physical deprivation. This is a portrait of a community from which famine seems quite remote – indeed, there is no need to mention the memory, threat or immediate reality of such a calamity. As a result, *Knocknagow* reads like an essay in rehabilitation, evoking physical resilience, moral durability and the inviolable spirit of home. Notwithstanding crippled Nora Lahy and the unfortunate Mick Brien, the strength of the populace is exceptional to a degree which, if not explicitly racial, at least indicates how belittling it is to be forced to function in ways not their own. This exceptionalism is noted even in peripheral events, as when the behaviour of guests at Ned Brophy's wedding reception is contrasted with that of 'guests of the same class' (216) at an English harvest home, as depicted by the novelist Charles Reade. When a local declares that 'myse'f can't see much difference betune us and other people' (252), it is in defence of Knocknagow people against a charge of being wild. Knocknagow people are as civilised as anybody else.

Native merits are broadly signified in such formulations as 'everyone in Knocknagow is a musician' (232) – itself perhaps extrapolated from Mary Kearney's telling Lowe that 'we Irish are a poetical people' (10). To represent the '*living* Present' (387) is also clearly important, however, in order to put a recognisable face on the novel's populist values. This face is worn by Mat 'the Thresher' Donovan, the community's archetypal male. True, Hugh Kearney, who saves the family by working to pay off its debts, is likened by Grace Kiely, his beloved, to 'Finn Macool' (314), an upgrade perhaps from 'some gallant young chief like Robert Emmet or Sir William Wallace' (94), Grace's earlier ideas of a hero. And Edmund, Grace's brother, 'had set his heart upon an open-air life' (395) of adventure, a future that seems scripted by Charles Lever. Those derivative representations of maleness are not Mat the Thresher's style. He does not cast himself in the role of leader, and though when evicted he is prepared to emigrate, and actually does go to America in pursuit of Bessy Morris, his bride-to-be, his most impressive feats are achieved on his native ground. Rather than having his head turned by thoughts of a heroic destiny or a wider world, as he makes his uncertain transit through Liverpool Mat renews his attachment to the faith, land and family that make home valuable to him. In America, the significance of that attachment is given full expression when an old neighbour says ''tis of'en I said Knocknagow was not gone all out so long as Mat Donovan was there' (583).

Yet, while there may be no doubt that 'Mat Donovan has something superior about him. And he is such a fine, manly, good-natured fellow . . . . He has made the name of Knocknagow famous' (283), his excellence should be not merely recorded, it also needs to be represented. Coming from the 'mild madonna' (124) Mary Kearney, that testimonial is unimpeachable, but Mat must be tested. Just like all his peers in the nineteenth-century Irish novel, he must go through the ordeal of action – or, in Mat's case, two ordeals, one physical, involving his athletic prowess and the other attesting to his moral courage when falsely arraigned for theft on the word of Beresford Pender, who intends the accusation to cover his own misdeeds. 'No surrender is my motto' (564), Beresford Pender proclaims; but it is Mat who does not yield, further evidence that he is emblematic of all for which Knocknagow is worth remembering.

Mat's trial is obviously important, but because it is based on Beresford's false representation it does not have quite the communal uplift and cultural resonance of his physical test. That simple – or perhaps elemental – trial of strength consists of a sledge-tossing contest, a pre-Olympic Games version of the hammer throw. Mat's opponent is the previously undefeated Captain French – 'a Tipperary boy, myself' (454) – who, in addition to his athletic ability, has a keen eye for male specimens, considering it 'a sin and a shame – that such splendid "material" should be going to waste' (448) by not being in the British Army. Mat's victory is not merely a feat of arms, so to speak, his winning throw is '[f]or the credit of the little village' (453), the local community being as worthy and empowering an inspiration as the empire that Captain French's army polices. As it expresses his labourer's way of life, Mat's strength seems more natural, more organic. And his exercise of it is an articulation of the fidelity that is such a vital component of Knocknagow's communal ethos, and testifies to able-bodied male assertiveness. This second aspect of Mat's triumph is later borne out not only by an encounter with a now one-armed Captain French but by a tableau of men mowing, 'with Mat Donovan at their head . . . like so many tall pikemen at drill' (498). It can hardly be denied that such a figure is, at the very least, capable of assuming peasant proprietorship, and even perhaps of resisting 'the crowbar brigade' (69), but it would offend against community values to associate its members with unseemly action. A preferred means of moving with the times, evidently, is Mat's eventually finding success as a cattle-dealer.

A breach of the peace would also offend against the type of novel *Knocknagow* aims to be. If 'we have, perhaps, lingered too long and too lovingly' (525) in the homes of Tipperary, this is so as to project scenarios in which conflict has little or no place. '[T]he faithful chronicler of the sayings and doings, joys and sorrows of Knocknagow' (155) must focus not so much on destruction as on what has been destroyed. Just as much of the work carried on locally is land reclamation, so the narrative restores the locals' inhering, unassuming, more sinned against than sinning image. Such a representation is a critique of landlord greed and arrogance, whose only products are depopulation and cultural loss. The assiduous reconstruction and projection of the natives' image counters the triumphalist claim of *The Times* that '[t]he Celts are gone with a vengeance' (584). And because '[n]othing is easier than sensation' (565), an ostensibly more literal approach is the method to be preferred in carrying out the duties of commemoration and the task of preservation. These devoted acts of restitution endow the past with a continuity that memory can honour, and, although as a novel *Knocknagow* seems to borrow from the embalmer's art, it is also a representation of land and people whose populist ideological undertow of uprightness and worth gave it a resonant afterlife.

# 1876

# May Laffan Hartley, *Hogan, M.P.*

*Beyond the titles of her works, little is known of the short-lived literary career of Dublin-born May Laffan Hartley (1850–1916). Her best-known work, rather originally for its time, is set among Dublin's poor. This is the eponymous novella of the story collection* Flitters, Tatters, and the Counsellor *(1879), admired by John Ruskin, among others. Mrs Hartley also published* The Hon. Miss Ferrard *(1877), a Big House novel of sorts;* Christy Carew *(1883), on the theme of mixed marriage; and* Ismay's Children *(1887), which has a Fenian background. These novels were all reviewed so negatively as to suggest that what were*

> thought flaws were in fact Hartley's typically daring perspective and free
> handling of somewhat controversial subject matter. Her refusal to provide
> works that seemed ladylike, or that were what might be expected from an
> Irish woman novelist, is perceptible in her satirical eye and her thematic
> focus on the allure and corrosiveness of institutional power. Her fiction
> also shows a keen awareness of this power's influence on the male mores
> of the day. A fluent style, witty social observation and an unblinking criti-
> cism of status are the most prominent features of Hartley's essentially
> worldly imagination. In addition, her work is neither pedantic nor
> moralistic.
>
> Many nineteenth-century Irish novelists still await the critical consid-
> eration that would further a complete and balanced view of the field as a
> whole. This is particularly the case with women writers, among whom
> May Laffan Hartley has one of the strongest claims to further attention.

Beyond a limited amount of basic information about John O'Rooney Hogan's educational background and the fact that '[o]n the maternal side he had inherited good blood, or the legend of it' (325), *Hogan, M.P.* is a novel without a past. The life of its times is sufficiently diverse and revealing to sustain the narrative, and the novel's representation of that life, although perhaps not entirely original, provides a convenient guide to the fresh fictional terrain mapped by Irish novelists in the 1870s. This terrain was undoubtedly shaped, in part at least, by the disestablishment of the Church of Ireland in 1869, and the emergence of the Home Rule Party in the years following. The old concerns with identity, affiliation and with the state and nature of the nation do not go away, but they begin to be dealt with from new perspectives and in different tones.

One illustration of such developments is the fact that *Hogan, M.P.* is almost exclusively an urban novel. Dublin and London are its principal, and almost exclusive, settings, with the former represented, perhaps surprisingly, in capitalistic terms, as though the city's claim to capital status may be more credibly based on class and money than on political entitlement or nationalist agitation. On the one hand, this is a Dublin of the emerging Catholic middle class, people who have become very much part of the commercial life of the city as 'whiskey people' (8) – bonders – and the like. As the novel's opening scene points out, these people are now educating their daughters, essentially with a view to their eligibility in the marriage market, thereby mimicking metropolitan manners elsewhere. And more representative of this newly prominent social presence is the novel's eponymous protagonist, the consequences of whose imitative and compliant behaviour in the money market constitute much of the narrative's novelty.

On the other hand, the stockbroker Cosmo Saltasche, as his name suggests, connects investors with the cosmopolitan financial world of London. This connection adds a hard-headed, if not indeed refreshingly cynical, dimension to proceedings, which contrasts revealingly with *arriviste* complacency. And there is also a political undercurrent to the connection, a suggestion that perhaps the Union could well be seen in the light of economic opportunity (or opportunism) and that the ebb and flow of financial interests shapes the practical politics of the day. This suggestion rests on the assumption that politics are basically nothing but practical. As in the case of the marriage market, this metropolitan focus shows a system at work, and Hartley's objective and unsentimental depiction of its mechanics makes a noteworthy break with both the tone and perspective of narratives with rural settings and conventional national concerns – *Knocknagow* is a case in point. The 'mongrel' (306) Saltasche is one instance of *Hogan, M.P.*'s apparent lack of interest in the national as such, and so too is its rather satirical account of provincial electioneering. Yet in both cases it is not so much that national issues are ignored as that their overdetermining effects are resisted. In one respect the epithet applied to Saltasche reflects the novel's interest in manners, but the context in which the label is attached reinforces its xenophobic, or even racial, overtones prompted by members of the Dublin élite – 'a class of Protestants' (ibid.) – objecting to him as 'a fellow come from God knows where' (ibid.) – and 'a Comtist' (307) to boot. And the informal and bibulous character of the Peatstown election might exhibit a greater degree of political consciousness if the promise made by a Fenian home from America of 'a real Irish Republic' (258) were taken seriously.

Another unexpected, independent-minded feature of *Hogan, M.P.* is its attitude to the clergy. In the novel's opening scene, the nuns of St Swithin's school are largely concerned that events meet with Bishop O'Rooney's approval (he is bishop of Secunderabad). This cleric – the protagonist's uncle – sees little point or value in 'Latin and Greek and mathematics for a pack of girls' (130). And his assumption that George Eliot is a man does not say much for his general level of cultivation. The bishop also exhibits a sectarian cast of mind, and finds his suspicions of Protestants extend to the Home Rule movement, to the emergence of which he expresses a grudging tolerance: even if 'it is neither sedition nor treason; neither, though it has begun . . . among the Protestants, and independently of the Church, is it irreligious' (164). To a certain extent, these episcopal positions establish a contrast between generations. The bishop is his nephew's would-be guide and mentor, but, while the younger man relies on the steady stream of legal business his uncle sends his way, he is also more literate and less reactionary, so that culturally and socially he appears to be representative of a fresh and future-oriented outlook. His travels in Europe reinforce his identification with 'a broader, larger life' (36). Moreover, the novel's view of the clergy is not merely a family affair. When Hogan travels to Peatstown, the constituency he is to represent in Westminster, he finds that the parish priest, Father Cockran, is on excellent social terms with the local aristocracy and opposed to Hogan, who bemusedly remarks, 'a priest sending a Protestant to Parliament – it is very strange' (250). This comment also, however, suggests that perhaps he has not quite outgrown his uncle's sectarian slant on things, and also that he does not notice the pragmatic rather than the programmatic nature of political alliances, even though his own candidacy illustrates it.

A third significant aspect of *Hogan, M.P.* is its feminist emphasis. This is embodied in Nellie Davoren, much more composed and self-possessed than Hogan, though, at nineteen, ten years his junior. Somewhat peripheral to the action, she lives at home in Green Lanes, where Saltasche also lives, although she is utterly removed from both the financial dealings and sexual entanglements of the stockbroker's world. Nellie represents an alternative to the Saltasche world, and Hogan's rejection of her in favour of the unloved but socially more influential Diana Bursford is a further indication of how easily he succumbs to selling out. Hogan's passive choice of enhanced social standing through Saltasche's machinations, election and marriage constitutes an unconscious form of adventurism, a kind of reflexive fortune-hunting. The culture of maleness represented by his behaviour prevents Hogan from being emotionally honest with either Nellie or himself, and contrasts with the girl's own open temperament and painfully artless expressions of feeling. Her eventual partner, Dermot Blake – 'very tall, broad-shouldered, and athletic-looking' (423) – is his own man, one to whom the label of adventurer applies only in the context of 'Yosemite or the North Fork' (426). Underlining Nellie's distinctiveness is her support for women's education, which is more cogent and forthright than Hogan's, and her arguments for it are additionally persuasive when seen in relation to her scapegrace brother Dickie, who squanders his Trinity College years and flees the country barely ahead of his creditors. Nellie also stands out in her attitude to the ladies whom her cousin, the socialite Dorothy O'Hegarty, entertains to tea: '[t]here was something unreal and artificial about them, polished and refined of manner and appearance as they all were' (102). Further, in her disregard for the marriage market, Nellie demonstrates an integrity that is notably lacking everywhere else in the novel, most plainly and destructively in the male, urban, much-approved world where Hogan attempts to make himself at home.

This is a realm whose public, institutional façade masks clandestine, underhand dealings devoted not just to 'selling short' (327) stocks but also trust in elected officials. Such two-faced activity has an unseemly emotional counterpart in Saltasche's private life, in the form of the affair he has with Adelaide, an exotic Brazilian beauty who has sacrificed her fortune and good name to a cruel and reckless army officer, Captain Poignarde. The latter's financial indebtedness to Saltasche seemingly emboldens the stockbroker to seek repayment in kind from the unhappy 'black swan' (318). Such is Adelaide's allure that Saltasche loses first his head and then his grip on his financial affairs. He and Adelaide abscond, but they fail to evade the law; and Saltasche, for all the male prowess implicit in the 'certain resemblance . . . discernible between him and the first Napoleon' (64), finds it impossible to accept the consequences of his financial and sexual betrayals. Ultimately, his Bonapartism is only skin deep; perhaps rather unexpectedly, *Hogan, M.P.* is in part a critique, however belated, of the romantic overreacher, the would-be world-changer, the ego with society as its plaything. John Hogan is nothing of the kind, but he does find the type irresistible, and if matters in his case are less sensational and more pathetic than in Saltasche's, the outcome for him is a variation on the fate of his sponsor.

Hogan's marriage to Diana is in many respects a misalliance, not exactly a betrayal as such but a confirmation of his own observation that 'mixed marriages are seldom happy' (89). And from one point of view it appears that what makes the match is Diana's pursuit of Hogan, rather than any great passion on his part. Conscious of being aged thirty-five and in danger of spinsterhood, Diana takes the initiative, selling herself short by capitulating to the generic, prefabricated social expectations of what a woman's life should be. Complacent Hogan accepts her attentions, but his attachment becomes serious only when Diana helps him out of a financial jam. She also comes to his rescue when he loses his seat in parliament by applying to her various well-born and well-connected relatives and acquaintances for a position for her implicitly useless, or at least helpless, husband. The appointment he eventually secures is secretary to the governor of an unnamed South Sea island, which will require full-time residence in Honolulu. Diana approvingly quotes Napoleon to Hogan: '*La carrière est ouverte au talen[t]s*' (368), but the irony of those words is for the reader alone to savour.

Just as the unconscious or unacknowledged substitution of money for love makes Hogan's marriage a false representation, so his parliamentary career is also a parody of service and principle. Its culmination in a position with a certain Ruritarian hollowness of office is a judgement on his futility. And the same applies to Saltasche. In all three cases, bad faith, trading in appearances and emotional inadequacy are prelude to decline and fall. The male-dominated system in which Saltasche and Hogan are invested, which represents them and which they represent, and that equates validation with embezzlement, is only as substantial as its façade. The liberty that appears to be the financial and marriage markets' strongest attraction is instead conducive to criminality, loss and exile. Such a set of final balance sheets shows *Hogan, M.P.*'s emphasis on crises as the outcome of attempting to make things happen. Its portrayal of the problematic nature of free choice masks the betrayals of the heart. True-blue Nellie Davoren alone embodies disinterested personhood, immune to Mammon and its self-seeking false representations.

Hogan embodies the crises in question not merely by his rather enthralled subservience to Saltasche, for whom he not only serves in parliament but also through the 'fine gift for literary imitation' (342) he exhibits in political articles written anonymously for the *Beacon*, Saltasche's London newspaper. (Such mimicry throws a satirical light in passing on the activities and influence of Irish journalists in the London media market of the day, a light also to be seen in W.P. Ryan's *The Plough and the Cross*.) In addition to his hireling character, Hogan also represents an atavistic predisposition to less than full engagement, a kind of Paddy-go-easy psychological heritage, an indifference to the use of his gifts for honest and upright purposes: '[t]here was a strong tinge of the peasant nature underlying all his polish: the ingrained hatred of work, the fatalistic indifference engendered by a social and religious system of long and complicated standing, the curious reverence and love of power and authority peculiar to those who have been oppressed' (325). Such an inheritance indicates a lack of self-confidence so comprehensive as to be self-cancelling. Hogan fails to represent himself because there is no proper framework, no structure of either moral obligation or intellectual self-consciousness upon which he might base an honourable role.

A centred, or focused, consciousness is not part of his makeup. For this reason the novel skimps his parliamentary career. (Elected to ensure passage of a bill allowing Lord Brayhead, a Saltasche client, to extend railway services to his industrial facilities, Hogan seems to have no idea of how to proceed.) And for the same reason, perhaps, 'his mind ran in rather a feminine mould. There were some parts of his character . . . which were not what the world calls manly' (ibid.). Like many protagonists in the nineteenth-century Irish novel, Hogan is neither equipped to operate persuasively in modern contexts not to 'keep to your own people' (23), as his uncle advises. As a supposedly 'self-made man' (369), what Hogan has made is a set of uncertain accommodations with, and dependences on, certain available systems. He evolves a way of life that only goes to show how little he has to call his own. His stunted awareness appears on his first visit to Peatstown, when 'he was astonished beyond measure at the Irishness of everything' (261), by which he means stage-Irish. He regards the locals as passing for theatrical types, whereas it is Hogan himself who performs the more insidious and serious version of fictive representation. And his misprisions extend to the more formal and official requirements of what he is supposed to be standing for, as is indicated by his ignorance of his constituents' overwhelming interest in land issues, rather than, as he had supposed, in Home Rule.

Its overlapping financial and emotional economies, of public and private double-dealing and self-aggrandisement, lend *Hogan, M.P.* a structural subtext that is more revealing than the incidentals of its plot. In this subtext the economy of personal relations predominates, revealing the inequitable rates of exchange between Hogan and Nellie, as well as the various manifestations, literal and metaphorical, of base coin, face value, false utterance and the like. The links between these manifestations comprise a world premised on counterfeit. That world functions not merely by cheating and the particular, narrow form of consciousness that goes into planning and carrying it out. It also acts through an awareness of how commonplace forms of social interchange – those of the drawing room, the reception, the representation of self before parents and peers – can be distorted, manipulated and given false currency. Hogan's career combines personal weakness and social opportunism. Each is a mirror image of the other. Each relies on strategies of concealment and evasion. Indeed, the types of social performance by which Hogan passes himself off seem to be central to the grooming of the young ladies of St Swithin's, whose soirées are staged 'in strict accordance with the precedents set by the last Castle entertainment' (50–1). And there is not a lot to be expected from Hogan's successor as the member for Peatstown, Dinny O'Hoolihan, 'a barrister whose principles it were a kindness to designate as uncertain' (459) and who was imprisoned for his part in the 1848 rebellion, which is not a credential in this novel.

Exposing characters with insufficient character introduces a note of scepticism to the depiction of Irish limitations, emphasising the degree to which they are self-made. This note, a *con brio* uptake of certain aspects of Trollope, is repeated to greater effect in *The Real Charlotte* and the work of George Moore. The recovery of Saltasche's embezzled funds may be the stuff of 'a perfect romance' (477), but the more important story has no romance in it. Its basis is choice, the instrument of realism. By giving free rein to his underdeveloped judgement, a 'paralysed' (488) Hogan ends up bereft of 'all his aspirations, all his hopes of distinction' (ibid.) – of all, in a word, that he vainly thought himself capable of representing.

# 1883

## Charlotte Riddell, *A Struggle for Fame*

*Charlotte Riddell (1832–1906) – née Charlotte Eliza Cowan – was born in Carrickfergus, County Antrim. In her early twenties she moved to London intent on a literary career, and almost immediately became the editor of the periodical* Home. *Shortly after this title ceased publication in 1866, she succeeded Mrs S.C. Hall as editor of* St James Magazine. *The two writers are alike in their remarkable productivity and in their ability to maintain high standing in rapidly evolving and competitive literary marketplaces.*

*Mrs Riddell's first novel,* Zuriel's Grandchild *(1856), was followed by some forty others (her full bibliography remains incomplete). Initially publishing under a variety of pseudonyms, most frequently F.G. Trafford, she broke through commercially with George Feith of Fen Court (1864). This work, although a Trafford novel, made her name, and was succeeded by such works as* The Race for Wealth *(1866),* Mortomley Estate *(1874),* Mitre Court *(1885) and* The Head of the Firm *(1892). Three Riddell novels have Irish settings –* Maxwell Drewitt *(1865), which has a Connemara background;* Berna Boyle: A Love Story of the County Down *(1884); and* The Nun's Curse *(1888), the action of which takes place in County Donegal. The majority of her works are set in and around the city of London and show a comprehensive grasp of business and legal affairs.*

*Mrs Riddell was also a prolific contributor to many of her day's leading magazines, particularly as an exponent of ghost stories. She also published a quantity of novellas. Some of her ghost stories draw on Irish settings and lore, and her contribution to these genres of Irish writing awaits further critical assessment, although her reputation, such as it is, has until very recently been based on these contributions. A full appraisal of her oeuvre would also reflect her invention of a new sub-genre, the financial novel, in which her representations of the male realms of loans, contracts and accounts, together with the treacherous fiduciary tides and whirlpools produced by the confluence of capital and ego, reveal the world of money's restlessness and uncertainty. As well as renewing the novel's traditional interest in the making and unmaking of fortune, these works also effectively assert the value of the woman's place and its emotional resources of trust, reliability and steadfastness which male authority and adventurism may deplete but never bankrupt. The admiration Mrs Riddell expresses for George Eliot does not mean that her own work is of the same calibre, but it is does suggest something of her ambition and sense of purpose. And if it does not attain a commanding perspective on the City and its system, her work reveals an unblinking awareness of the nexuses of self-interest, class interest and financial interest that shape both the location's and its practices' moral landscape and personal exactions.*

The arduous nature of the lives of nineteenth-century women authors did not deter large numbers of them, including a sizeable contingent of Irish women, from pursuing the profession of letters. Their collective experiences, both as writers and as women, as both workers in a volatile marketplace and highly individuated artistic temperaments – as, in a sense, double outsiders – are typified in the perhaps predictable but nevertheless keenly felt ups-and-downs of the career of young Glenavy Westley, the protagonist of *A Struggle for Fame*. From her arrival in England from the north of Ireland on 17 October 1854, her progress is marked more by attempting to become famous – connoted by the initial condition in this novel's title – than by the successful outcome denoted by fame. Atmospherically grey and featuring dramatically muted reworkings of some venerable tropes of the picaresque and the *Bildungsroman*, Glen's experiences confine her to a 'very transition [*sic*] state' (I, 20) long after her arrival, with all the difficulties of finding the right direction and otherwise adjusting to the challenges of a 'modern Babylon' (II, 206) which this implies. Images of tempestuous seas and perilous passages recur to reinforce the young woman's embattled state, and also to suggest the possibility of her becoming a castaway, an outcome in sharp contrast to her tomboyish though 'not unfeminine' (I, 260), early years in the shoreline home of Ballyshane, County Antrim. With the exception of Lever's *Luttrell of Arran*, accounts of women in exile do not figure very prominently in the nineteenth-century Irish novel, and Glen's removal to England – although the result primarily of social embarrassment – anticipates those narratives of displacement developed by George Moore and George Bernard Shaw. Like them, Glen (and Riddell, whose persona she is) pursues a 'new line' (III, 52) in literature, but, in contrast to their focus on social contexts, she dwells on private dilemmas of integrity, conscience and doing the right thing in an alien environment. But she resembles her illustrious fellow-countrymen in viewing her material problematically, revealing flaws in the system even while seeking to represent herself in the system's terms.

Such dilemmas recur with differing degrees of emphasis in *A Struggle for Fame*'s various subplots, many of which have to do with the self-representational activities of writing and publishing. They are central to the release of the sensational personal material by the best-selling 'handsome virago' (II, 86), Lady Hilda Higgs. The literary fate and marital fortune of Glen's opposite number, the opportunistic man of letters Barney Kelly, and of his cousin Mat Donagh illustrate their vapid identities. The family entanglements and hapless business career of Glen's long-suffering husband, Mordaunt Logan-Lacere, also reveal inner hollowness. And the sharp publishing practices of the upstart Felton is the ultimate expression of the falseness that the other subplots also represent. It is Glen alone who registers these difficulties' moral and emotional impact. She will not offend her nature by adopting the worldly extemporaneity, flightiness and superficiality of metropolitan manners. Nor can she subject herself to the cold-heartedness of her in-laws, much less to their 'prejudice against everything Irish' (III, 71). Initially portrayed as an 'impetuous child' (I, 15), Glen is less a wild Irish girl than a woman who, 'when women as a rule were not pushing' (I, 103), embodies an impressive sense of her own worthiness and the independence of mind to assert it in literary form. And her guiding conviction that 'I can make a future for myself' (I, 282) is eventually borne out, even if 'the grapes of life' (II, 39) for which she somewhat naively reaches prove to be more sour than sweet. Success in the market is important to her; she is as hard-working and enterprising as she is meek and forbearing. Yet, for her, fame is not entirely limited to cultural and economic attainments. She pursues those as a means of living for herself, with herself, and within herself. Neither her address in Bloomsbury nor the Hampshire cottage where she lives at the novel's end may represent Virginia Woolf's 'room of one's own', but they do suggest themselves as prototypes of that celebrated place of autonomy, safety and productivity. Identifying Glen as 'only a woman' (I, 222) is ironically meant. How she acquits herself in a competitive and materialistic milieu shows that if her sex is a barrier to her ambition to be published, it is the invaluable resource from which she draws the sympathy and the psychological strength represented in her writing.

Indeed, the difficulties she encounters arise almost entirely from the world of men, that external sphere of action, business and chancing one's arm. The novel's insider's view of the publishing world shows the prevalence of all three of these elements, as well as providing details of editorial decisions, remuneration and the whole apparatus sustaining contemporary 'novel mania' (III, 138). In this particular sector, risk, bravado and devious dealing are requirements, and it is so industrious, competitive and prolific as to represent a model of mid-Victorian capitalism in full spate. Its retinue of advertising agents, bribed reviewers, mountebanks and similar denizens of 'the realms of Bohemia' (I, 204) provide the type of social chorus familiar from Dickens' portraits of London life. And these rather cartoonish demi-mondaines are all more or less grotesque variations on Glen's situation, being misfits, adventurers, self-promoters and confidence men, whose socially marginal status derives some semblance of currency from publishing houses, establishments that the homeless, itinerant Glen is also inclined to regard as refuges. Glen also believes that her talent will enable her to rise above the cheap superficiality and market values typical of the publishing scene, but in certain crucial respects she represents a continuing struggle between 'the children of this world, in the shape of hard and stern capitalists' (II, 39) and those, such as authors, who are 'over-apt to consider themselves children of light' (II, 40). That Glen does in time succeed in holding her own as an unworldly, idealistic contrast to this diverse display of male adventurism is a tribute to her self-reliance, however shaky, and her pure-minded imaginative aims, however discouraging her apprenticeship is in realising them. As an exception to publishing industry norms, she stands in opposition to false representation. That stance portrays her struggle for fame as essentially a quest for self-representation.

The main structural device of *A Struggle for Fame*, then, is that of contrasts, and the contrast that does most to establish Glen's literary fortunes is the one with her 'fellow-pilgrim' (I, 309) Barney Kelly. Having come to England 'for the flesh-pots' (I, 170), he immediately attempts to act independently by rejecting his relation Mat Donagh's offer to be his 'Mentor' (I, 71) and by alienating a more powerful family connection, Judge Balmoy. As a result, Barney soon finds himself as 'stranded' (I, 210) as Glen herself. But, despite considerable evidence to the contrary, he is as convinced as she is of his literary ability, and proceeds to make a rather rakish progress through London's thriving hack journalism scene. Barney's forays into periodical writing show the typically scapegrace, improvised, mercenary and – from an imaginative standpoint – old-fashioned adventures of a *pícaro*, culminating in the fortune-hunter's perennial dream of marrying money. In comparison, Glen's sensibility seems modern. Admittedly, she too exhibits aspects of an outmoded stock character, the self-sacrificing Griselda. But in her artistic commitment and even in the alleged 'cynicism and realism' (III, 325) of her work, she is her own person to a degree that is well beyond superficial Barney's reach. As though confirming Barney's shallowness, his attempt at a novel is 'heavy as lead' (III, 229) and falls flat.

Public Barney and domestic Glen, flashy Barney and modest Glen, mercenary Barney and a Glen who will not sell her talent unless doing so helps her husband, a Barney who eagerly initiates a marriage plot and a Glen who seems likely to keep her vow that 'I shall never marry' (I, 261) – the contrasts between the two are drawn in broad strokes. Irishness is their only common ground, but, though neither of them denies their origins, Barney is much more assertive about his nationality. If she has 'something to say' (III, 55), it evidently does not need to be framed in national terms, while Barney's claim that 'I haven't found my accent or nationality the slightest hindrance to me in literature; quite the contrary' (II, 15) has to be considered in the context of his marketplace compliance. For him, Irishness is a flag of convenience, a means of distinguishing himself from a myriad ink-stained rivals, and his declaration to Glen that 'I feel quite proud of you as a country-woman' (III, 344) is the condescension of a journalist to an author, suggesting that he relies on a classification to validate his feeling while she tacitly demonstrates her superiority by not requiring one. Paradoxically, Barney's Irishness has facilitated his English success, while non-national Glen remains throughout 'still an alien' (II, 161), distant inward and struggling. Hers appears to be a personal identity only, and not even a marriage proposal from her Ballyshane sweetheart Ned Beattie can change that.

Confining Glen to her authorial struggles and to a preoccupation with fame as the sole antidote to them risks narrowing unduly how she is represented. Her asocial, deracinated and largely loveless state is further limited by her narrow education and lack of intellectual curiosity – '[s]he had not even a speaking acquaintance with any -ology' (II, 262). Glen's fitness for the life she has chosen is constantly in question. Such an approach extends the narrative less through plot development than repetition, and, while the result portrays her as being between a 'has been' (I, 4) in County Antrim and the cream of English novelists, that condition is based on tensions that she passively accepts much of the time. Her personality alternates with a bland predictability between dreams of literary success and depictions of 'dogged perseverance' (III, 332). The latter are marked heavily by her obligations as a dutiful daughter and devoted wife, roles that, despite Glen's undoubtedly sincere embrace of them, countermand the writing life's will to self-representation.

Barney Kelly's bohemianism is no doubt a crude and adventitious version of that life, and its tawdry hues are not to be compared to those of Glen's Pre-Raphaelite palette – 'the colours modern humanity had so long wished for' (III, 56–7). Yet bohemia's knockabout social milieu – its performative incentives, its convivial camaraderie, its getting and spending, its vulnerability to the transitoriness that it lives by – conveys a den-like closeness that Glen's refined sensibility and domestic responsibilities deny her. As in the publishing world, so also at home; Mr Westley and Mr Lacere, to whom she believes she is beholden because of their respective roles as father and spouse, mostly represent male obtuseness and impotence. The failure of both these central figures to nurture and emotionally support Glen creates in her a conflict that compounds her authorial struggles, not merely because of its intimate, personal character but also because of both men's depersonalising, self-inflicted economic insufficiency. Their inability to represent themselves financially parallels and exacerbates Glen's attempts to represent herself through the values of her initiative and talent. Money's apparently arbitrary circulation, its speculative allure and its impersonal authority provide a context for the uncertainty of Glen's dealings with publishers and her works' public reception. Money is the signature of a system of commodification and exchange which can neither value nor reward the disinterested service that requires that she 'saw to everything a girl might, and to many things most girls never do' (II, 136).

Dealing with publishers, Glen learns that 'unless a woman goes down into the thick of the conflict, she is far too apt to take the man's representation as facts' (III, 144). But she cannot assume this approach to her weakling, financially irresponsible father or her emotionally remote and financially overburdened husband. Instead, like the heroic personages of her childhood reading, with their 'great deeds of courage, endurance, [and] devotion' (I, 224), she stands by her hollow menfolk, and in the case of Lacere sacrifices her commitment to writing 'original books' (III, 226) and tells herself 'to regard authorship really as a profession' (III, 175) and thus to producing serials notable only for their 'utter absence of all art' (III, 298). As though to underline the cost of her subservience, neither of the men whose weakness controls her believe in Glen the writer, though they are ready to accept the income it provides. Even when she has reached her 'pecuniary zenith' (III, 264), Glen is powerless to avert her husband's 'ruin, utter and complete' (III, 316), and his unexpected death merely reinforces the sense of waste, impotence and humiliation of their marriage. This latent critique of the marriage plot is a further manifestation of proto-modernist undercurrents in *A Struggle for Fame*, particularly with respect to the emergence of the New Woman and the ways in which the novel form portrayed new-found expressions of feminine self-representation and the cost of upholding it.

Glen's entry through 'the golden gates of Fame' (II, 138), so ardently desired and so long sought, leads not to metropolitan acclaim but to Hampshire self-sufficiency, further confirming that the subject of her story is the struggle for her own form, her own perspective, her own say. Yet there is also a sense that her efforts represent not only a self-aware attempt to earn the respected reputation and cultural assimilation that both 'the mere force of the machinery' (III, 98) of publishing and an accepting readership provide. Her struggle also suggests itself as an unconscious desire to sublimate subservience to the male regimes that delimit woman's purpose and potential, to create a space between authorship and male authority. Remuneration is not to be dismissed; it represents a degree of integration with the system of production and circulation that is rewarding as far as it goes. But self-representation on one's own terms is a more significant achievement, and the struggle for that delineates a divided, embattled, exceptional Glen whom nobody will consider worthy if she herself does not. Seeing Glen in this light emphasises *A Struggle for Fame*'s preoccupation with agency and independence. The novel's treatment of this concern may not necessarily make it a parable of life under the Union, but its anxieties regarding displacement, affiliation and recognition are difficult to dissociate entirely from the problematical matrix of hopes and insecurities, belonging and estrangement, participation and rejection characteristic of nineteenth-century Anglo-Irish relations.

# 1885

# George Moore, *A Mummer's Wife*

*George Moore (1852–1933), a member of a prominent family of landlords and parliamentarians, was born at Moore Hall on the shores of Lough Carra in County Mayo. He was educated at St Mary's College, Oscott, near Birmingham, and, despite his artistic aspirations, was intended by his family for the army. In 1873 he inherited the family estate and set out for Paris. There, in the company of such artists as Manet and Degas, his eyes were opened to modern sensibilities. His painting ambitions came to nothing; instead, his sense of artistic purpose became influenced by the novels of Émile Zola. Moore introduced those works' Naturalism to the English novel, sparingly in his first novel A Modern Lover (1883) and in more full-blown fashion in A Mummer's Wife. The back streets and human weaknesses depicted in both these novels broke many Victorian cultural taboos. Moore insisted on his right to break them, notably in the pamphlet Literature at Nurse (1885).*

*Other novels in similar vein followed, including A Drama in Muslin (1886) and his most celebrated work, Esther Waters (1894). Now resident in London, Moore became one of the founders of the Independent Theatre, which staged the European avant-garde dramas of the day. This experience led to his recruitment by W.B. Yeats to assist in the establishment of the Irish Literary Theatre, and he moved to Dublin in 1901. Works written there include* The Untilled Field *(1903), the first collection of modern Irish short stories;* The Lake *(1905), a novel; and* Memoirs of My Dead Life *(1906), one of Moore's various path-breaking experiments in autobiography, the most noted of which is the three-volume* Hail and Farewell *(1911–14). Published after his return to London in 1911,* Hail and Farewell *became a* succès de scandale *for its portraits of the Irish Literary Revival's leading personalities.*

*Moore was an inveterate reviser of his own work, and much of his later life in London was devoted to rewriting previously published material –* A Drama in Muslin *became* Muslin *(1915);* A Modern Lover *reappeared as* Lewis Seymour and Some Women *(1917). Among his later works, the controversial* The Brook Kerith *(1916), whose protagonist is a Jesus who survived crucifixion, stands out. His final novel is the somewhat neglected* Aphrodite in Aulis *(1930). And as a short-story writer, Moore continued to expand that form's scope and technique, here too drawing on modern European models. In addition, his oeuvre also includes some important, typically idiosyncratic, critical works –* Parnell and his Island *(1887),* Impressions and Opinions *(1891),* Modern Painting *(1893) and* Conversations in Ebury Street *(1924).*

*The impact of Moore's novels on English literary and cultural life has its origins not only in his Zolaesque forays and his critical, or in some respects theoretical, turn of mind. It also owes a good deal to his being an outsider, a persona he also cultivated when a member of Dublin's artistic élite. Yet the reputation he earned in Dublin as an erratic dissident and in London as an unpredictable controversialist obscures his independence. Culturally combative and aesthetically innovative, Moore was in the forefront of the late nineteenth-century incursion of Irish writers into English letters, permanently changing the literary landscape of that country as well as suggesting new directions for Irish writing, some of which the young James Joyce pursued.*

The graphically detailed bout of asthma at the beginning of *A Mummer's Wife* sets the stage for not only the novel's brand of realism but also for its preoccupations with both breakdown and the weaknesses of the flesh. Ralph Ede survives his attack, but his recovery also reveals that his wife Kate suffers from more subtle and complicated forms of suffocation – environmental, domestic and spiritual. This arresting opening is just one instance of the novel's originality. Its setting, the town of

Hanley in the Potteries district of the English Midlands, representing an industrial modernity far removed from the nineteenth-century Irish novel's typical landscapes, is another. The mean urban scene in which the Ede drapery shop is located reveals a drabness that, if not necessarily at the heart of the nation of shopkeepers, hardly valorises material life in the heyday of empire. And the demands of Kate's mother-in-law, the effective head of the household, are exacerbated by the narrowness of that lady's Low Church ethos and observances. Understandably, Kate longs for relief, even if she has only novelettish notions of what form it might take, and when an alternative presents itself in the shape of Dick Lennox, the head of the mummers, it is not difficult to sympathise with her falling for him and for his way of life. Eliciting sympathy for Kate the sinner is another aspect of *A Mummer's Wife*'s originality, as is the implication that, if 'all things belonging to her had to be broken' (90), it would mean a change for the better.

Dick Lennox is the actor-manager of Morton and Cox's Operatic Company, a travelling show, and Kate's enchantment by what she sees on stage helps her to sublimate the power of 'coarse, large, sensual Dick' (93), an obvious contrast to sickly Ralph. The Ruritarian levity of the company's repertoire of French operetta and Dick's 'animation' (66) become complementary facets of Kate's desire. She elopes with him and the company. Before this, 'of pleasure, or even of happiness, she knew nothing' (69). Now Kate's knowledge of both expands exponentially, and the thespians' boozy, lecherous way of life soon banishes her provincial inhibitions. The company's travels take her to England's main industrial centres, all of which disclose an avid appetite for the tawdry therapy of *opéra bouffe*. Her eventual divorce from Ralph is arrestingly lacking in drama and seems no more than a legalistic reflex. Not alone does she marry Dick, she also becomes a leading light in the company, adopts a stage name and becomes a figure of 'delicious' (234) allure. This transformation in self-representation is formalised in the chorus of her signature song – 'Look at me here, look at me there' (*passim*). In short, 'the fierce longing for change she had been so long nourishing' (167) now appears to have borne abundant fruit. And soon she is pregnant.

All the world is not a stage, however, and 'the date that marked the turning of the tide of prosperity that till now had favoured the "Co." was Kate's marriage' (264). The practical economics of touring are one reason for this decline, and so is the nature of touring itself. Temporary seasons, hit and miss productions, unpredictable audiences and

backstage intrigues contribute to a way of life that is unsettled and dis-
continuous. A pattern of build-up and let-down is endemic to theatrical
life and that pattern both appeals to and betrays its adherents' vain
pursuit of fortune. Kate's belief that '[s]he would go on acting, and Dick
would continue to love her' (260) reveals a temperament peculiarly
unsuited to her adopted way of life. Only a character with Dick's unassailable ego and amoral resourcefulness can master such a flimsily
structured *métier*. And his resilience emerges in the rapid formation of
the Constellation Company – nothing but stars – that succeeds Morton
and Cox. But the Constellation is much more short-lived than its predecessor, leaving Kate to poverty-stricken childbirth. Post-partum
depression overwhelms her. She fortifies herself with brandy against it.
Her child dies; her alcohol dependence increases. Dick sees to his
theatrical affairs, not all of which are confined to the stage, so that Kate
is now afflicted by jealousy, which 'accentuated the neurosis, occasioned by alcohol, from which she was suffering' (317).

Her singing career is obviously over. Her marriage is doomed.
Instead of acting in the escapist roles in which Dick cast her, Kate is
reduced to acting out the inescapable roles that her relationship with
Dick has conferred. 'She was all pain, but, worse still, a black horror of
her life crushed and terrified her' (336); a body, merely, unadorned and
without a sustaining context. Acting on her desires has trapped her; an
'incapacity to act maddened her' (338). Deprived of both married life's
affirmative potential and the theatre's limelight, Kate has no means of
authentication, and she confirms the absence of a basis for representing herself in increasingly self-destructive behaviour. Throughout,
Dick has typically been seen as 'a mere mass of sensuality' (271), but
the deterioration of his marriage makes it difficult to determine who
now is the beauty and who the beast. Furthermore, the scene of the
action has moved to London, where Kate's domestic difficulties are
reinforced by 'that awful sensation of being lost amid a myriad beings'
(325) that the city conveys. This response makes the public sphere
impossible to comprehend, much less to find a footing in. The city's
alienating mystique is depicted as both lurid and cosmopolitan, and
Kate has her most telling encounter with it while wandering along the
Strand, the resort not only of theatre-goers but of prostitutes. On at
least one occasion, Kate is picked up, though her recollection of it is
imperfect, making both act and recall symptoms of the increasingly
uncertain grip she has on herself, rather than pretexts for moralising. If

the actor's life is one that can 'never run a year without getting entangled in some difficult knot or other' (267), Kate is clearly entangled beyond extrication, at best no more than a debased and marginal player in the spectacle that is the imperial capital.

Typically, Kate's London is limited to her insalubrious Islington surroundings. Her foray into one of the city's cultural showcases, besides being one of the first times an Irish novelist ventures onto London's streets and depicts the fugitive, transient, heterogeneous activity that animates them, is a statement focusing less on urban grandeur than on the variety of ways in which it is impossible to determine the crowd's directions and objectives. In the levelling democracy of the pavement, Kate's displacement is given its most resonant representation. Loss of her native Hanley, loss of her child, loss of her profession, loss of self-possession find their public counterparts in the incessant impermanence of the passing throng. Kate's surprise – indeed implausible – street-side encounter with her ex-husband Ralph highlights Moore's paradoxical representation of a structure of unpredictability. This encounter, too, leads to nothing; its occurrence merely accentuates not only how lost Kate is but that being lost is at least as representative of modern urban life as the great city's projections of pomp and circumstance, fashion and wealth. Weak, destitute, *distraite,* in her depleted humanity Kate has become a remnant, an afterthought, a husk of her former desires. But in her abjection, she represents a critique of the surfaces that seduced her, the world, flesh and devil that colour and empower that realm beyond the traditional roles of wife and mother. Life in Hanley falsely repressed Kate's desires; life after Hanley falsely fulfilled them. A consciousness of how best to represent herself is thwarted no matter where she turns. Her awareness consists of loss, pain, negation, abandonment – the reverse of what she had hoped for.

The spirit of the critique rehearsed in *A Mummer's Wife* is also evident in Dick Lennox's activities. Opportunistic as ever, he has taken up with a Mrs Laura Forest, author of 'classical cartoons' (319) and a devotee of Eastern religion. Allowing for differences in class and temperament, Laura Forest's venturesome extravagances oddly resemble Kate's elopement, with the former being taken in by exotic displays in terms of whose dubious authenticity she now represents herself. Nevertheless, her artificial, unearthly and sexless high-mindedness starkly contrasts with the lower depths into which Kate's flesh has led her. The one part that Kate is now thought fit to play is that of 'the mad woman' (342) in *Jane Eyre*; whereas in Laura, Dick has 'hopes of turning his strange acquaintance to account' (320) and begins work on a comic opera based on her experiences. Laura's ostensible repudiation of the things of this world contrasts her with Kate's initial desires, while her advocacy of 'a radical change in hereditary environment' (391) challenges a fundamental tenet of Zolaesque naturalism. Laura's loftiness brings to mind the enthusiasm for the occult that emerged during the 1880s, and which may be regarded in this context as a type of higher escapism. As such, the nature of her appeal to an operetta impresario is self-explanatory. Dick is as unlikely to be carried away by Mrs Forest's uplift as to be depressed by Kate's decline. He occupies the middle ground, the sphere in which both women are essentially regarded as business propositions, his attachment to them a pragmatic improvisation comparable to the free hand with which he treats his imported French productions. The temporariness and artifice of these productions are not only reproduced in his treatment of Kate; those two characteristics are also versions of the urban experience. If Mrs Forest takes Dick Lennox for 'one who looked nobler than the rest' (319), she is as mistaken about him as Kate has been. Worldly Dick knowingly plays false, thereby distorting Kate's pursuit of an alternative framework for self-representation.

Although, in his final appearance at Kate's deathbed, Dick is likened to 'a big and ponderous animal' (394), from the start Kate has thought of him as 'in a word, human' (93). Dick sees little reason to demonstrate that there is more to him than appetite (another reason why he and Laura Forest are an odd couple). Yet he does not quite reject the disturbed Kate out of hand, and initially attempts to withstand her increasingly belligerent and irrational reactions to him. But after Kate's unsuccessful committal to institutional care, Dick breaks with her, accelerating her deterioration. All that she has left is the knowledge that 'she felt, she lived, she was conscious. Oh yes, horribly conscious' (365). But this faculty – the one that perhaps concerns the modern outlook above all others – rather than leading Kate to an understanding of what's become of her, prompts fantasies that Dick 'would take her back, and they would live as the lovers did in all the novels she had ever read' (377). Clearly, Moore intends *A Mummer's Wife* to be very far removed from the kind of fiction that Kate has in mind, and the story ends not on a note of putatively redemptive love but with much more persuasive scenes of breakdown and destructiveness, the comprehensive nature of which seems to be a malevolent flowering of the squalor, impotence and emotional exhaustion suggested by the novel's opening.

Kate finally attains the permanent oblivion that drink promises. But it is not only her craven need of alcohol that destroys her; in addition, she is also fatally undermined by the disorders of consciousness that drunkenness induces. Such problems, however, pre-date Kate's drinking and have their origin in the quality of consciousness she possesses before entertaining Dick's attentions. It may be argued that she falls for Dick precisely because of her naïve and sentimental emotional makeup, fed by insipid romances but otherwise parched by the joint effects of a narrow materialism and a religion of constraint. The result of such formative influences is a false consciousness, one that must inevitably be susceptible to the surface allure of a Dick Lennox production. His shows lend a captivating legitimacy to falseness, so that 'in all she saw there was a mingled sense of nearness and remoteness, a divine concentration, and an absence of her own proper individuality' (136). The only social foothold that Kate can secure is through her stage representations. When the mask that substantiates her escape from Hanley and the Ede household is no longer available, she has neither the incentive nor resources to sustain alternative performances.

In addition to its thematic and cultural interest – its feminist orientation, crisis of agency and closely observed class gradations – *A Mummer's Wife* is significant for its narrative method. Maintaining the guise of conventional third-person omniscient storytelling, it at the same time subverts that guise by enacting a tissue of discontinuities and incoherences. The unities of plot yield to the disruptions of drives. An ending in which all is restored and reintegrated is supplanted by irremediable dissolution followed by a dead stop. And in his refusal to judge, the narrator conveys an apparent indifference to audience expectations. The use of time is central to the novel's obviating of a cause-and-effect, motive-and-mystery structure. Rather than proceeding at a regular rate, or in a manner that relies on the calendar, the seasons, the social round, the workday, it focuses on moments, scenes, turning points, gestures, and extends their impact, especially on Kate's consciousness. These excerpts from the time continuum give rise to a rhythm that provides the reader with a sense of coherent development while at the same time revealing that Kate is deprived of it. The moment is treated like a musical note, to be extended or abbreviated as emotional expressiveness requires, a particularly fitting means of notating Kate's attempts at self-representation in view of her musical talent.

This derivation of an aesthetic strategy from unlovely subject matter makes it difficult to consider Moore as simply a follower of French literary fashion or as merely intent on making a name for himself as an *enfant terrible*. The latter reputation might lend him an Irish coloration in the reading public's mind, yet *A Mummer's Wife* has no apparent interest in being thought Irish. Or perhaps it is more accurate to say that it relocates in English settings the squalor, impoverishment, ignorance – the whole spectacle of failure – that typify Irish conditions. Removed from their usual location, these conditions' supposedly national character are more affectingly restated as aspects of human limitation, or as consequences of Kate's desire for 'some ideal fatherland' (140) in Dick. The impossibility of regarding Kate as merely embodying those two staples of Irish stereotype, drink and staginess, challenges the value of generic and prescriptive modes of thought, and suggests independence of mind as a precondition for other forms of independence.

# 1886

## Rosa Mulholland, *Marcella Grace*

*Rosa Mulholland (1841–1921) was born in Belfast, but spent her writing life in Dublin, where she was married to John Gilbert, the noted historian of the city; on his knighthood she became Lady Gilbert, a name under which some of her writings appeared. Initially intending to be an artist, Mulholland – with Charles Dickens' encouragement – turned to literature. A number of her early stories and a novel, Hester's History (1869), were published in* All the Year Round *under Dickens' editorship.*

*These early short stories were also reprinted in the* Irish Monthly, *the leading Irish periodical of the day, in which much of her subsequent writing also appeared, including* Marcella Grace, *and such was the number of her contributions to it that it is tempting to think of her as the tutelary spirit of that important publication. Together with its editor, her brother-in-law Father Matthew Russell, SJ, Mulholland helped to promote literary taste and cultural purpose for the instruction and edification of Ireland's emerging Catholic middle class.*

*A high-minded, Catholic and in certain crucial respects High Victorian outlook informs her prolific output of novels, poems and short stories, as well as much children's fiction. Her works' essentially sentimental, inoffensive and appeasing inclinations gave them a wide readership, as their*

*many editions confirm. But* Marcella Grace *met with the unique
response of a novel rebutting its point of view – the anonymous* Priests
and People: A No-Rent Romance *(1891). More interesting, perhaps, is
Mulholland's recurring treatment – in such novels as* A Fair Emigrant
*(1888),* Gianetta *(1889),* Onora *(1900) and* The Return of Mary
O'Morrough *(1908) – of poor girls in peril and their capacity to withstand whatever threatens or constrains them. Less noteworthy for the
quality of her imagination than for her cultural values, Mulholland is
also important for the example her career provided for the generation of
Irish women writers – Katharine Tynan, for instance – that came to the
fore in the Irish Literary Revival.*

The style and size of Marcella Grace's home in Weaver's Square in
Dublin's Liberties sets it apart from neighbouring dwellings, and the
lives of those who live in it are also rather out of keeping with the
locality. Marcella's irascible father is a poplin weaver, but his business is
in decline and his patriarchal manner is overbearing and repressive
and ignores the fact that, aged twenty-one, Marcella has reached the
age of consent. He continues to treat her with ill grace and his refusal
to teach her to weave leaves her without occupation, fortune or a discernible future. Another expression of his belittling of Marcella is his
habit of regarding her as a misfit, a possessor of 'the cursed proud
blood of strangers' (24). The allusion is to the girl's late mother, a lady
whose marriage was obviously a misalliance. But '[t]he instincts of her
mother' (ibid.) are all Marcella has to rely on. These place her 'standing
a little apart' (18) from the neighbours, though when they are in need
Marcella is the first to lend an unselfish helping hand. Such willingness, like her fidelity to and care of her father, is an indication of her
refinement and its accompanying *noblesse oblige*.

An opportunity for another good Samaritan act is presented when,
after the murder in a nearby street of the absurdly named landlord
Gerald Ffrench-Ffont, Marcella shelters a fugitive whose 'look of noble
resolve and manly determination' (28) impresses her. Such an appearance overrides any misgivings she might have, given that 'the times were
troubled' (ibid.) – the 1880s, that is; one of *Marcella Grace's* most significant aspects is its attempt to be contemporary. The fugitive is Bryan
Kilmartin, and it is with his destiny that Marcella's future is hereupon
united, as is Bryan's with hers, though it is through the pressure of public
concerns that their union becomes indissoluble. As a former Fenian,
Bryan is a suspect in the Ffrench-Ffont murder and though now, at the
age of thirty and with a Cambridge degree, he holds quite respectable

Nationalist views, it is still difficult for him to live down his earlier enthusiasm for the politics of physical force. Marcella turns out to be his salvation, a role that is consistent with her laying on the people of a 'world-forgotten' (104) area of the west of Ireland the bountiful, irenic hand of the benevolent landlord. That role represents the Marcella who 'in her secret heart . . . was on the side of the powers that be' (31). And it is this outlook that essentially enables Bryan to survive his various trials and sufferings. Indeed, Marcella's righteousness enables her to suffer in kind with him.

Initially, however, it is not clear to either of them what the other represents. This is largely because of an unexpected change in Marcella's fortunes. In one of the many recognition scenes on which the narrative is structured, Marcella fortuitously encounters an aunt she did not know she had, Mrs Timothy O'Flaherty O'Kelly. She is the absentee landlord of Crane Castle – full address, 'Distresna, Back o' the Mountains, in Connaught' (37) – a property adjoining Kilmartin's. Annoyed by the severe criticism of a local priest, Father O'Daly of Ballydownvalley, for neglecting her landlord's responsibilities, Mrs O'Kelly is also distressed by having no heir to the property other than a detested distant relative. Marcella's facial resemblance to Mrs O'Kelly's late, errant sister is a most welcome surprise, and she at once begins grooming the girl to be 'an Irish Cinderella' (59), beginning with an attendance at the St Patrick's Day ball in Dublin Castle, an event at which Marcella is able 'to live like the heroine of a fairy romance' (62). Such a role, however, is only the most far-fetched of the ones she is expected to play in compliance with the new identity Mrs O'Kelly has in mind for her. Thus, when she is introduced to Bryan at the ball – and is struck again by his representation of 'all that was strong, chivalrous, and stainless in manhood' (32) – her name is said to be Miss O'Kelly, a relative of Mrs O'Kelly recently returned from the Continent. Bryan does not recognise her as his Liberties deliverer, though he does regard her as a woman of his dreams, suggesting that initially, at any rate, a crucial dimension of whoever Marcella might be is that she be seen. Her visibility is perhaps the most important feature of her new status; its value is shown in a different way apropos of Bryan when she is able to see through Mrs O'Kelly's false representation of him as a Fenian firebrand and no friend of landlords, despite the fact that he himself is one.

The fabrication of an upper-class identity for Marcella continues to be a source both of ambition and confusion to Mrs O'Kelly, partly because she 'want[s] a daughter' (59) and also as a result of Marcella's constancy to her father, though her devotion is rather shockingly devalued by Grace's attempt to get more from Mrs O'Kelly than the fifty pounds a year she has offered for his daughter's service. But this unseemly haggling is cut short by the weaver's death. Shortly thereafter, Mrs O'Kelly also passes on, and Marcella learns from Father O'Daly – who has befriended her – that she is the heir to Crane Castle and must leave at once for the west; she has no intention of being an absentee. Since Crane Castle is unprepared to receive her, Marcella stays with Bryan's mother in her island home of Inisheen. In that house a harp is prominently displayed and there are paintings on the walls of the old Irish Parliament and of Robert Emmet in the dock (the latter foreshadowing what is to befall Bryan; the connection between him and Emmet's uprising has already been made when Marcella sees newspaper placards with pictures in which Ffrench-Ffont resembles Lord Kilwarden). These images not only convey political tradition and national sentiment; they also suggest the forms available to Bryan should he choose to represent himself as either the 'warm Nationalist' (203) he is said to be or as the imbiber, from his mother, of a 'romantic love for his country' (162). Bryan's position between these self-representational frameworks emerges when he arrives in 'his little Connaught kingdom' (87) hounded by certain Fenian elements who wish to incriminate him in the Ffrench-Ffont affair. (These elements are, according to Bryan, 'creatures of a debased Fenianism' (130), and are ultimately revealed as members of 'the Irish Invincibles' (264).) Once again, shelter, enclosure, retreat from the public scene and a woman's protection typify Bryan's behaviour. The pattern such reactions comprise is resourcefully varied and developed over the course of the novel.

Marcella, adopting a more benevolent form of clandestineness, carries out, disguised and unannounced, a campaign of good deeds amongst her tenants. (The motif of the unrecognised, uplifting lady recurs in Yeats' *The Countess Kathleen* (published 1892) and *Cathleen ni Houlihan* (produced 1902).) Her charity, sweetness and light soon make her beloved by all, a reception that Marcella appears to reciprocate in thinking '[w]ere not these poor over-joyed creatures her actual children?' (121). And Crane Castle is *en fête* when she concludes 'the little play she had been enacting for the benefit of her people' (119) by revealing that she is their new landlord. The state of her property, compared to that of Bryan the improver's, makes it clear, however, that she has much to do to make good, a condition that recurs in different forms to exemplify Marcella's almost compulsive voluntarism. Undaunted by the task ahead, Marcella dedicates herself with unsparing zeal and utter lack of class-consciousness to her duties, so much so that her companion, the chilly and aloof Miss O'Donovan, believes her to have been caught 'by the radical wave .... I feel sure she has a democratic strain in her somewhere' (125). These suspicions mushroom into the spectre of Marcella as 'a furious radical woman who had spoken on platforms about women's rights, and walked about the country in a jacket like a man's' (126), further complicating perceptions of her status and legitimacy, as well as prompting the reader to a balanced and proper assessment of their motherly nature and Marcella's gently ameliorating ways. But whether expressed radically or otherwise, Marcella's virtue is no prophylaxis. According to the urchin Mike, who has become particularly attached to her and who possesses 'the quickness of perception of his race and class' (109), Bryan is a marked man. In addition to the Fenian threat, the authorities still suspect him of the Ffrench-Ffont murder. A detective – a rather novel representative of the law, though one in keeping with the novel's contemporaneity – calls at Crane Castle, and Bryan is arrested on information laid against him by his erstwhile comrades.

This development creates the crisis on which the story turns, and in part it is a crisis of self-representation. As a witness to some of Bryan's movements on the night of the murder, Marcella can tell the truth (thereby revealing that she is not an O'Kelly but a Grace – pun presumably intended), in which case Bryan will almost certainly hang. Or she can maintain her O'Kelly identity and perjure herself in the hope of saving Bryan. Conscience-stricken, she opts for the latter, but Bryan insists on truth before all else: '[w]e are both too keenly alive to the beauty and harmony of life regulated by the moral law to be able to smile in each other's faces while conscious of having gained our happiness by so hideous a lapse from it' (184). She should let Bryan be her guide, for as he remarks, 'I am the man, and I must be the master' (182). Yet Bryan too is beset by difficulties of self-representation. The prosecution accuses him of class treason, for not only has he allegedly killed a man but 'still worse, his fellow-landlord' (191). His supposed confederates are 'the leaders of Communism and Socialism' (ibid.), and his allegiance is 'to Fenianism in its more modern and deadly form' (192); that, according to press reports, includes being 'an agent for the

American dynamite party' (145). Only the death of one of his informers and a death-bed confession by the other save Bryan from the gallows; his sentence is commuted to life imprisonment in Dartmoor.

Marcella and Bryan correct those false representations, however, by declaring their true selves in a marriage ceremony conducted in prison by Father O'Daly. The priest now assumes a paternal interest in Marcella, keeping both her spirit and her Catholic faith alive, and retrieving her from the depressed immurement in Crane Castle, whereby she replicates her beloved's banishment. Rather than deny the world, Father O'Daly helps her to affirm it by substituting for a local teacher. He also teaches her Irish, and soon she is instructing her tenants' children how to read and write in their native language. This cultural turn proves to be most therapeutic, demonstrating to Marcella her continuing usefulness while also providing a source of entertainment to the imprisoned Bryan, to whom she writes at length about it. His letters to her convey the undimmed 'vigour and noble temper of his mind, the manliness with which he accepted his misfortune' (232) – that is, his essential integrity, a quality that Marcella's unflagging sense of duty also valorises. But if Bryan remains with her in spirit, Fenianism is a more palpable presence. James Barrett, the brains behind the plot against Bryan, turns up in disguise at Crane Castle and threatens Marcella that if Bryan does not undertake to rejoin his old comrades on his release, she will suffer for it: 'you stand between us and the people . . . but if you don't change your hand, and work for us, you'll have to go' (244).

As though to confirm Barrett's noxious presence, fever breaks out in the locality. 'There are no Sisters of Mercy within reach' (236), so Marcella in effect impersonates them, devotedly caring for peasants 'deplorably ignorant of the first principles of nursing' (ibid.). Then Mike, her willing acolyte, is shot, and so would Marcella herself have been had not the diseased Barrett, the gunman, collapsed. Marcella nurses him back to health partly in the hope that, once recovered, he will confess his misdeeds, but largely because of her present role as 'almoner of heaven's mercy' (256). This role is vindicated when Barrett, acknowledging her goodness, declares that 'for once in my life I'll do an honest turn to somebody' (261). A death-bed confession follows, in which it emerges that Barrett became a Fenian in response to landlord injustice, and he draws the moral of his story by acknowledging that 'if most landlords were like Mr. and Mrs. Kilmartin, I and the like of me would never have been what we are' (264). The confession is taken down and signed, so that it has legal force and thus can secure Bryan's release. A future eliminating the peasantry's 'two mortal fears – dread of the landlord, and dread of the secret societies' (241) is now in prospect, one that strikes Marcella as 'a dream' (265). But Father O'Daly reminds her that, on the contrary, what has transpired is a manifestation of the reality of 'God's love and God's mercy' (ibid.).

Marcella '[i]n her heart . . . leaned to the side of landlordism' (104), and the novel points out this path as the one of righteousness. Religious resonances support this indication. The timely intervention of a benevolent Providence is frequently invoked. Bryan is not only a victim of false representation, he is also 'my martyr' (222). Marcella herself is also very nearly sacrificed, while her 'motherly love' (238) works something of a miracle among her epidemic-stricken though ever-faithful tenants. Occupying a position between Fenianism on the one hand and Bryan's Rackrent-like forefathers on the other – who, as he says, 'sold my birthright for a mess of *poteen*' (97) – Marcella is represented as a member of the Ascendancy of the spirit. And her strong faith in property's rights and responsibilities imparts a moral tutorial to more worldly members of the landlord class. If Bryan is no revolutionary, the same is equally true of Marcella; their politics forms a bond. But though the exceptional uprightness that their bond maintains is articulated by their improving custody of land and people, they share a more fundamental resource in their inner lives, to the quality of which Catholic imagery and sentiment testifies – when Marcella gives milk to a peasant infant, 'the mother knelt speechless watching her, no more daring to interfere than if it was the Holy Mother herself' (106).

As a so-called 'Donna Quixote' (171), Marcella represents the kind of secular, but not worldly, saintliness that alone saves herself, her beloved, her tenants and the socio-economic status quo. In her meekness and mildness, the availability of her other cheek, her patience, prudence, dutifulness and devotion, she is more a vessel of virtue than a three-dimensional character, a rhetorical projection in which the complications of race, gender and class that her experiences bring to light are secondary to the requirement that she always be represented as returning good for ill. The insistence throughout on the fineness of Bryan and Marcella is a plea for the principles that they represent to be recognised for their pre-eminent value to the discourse of the day. The innocence that is the hallmark of *Marcella Grace*'s two main characters also decisively colours the novel's political leanings, of which the creation of a set of more perfect unions (between city and country, landlord and peasant, Irish justice and English jails) is the most obvious. Marcella and Bryan represent themselves in terms of good deeds and good faith. Their story is based on the romantic, or at least romancing, assumption that theirs is the goodness that will eliminate landlordism's conflicts and contradictions – an assumption that requires readers to accept as synonyms charity and condescension, spiritual values and social policy, and an ethical sublime with ideological special pleading.

# 1887

## George Bernard Shaw, *An Unsocial Socialist*

*George Bernard Shaw (1856–1950) was born in Dublin, where he spent the first twenty years of his life before leaving for a literary career in London. Early attempts to establish himself as a novelist failed, and Shaw eventually discovered his métier in the theatre (his first play, Widowers' Houses, was staged in 1892). A lengthy succession of popular, provocative and culturally searching plays followed, securing his eminence in world literature. The outspoken treatment of daring themes caused some of Shaw's early plays to be banned, and in some respects he stands in a similar relation to the English theatre as George Moore does to the English novel. As a determined controversialist who frequently masqueraded as a jester, Shaw used paradoxical utterance and iconoclastic thought to establish himself as a formidable public intellectual. His engagement with English public life and manners is expressed not only through his creative works but by his socialist activism (he was a founding member of the influential Fabian Society) and the voluminous criticism that is the cultural pendant to his political ideology.*

*The sharpness of Shaw's rhetorical weaponry and the zeal of his reformist views are not only evident in his Fabian pamphlets, but in the criteria of taste and value enunciated throughout* Our Theatres in the Nineties *(3 vols., 1932) and* Shaw's Music *(3 vols., 1981; revised edition, 1989). Shaw's artistic beliefs led him to identify with such early modernists as Wagner and Ibsen, though he disguises the earnestness of those two influences by subversive logic. The intent and effect is to provoke the audience to think. This intention is not confined to the stage; his unpopular opposition to the First World War in* Commonsense about the War *(1914) is one of Shaw's numerous direct, polemical interventions in public debate. In the post-war period, Shaw's theatrical stock* declined somewhat, the success of Saint Joan (produced 1923; published 1924) notwithstanding, while his international standing as a man of letters increased. He received the 1925 Nobel Prize for Literature. His enthusiasm for Europe's interwar dictators ensured that Shaw remained on the ideological front line; his outlook is most fully stated in The Intelligent Woman's Guide to Socialism and Capitalism (1928; expanded in subsequent editions). Shaw's other causes included reform of English by simplifying conventional spelling, and he endowed the development of an alphabet for that purpose.

With the exception of John Bull's Other Island (produced 1904, published 1907), few of Shaw's works deal directly with Irish matters, and in general his published views on his native country, and in particular on his native city, are far from flattering. But he did espouse Irish causes, defending both Sir Roger Casement against charges of treason and the Easter 1916 Rebellion, although he was not a separatist, as his How to Settle the Irish Question (1917) makes clear. In each of these instances, Shaw's contrarian viewpoint endows the issues with a greater degree of intellectual cogency than was typical at the time. A selection of Shaw's occasional journalism on Irish themes, The Matter with Ireland (1962), is a reminder of his continuing interest in the country. None of Shaw's five completed novels – Immaturity (written 1879; published 1931), The Irrational Knot (written 1880; published 1905), Love Among the Artists (written 1881; published 1900), Cashel Byron's Profession (written 1882; published 1886) and a work entitled An Unfinished Novel (1958) – has an Irish setting. These are generally regarded as his weakest works, and deserving of critical attention only for the light they throw on the mature dramatist. And indeed their essential staginess is to be seen in their intricate reliance on exits and entrances, their overdependence on dialogue and speechifying, and their abundance of indoor settings. In addition, however, Shaw's novels are a series of forays into a society whose workings are found strangely difficult to justify, whose manners and morals are assumed rather than thought through, and whose clarity of motive and honesty of desire seem less than complete. The view of this society is that of an outsider compulsively drawn to the point of critical exasperation with the surfaces and complacencies surrounding him, to which he responds with a critical vehemence whose style and ideas seem hardly English.

The title of the last of what Shaw called 'novels of my nonage' contains a number of noteworthy resonances. It places to the fore, for perhaps the first time in an imaginative work in English, the term socialist, alerting the reader to the novel's polemical and provocative aims. Moreover, the reader may also expect these aims to find expression through a character who typifies a paradox, if not a contradiction, somebody who cannot be expected to be the upstanding, reliable, valiant, moral and sentimental protagonist familiar to the Victorian novel. The title also seems to promise that the story will dwell on the incompatibility of, or tension between, two opposed outlooks, or arguably two different modes of social identity – again, not standard novel fare. And within the title's two terms a particular time and space are disclosed in which the dialectic between the pair of titular terms is established, and where the drama between them is staged and formalised. These activities, while they may make free with deadlock, are unlikely to conclude in it. The creation of a necessary interim, a place and a moment in which differences can play out, is achieved in *An Unsocial Socialist's* two principal settings, Alton College and Brandon Beeches. Both are temporary accommodations, way stations en route not so much to more desirable domiciles but to that rarer position, a more enlightened and self-aware mode of self-representation. In outlining a path to that position, Shaw's novel is an early essay in modern consciousness.

As though to highlight not only the desirability of such a point of arrival but also its distinctive dialectics of becoming, the first part of the novel is largely devoted to Alton College and environs. The educational policy of Miss Wilson, the college head, is based on a Rousseauesque – or even Edgworthian – conception of 'moral force' (16), by which students develop according to the amount of responsibility they take for their thoughts and actions. But the limits of Miss Wilson's intentions are continually exposed by the threesome on whom the narrative initially focuses, Agatha Wylie, Jane Carpenter and Gertrude Lindsay. Of these, the most rebellious and outspoken is Agatha, and although, as Miss Wilson tells her, 'you are old enough and sensible enough to know the difference between order and disorder' (50), Agatha's indifference to maintaining this distinction threatens her with expulsion. Moreover, her complicated involvement with the unsocial socialist himself, Sidney Trefusis, not only occasions this threat but also gives the story its admittedly fitful impetus. This ostensibly unsuitable entanglement exposes the shibboleths that inhibit choice, action and change, thereby revealing the unsocial character of social convention. In that sense, unsocial is a synonym for unthinking.

A connection of sorts between Sidney and Agatha pre-dates the action. Sidney is married to Henrietta (Hettie; *née* Jansenius), and her father, a prominent Jewish businessman, is Agatha's uncle and guardian. But she, 'with the instinct of an anarchist' (46), rejects his patriarchal supervision, a gesture that parallels Trefusis' abandonment of his marriage when it is a mere six months old. His reason is that Hettie is so beautiful that she distracts him from his work, which is to spread the socialist word. The novel devotes comparatively little attention to Trefusis' claim that 'I am helping to liberate those Manchester laborers [sic] who were my father's slaves' (76), preferring to dwell on his opposition to the falsity of polite society's mores. But both Agatha's and Trefusis' rejection of their heritage, especially its economic advantages, and the fact that the rejection is linked to a repudiation of the father and the power he connotes, unites them in their separate, equal, alternative lines of development. Together they form the novel's dialectical axis, that interplay of thought and feeling that replaces conventional fiction's action. And while Agatha's resistance to the Alton regime is neither as outlandish nor as comprehensive as Trefusis' assertion that '[m]odern English polite society, my native sphere, seems to me as corrupt as consciousness of culture and absence of honesty can make it' (67), there is in both a sense of vital, spirited will to see through prevailing structures. The essentially rhetorical manifestation of that *élan* will ensure that it appears only logical (though not necessarily plausible) that Agatha falls for Trefusis – or at least for a version of him.

Having left Hettie, Trefusis takes a cottage near Alton and assumes the persona of a yokel named Jeff Smilash. He soon makes the acquaintance of the three schoolgirls, as well as Miss Wilson, and annoys everybody he encounters by acting with a gormless cleverness that makes him seem like a secular version of a holy fool, forever posing embarrassingly direct questions and turning received views and practices on their head. Manipulating false representation, particularly in terms of class and knowledge, extends the novel's dialectic between unsocial and social. Trefusis is fully conscious of his strategy and of its pleasure-giving revolutionary jokiness. Not surprisingly, he boasts that 'I take an insane pleasure in personating' (99) a figure who is his equal and opposite in class terms, and whose 'mummery' (62) disturbs its various audiences. The nature of this disturbance is not uniform, however. Physical disturbance is predictably created when on a dark and stormy night Smilash brings a poor shepherd and his family to the school and insists that they receive shelter and care. But Agatha, who witnesses the scene, is emotionally disturbed by Smilash's performance, and persuades herself that she sees in him 'my ideal hero' (92), even if she also wishes to convince herself that she is above regarding men in such a light. 'I am not a romantic fool' (109), she writes to Hettie, though – in the kind of false consciousness and projection from which An Unsocial Socialist derives a good deal of comedic play – 'he is very much in love with me' (ibid.). Alarmed at this development, Hettie rushes from London to Trefusis' cottage, a journey in wretched weather that results in her literally catching her death.

Hettie's death is arguably the novel's most testing incident – for the reader and for Trefusis (who has by now abandoned the Smilash act). 'Nothing is sacred to you. This shows what Socialists are!' (130), the mourning Jansenius tells his son-in-law, showing him the door. The test for Trefusis is to keep his head. To do so he relies on the intense, contrarian rationalism whose most arresting expression hitherto has been his separation from Hettie. (The test for the reader is to accept how Trefusis disciplines his emotional reactions. He uses his unsocial critical persona to overcome the force of the irrational registered by his wife's premature demise.) His refusal to concede that 'my feelings are a trumpery set of social observances to be harrowed to order and exhibited at funerals' (127) is one aspect of his reaction. Another is to see Hettie's death in the context of the countless other needless deaths 'hidden in a back slum' (125) that have no effect whatever on Jansenius – or, by implication, on what the city man represents. These differences are given concrete form in the tombstone that Trefusis erects with an inscription recording nothing more than Hettie's dates of birth, marriage and death. The majority consider this offensively cold-hearted but it might also be thought an acknowledgement of the inadequacy, in the circumstances, of conventional sentiment. And, as though his wilful, adversarial, private behaviour is a rehearsal of his public role, Trefusis immediately turns to revolutionary activity, including a 'suspected connection with a secret society for the assassination of the royal family' (137).

Yet details of quite what his political commitments represent are kept to a minimum and at a distance. They are projected as desires, as a romance of possibilities whereby will and reason will exert power that is neither imperial nor national. If Trefusis is the paladin of a paradoxically romantic quest, Agatha is his opposite, foregoing romance as a prototypical New Woman. Her formal education concluded, she is antagonistic both towards Trefusis and the fashionable life that she is expected to take up. She has no interest in the marriage market, and her attempts at a career prove inconclusive at best. At a loose end, she joins her two old school friends at Brandon Beeches, the home of Jane Carpenter, now unhappily married to Sir Charles Brandon, a dilettante. This gathering somewhat focuses the novel, and a high-quality drawing-room comedy ensues, with all the mistaken identities and representations common to that genre, though without that genre's typical protestations of innocence. Supplying the spark to the combustible elements of the house party is none other than Trefusis, who, duplicating his earlier proximity to Alton, so happens to live quite near, at Sallust's House. He first appears in this setting leading a demonstration to reclaim a right of way through Brandon Beeches, and he continues to be an intrusive presence throughout – a *deus ex machina* who cannot deny his own omnipotence.

If Trefusis' political watchword is 'Socialism or Smash' (207), his mission at Brandon Beeches is regulation of the marriage market. His campaign, directed at the three Alton alumnae, aligns social change with sexual politics, with the same intention of challenging prevailing, unreflecting power relations. With respect to genre, the result subverts drawing-room comedy's conventions by removing their patina of harmlessness. A sense of play is retained, but this is serious play, earnest and socially conscious, intended to eliminate illusion and to make the choice of partner deliberate and knowing, not 'a silly love match and a failure' (248), which is how Trefusis describes his marriage to Hettie. Hard-headed, as opposed to soft-hearted, this new approach is another aspect of the novel's critique of the approved forms of romance. These forms' inadequacy is evident in the partnerships at Brandon Beeches, which represent instability, alienation and constraint, deriving from the false consciousness of attempting to love 'story-book fashion' (221). A more adult form of loving – free, between equals, not prearranged – is the alternative, although old ways are not that easily dispensed with, as Gertrude's attachment to Trefusis shows (as is his wont, he talks her out of it, preferring Agatha). Embracing a self-aware, adult expression of adult desire – what the Brandons' marriage might well consider – asserts vital individual consciousness, autonomy and power, and replaces the preconditioned posturing demanded by the marriage market and its culture. Such a development could not only liberate women like Agatha, who does not accept that 'a lady's business in society is to get married, and that virtues and accomplishments alike are important only as attractions to eligible bachelors' (139), but also others not so obviously endowed with minds of their own, or with ideas of how they should represent themselves, such as Gertrude Lindsay. The New Woman may be the Unsocial Socialist's significant other.

Trefusis notes that 'we Socialists need to study the romantic side of our movement to interest women in it' (215), a strategy that, sexist as it sounds, points towards common objectives shared by a new politics and a new feminism. Each new departure also indicates a different approach to forms of social and sexual representation, the former over-riding class barriers and the political and economic artifices that keep them in place, the latter dismantling sexual stereotypes and the emotional and cultural modes of exchange that propagate them. Of these, the reform of the marriage market is the most obviously unsocial, because it implicitly claims that personal, private, intimate concerns should be regulated by the rationality on which socialism has the revolutionary nerve to pride itself. Moreover, both forms also reconfigure the notion of union, whether that enshrined by the social or by the marriage contract. And a fresh conception of convergence, articulated as a revolutionary strategy of choice, self-determination and the calculated reasoning of ideological awareness, offers at the very least a set of suggestive prompts to those who are also concerned with 'what we have done to get our rents in Ireland' (210).

For all his ability to play fast and loose with prevailing attitudes, practices and systems of value, Trefusis' radicalism remains embryonic, a matter of potential rather than accomplishment. He faces the future in a resolute and unusually doubt-free frame of mind. His unsocial disregard for present usages may indeed be a necessary overture to the socialism yet to come, but possibility and promise are the stuff of romance and its ethos of quest. In his letter to the author that concludes *An Unsocial Socialist* – yet another of its many expressions of dissatisfaction with the novel as a form – Trefusis informs Shaw that 'I can only congratulate you on the determination with which you have striven to make something like a romance out of such very thin material' (259). Without romance, however, how little there would be. Instead of replicating its old jaded associations, romance here suggests the rudiments of a modern psychology, a portmanteau carrying ego, passion, individuality, sexual identity and various other incentives to personal representation necessary to resist the restrictive endowment of a century which, in Trefusis' words, 'will be infamous in history as a time when the greatest advances in power of man over nature only served to sharpen his greed and make famine its avowed minister' (250).

# 1890

## William O'Brien, *When We Were Boys*

*A native of Mallow, County Cork, William O'Brien (1852–1928) was in his day one of the best-known figures in Irish public life, first as one of Parnell's lieutenants and subsequently as a leader of the United Irish League, which he founded in 1898. His first career was journalism, in which he quickly made a name for himself with a series of articles entitled* Christmas in the Galtees: An Inquiry into the Condition of the Tenantry of Mr Nathaniel Buckley *(1878). First published in* The Freeman's Journal, *this exposé was followed by O'Brien's 1881 appointment by Parnell as the founding editor of* United Ireland. *In a generation of gifted Irish journalists, O'Brien's dramatic sense and rhetorical flair made him one of the most notable. He also drafted the 'No Rent Manifesto', one of the key documents of the Land War, during one of his jail terms. He was elected to parliament in 1883 and was almost continually re-elected until 1918; he twice served as MP for Cork city.*

*His post-Parnell career was largely devoted to maintaining the United Irish League, whose influence on the activities and makeup of the Irish Parliamentary Party in the early years of the twentieth century was strengthened by various O'Brien-owned newspapers. O'Brien also continued to write prolifically, producing the memoirs* Recollections *(1905) and* Evening Memories *(1920), much political commentary, including* An Olive Branch in Ireland *(1910) and* The Downfall of Parliamentarianism *(1918), and essays on life in Ireland and elsewhere, many of them collected in* Irish Fireside Hours *(1928).*

*In addition to* When We Were Boys, *O'Brien wrote one other novel,* A Queen of Men *(1898), a historical romance about Grace O'Malley. Both works are vehicles for O'Brien's idealising outlook and his stylistic exuberance. The presence in Leopold Bloom's library of* When We Were Boys *is perhaps one indication of its wide popularity, although the bookmark on p. 217 noted in* Ulysses *may mean that Bloom, or Molly, did not finish reading it. (On the page in question Reggie Neville – yet another boy – arrives in Ireland, a typical instance of how conventionally overstuffed* When We Were Boys *is.) As the note at the end of* When We Were Boys *states, it was written during two separate spells of incarceration, during the second of which the author did not have access to what he had written earlier. This drawback does not noticeably impinge upon the work's wealth of incident or congested plot. O'Brien was not really a*

*novelist, and his conception of the form relies on the episodic and coinci-*
*dental in ways that the typical romance made familiar and predictable. At*
*the same time, for all its narrative* longueurs, *its oddly Leveresque priv-*
*ileging of daring and adventure, and its ideological overstatement, the*
*states of mind of* When We Were Boys *represent not only the energies*
*and confrontations of an earlier time but also point to some of the dreams*
*of action entertained by members of an Irish generation facing the twen-*
*tieth century.*

'When boyhood's fire was in my blood' – the opening line of Thomas
Davis' 'A Nation Once Again' is one the career of Kennedy (Ken)
Rohan, the youthful protagonist of *When We Were Boys*, irresistibly suggests. The incendiary element takes a number of instructive forms –
personal, romantic, ideological, revolutionary – as he embarks on the
journey to maturity. These forms not only test and temper the mettle of
Ken's incipient manhood. In addition, they are shown to be interrelated, not only by the responses in thought and action that they
prompt but by the desire from which they all essentially originate.
Ken's path takes him from seminarian to convict by way of a series of
seductions, enticements and romantic entanglements, each more
intense than its predecessor, its highest point being participation in the
Fenian rising of 1867. That momentary outbreak's social and political
implications are by no means neglected in the novel. But the rising is
also the *ne plus ultra* of attempts to represent Ken as not only a guiltless
victim of youthful hotheadedness but as an exemplar of the virtues that
come with such a temperament. His generous, willing spirit is what the
novel ultimately invites the reader to admire, not the body in chains of
his final appearance, even though the two views represent *recto* and
*verso*, as it were, of the novel's title.

In a sense, however, it is surprising that the reader's last look at Ken
Rohan is as he is being shipped off to an English jail, even allowing for
the work's projection of the felon's lot as both a personal apotheosis
and the continuation of a glorious national tradition. Ken is the son of
the mill-owner of Drumshaughlin, a community in the scenic Beara
Peninsula whose members collectively represent a knowingly diversified portrait of provincial Catholic middle-class life. This group's
public profile is piously orthodox in moral tone, mildly nationalistic
and to that degree politically progressive – or in the case of Ken's
father, 'Radical' (13) – in ideological outlook, and to all appearances
reasonably secure economically, though, as events show, the secular

realms of politics and economics may not be as soundly structured as they appear. But, with the Famine still in the quite recent past, and Drumshaughlin being suggestively located in the shadow of Hungry Mountain, this class' rather heavily underlined state of material and cultural solidity, complete with copious meals, musical evenings and polished though not artificial manners, is a sociological revelation. From a fictional standpoint, the sense of at least ostensible material security is a further elaboration of the class-based romance of self-sufficiency found in *Knocknagow*. In such an environment of peace and relative prosperity, Ken might profitably follow his father's footsteps, not necessarily by succeeding to Myles Rohan's mill but by following his example as a sober, industrious, conventional authority figure. If Ken's 'knowledge of the real world was as scanty as his travels in the worlds of poetry, history and adventure had been extensive' (5), his embarkation on a clerical career at the novel's outset suggests a life of orthodoxy, tradition and virtuous endeavour that seems not to stray so very far from his father's ethos.

Rather than consolidate that ethos, however, St Fergal's seminary gives seventeen-year-old Ken the opportunity to experience 'his first rebellion' (33). This takes the form of friendship with Jack Harold, nephew of Drumshaughlin's Father Phil and son of a French doctor, a revolutionary of the generation of 1848. Jack is trouble, but Ken finds him irresistible, being too innocent to see him as a false representative of the militancy he so enthusiastically espouses. Jack's penchant for superficial role-playing is initially signalled by his appearing in black-face at Ken's bedside, while his general unsoundness is suggested by a 'certain air of foppishness [that] might have given him a character for effeminacy' (28), a possibility that the text defers at this point. Instead, Jack's attributes are initially the basis for displays of unmanly promiscuity, both personal and ideological. At first Ken is captivated by Jack's affectations of metropolitan sophistication, his irreverence and his political lineage. An ill-fated escapade leads to Ken being accidentally shot, and once blooded he determines not to return to St Fergal's but to pursue dreams of revolutionary glory, even if they mean being, as the president of St Fergal's warns him, 'entangled in a secret society which is under the curse of your Church' (126).

Meanwhile, conditions in Drumshaughlin are becoming increasingly uncertain owing to the dereliction of its landlord, Ralph Westropp, Lord Drumshaughlin. Beached in his London residence, beset by gout and debt, his lordship dolefully luxuriates in the fate of belonging to a class of what he calls 'hybrids. We've forgotten how to be Irishmen and we'll never become Englishmen' (58). His Irish property is in the hands of his good-natured, sport-loving, throwback of a son, Harry, resulting in neglect that is exploited for his own ends by Hans Harman, the estate's hard-hearted agent, whose methods, as he boasts, have raised 'rack-renting ... to the utmost limit of high art' (373). Harman's embezzlement of rents is eventually revealed, as is his conspiracy to swindle Lord Drumshaughlin out of his property, a scheme that relies on a tissue of false representations. Such economic self-seeking threatens Myles Rohan's mill, and that pillar of the community is physically weakened by pressure from Harman, with eventually fatal results. Moreover, Harman 'was consumed by a hatred of Ken Rohan' (406) while being drawn to Jack Harold, who cynically allies himself with the agent, although what Harman wishes to use Jack for is of a more intimate nature than his superficially avuncular manner suggests.

Both the novel and Ken's career proceed on two fronts. One of these concerns preparations for the arrival of a regiment of Fenians from America who, together with local forces, intend to change utterly current social and political conditions. The second is the preservation of the Drumshaughlin estate, a task that his lordship's daughter Mabel sets herself, forsaking London salon life and residing in her ancestral home to do so, despite her father's belief that her brother Harry is 'involved deeply in an atrocious communistic conspiracy' (200). At first sight, these two fronts appear incompatible, but the warmhearted, scapegrace Harry welcomes the possibility of insurrection, largely as a way to extend his repertoire of male activities, while Mabel's Irish experiences inspire her to declare that 'I am born a rebel against a great deal that passes for law in England and against almost everything that is called law in Ireland' (209) – a rendition of 'The Wearing of the Green' has inspired her to take this position. For his part, Ken has discovered that 'youth, strength, friendship, love, country, adventure, glory, heaven, were all realities in the rosy lands through which the tide of his young blood was bearing him' (134). This rush of feeling is partly the result of his wanderings amidst the local scenery, and partly from flirting harmlessly with local girls, Mabel included. Most importantly, Ken's growing acquaintanceship with Captain Mike McCarthy, a veteran of the American Civil War, sent ahead by his Fenian comrades to assess the lie of the land, kindles the desire that sublimates the uplift caused by girls and scenery. Land and liberty, material concerns and spiritual values: these integers of amiable social accord make common cause in Ken. The broad cast of characters who picnic together at Gougane Barra suggests a prototype of his nascent utopianism. In their ease of manner and elevated conversation, the picnickers enact an alternative that might regulate what Ken thinks of – in terms that wed horror to awe – as 'this great, half-instructed, human-hearted giant of an age of ours' (289).

This phrase suggests Ken's struggle to establish himself in his own times, a struggle represented by his somewhat inconclusive progress as a journalist, parliamentary candidate and, above all, revolutionary. What empowers and vindicates him is failure, which takes the form of his identification with a rather attenuated sense of a usable past. This sense reaches its apotheosis with his appearance in the dock of Green Street courthouse, 'that sad, royal house of Irish Patriotism, of which the gallows is the genealogical tree' (537). His keen appreciation of the precedent set by the words and deeds of Lord Edward Fitzgerald, Thomas Davis, Thomas Francis Meagher and related historical figures provides him with a birthright and a sense of tradition. Thus authenticated, Ken is a more worthy representative of the people than his election opponent Glasscock, who '[l]ike most men of his faith and of his year in Trinity . . . had tipped the "true and blushful Hippocrene" of Young Irelandism' (469) only to become the Irish Attorney General. What ignites Ken's rebel spirit in the present is the energy and commitment of Irish-America (in a concluding note, the author remarks of his work that 'the sketch idly begun grew insensibly into something like a picture of the transformation which the progress of American democratic ideas has brought about in Irish society' (549).) One reason that Ken looks up to Americans is that they are not boys. Those who eventually arrive have not only been tested in war, but are, in Harry Westropp's words, 'devilish fine fellows – as hardy as cannon-balls, every man of them!' (441). Such models of male accomplishment and maturity, and particularly their most imposing and experienced 'General', bring not only force of arms and organisational expertise to the cause of Ireland, but implicitly represent a political outlook that, like their physical presence, is 'as large as life – and that's large enough' (421). Vivid reminders are supplied by Captain Mike's reminiscences that they have already proven their worth as 'the men who carried Cemetery Heights at Gettysburg' (349). They are by no means the

'Garibaldians . . . infidels . . . Reds!' (172) denounced from the pulpit by the Drumshaughlin parish priest. Clearly such comrades are much more worthy of Ken's attachment than Jack Harold, whose flights of revolutionary fancy they tacitly repudiate. Jack ends up sailing to America, where what he has called 'my poor Daedalus wings' (257), clipped during his Irish double-dealing, may spread anew.

If American Fenians and their democratic energies represent one modernising tendency, another is shown by the way Harman's depredations are discovered by Joshua Neville, father of Mabel Westropp's gauche intended, Reggie. An ironmaster by trade, and a geologist by avocation, Joshua Neville lives up to his image of being the salt of the earth by his exhaustive investigation of the Drumshaughlin estate accounts. Patient, detailed and persistent, he represents the qualities required to unearth Harman's defalcations. Unprejudiced and level-headed, this father figure embodies a forensic, less emotive brand of leadership whose effects on Irish conditions may be as modernising as those of democratising Fenians; and the picture of a middle-class industrialist saving a landed aristocrat from his own physical and psychological absenteeism identifies one more colour on the novel's political spectrum. The ironmaster is not entirely disinterested, though his hopes of introducing 'blast-furnaces and steam-ploughs and all the rest of the modern apparatus for blinding and deafening people' (224) do not bear immediate fruit. A development that threatens a landscape that for Ken has 'something of the sanctity of a cathedral . . . and something of the mystery, beauty, and inspiration of the Future' (138) is of more than economic consequence. Yet, while his potential despoliation remains unrealised, Joshua Neville's actual intervention contrasts tellingly with the pallid and pointless bog-draining initiatives of Jelliland, the Irish Secretary, one of Lord Drumshaughlin's government cronies. And it also contrasts with the abortive Fenian Rising, in which the lack of a systematic approach among the locals convinces the Americans to withdraw in anger. Whichever the system, entrepreneurial or democratic, Ken seems adrift between them.

Joshua Neville and the American 'General' are both essentially pragmatists, but this is a philosophy more honoured in the breach than in the observance by the novel's action. The debacle perpetrated by local forces exemplifies the unpragmatic ways of 'your true Celt' (396). Harry Westropp's death, the separation of the 'Flying Column' (454) from other fighting units, the activities of a local Judas, and ultimately Ken's arrest show the fecklessness in local ranks. Yet the Rising's mismanagement and futility, rather than being a critique of Ken's boyishness, augment its appeal by adding bathos to his high-mindedness, as though defeat valorises his youthful desires. There is no indication, and no perceived need, that this boy may yet be father of the man. This portrait of Ken also implies that physical and material concerns may be left to others. To him remains the high ground, the lofty principle and the pure heart, an all-important spiritual homeland (its grandeur suggested by the topography of the Beara Peninsula) that conflates the patriotic and the divine, for '[i]f there is a more detestable thing on earth than a priest without a country, it is an Irish patriot without a God' (158). Yet, ultimately, Ken represents himself less in Catholic terms than in those of a nationalist sublime, an atemporal symbolic construct that is a vital, independent-minded counter to the strangers' pragmatism and that transcends 'that ugly apparatus of steel rails, telegraph wires, gaspipes and main drains that we call civilisation' (228), even while, in all innocence, falling for the allure of democracy.

The Fenian Rising is one of those acute crises in which protagonists find themselves as the Irish novel moves from the nineteenth century into the twentieth. Ken's desire to represent himself as the self-sacrificing son of a noble cause reveals that cause's amorphous composition, its vaporous pieties and abortive strategies; its immaturity. But if the national struggle is eclipsed – temporarily, as the narrator sees it: 'A Rising is (I may not yet quite say, used to be) a sort of Silver Jubilee in every generous Irish life' (434) – the sentiments that animate it remain undimmed. Such sentiments are pre-ideological; they derive from a natural endowment of qualities like spontaneity, liberality, candour and passion, not from the nurture of militancy. And in his abundance of these qualities, Ken seems to be a promising agent of the romance of union rather than of the violence of separatism. He brings out the 'Wild Irish Girl' (209) in Mabel; helps the Drumshaughlin peasantry to understand their economic interests; welcomes the collaboration of Harry Westropp and Reggie Neville; and rouses those 'Irish Parisians' (503), the citizens of Cork, with his parliamentary programme. He is an unwitting coordinator of a skein of sympathies and affections, typifying a community whose heart is in the right, pastoral, amenable place. Yet, when it comes to a choice between social harmony and revolutionary triumph, Ken cannot decide. Joshua Neville tells the fettered Ken that '[t]his is NOT THE END' (549), but it is as if the youngster is not sure whether the reference is to his body or to his spirit. As his jail-bound ferry sets off downriver into a fog, he for once is silent.

# 1891

## Oscar Wilde, *The Picture of Dorian Gray*

*Oscar Wilde (1854–1900) was born in Dublin and received his early education at Portora Royal School, Enniskillen, County Fermanagh. Entering Trinity College, Dublin, on a scholarship in 1871, he excelled as a student of classics; Greek literature and culture were mainstays of his artistic formation. His career at Magdalen College, Oxford, where he held a scholarship for four years from 1874, was no less impressive. There the aesthetic and cultural doctrines of Walter Pater and John Ruskin became major influences. From Oxford, Wilde entered the world of the London professional writer, and from 1879 the metropolis was the lieu théâtral of his literary success, his social lionisation, his flamboyant image and his reputation as a wit and* raconteur. *As is well known, London also saw the eclipse of his name and fame.*

*Literary success came largely through the theatre in the 1890s, but in the preceding decade Wilde produced a variety of work, mainly in prose, whose intellectual value and aesthetic appeal has been overshadowed perhaps by his plays and also by the culture of notoriety from which it remains difficult to dissociate him. His earliest journalism was aimed at the diverse Irish readership served by the* Dublin University Magazine *and the* Boston Pilot, *while his verse, some of it tinged with the Catholicism in which Wilde showed an interest in a number of his mature works – including the epistolary monologue* De Profundis *([1905], 1962) – appeared in the* Irish Monthly. *The emergence of Wilde's public persona owed much to his year-long lecture tour of the United States, beginning in 1881, in the course of which he acquainted a wide variety of auditors with not only his Ruskinian views on beauty but also his Irish artistic and political heritage. This American year also led to an 1883 New York production of* Vera, *Wilde's first play. The consolidation of his reputation as a speaker was followed by that of his aesthetic principles resulting from encounters with leading contemporary French authors. Of these, the Symboliste group exerted the greatest influence, although somewhat adulterated traces of Zola are evident in* The Picture of Dorian Gray.

*A two-year editorship of the periodical* Woman's World, *beginning in 1887, furthered Wilde's views on art as a dimension of living, and his aesthetic outlook also found more developed expression in such notable essays as 'The Truth of Masks' and 'The Critic as Artist'. These essays were collected under the quietly assertive title* Intentions *(1891), and their theorising of artistic practice, an important aspect of twentieth-century literary Modernism, together with their adaptation of Platonic dialogue (a Modernist strategy too), are additional indications of Wilde's innovation and originality. This period also saw the publication of* The Happy Prince and Other Tales *(1888), Wilde's first collection of stories. Two other collections –* A House of Pomegranates *and* Lord Arthur Saville's Crime and other stories *– appeared in 1891. The stories in the latter collection have more conventionally social subject matter, but Wilde's other stories are imaginatively more appealing; their ostensible fairytale form and content use that genre's perennial interest in youth and beauty both for their own sake and also to mask representations of power, desire, hierarchy and related themes. Wilde's use of this form is contemporaneous with, and in certain respects is not dissimilar from, that of W.B. Yeats. And fairytales are often thought to reflect Wilde's Irish heritage, the form linking him through his father's interest in legend and folktale to a distinctively Irish nineteenth-century cultural terrain. This connection is also suggested by two of Wilde's forenames, Oscar and Fingal.*

*Wilde's apparently irresistible rise to fame during the first five years of the 1890s began with the publication in* Lippincott's *Magazine (Philadelphia) of* The Picture of Dorian Gray *(1890); a revised, book-length version appeared the following year. Attacked by prurient London critics, the novel outlived its moment to attain the status of* Frankenstein *or* Dracula, *whose patrimony of gothic melodrama it partly shares. But the work is also a systematic, if not indeed somewhat programmatic, elaboration of Wilde's own artistic and cultural positions, a restless dialectic between freedom and morality, art and experience, social self-representation and private self-awareness. Wilde was uniquely placed to appreciate such dualities, not only as a London insider with an outsider's background but also as an artist whose evident delight in façades was matched by his spirit of critique.*

Among the connotations of the term 'Victorian' is a comprehensive range of expectations and prescriptions governing personal behaviour, a series of codes that presume to blend manners with morality and that produces a well-defended and unified consensus regulating matters of propriety, taste, class, duty and freedom. One of the many significant aspects of *The Picture of Dorian Gray* is its representation of the reverse of these norms as a compelling reality. Lord Henry Wotton's claim that '[t]he aim of life is self-development . . . the highest of all duties, the duty that one owes to one's self' (17) is one version of such a reversal that impresses the youthful, impressionable and 'unspotted' (15) Dorian. And in responding to Lord Henry's stimulus, the young man represents a crisis that occurs in an ultimately untenable area between public appearances in fashionable milieux and a withdrawn, secret, private space where his image disintegrates. Dorian's public venues – the drawing room, the theatre, the dinner table – are where his face ostensibly fits; his presence there need only consist of representing himself conventionally. His portrait, in contrast, shows a Dorian that not only his friends are not allowed to see but from which Dorian himself hides. The picture's confinement to an abandoned schoolroom is an additional reminder that it is a source of knowledge, memory and conscience – those essential components of an inner life – which Dorian disregards, a failure that costs him everything. As so often in the nineteenth-century Irish novel, the protagonist's 'double life' (175) seems as irresistible as it is unsustainable. But in *Dorian Gray* there is no conclusion in compensatory unity.

Duality is not only a condition that Dorian discovers through experience and wishes to suppress. It exists from the beginning. Indeed, it may be regarded as a parental bequest. For although the story of his mother's elopement and his father's death by duelling seems, at best, redacted incidents from *The Memoirs of Barry Lyndon*, in Lord Henry's view it suggests 'a strange, almost modern romance' (35), an episode of the righteousness of passion and of repression's murderous consequences that resonates with his lordship's criticisms of the conventions of his day. As such, the story is a further incitement for Lord Henry to shape Dorian according to his modern combination of theory and desire, the result of which will be not only to transform the youngster into 'a marvellous type' (36) but also to allow Lord Henry '[t]o project one's soul into some gracious form . . . perhaps the most satisfying joy left to us in an age so limited and vulgar as our own' (35). Thus Dorian will represent a 'return to the Hellenic ideal' (18) – a return to the unrepressed – as well as an occasion of delight. The combination of outward form and inner sensation offers Lord Henry a rare experience of uncritical wholeness. Yet this ideal is not merely the product of the older man's designs; it also requires belief in Dorian's surrender to them. Witty, debonair, cultivated and imperious as Lord Henry is – in many respects a representative of the age that he affects to despise – he exerts his power over 'this son of Love and Death' (36) as though Dorian's choosing to do what he is told is irrelevant.

Just as Basil Hallward has found Dorian irresistible, so Dorian finds Lord Henry. The portrait painter, however, has the discipline, the technique, the courage and the sense of form to respond to what intensely strikes him about the beautiful teenager. He creates a memorial of it, preserving and honouring it, so that it will by virtue of its aesthetic authority become a cultural icon, a creation that will typify a certain moment, a certain season, by outlasting it. In this case, too, Dorian lends himself to how he is being represented, so much so that he accepts the substitution of his actual, temporal presence by the formalised space of his portrait. The thought of such a reversal is a prototype for Lord Henry's refashioning of Dorian as his intellectual and cultural puppet. Basil does not have the courage of the conviction with which he painted the portrait, and in his reluctance to own up to his work on the grounds that 'I have put too much of myself into it' (2) attempts to repress the picture's full impact. Refusing to exhibit a painting is a form of false representation. In contrast, Lord Henry is too forthright in opening Dorian to adventures in the psychological and spiritual terrain that prevailing conventions keep in the dark, arguably putting so much of himself into his refashioning project that Dorian represents his mentor more than himself. Lord Henry's overdetermined reconstruction is, in its desire to be conclusive, also false. These different but interconnected valences of motive, power and personality, relating but also separating life and art, together comprise an intriguing panorama of the metropolis' cultural inner life, its taste and values, masks and dreams, its evasiveness and sense of purpose, its notions of form and its efforts to escape self-inflicted *ennui*. This depiction represents a more complicated and penetrating view of the deceptions and limitations required to keep surfaces intact than Lord Henry's rather glib objections to 'the sickly aims, the false ideals, of our age' (22) and the facile and 'so cynical' (81) paradoxes from which he derives an exhibitionistic, if not narcissistic, pleasure.

Dorian is the joint but contradictory creation of Basil and Lord Henry. He represents their social position and their cultivation, but also the distance between their two conceptions of him, a gap that desire can bridge but that experience can only widen. Neither version of Dorian can live up to what has inspired it. Hallward's artistic breakthrough must remain a secret. He worries about the public sphere on Dorian's behalf, and reproves him for having lost 'all sense of honour, of goodness, of purity' (151) when what he might have offered his friend is a less moralistic expression of the love he bears him. Dorian does not need criticism; he needs to be saved from the artifice, or

myth, he has embraced. The new thing into which he has been fash-
ioned should be something worth having – a persona that is less
destructive of his inner life, an ideal that will transcend the polarised
world of the spoiled élite and the sordid masses that people the
metropolis. In response to Hallward, he retains allegiance to the 'new
Hedonism' (22) advocated, though evidently not very assiduously
practised, by Lord Henry. He defends himself to Hallward by claiming
that 'I know the age better than you do' (153), as Lord Henry himself
might well assert and as the corrupt self-representations to which Lord
Henry has directed Dorian indicate. Dorian has seen beneath London's
veneer. Hallward can maintain his naïve, or romantic, or uncritical
hope that Dorian still has the potential to be 'fine' (151). Dorian is the
artist's compensation for the fact that 'English society is all wrong'
(ibid.) – because there is no evidence of dissipation to bear out his
concerns. But when Hallward sees the portrait, he cannot accept the
decay it depicts. Reversing the structuring terms of life and art, Basil
becomes the picture's actual, physical casualty, just as Dorian's suppression of what he sees renders him the portrait's moral victim.
Preserving that suppression by means of murder is a paradox more
bitter and telling than any of Lord Henry's; and Hallward's death initiates the dialectic of terror and safety – the conflict inherent in Dorian's
'devil's bargain' (189) – that intensifies somewhat melodramatically
after he kills one of his progenitors.

Hallward's criticism of Dorian is misplaced though well-meaning.
Lord Henry's indulgence of his protégé, through which he has chosen
to transmute his own *taedium vitae*, is also plainly misguided, though
in this case the critic evades the dangers that result from his representation of Dorian. Under the patronage of his lordship's theories, Dorian
foregoes memory and 'freedom of will' (190); he is advised to ignore
remorse of conscience and to cultivate what Lord Henry claims to be a
distinctively male accomplishment, 'the triumph of mind over morals'
(47). Dorian 'never fell into the error of arresting his intellectual development by any formal acceptance of creed or system' (133), but that
does not prevent him from exemplifying his sponsor's admission that
'[d]ecay fascinates me' (195). Such is Lord Henry's power over Dorian
that, even when the latter finds himself 'prisoned in thought' (188),
conscious to the point of breakdown of what he has permitted himself
to represent, he still accepts that '[y]ou are the type of what the age is
searching' (217). This assertion may indicate that Lord Henry, like Basil

Hallward, has no alternative but to maintain the necessity, and hence the indestructibility, of his creation, but it confers on Dorian a degree of consistency and affirmation whose aim effectively is to nullify the hidden life that the condition of his portrait signifies. The manner in which Dorian's two influences blur art and life suggests, perhaps, the prevalence of category errors in the culture at large, a condition that Lord Henry's paradoxes and his 'experimental method' (58) toy with.

Yet, while the two older men's artistic and cultural power over Dorian is considerable, there is also a certain degree of complicity in the young man's relinquishing himself to it. Such partnership in a knowing reconstruction of his nature is, from his point of view, not difficult to understand, given its aim of preserving his youth, beauty, lack of affectation, and amiability. The fairytale appeal of both vivifying frameworks, their conquest of time, their assertion of innocence in the face of experience, speaks for itself. And the possibility that, in embodying Lord Henry's doctrine, life might be intensified and complicated to represent 'the emotional coloured life of the intellect' (57) has a rare sheen of romance to it. (As to romance, Basil admits that keeping things hidden 'seems to bring a great deal of romance into one's life' (4). In certain respects, *Dorian Gray* is a swan song for romance.) Such heightening may be more clearly perceived in the light of an alternative romance, that of Dorian and Sybil Vane. This brief episode – a cockney Romeo and Juliet – seems more in keeping with Dorian's age and inexperience, as his announcement that it is 'the greatest romance of my life' (48) indicates – how many others can there have been? This is an attachment that has grown out of *his* life, not out of an existence on which he must model himself. And although the role of 'Prince Charming' (53) in which Sybil casts him – she being an equal partner in the experience of intense youthful feeling – accentuates the fairy story aspect of the encounter, there are more far-reaching elements to what the young couple represent. Among these is the opportunity to cross class boundaries, as daring and worthwhile an enterprise as any manifestation of the new hedonism. And, though Dorian seems unaware of it, his falling for Sybil is a reiteration in his own terms of the love match that gave him birth. Moreover, Sybil's on-stage failure before Lord Henry and Hallward suggests that she has no need of role-play now that a real-life romance is within reach. To judge the state of her feelings by theatrical criteria trivialises what she holds most dear. When Dorian leaves her – after removing the image he has conferred on her – she has nothing to live for. And Lord Henry's endorsement of Dorian's 'callousness' (91) is telling. The morally solipsistic dictum that '[i]f one doesn't talk about a thing, it has never happened' (107) – suggesting that if something is out of sight means it is also out of mind – is one of his more puerile notions.

Rejection of Sybil in effect denatures her. Unspotted, she too, like Dorian, is destroyed. And her name – prophetic, far-seeing – characterises her as a pointer to the artificial persona, the orchestration of appetites and pursuits, which inform his behaviour after her death. In view of how the East End is represented later on in the novel, and the threat of James Vane both to Dorian and to his country-house context, perhaps Dorian should have allowed nature to have taken its course. He and Sybil could have embodied the kind of ideal worthy of an exhausted civilisation, a union marked by tolerance, entered into with a clear conscience, and obviating Lord Henry's assumption that 'we are all afraid for ourselves' (74). This union, too, is a romantic scenario, and the amelioration it putatively represents may at best be regarded sceptically, as James Vane's suspicions of '[t]he young dandy' (66) confirm. Arguably Dorian sees Sybil in the same terms as he himself has been seen, and thinks her art is synonymous with her life, which leads to disillusion and destruction, a portent that he cannot imagine Sybil transmitting. Yet the attraction also has spontaneity, generosity and mutuality, qualities that the decadent Dorian later spurns, demonstrating further how depthless he has become – as depthless as paint on canvas. Romance or not, he and Sybil would at least have represented their independence. Such an attainment would portray a Dorian who would not be the subject of others' designs, consigned to an unchanging, ahistorical condition of fabricated identity and sponsored agency, the validity of which resided primarily in the eye of controlling beholders. That portrait would perhaps have a particular appeal to Irish readers, especially since it would counteract the condition of a subject who can only represent himself by being transgressive.

# 1892

## Emily Lawless, *Grania: The Story of an Island*

*The Honourable Emily Lawless (1845–1913), daughter of the third Baron Cloncurry, was born in County Kildare. Through her mother, she had a strong west of Ireland connection. This emerges in her first well-known novel,* Hurrish *(1886), set in the Burren, with a plot featuring the Land*

*League. It was Lawless's third published novel; its two predecessors – A*
*Chelsea Householder (1882) and A Millionaire's Cousin (1885) – are*
*lesser works in the drawing-room vein that their titles suggest.*

*Lawless also published two historical novels, With Essex in Ireland*
*(1890), a first-person account in journal form of the eponymous*
*Elizabethan's Irish activities, and Maelcho (1894), also set in Elizabethan*
*times. A final novel, The Races of Castlebar (1913) – a pastiche of a*
*contemporary account of one of the 1798 rebellion's most noted military*
*events – was completed by Shan F. Bullock. The historical bent of Lawless's*
*imagination is also shown in her poetry and short fiction. In the latter*
*genre, her Traits and Confidences (1898) also includes stories with an*
*autobiographical basis. Among her non-fiction works are Maria*
*Edgeworth (1904) and Ireland (1888; revised edition, 1912).*

*Emily Lawless's fiction does not demonstrate the penetrating gaze that*
*Somerville and Ross turned on the class to which she and they belonged.*
*Nor do her novels show any marked attachment to either the literary*
*style or cultural aspirations of the Irish Revival or to other contemporary*
*interests and outlooks. But her works reveal a thoughtful and sympa-*
*thetic disposition towards her native country, expressed most directly in*
*her appreciation of natural surroundings and conveyed in somewhat*
*plain but supple prose. Through her aristocratic background, she also*
*had access to London's élite social circles. Among her literary admirers*
*were such luminaries as George Meredith and Mrs Oliphant, a partic-*
*ular friend and literary influence; and Algernon Swinburne expressed his*
*keen admiration for Grania.*

*Displacement is a prominent theme in her work, possibly signalling*
*the author's consciousness of certain anomalies in her cultural standing*
*and artistic perspective, despite her oeuvre's favourable Irish reception.*

Although the sea on which the story of Grania O'Malley begins and
ends is 'almost her element' (81), it is less from how she fares on it than
from her efforts to eke out a living from the rocks of her native
Inishmaan that Grania attains her singular stature. Indeed her singularity derives from how she contends with the ebb and flow of her
position of being between land and sea, literally and figuratively. She
endures to a far greater degree than anybody else on the island the fluc-
tuations, meteorological and otherwise, of '[t]he "Old Sea," as the
islanders call the Atlantic' (80). And she is the only member of the community who confronts head-on her domicile's unyielding terrain.
Uniquely, Grania possesses not only a physique capable of unremitting
hard labour but a will to match. And she alone has the *élan vital* necessary to face the many vicissitudes, limitations and uncertainties of

island life 'thirty years ago' (49). The current of her vitality is sufficiently strong for her to experience passion and desire, and in such terms she can dream of a future. Grania is a body and a spirit, and her capacity to draw on the energies of both places her head and shoulders above the dispirited men and exhausted women who typify Inishmaan people. Moreover, her exceptional endowments appear to owe something of their racial and sexual distinctiveness to her mother, Delia Joyce, 'a tall, wild-eyed, magnificently handsome creature, with an unmistakable dash of Spanish blood in her veins' (62). Honor, Grania's older half-sister, credits Delia with 'the walk . . . of a queen' (125).

Delia died soon after giving birth to Grania, however, depriving her daughter of nurture but unwittingly ensuring that the girl's '[h]onesty, strength, courage, love of the direct human kind . . . came to her direct from the hands of Nature' (86). The power of this birthright is clearly seen in the contrast between Grania and her sickly sister Honor. As befits a child of nature, Grania is almost always active and outdoors; Honor is a housebound invalid. Honor's thoughts dwell on mortality and immortality; earth-bound Grania has neither time nor inclination for abstractions. Given her physical condition as well as the example of both girls' alcoholic father Con, Honor not surprisingly takes the view that 'men is a terrible trouble' (123); Grania is incurably infatuated with ne'er-do-well Murdough Blake. Yet, one-dimensional though Honor is, she has her uses. She carries out 'semi-sacerdotal duties' (73) – baptism, for instance; and as 'a saint – a tender, self-doubting, other-wise all-believing soul' (67), her essentially disembodied existence provides a necessary thematic counterweight to Grania's much more physical presence. In addition, Grania's faithful nursing of, and general tenderness towards, Honor tempers an entirely Amazonian perception of her, and she respects the fact that 'all women are not made like' (147) her virginal and long-suffering half-sister, a revealing aside on gender formation.

The pastoral services that Honor provides are necessary because the church at Inishmaan is a ruin half-buried under a drift of sand, and Father Tom, the nearest priest, is based in Kilronan, a circum-stance that adds to the representation of primitive, or at least pre-social, Inishmaan. And the absence of a priest is a resonant factor in the novel's conclusion. The ruined church is in keeping with the 'impression of ugliness' (92) that Inishmaan in general imparts. Its terrain is so harsh and ancient as to be 'unknown to geologists' (69), and its 'seven or eight so-called Cyclopean forts' (75), together with the roofless church, suggest that mainland institutions have not gained much of a foothold on 'the most retrograde spot . . . within the four seas' (57). To reinforce this vista of dereliction and abandonment, there is an out-of-place villa 'intended to imitate some small Greek or Roman temple' (79), the former property of a justice of the peace. Even if it has become 'a mere dirty, disreputable little "shebeen-shop" inside' (163), from a distance 'it shed an air of classical dignity, of half-effaced importance and prosperity' (158), and its former owner likewise is considered a relic of old decency by Grania's neighbour, Peter Durrane, '[a] queer old ragged Ulysses' (167). The idea of order implicit in the villa's design, and in the work of its erstwhile occupant, contrasts with the novel's greater emphasis on the island's marginality, remoteness and its tenuous character as a place of settlement. Inishmaan's uniqueness, admittedly remarkable, does not necessarily serve its best interests, and in any case is largely represented by tokens of the past.

For the most part, the islanders also are dilapidated and bereft. In addition to Honor, Inishmaan's women and children are afflicted somehow or another. Shan Daly's starving family seem 'full of ancient primordial horrors' (72); the storyteller Peggy O'Dowd might be 'taken for some sort of queer vegetable growth – a fungus, say, or toadstool' (102); the deaf-mute O'Shaughnessys are 'pariahs' (77) because of their disability, and the way they sign to each other resembles the action of 'some sort of ugly complicated toy' (82); their nephew Teigue is a simpleton; Shan Daly himself seems excessively primitive, possessing both 'the eyes of a wolf or other beast of prey' (50) and 'the harsh inarticulate cries of some infuriated ape' (53). It is debatable 'if there are such things as typical peasants or, indeed, any other varieties of human being' (61), and perhaps Lawless's physiognomies and other spoiled forms of self-representation are meant to suggest the inadvisability of facile classification and of the snap judgements that go with them. In all, however, these natives seem a lower form of life compared to the physically splendid Grania and the air of self-sufficiency and energy her build conveys. Lacking in structural support and prey to an unnervingly wide range of misfortune, the lives of Grania's neighbours verge on the entropic. Perhaps as a child Grania was 'a born aristocrat' like 'all children' (78), but such a generalisation hardly applies to puny and pathetic Phelim Daly, Shan's son and heir. Phelim is a token of an emaciated future, just as idle, drunken, vainglorious Murdough Blake represents the aimless present – 'a more typical young man it would be difficult to find' (86). In such a community, even Grania's youthful desire for 'life, life! sharp-edged life, life with the blood in it' (126) succumbs to weakness and lack of will.

The main reason for Grania's unfortunate fate is that she has found in Murdough Blake an object that is both impossible and unworthy. From childhood, Grania has had a strong attachment to Murdough. His boasting and logorrhoea hold her in thrall – '[f]or words, unlike Murdough, she had no talent' (87). As a 'well-developed specimen of youthful manhood' (93), Murdough may appear to be Grania's match, but his values, such as they are, have nothing in common with hers, being confined to airy notions regarding his own entitlements. His onrushes of verbiage about money and horses has 'nothing about it that she could attach any idea to' (97). Having no work of his own to do, Murdough might be expected to lend Grania a hand with hers, but that thought 'had long seemed to both of them a sheer absurdity' (98), a small indication that Grania is complicit in the unequal partnership. Indeed, in a phrase whose resonances attain full expression in the novel's climactic sequence, '[a] vast, untravelled sea stretched between them' (114). In addition, Murdough seems to be affected by a half-baked vision of modernity, in which everything 'beyond that grey wash of sea . . . hung before his eyes as a region of dangerous novelties, dazzling, almost wicked in its sophistication' (66).

Such imagining may be an expression of Murdough's callowness, but his aim to mask his origins by acquiring 'the good English' (94), and his later, far-fetched, hopes of becoming a ship's pilot suggest a desire for forms of self-representation other than Grania's island-grounded ones. This desire is perhaps a sign of Murdough's superfluity, his chronic passivity and his unstructured, alcohol-addled days. 'A quarter of a century ago no golden political era for promising young Irishmen of his class had yet dawned' (85), and that may be an influence on Murdough's lack of a consistent *raison d'être*, though it is also the case that any such era would not be likely to reach out to Aran for recruits, 'especially recruits who are innocent of any tongue except their own fine, old useless one' (ibid.). The absence of a cause, a principle, an affiliation, a self-actualising public structure – and the consciousness and perspective that such frameworks would provide – leaves Murdough emasculated. Not only is he sexually diffident to an unmanning degree, he is also in a state of moral inanition, deprived of the strength, competence, enterprise, worldliness and *savoir faire* that are conventionally thought of as the male birthright, not least by men themselves. Murdough is no citizen-prince like *Knocknagow*'s Mat the Thresher. Nor does that bother him.

Yet Grania clings to him. In keeping with her fidelity to blood and soil – to Honor and to their 'croggery' (141) – she remains faithful to Murdough to the point of helplessness. Implausible as this attachment might seem, it is a further expression of the passion and sensuality evident in Grania's general lust for life. The power of those elements is palpable when the two go fishing and, in a scene where the sea seems a vessel of sweetness and light and where an unwonted calm, warmth and innocence suffuse the moment, Murdough – at Grania's prompting – kisses her. Now she is no longer what a neighbour calls 'a very wild queer girl . . . [who] goes out to the fishing just like a man' (131). For her too, '[t]he common heritage was at last hers . . . . They loved; they were together' (175). Her world has changed, and though 'the iron convention of their class would have forbidden anything like open demonstrativeness' (173), the internal effect of intimacy cannot be denied. Or at least Grania cannot deny it (she never denies anything that impinges upon her). For Murdough, however, a kiss does not at all imply a change, much less a compact, as becomes clear when, at a fair in Galway, he abandons Grania to the unfamiliarity of the town and the indignity of waiting for him, 'used as she was to moving at her own free will amid the solitude and austere silence of her own island' (178).

Initially the trip to town appeals to Grania. 'It was good to look abroad' (ibid.), and she even entertains thoughts of 'that Dublin which Murdough was always talking about and pining to get to' (ibid.). But the crowds and the bustle alienate and distress her, and the cabin in which she shelters from a downpour presents a spectacle of impoverishment and suffering that evince feelings that are 'exactly the reverse' (181) of what she had felt in the fishing boat with Murdough. The whole day away from Inishmaan is 'a turning point' (183) and leads to a period of discouragement for Grania during which she not only breaks with Murdough but wonders if Honor's self-denying view that life is 'just a dream' (125) may be true after all. There are moments when 'a sense of having regained her old liberty' (189) returns, but Murdough's indifference has exposed her to the pain of self-awareness, of emotional rejection and a more intimate recognition of defeat than she had previously known. New to being vulnerable, her experience of which is reinforced by Honor's continued deterioration and the theft of her hard-won turf by Shan Daly, Grania finds it difficult to cope. The diminution of her inner strength preys on a mind that 'still worked as a child's mind . . . with a sort of dim diffuseness' (199). Such a mentality is insufficient for self-representation, and together with a shortage of material resources, she cannot readily see her way forward. Her 'wild, untamed vision of strength and savage beauty' (200) impresses a party of English visitors to Inishmaan. But it is also an image of somebody at bay. Her appearance does not represent a whole person. Her earlier immediacy of manner and forcefulness of character has been sapped by memory, by hurt and by a nagging, inarticulate realisation of displacement or usurpation.

She permits Murdough to resume contact, even though his drinking – '[l]ike most Irishwomen of her class . . . this was to her the sin of sins' (163) – has increased, he has acquired Shan Daly as 'his jackal' (208) and generally appears to be drifting from bad to worse. He exploits Grania financially, and as a *coup de grâce* the would-be pilot refuses to accompany her from fog-bound Inishmaan to fetch the priest for the dying Honor. Instead, Grania sets out with little Phelim Daly, the poorest possible replacement, though he does survive the ill-fated journey through the 'mountain made of smoke' (218) and summons Father Tom. Murdough, in effect, sacrifices Grania to his own fecklessness and, in what seems to be a complementary gesture, she sees no alternative to sacrificing herself for Honor. Her final voyage is a dramatic and well-sustained tribute to Grania's will, courage and self-assertion. The sequence is also an impressive statement of the high regard in which the author holds her. Yet the action through which Grania attains optimum self-representation is also the one that takes her life. The pathos of that outcome is most evident in her final moment as, buoyed up by a mass of kelp, she imagines that Murdough 'was lifting her in his arms' (237). This illusion of consummation, sustained by drift and uplift, is comparable to the 'floating mirage' (238) that Honor experiences as death takes her.

The impact of the Aran Islands on the nineteenth-century Irish imagination is an important and revealing chapter in cultural history, the significance of which begins to emerge at century's end when the place's linguistic and anthropological distinctiveness became more widely known and valued. To this chapter, *Grania*, published six years before J.M. Synge's first visit to Aran, undoubtedly adds some worth-while pages, even if the period dealt with looks back to Charles Lever's *The Martins of Cro' Martin* (1856) and *Luttrell of Arran* (1865). In addition to its Victorian interest in mapping and typifying, however, *Grania* also reveals a modernist fascination with the primitive. This dual perception, an attempt to combine the essential with the exceptional, reproduces itself in the narrative's every aspect. Splendid as Grania is, she cannot avoid being a victim. Metaphorically speaking, she is said to be 'a very isolated, and rather craggy and unapproachable, sort of island' (85), but her standing is eroded by the sea of troubles consisting of Honor's physical weakness and Murdough's moral cowardice. On finally parting with Murdough, Grania feels 'torn in two' (219), a condition also represented in her story by the failures of soil to support blood and of sexuality to engender continuing life. Despite her totemic presence and dauntless energy, Grania is unable to go it alone and has no future. Her independence – 'I would not be bid . . . not by anyone' (106), she tells Honor – cannot attain a stable form of representation. And her fate suggests a modern uncertainty as to what to do with the native, the unaccommodated, the pre-citizen, so to speak, the poor person rich in natural faculties, the emblematic yet exotic outlier in whom grandeur and futility contend. It does not seem right or proper that such a person should suffer from attaching herself to a layabout whose big talk consists of false representations. Nor does one life in the here and now seem an equitable price to pay for another's in the here-after. Such doubts are also part of Grania's bequest, and their relevance to an island rather larger than Inishmaan may be inferred from the problematical intersection of past and future which her story enacts.

# 1894

## Somerville and Ross, *The Real Charlotte*

*The literary partnership of Somerville and Ross consists of the cousins Edith Somerville (1858–1949) and Violet Martin (1862–1915), who wrote under the pseudonym Martin Ross. Both were members of noted Ascendancy families. Born in Corfu, Somerville grew up in Drishane House, Castletownshend, County Cork. She studied art in London and Paris. Martin was a member of the Connemara family of that name (Charles Lever draws on its history in The Martins of Cro' Martin (1856)). Family connections do not quite account for the almost uncanny closeness of a writing partnership that survived even Martin's untimely death, Somerville retaining their joint signature on the basis of continuing spiritualistic contact.*

*Their best-known works remain the stories of the Irish R.M. series –* Some Experiences of an Irish R.M. *(1899),* Further Experiences of an Irish R.M. *(1908) and In* Mr. Knox's Country *(1915) – which, though anathematised by nationalist critics, have, with their blend of light touch and knowledgeable characterisations, a distinctive place in the Irish short story's development. Their novels, however, beginning with* An Irish Cousin *(1889), are less concerned with the horse-and-hounds aspects of Big House life than with questions of continuity and integrity, of retaining possession while maintaining self-possession, together with variations on themes of union. (Martin, in particular, was active in Unionist politics towards the end of her life. Both women were also involved in the suffrage movement.) Important novels include* Mount Music *(1919) and* The Big House of Inver *(1925), though the absence of Martin's wit make these somewhat stiff. Other novels include* Naboth's Vineyard *(1891),* The Silver Fox *(1898) and* An Enthusiast *(1921), the last based on the career of the reformer Sir Horace Plunkett. Noteworthy among many non-fiction works are* Through Connemara in a Governess Cart *(1893), the autobiographical* Irish Memories *(1917) and* An Incorruptible Irishman *(1932), a biography of both Somerville's and Ross's grandfather, Charles Kendal Bushe (1767–1845), an opponent of the Union who became Lord Chief Justice of Ireland.*

*Somerville and Ross elevated the literary standing of the Big House at a time when its social prominence and economic significance were already in decline. Perhaps in acknowledgement of this turning point, they distance themselves from their material by their typical narrative strategies, particularly their satirical sense, which recalls, even as it surpasses in nuance and attack, that of Maria Edgeworth. Often read as comedies of manners, the works of Somerville and Ross also display more tight-lipped types of expression – admonitory, judgemental, valedictory – as they attempt to contain the uncertainty that is their chief preoccupation.*

Charlotte Mullen lives in Tally Ho Lodge, in the little County Galway town of Lismoyle. A small-time rentier, she has, at the age of forty, reached the point where the realisation of her social and personal ambitions is of paramount importance. Her social goal is to become a lady of the manor, and she also hopes for more from the unhappily married Roderick Lambert, agent of the nearby Dysart estate, than the easy social relationship that they already have. Her hunt for an upgraded version of self-representation – both for status and emotional satisfaction, for authentication in terms of class and sex, for the union of her outer persona and her inner needs – eventually proves a rather more complicated undertaking than the crude, if cunning, Charlotte can manage. Initially, however, her combination of forthright manner and inflexible will suggests that there is little that can stand in the way of her aspiring reinvention.

The lengths to which she is willing to go to secure the desirable property of Gurthnamuckla is an early indication of Charlotte's readiness to ride roughshod over anything that comes between her and her ambitions. The sight of this place elicits from her 'a sigh that was as romantic in its way as if she had been sweet and twenty' (53), but there is nothing soft-hearted about her treatment of the current occupant, Julia Duffy, whose eviction and institutionalisation in Ballinasloe mental hospital Charlotte takes in her covetous stride. A mixture of ruthlessness and amorality is not too subtly contained by Charlotte's outward show of affability and social inclusion. Ostensibly a member in good standing of the local Protestant community, Charlotte is at the same time given to the sharp practices that weaken social bonds. Not only does she become a victim of a self-generated conflict between means and ends, she also shows the vulnerability of her small band of co-religionists, who rely on reputation and social unassertiveness to maintain their position. She pursues so passionately her twin aims of higher social status and greater social visibility in the acceptable form of partnership with Lambert that it appears as though she has never quite settled in her own community, and she is dogged by intimations of being a misfit, lacking the gentility that is Lismoyle's pseudonym for passivity. Somewhat simplistically, perhaps, an ugly congruence is posited between Charlotte's unappealing physiognomy and a moral interior that too often yields to 'the anarchy of the lower passions' (229).

Charlotte's defeat results from her difficulty in coordinating a temperament that tends to override a balanced, accepting sense of her place in the social order. Yet, complying with such acceptance would be to deny herself agency. But her problems arise less from agency as such than from a failure to rein in her headlong progress (the authors' imaginative adaptation for purposes of social dissection of the blood sports with which their work is conventionally associated is revealing), and the transgressive breaches of good faith that litter her path, like so many divots from the common ground she shares with her Lismoyle neighbours. Moreover, she does not fall alone. Indeed, it might be argued that she would not have been dismounted, so to speak, were it not for her cousin Francie Fitzpatrick, although, since Charlotte invites this young woman to Lismoyle from the 'immutable, unchangeable' (3) stagnation of her northside Dublin home, here too the consequences are on her own head.

Francie is the decisive instance of Charlotte's efforts to impose herself reacting against her. In Francie's case, what Charlotte believed to be susceptible to her control proves beyond it. Half Charlotte's age, Francie is pretty and flirtatious, and perhaps because she possesses 'the gaiety and soullessness of a child' (68) she is also 'wholly without the power of self-analysis' (120). Already having caught Lambert's eyes, Francie quickly attracts the attention of two other male admirers. One is Lieutenant Gerald Hawkins, a member of the Lismoyle garrison, whom the impressionable girl regards as representing 'those heroes of romance' (37). The other is Christopher Dysart, heir to the local estate and an embodiment of 'the modern malady of exhausted enthusiasm' (179). That Francie favours both a bumptious soldier of the queen and a vapid *fin de siècle* figurehead testifies to '[h]er emotional Irish nature, in all its frivolity and recklessness' (274), characteristics that bear a family likeness to Charlotte's difficulties with self-control. Of the two swains, Charlotte is in no doubt that Christopher's prospects – land, title, Big House – are to his overwhelming advantage; and to hers. As the future Lady Dysart, Francie would obviously elevate Charlotte's standing. Her cousin's continuing infatuation with Hawkins, and her failure to take advantage of Dysart, persuade Charlotte to dispatch her back to her family, whose dismal fortunes are indicated by their current address, Albatross House, Bray.

This break between the two antithetical relations is preceded by – and is, in a sense, intended to arrest – trouble elsewhere. As a recipient of Lambert's attentions, Francie has developed into an infuriating threat to Charlotte, whose idea of re-establishing herself with her love object is to inform Lambert's hypochondriac wife of his behaviour, and also by confirming her worst fears by reading Francie's letters to him – further evidence of the lengths to which Charlotte's unchecked emotions can carry her. In this encounter with Mrs Lambert, 'the real Charlotte had seldom been nearer the surface' (173). Again, excess leads to crisis; Mrs Lambert suffers a fatal collapse. Instead of ensuring that Lambert remains tethered to a dead marriage, Charlotte has been instrumental in freeing him from it. Before long, events mock Francie's parting words when Charlotte sends her packing: 'I'll not deprive you of him . . . you may keep him all to yourself' (193). On the contrary, in keeping with the novel's elaborate counterpoint of projection and rejection, of what the ego proposes and the world denies, the very opposite takes place. Lambert weds Francie, inflicting on Charlotte 'the hardest blow that life could give her' (229). A woman scorned, 'the weight of the real Charlotte's will and the terror of her personality' (192) are now revealed as she exacts her revenge on Lambert. The result is the permanent frustration of her attempts to nurture an emotional attachment in him, and the irrepressible release of her primitive, impassioned nature.

In addition to snooping through Lambert's bank accounts, where she finds damning evidence of embezzlement, Charlotte also learns that he has cheated on a land sale. Charlotte's father preceded Lambert in the Dysart agency, so she is aware that the position 'had always been considered to confer brevet rank as a country gentleman upon its owner' (22), an awareness that has influenced both her social aspirations and her sense of Lambert's desirability. But Lambert is no more a gentleman than Charlotte is a lady. His first marriage was motivated strictly by fortune-hunting; he seems indifferent to the fact that a number of Dysart tenants have 'pledged themselves to the Plan of Campaign' (57); and his disregard for his employer's interests – and those of the social system that the Dysart estate represents – replicates on a social level his emotional indifference to Charlotte. Lambert's false self-representation places him at the real Charlotte's mercy. She reports his misdeeds to Sir Christopher (as he has become), though the latter's somewhat dilatory and spineless reaction indicates that maintaining the estate and what it stands for is not merely a matter of money but also requires leadership. Had Sir Christopher been a leader, Charlotte would not have had to prod him into action, nor indeed would Lambert have been able to indulge his own lack of self-command. The old social hierarchy would be intact, not prey to upstarts and wasters.

Charlotte's revenge on Lambert is the dark and destructive obverse of the partnership she once envisaged. Lambert 'had always been uncomfortably aware that she was intellectually his master' (252). Now she is his economic superior as well, demanding he repay her money she gladly loaned him and refusing to help him make good his Dysart shortfall. By this point, she has entered into her kingdom of Gurthnamuckla, but her reign as a person of property is indelibly tainted with the knowledge that her inner life, her feelings of love and the promise they portended, have been 'twisted to burlesque by the malign hand of fate' (236). The dream of union – of union as progress – is shattered. And while the invocation of fate can enhance the reader's sense of 'ignoble tragedy' (ibid.) that has befallen her, the novel's mordant and sometimes acerbic ironies show how Charlotte's attempts at reinvention push her to depths that she had hitherto concealed from herself and from Lismoyle.

The union between Francie and Lambert is also beset by internal weaknesses. Francie 'had never pretended either to him or to herself that she was in love with him . . . . There was nothing in the least romantic about having married him, but it was eminently creditable' (232). Lambert is, not unexpectedly, rather less attentive as a husband than he was as a suitor. Hawkins is still an importunate presence whom Francie – despite her 'Irish girl's moral principle and purity' (274) – fails to resist, with fatal consequences. In flight from Hawkins, Francie is unseated from her horse while disrespectfully galloping past the funeral of usurped Julia Duffy of Gurthnamuckla. This lamentable juxtaposition occurs while Lambert makes his final appeal to Charlotte. The latter is repairing a deteriorating Gurthnamuckla potato shed, but it is clear that her true *métier* is hammering nails in Lambert's coffin, particularly in the light of her telling him, 'you look as if you'd been at your own funeral' (290). Though neither Lambert nor Charlotte know it yet, there are other funerals, recent and imminent, whose literal impact and figurative resonance comprise a wake left by Charlotte's excesses.

Lady Dysart 'was an Englishwoman and, as such, constitutionally unable to discern perfectly the subtle grades of Irish vulgarity' (12). She takes Charlotte as she finds her. But *The Real Charlotte* is not as uncritical and indeed her ladyship's complacency does not escape its scathing perspective. Throughout, vulgarity is the term that consistently registers the narrator's cutting standpoint. It is a codeword for excess or lack of proportion; for not knowing one's place or, worse, not keeping to it; for allowing the ego's grasping impetus to overrule straight dealing, good order and proper manners necessary for communal well-being and stability. Vulgarity's signature is overdoing things, which is all the more necessary to avoid in the minority community like Lismoyle's, where the done thing and predetermined self-representation are not merely social amenities, they underwrite a disciplined observation and perpetuation of status, difference and self-possession. For Charlotte, the land hunger implicit in her desire for

Gurthnamuckla is not easily distinguished from the desire that impels her to make Lambert her own. And there are additional reasons why, even before she begins to plot, she seems out of place and unfitting. Her unprepossessing looks, 'strong, acrid voice' (174) and other features make her an exception to conventional standards of femininity. While her father held the Dysart agency, on the female side her grandmother was 'a barefooted country girl' (12) – hence, Charlotte's 'Irish peasant woman's love of heavy clothing' (150); and she has 'a strain of superstition in her that, like her love of the land, showed how strongly the blood of the Irish peasant flowed in her veins' (223). If, as a Dysart English house guest maintains, 'Irish society was intolerably mixed' (42), Charlotte is too much of a mixture, coarse and cunning, volatile and vindictive, in part a daughter of the people and in part an eager *habituée* of fashionable events. If the designation Anglo-Irish connotes an idea of balance, of accord between self and system, Charlotte can never be more than a caricature of it. And her efforts to represent herself as anything more exposes, among many other aspects of her character, a hasty and unready run at independence.

Francie's differences from Charlotte do not mask their kindred in certain fundamental respects. The girl's *parvenu* status makes her seem an outsider, too, and her vulgarity is as pronounced as Charlotte's, as her social gaucherie attests. But in youth and experience, Francie can only be a plaything who risks being broken when the players tire. As for Lambert, he is obviously more of an insider than either of the two women. Yet the veneer of his occupation and appearance covers a personality that must allow cavalier materialism to have its way at all costs. His indulgence in headstrong behaviour emerges when he almost drowns Francie in an avoidable yachting mishap, an incident recalled later as '[s]he swept towards her ruin like a little boat staggering under more sail than she could carry' (278). Charlotte's vulgarity is a symptom of her general overreaching; Francie's of her social insecurity. But Lambert's recklessness shows a temperament more crass than either. For all three, ambition and desire are derailed by the very energies employed to realise them, disestablishing intended forms of union and the expectations of loyalty on which those forms presume. In addition, the way of life – the manners, appetites, methods and morals – that the threesome represents also contravenes those of their own community; and, Charlotte's origins notwithstanding, they obviously have no identity of interest with

Catholic society, here largely represented by a chorus of service providers, querulous, powerless and unillusioned, though also more dangerously in the know than anyone but the two-faced Charlotte recognises.

The middle ground that Charlotte, Lambert and Francie occupy mixes Lismoyle's two traditional worlds, high and low. Yet in neither are they quite servants or masters. In a sense, Charlotte is kin to John Hogan of *Hogan, M.P.* in her economic aims and self-advancing instincts, but the moral compass that Charlotte boxes is empowered by a strongly subjective sense of entitlement; unlike Hogan, she is no catspaw. If she represents an emerging class it is one that can assert its interests only by betrayal. For all the satirical verve and narrative fluency that make *The Real Charlotte* one of the most artistically accomplished nineteenth-century Irish novels, the work also sounds notes of judgement, misgiving and indeed warning. Dysart's spine-lessness, Hawkins' philandering and Lambert's slackness make them unworthy, uncomprehending, representatives of the social system that they must live up to, their inadequacy tellingly replicated in the indif-ferent quality of their maleness – also like Hogan. The hegemony that these men's conduct should honour is undermined by their failure to identify actively with its collective, supposedly unifying interests. The consequences of failing – their failure as gentlemen – are seen in the inclination to exploit Francie rather than to save her from herself.

Charlotte, perhaps unexpectedly, is 'a great and insatiable reader' (20) whose tastes include 'works of fiction of a startlingly advanced kind . . . many of them French' (ibid.). Such works deal with, to cite a Zola title, *La Bête Humaine*, and highlight the monstrous appetites and blighted destinies that bloodlines bequeath. The real Charlotte Mullen is something of a rough, modern beast, but, as her reality is uncovered, so is that of her social context. The novel's depiction of an imbalanced coexistence between self and world conveys degrees of moral drift and social slippage that show *The Real Charlotte* – a story of missed opportunities – reaching well beyond its surface's diverting immediacy to disclose unsuspected cracks in the codes and struc-tures, loyalties and obligations, that constitute the supposed compatibility of Anglo and Irish.

# 1897

# Bram Stoker, *Dracula*

*Abraham Stoker (1847–1912) was born in Clontarf, Dublin. After a successful social and academic career at Trinity College, where he read science and went on to take a master's degree in mathematics, he studied for the bar and became a member of London's Inner Temple. Instead of practising law, however, he took an administrative position at Dublin Castle. His career as a bureaucrat led to his first book,* The Duties of Clerks of Petty Sessions in Ireland *(1879) – the importance of efficient organisation recurs throughout his fiction. But by the time the book was published, Stoker had abandoned the civil service for theatre management in London.*

*Reviews he wrote as a Dublin playgoer led to Stoker's introduction to the actor Henry Irving. And when Irving began his occupancy of the Lyceum Theatre in 1878, Stoker became his business manager, a position he retained until 1902, during which time the Lyceum was among the Anglophone world's most noted theatres. Stoker commemorated his years with Irving in a two-volume tribute,* Personal Reminiscences of Henry Irving *(1906). Irving's imposing physical presence and arresting personality are thought to be bases for Count Dracula.*

*Stoker's writing career ran parallel to his managerial commitments, and while Dracula's success and longevity has overshadowed his other fiction, he did produce a reasonably substantial oeuvre. His early novels, of which* The Snake's Pass *(1891) is perhaps the best known, are adventure stories akin to those by contemporary authors such as Robert Louis Stevenson and H. Rider Haggard; and it might be said that Stoker's later works are, from the point of view of genre, intriguing variations on the remote settings and sense of duress typical of such narratives. Stoker's post-*Dracula *works include* The Jewel of the Seven Stars *(1903),* The Lady of the Shroud *(1909) and* The Lair of the White Worm *(1911), each of which is a restatement of the threats and vulnerabilities so comprehensively represented in the work that has secured the author's undying reputation.*

*The fears that Stoker's novels bring to the fore are so numerous, so deep-seated in individual psyches and so menacing to public well-being, as to suggest that the present and all that has gone into making and sustaining it is in a permanent state of imminent eclipse. The obscurity of the danger, the uncertainty of a way forward, the weakness of the flesh and the frailty of the spirit that typify the troubled moment can be allayed only by efforts of an extraordinary intensity, dedication and resourcefulness by a small corps of volunteers. Such parlous conditions are central to much popular literature of the day, writings descended from mid-century sensation novels, among them those of Sheridan Le Fanu. The fears of Stoker's works are more wide-ranging, and derive not only from alien sources of psychological and cultural power but from an awareness of uncertainties produced by an accelerating and expanding modernity, challenges to imperial authority, changes in men's and women's social behaviour, and the neuroses created by a fin de siècle cultural atmosphere overcast with preoccupations regarding race, disease and degeneration. Such concerns raise questions about morale, control and order, about hierarchies and the unities they impose, and about the threat of the other. Defending metropolitan civilisation also requires that no alien, undeveloped area such as Dracula's Transylvania (a metonymy for all marginal regions, Ireland included) resurrect itself, rejuvenated by cultural traditions and mental energies that have remained un-dead – to borrow the term that was originally intended as Dracula's title.*

Bram Stoker's Count Dracula is not the camp exotic in a dress suit that latter-day cinema audiences have found so titillating and intriguing. On the contrary, Stoker's vampire is an evil to be extirpated, a threat to be taken with the utmost seriousness. This blood-sucking menace from beyond the pale must be dealt with by the most strenuous efforts across a coordinated number of fronts. And it is on these efforts that *Dracula* essentially focuses. It is not only that the Count is invasive and insidious, that his methods are repellent and his nature inhuman. In addition, his actions and character undermine those fundamental institutions such as marriage, medicine and the law which lend cohesion and substance to the all-important secular order. Should the values of mutuality and interdependence upon which these institutions rely be degraded, or the sense of duty that maintains them weaken, a terminal crisis will ensue, fatal alike to personal identity and social discipline. In a sense, *Dracula's* 'chivalrous' (258), self-appointed group of defenders anticipates the ethos of taking up 'the white man's burden' propounded in the eponymous Rudyard Kipling poem of 1899. (Part of the burden is to police the 'Half-devil and half-child' of which the alien other is compounded, a description that also applies to Count Dracula.) The upshot is a narrative of a clash of civilisations, of opposing powers, and of the various types of strength these powers embody.

The imminence of crisis, of the extreme, of being 'hedged in with difficulties, all of us' (128), obviously also helps to magnify the alien's mysterious persona. Dracula's origins in 'one of the wildest and least known portions of Europe' (8); his capacity to represent himself falsely as a winged creature or grotesquely as a ravening male predator; his capacity to operate outside the normal space–time continuum; these and numerous other distinctive attributes combine to form, in terms of the familiar categories of species, nationality and social functioning, an otherness that seems as impenetrable as it is irresistible. And his distressing, subversive enterprise seems a perversion of the very resources that are brought to bear against it – not only professional ones like medicine but also equally vital ethical, moral and spiritual assets. Dracula's demonic drive articulates a system, grounded in historical heritage and expressed through a regressive pattern of essentialising and return; and it will take a system to counteract him. The superiority of the latter system and a demonstration of its value in action is what must be brought about. Thus, Dracula's undoubted power, the malign character of which is revealed not only in his repulsive physical methods but in his intention to enslave, is a test, a trial, an ordeal. And as the Count's vampirism targets inner mortal realities – affective, mental, sexual; a nexus signified by life-sustaining blood – the means to resist it must themselves draw on interior qualities such as faith, intellect and trust. Seeing those qualities in the clearest light, however, comes only when the threat to them attains critical mass, suggesting that there is a certain dialectical relationship or even complicity between attack and defence, menace and remedy, the dark world of Dracula's 'earth-home, his coffin-home' (255) and the realm of 'lights' (196) where those willing to devote themselves to a 'great quest' (232) reside.

The antagonists feed off each other, each seeking the triumph of its own world-view. Dracula and his opponents have the same goal, the validation of their power; and both take taboo-breaking liberties to secure it. Between the two there seems to be something of the intimacy that is said to exist between quarry and prey, an association underlined by the pursuit of Dracula having been unwittingly rehearsed by 'our hunting parties and adventures in different parts of the world' (325). (This is an instance of how Stoker adapts a staple of the adventure story to serve his novel's more far-reaching, though no less adventurous, objectives. Further, Dracula's parasitism and his interloping, fly-by-night manoeuvres recast the activities of the typical adventurer – the cad, the snake in the grass – with which nineteenth-century Irish and Victorian novels abound.) The opposing parties' secret sharing constitutes the narrative's dual reality, represented most explicitly in the 'dual life' (214) attributed to Lucy Westenra, Dracula's principal victim, whose fate is the immediate pretext for the 'stand-up fight with death' (158) of the novel's action. More generally, as may be seen from the opening sequence detailing Jonathan Harker's business trip to Castle Dracula, the dual character of conditions reveals itself in the coexistence of the everyday world of domestic custom and business affairs with the activities of a foreign body that degrade the idea of home and use commonplace dealings as a screen for subversion. Further, Harker considers himself complicit in the horror he has unearthed by facilitating Dracula's removal to London. 'The very thought drove me mad' (60), he reports, and not only does he eventually break down, so do those ties, commitments and forms of communication on which both valid self-representation and reliable social interaction are based.

As guest-turned-captive, Harker is one more example of being in the critical position of *between*. He is cut off from his beloved Mina and from the forms of self-representation afforded by his practice of law; and the distance that he is from these two regulating and validating mainstays – the geographical distance and the distance from secure perspectives – ensures his inability either to advance or return. Yet, to appreciate fully the implications of Harker's plight, a more intense drama of physical confinement and psychological duress, complete with a helpless but appalled audience (or witnesses), is required. Beginning on a conventional dark and stormy night and the running aground of what is effectively a ghost ship, the *Demeter* (the name of the Greek goddess associated with the life cycle – or, arguably, eternal recurrence), this drama unfolds through the deterioration of the spirited and much-desired Lucy Westenra. The spiritedness for which her good looks were the outward sign is transformed by some strange internal storm, a riot in the blood expressed in terms of a personal entropy, of which the most serious consequence is the contamination of the 'clean grit' (67) that her American suitor Quincey Morris prizes in her. The degenerating, increasingly 'bloodless' (121) Lucy no longer represents the ideal of womanhood that her three admirers have esteemed. Apart from any other consideration, her seduction into the ranks of 'the wanton un-Dead' (393) compromises her sexuality. Blood donations are the form that physical intimacy must now take, and though his donation convinces Lucy's fiancé Lord Godalming that 'she was his wife in the sight of God' (185), the contrast between such a union and the expressions of companionable reciprocity that typify the marriage of Harker and Mina reveals the pathos of his lordship's attempts to keep his ideal of womanhood alive.

Lucy's passive seduction into deviancy is one representation of Dracula's terroristic power. The threat is not only sexual and intimate, though that in itself is sufficiently disturbing to conventional social constructions of the feminine. In addition, Lucy's physical downfall has larger implications for mating, the marriage market and the maintenance of blood lines (her betrothal to Lord Godalming points to such concerns). The violated and abandoned female body has an emblematic force in addition to, and perhaps sublimating, its sexual nature; in it may be seen the defacement and abjection of an ideal that disciplines and reorients the beast in man, the mark of which is one of the vulpine Dracula's most graphic characteristics. This ideal is central to the gentlemanly code the observance of which was a crucial means of substantiating the Victorian era's claim to be a civilisation. But Dracula doesn't stop at female despoliation. His assault on the male is equally consequential, as the case of Renfield and its implications reveal. Here, as a counterpart to Lucy's bodily travail, the mind is under attack. And rather than being a representative of all that is good in his sex, as Lucy is of hers, Renfield's deviancy is active, dissident and exceptional to such a degree that 'a new classification' (80) is required to deal with his zoophagous mania.

Lucy is mastered by the vampire; but, for Renfield, Dracula is freely and provocatively acknowledged as 'the Master' (111). (Mastery is a recurring preoccupation; John Seward, Jonathan Harker and Van Helsing are at various points all considered masters, a designation signifying expertise, intellectual prowess and independence. These three characters' combined possession of different aspects of mastery makes them central to the élite corps that ultimately triumphs over the dark invader.) The assault upon consciousness that constitutes Renfield's condition represents him as a different form of threat, one who has broken ranks with male composure and self-discipline, who has required isolation from the realm of good order, institutional compliance and bond of trust by means of which the male maintains coherent self-representation in the world of his peers. As Dracula's creature, Renfield offends not only behaviourally but conceptually against the shared male ethos of the daylight world, and its presumption of intelligence and its faith in remediating wholeness. And again, the afflicted one is essential to the eventual diagnosis and casting out of Transylvanian possession.

Rejected by Lucy, Seward, the third of her swains, wishes for 'a good unselfish cause' (80) in which to immerse himself. Although he is Renfield's keeper, he does not see that patient leading to such a cause but regards him in strictly clinical and institutional terms. Seward's asylum is a little too conveniently next door to Carfax, the house that Harker sold to Dracula, but he has little inkling of his neighbour's boundary-breaking influence. Such limited perception testifies to Seward's professional focus. It also allows Lucy's fate to be the basis of his further endeavours, beginning with his recruitment of the father figure, Van Helsing – the good, learned, Christian foreigner who contrasts to such decisive effect with Dracula and his 'child-brain' (322), in whose 'barren land . . . the forces of nature . . . are occult' (340). Led by his old mentor's example, Seward is able to look past 'our scientific, matter-of-fact nineteenth century' (254); that is, to go beyond his forensic interest in Renfield and to acknowledge a realm that lies outside 'rational explanation' (217). This realm is represented not merely by the un-Dead but also by the symbol of redemptive and eternal life, the Host, which Van Helsing uses, 'going down his own road' (213) – that is, the evidently one necessary and sufficient road. The resultant broadening of perspective and introduction to new methods also enables Seward to accept the shocking treatment of head and heart, ensuring the death of Lucy's vampire persona. The dual emphasis on both the seat of affection and of cognition, and the sense that these properly make up a union, is elaborated upon in the further progress towards Dracula's end and its interdependence of theory and action, faith and method, and heartfelt commitment and mental endurance exemplified by the group of embattled attackers who, like 'old knights of the Cross' (341), take their crusade to the infidel in order to preserve England's home and beauty.

An important credential of this 'little platoon' (to use a phrase of Edmund Burke's) is its maleness; the importance not only of the existence of 'good, brave men' (331) but that the men concerned are aware of their maleness and of the virtues and obligations it connotes. Lord Godalming exhibits his 'stalwart manhood' (179) in carrying out the gruesome last rites on his beloved; and Quincey Morris is no less a man – indeed he attains what seems to be intended as the racial ideal of 'a moral Viking' (185) in assisting him. Seward is man enough to risk 'the perils of the law which we were incurring in our unhallowed work' (213) at Lucy's tomb. Membership of the group reveals Jonathan Harker as 'never so resolute, never so strong, never so full of volcanic energy, as at present' (243). Most notably, Mina Harker, though she chooses 'meekness and righteousness' (307) over the self-empowering outlook of the New Woman, is admired by Van Helsing for her 'man's brain' (250). He particularly approves of the organisational acumen that he and Mina share and which lends to the crusading enterprise a sense of inner order and collective purpose which is continually challenged by the urgency of Dracula's machinations, his speed of action and above all his capacity for false representation. Mina's tireless managerial efforts, her combination of the conventional marriage and familiarity with modern technology, and her creation of 'a whole connected narrative' (240) comprise one version of 'the world of thought' (132) that Van Helsing embodies. It is this world that, not merely by virtue of its intellectual content but by the care and insight with which that content is availed of by disinterested 'men of the world' (273), eventually triumphs, though not without Quincey Morris' 'belief in Winchesters' (345) and Mina's own acknowledgment of 'the wonderful power of money' (378).

Mina's diligent application, her total devotion to the cause, is an individual exemplification of the values represented by the corps as a whole. In addition to both their superior intellectual abilities and the moral qualities that their manhood is claimed to enshrine, trust and the 'power of combination' (254) are also essential elements in Mina's makeup, as her eventual inclusion in the group's victory indicates. Yet she also has undergone the 'baptism of blood' (343) of her friend Lucy, and her graphic representation of that initiation shows her to be among the group's enemies, even as she is one of its key members. Brain sides with good; blood absorbs danger. In this duality Mina recapitulates a more intense and decisive iteration of Jonathan's earlier *between* condition, one that is both at the service of loyalty and union while simultaneously in the grip of a debased and debasing perversion of such cohering affiliations. The presence under the skin of subversion and its deviant authority will remain unless the will and the means to 'unmask' (200) prevail. And perhaps depicting the interface between union and disunion has a particular resonance in Irish conditions, where, in addition, blood-sucking has a distinctive metaphorical bite. It is also the case that the publication of *Dracula* roughly coincides with attempts to resuscitate Irish national self-respect through rhetorical and organisational engagement with cultural traditions hostile to 'this enlightened age' (341), while another spectral cross-current emerges in the commitment to extirpation and remediation of a small, self-appointed group of Dublin activists.

# 1901

## P.A. Sheehan, *Luke Delmege*

*Patrick Augustine Sheehan (1852–1913) – commonly known as Canon Sheehan; he was raised to that clerical rank in 1903 – was born in Mallow, County Cork, and trained for the priesthood at St Patrick's College, Maynooth. He was appointed parish priest of Doneraile in 1895, a town with which his name has remained closely linked, partly because his writing life was spent there.*

*Sheehan's first novel is* Geoffrey Austin, Student *(1895), and he is primarily known as a novelist, but his wide-ranging output includes children's books, devotional literature, a volume of poems and a collection of sermons. His early essays, particularly those on education, gained him a reputation in intellectual circles. Subsequently, he published two collections of essays,* Under the Cedars and the Stars *(1903) and* Parerga *(1908), 'a companion volume'. These works reveal a well-stocked, sophisticated intelligence. A supplement to these works is* The Literary Life and Other Essays *(1921). And related to his non-fiction is his novel* The Intellectuals *(1911), a work notable not only for its title but for its anti-sectarian argument. Constructed as a set of conversations between speakers from different parts of the United Kingdom openly exchanging views, this novel shows a more obviously engaged and public-spirited author than Canon Sheehan is popularly thought to be.*

*His reputation, however – and Canon Sheehan is one of the most widely known nineteenth-century Irish novelists – is based on such works as* My New Curate *(1899),* Glenanaar *(1905) and* Lisheen; or The Test of the Spirits *(1907). The Doneraile conspiracy of Daniel O'Connell's time is the setting for* Glenanaar, *and* The Graves of Kilmorna *deals with the Fenian Rebellion. Another historical novel,* The Queen's Fillet *(1911), is set in the French Revolution. These works are written in a straightforward, though not necessarily plain, style and are simply plotted. With some notable exceptions, Sheehan's intellectual energies and engagements are implicit in his sympathies rather than articulated in sermonising.*

*A particular fictional interest of Sheehan's is the priesthood, and his treatment of it significantly redresses the numerous caricatured clergy in the nineteenth-century Irish novel. His priests are largely portraits in humanity who experience their roles as conflicts between duty and tolerance, the fallible parishioner and the moral law. They invariably tread the path of righteousness, and are never allowed to lose faith. Their representation can have an air of tout comprendre c'est tout pardonner about them, evident in a sometimes avuncular attitude to their flock and in the flock's fundamental harmlessness and compliance. The possibility of goodness outweighs the reality of sin in these works, and perhaps this outlook is the reason why the typical Sheehan protagonist is a young man, inexperienced rather than culpable, hotheaded rather than defiant. Nevertheless, Sheehan's detailed knowledge of the provincial Catholic petit bourgeoisie, his principal milieu, does extend the scope of the Irish novel, and also tacitly establishes a sense of provincial distinctiveness that is regarded as a proud possession by those who embody it. The result is an illuminating form of cultural pastoral that ultimately projects a sense of the security and benevolence of the relationship between priest and people, and that is all the more valuable and worthy of trust when other social and political connections between the faithful and their representatives are rife with worldliness and instability.*

Despite having graduated 'First of First' from Maynooth and being 'fond of analyzing – a dangerous habit' (25), young Luke Delmege has a lot to learn. And how he learns it and what conclusions are reached comprise this 'life-history' (12), written after his death by one of his fellow-priests in the belief that 'life has a lesson' (13). This choice of form and sense of purpose presuppose that the tortuous path on which Luke's personality and ideas embarked constitute a particular kind of good from which others may derive instruction and awareness. From that point of view, *Luke Delmege* is a novel of consciousness, and indeed is a noteworthy early instance of an Irish novel devoted to the thorny reality of that realm. Thus, the conflicts, problems, trials and difficulties that Luke experiences, in addition to the manner in which these are ultimately overcome, have an exemplary interest. In being a problematical figure, Luke becomes a representative one.

His experiences crystallise his generation's difficulties in stabilising such categories as faith and fatherland, the lure of the modern and the tug of tradition, metropolitan manners and rural verities. Luke is both a young man from the remote Munster countryside and a student of outstanding academic ability. He rejoices in the novelties of thought, and has a particular relish for the bracing uplands of German theology, but he must also abide by clerical orthodoxy. His 'plastic Irish nature' (171) enables him to adjust superficially to the tone of English presbyteries, but everywhere he remains 'as much alone as Werther and his stars' (146), as a colleague remarks, and the seven years he spends in England as a young priest almost cost him a sense of his nationality. Institutional life and its obligations offer Luke a discipline and structure that, for reasons of intellectual pride and reformist ardour, he finds irksome. And if his understanding of his priestly self and of how he should be representing himself in it almost invariably lead him astray, so does his wayward inner life ensure that he more often than not gets in his own way. Luke's forthright opinions are controversial partly because they are the product of 'a hundred, naked, quivering nerves' (78). His lack of 'that first accomplishment, self-control and reserve' (53) results in such excesses as an apparent inability to talk to anybody without arguing. And, 'like so many other fools . . . a dread introspection of self' (42) besets him, and is made worse by 'his singular and irremediable mistake of supposing . . . that human action was controllable always by those definite principles that he had been taught to regard as fixed and unchangeable truth' (43).

Priggish, immature, intellectually ambitious, impatient with authority, Luke has arguably too much to contend with, even if some of these flaws may be regarded as an overflow of the youthful virtues of passion, conviction, idealism and hope. Yet the burden of the young man's mentality also generates a narrative strategy. A range of challenges – unfamiliar settings, disputatious clerics, intellectual adventurism – are required, as though to enact a pilgrim's progress. The view of the barriers Luke must overcome, the impressions he has to dispel, the reconciliation he is obliged to embrace, represent the magnitude of what is at stake. A rhythm of departure and resettlement marks the recurring occasions when Luke seems out of place, with each new curacy an unexpected variation on his continuing problems of ego and attachment. There is even a hint in his name of being a born outsider, the Palatine origins of which give Luke a somewhat metaphysical German connection. It is while vacationing in Germany that he experiences 'a turning-point' (263), even though the turn takes a long time to complete. And while his surname might prove 'wholesomer' (73) in England than a typical Irish one, especially 'if you pronounce it in the French fashion' (ibid.), there is a sense that Luke cannot help but be an exile on the English mission.

The complicated intertwining of office and domicile, thought and purpose, and the ideations that they prompt reveal how unformed this new curate is. In London, 'what he afterwards regarded as the strongest characteristic of this English people – their surprising "individu-alism"' (97) – introduces him to a worldly, understated, personalised range of outlooks that shows a dogmatic priestly persona to be bump-tious and overbearing. But Luke persists in his overdetermined view of how he should represent himself, maintaining his conception of pastoral duty as an essentially intellectual responsibility (though his sermons go over everybody's heads), while hoping that 'he could break through the crust of self-opinion that gathers around the right of private judgment' (166). Yet his critical attitude to Protestantism, expressed in such claims as 'they found their liberty in the assertion of individual freedom; sensuality followed' (158), does not affect a growing conviction that there is little difference between the English and the Irish, if only a 'valiant knight' (178) would point out the sim-ilarities. But his position on national differences seems another instance of Luke's committing the error of false representation, or 'the fatal sin of self' (489). Like the many other assertions in terms of which he misguidedly represents himself, his chivalric fantasy is moti-vated by ego rather than service. And as such, it is a symptom of the modernity to which Luke aspires and of which his career is a criticism and a rejection.

The primary representation of that modernity is the metropolis itself, which Luke essentialises in physically repellent terms. In its spirit-crushing life, the city resembles being 'imprisoned in some huge, infernal Tartarus of cranks and wheels' (98), while at a more localised level the urban scene confronts Luke with 'the dread embodiment of vice' (89) in the person of an Irish prostitute. In dreams, the city appears to him 'as a huge dead carcass' (92) – not a victim of Dracula, perhaps, but the image of a pathology nevertheless. And these arguably derivative general views of London are represented in more intimate terms by the fate of Luke's friend Louis Wilson. He is the nephew of the canon who is Luke's first mentor, and whom Luke has come to know when he and his sister Barbara visit their uncle. Louis is a laudanum addict and Barbara has asked Luke to keep an eye on him. Doing so leads the young priest into advanced circles of modern views and free thought. But even this milieu does not satisfy Louis; nothing will deter him from his trips to 'a Mahometan paradise' (110), which like those of Dorian Gray, inevitably end in squalor. Barbara Wilson's self-sacrificing attentions to her self-destructive brother greatly impress Luke, although here again he is slow to recognise the more than individual example that Barbara embodies. To comprehend what seeing Barbara as 'a spirit and a symbol' (263) means, and to find a mode of valid self-representation in her disinterested, ego-free conduct, requires a dramatic recognition scene featuring a fallen woman in the Good Shepherd convent, Limerick.

Offsetting London's nightmarish effects is the city's Irish community – emigrants who lend 'lambent flashes of Celtic wit and humour' (93) to the scene, and the 'Irish *guerrilleros*' (141) who sit in the House of Commons, practitioners of 'Ulyssean' (137) cunning under the leadership of 'the Silent One' (141) – a notable change from the days of *Hogan, M.P.* When Luke returns home to his sister's wedding – a bacchanal of which he takes a dim view – he sees 'a land of desolation and death' (206); it is the provincial town of Aylesburgh, his new English appointment, that he considers 'home' (213). Again, where Luke stands and how he affiliates is prematurely presumptuous. Aylesburgh exposes Luke to an intellectual clique of Catholic modernists, and though he does not neglect 'the primary obligation of a Catholic priest – the care of the poor' (229), particularly the Irish slum-dwellers of Primrose Lane, he does fall for the radical theological views of Amiel Lefevril who, among other questions, asks 'Is it not higher and nobler and loftier to act and think for the abstract *idea* of benefiting humanity?' (223). Luke's attraction to this idea no doubt derives from his own 'final temptation, to which he succumbed . . . namely to live in ideas, not in action' (133). But he soon finds Lefevril's doctrine challenged by priestly duty. In what reads like a parable, and is something of an analogue to the ruin of Louis Wilson, Luke is called to minister to an Irish soldier about to be executed. The condemned man's story is not merely one of misplaced loyalty but also an archetypal tale of '[t]he proud and effeminate imperialist, fresh from the voluptuousness of the capital, and the strong-thewed gladiator of Scythia' (245). To Luke, the soldier represents '[t]he history of a vagrant and ubiquitous race' (249), although his own intellectual wandering and spiritual seduction make the description more applicable to himself than he realises.

An appointment to an Irish parish where 'prairie conditions' (301) prevail – and where he feels like 'a soldier . . . [on] outpost duty' (304) – does not awaken national feeling in Luke. He continues to put his own thoughts, reactions and preachments first. Ireland, however, is a place where thought and action have an unexpectedly complicated interrelationship. Luke's position – 'I see nothing before us but to accept the spirit of the century, and conform to the Anglo-Saxon ideal' (333) – gradually becomes untenable as his various subsequent appointments reveal an unwonted self-respect and 'manly independence' (349) among many of his parishioners. The questions of the day press in on him, and the situation of the country, with 'English omnipotence . . . pushing from behind [and] American attractions . . . dragging us in front' (365), elicits his questioning but eventually affirmative engagement. This Luke expresses in the persona of 'a thorough democrat' (347) heading a branch of the Land League, as a seeker of 'a *via media* between modern civilization and Irish purity' (365), and as the violent, though unsuccessful, defender of his parents against eviction. He may still cite 'Vico and Campanella' (334), but self-representation now combines intellectual energy and collective interests (racially inflected though the latter are). Luke is now able to embody the public moment, as his finest rhetorical hour – a sermon on Calvary and Cremona – attests. This oration highlights a unity of sacrifice and service, and his connection between spiritual strength and historical precedent meets his congregation's warm approval.

Despite the impact of 'the great resonance of the new spirit that was just then stirring the dead clods of Irish life' (350), the single most powerful influence on Luke is Barbara Wilson's composed persona. Her service in the Good Shepherd convent, that haven of 'soiled womanhood' (451), embodies the dialectic of doing and being among the perhaps surprisingly large 'happy sisterhood, working in perfect silence and discipline' (ibid.). In assisting these women, Barbara is a credible and edifying representation of his own ambition 'to dovetail professions and actions' (10). She is a 'supreme example of self-abandonment' (453), the desideratum that all Luke's ardour, posturing and advanced views distracted him from attaining. Her incorruptibility also embodies the ideal of Mammon-rejecting independence being advanced as the national ethos, leading to his conclusion that '[t]here can be no question that such a lifetime of heroism and self-sacrifice is closely symbolical of our beloved country' (486). By maintaining her spiritual integrity, Barbara is the *echt* representative of 'the race which has given to the world in its apostles and martyrs the highest examples of altruism' (489).

In a sense, the power of Barbara's unworldliness both redresses and validates Luke's career. Were it not for his journey through error, he would not need to learn and uphold her self-forgetting and devotion.

And her unassuming and almost wordless sanctity, cloistered in fidelity and rectitude, contrasts instructively with the psychological ups and downs, the many parishes and the general restlessness of spirit that precede Luke's chastening recognition of humility and simplicity as the lineaments of his proper spiritual home. Perhaps Barbara's attainment of a rarefied level of self-representation is attributable to the archetype of womanhood composed of caring, steadfastness, purity and related virtues. She seems literally to be the angel-of-the-house ideal of the feminine. And in her is confirmation that 'the one thing that takes the place of gold and consols, scrips and shares, is the divine economy of the Church' (370).

Yet, despite Barbara's example, and Luke's own eventual 'life of an anchorite' (491) – paralleling her profession as a nun – his is predominantly a story of misjudgements and flawed enthusiasms. That is partly the nature of the novel form itself, as we are reminded when Luke asks 'Do you think that anyone would read a novel, if it were not about something painful?' (11). The matter is not merely one of novelistic form, although it is a sign of the Irish novel's development, belated and erratic though it may be, that *Luke Delmege* is a fully and knowingly formed *Bildungsroman*. As much to the point, however, is that painful matter conveys a condition of crisis. The novel is not only concerned with the fact that 'Mammon is sending his apostles and missionaries among us' (363), or that in response the Irish national movement should assert its exceptional character by keeping faith with 'seven centuries of fire and blood' (365). The conflict between these two contexts is critical enough. In addition, however, the Church itself is in crisis as a result of a modernist movement spearheaded by the kind of thinkers Luke encountered in Aylesburgh. There seems to be a crisis of leadership, as Luke's characteristic impatience with prospective father figures indicates. His unsound ideas, his impulsive assertions, his egotistic self-indulgence and his many other manifestations of false self-representation suggest the absence of a spiritual home and of a man to obey. Overcoming such deficiencies and reaching a state of spiritual manliness are given both national and religious connotations; indeed, they have connotations of a religion of nationhood. But Luke's most significant representation of himself remains that of a young man at a crossroads, not quite comprehending modernity while at the same time acting superior to tradition. Such a portrait of a problematical young man confronts not only its own present moment. It also looks forward, as is suggested by the effective revision of its themes in W.P. Ryan's *The Plough and the Cross*, towards ways in which ideologies of 'futurity and fate' (7) will be framed in Ireland in the coming times.

# 1905

## Shan F. Bullock, *Dan the Dollar*

*Shan F. Bullock (1865–1935) – né John William Bullock – was born near Newtownbutler, County Fermanagh. Most of his life was spent as a London civil servant, though he was also known within the capital's literary circles. It was in London that he changed his name to Shan Fadh ('Long John'), the eponymous protagonist of a short story by William Carleton, an author who would appear to be Bullock's antithesis.*

*His fictional output includes the semi-autobiographical* By Thrasna River *(1895),* The Red Leaguers *(1904) and* The Loughsiders *(1924), as well as several volumes of short stories. Bullock also produced a small amount of minor poetry; the somewhat hagiographical* Thomas Andrews, Shipbuilder *(1912), a biography of the* Titanic's *designer; and* After Sixty Years *(1931), an autobiography. Predominant features of his fiction are the land and people of his native place, but Bullock also published a number of novels with a London setting, including* Robert Thorne *(1907), a carefully detailed portrait of a low-ranking civil servant quite in keeping with the middlebrow English novel of the day.*

*Bullock's representation of the unassuming countryside where he grew up – with its watercolourist's eye to nature, its class-conscious fascination with local folkways and speech patterns, and its intimate knowledge of the area's economic life – draws attention to the regional dimension of Irish writing, though this is a less prominent presence in the nineteenth century than in the twentieth. Landlords, politicians and other embodiments of social and administrative activity are notable by their comparative rarity in Bullock's rural canvases. The concerns of the moment are sublimated in the seasonal round, the repetitions of the workaday and an appreciative respect for pastoral's protective familiarity. The stock type and picturesque setting common to Irish representations of the rural are here embodied in the stoical native and his toilsome fields. And absence of change is rendered as though it were fate.*

Sarah and Felix Ruddy, a couple in their mid-sixties, are failing tenant farmers on a 'bad to middling' (53) smallholding in the townland of Shrule, the third in a series of such unsuccessful rentals that has left them heavily in debt and without prospects or resources. Set '[s]ome fifteen years ago' (5), the novel opens as the pair make their way to Lismahee fair, Sarah to sell their lean and ancient cow, Felix to make a few pence from his crop of apples. Selling the cow is a last resort, but Felix takes the sale in a stride so easy-going and inattentive that his name seems not so much to connote happiness as fecklessness. Perhaps the fact that, as the offspring of a mixed marriage, he is of 'true Irish blood' (39) has something to do with his temperament; or possibly it is because Felix regards himself as 'a bad Protestant' (82). In any case, he is Sarah's 'opposite' (7). She not only 'gives the impression of vigour and determination' (6), but is also the more enterprising of the two. She is also of exclusively Protestant stock. Differences of temperament and origins to one side, however, the pair are united not only in their immediate economic objectives but in the knowledge that 'sure as fate the reckoning day would come' (30) when they must forego life at Shrule.

Such a turn of events would also foreclose the future of the two adoptees who comprise Felix and Sarah's family: their nephew Phelim, who helps them work the land, and Mary Troy, their housemaid. Phelim is a fiddle-playing dreamer and an *aficionado* of myths and folktales. He lives in a place of his own, though he is not entirely the eccentric or outsider that his manner or residence might suggest. Mary, a Catholic, lives in, and while Sarah 'like a good Protestant . . . had small faith in Catholic prayers' (47), as a rule she keeps her sectarian attitudes to herself. In her domestic capabilities Mary resembles Sarah, and their relationship is akin to that of mother and daughter. Phelim resembles Felix. Time is the most salient dimension of the women's realm, whereas space is essentially where Phelim and Felix live – the latter's disregard for the clock is expressed in his 'philosophy of life . . . [t]ime enough, ah oceans of time' (8). Both these dimensions are given a different shape and a different interrelationship when modernising Dan, son of Sarah and Felix, returns from America. Initially, however, the lives of 'these poor Irish folk' (76) are as one, united in essentials, which is all they know: '[t]heir wants were few, their hopes small, what concerned them chiefest were the primal things of life, the crudities of bare existence' (73). Such narrowness is accentuated by Felix and Sarah's indebtedness to the moneylender Henry Ray. 'As well argue with fate itself' (66), they conclude, as seek relief from the twenty per cent interest rate imposed by this capitalist with the vaguely bloodsucking nickname 'Ray the Spider' (111).

Yet no sooner do the Ruddys' finances reach their lowest ebb than Dan reappears after twenty years in America. According to one of the myths Phelim cites, 'Finn and his people are still alive yet . . . and will get loose some day and walk again' (58). Dan, with the 'Napoleonic . . . cast and expression' (108), at first seems like the modern equivalent of such a revival, not least because he is such a stranger (Sarah does not recognise him at first), behaves in a masterful manner and spends so freely that, as the nickname with which a Lismahee wit tags him indicates, his name is money. Though the books Dan sees in his parents' front room – *The Pilgrim's Progress* and *Robinson Crusoe* – suggest alternative and just as appropriate ways to frame his identity, his self-confidence and resources do make him as seemingly almighty as the dollar. He tells Sarah that the person she welcomes home is 'what I have made of myself' (87), which also makes him a blatant and provocative contrast to Felix and Phelim. With regard to the former, Sarah concedes that 'God meant him to be always like a child' (94), while Dan regards Phelim as the archetypal Paddy, 'lazy, unenterprising, worthless, a very growth of these barren hills' (126). Dan may not intend to be a threat to local manhood, or in the light of developments, he may not much care if he is or not, but he does represent a male style that is thrusting and forward-looking, and is thus a critique of the passivity and oddly complacent self-effacement that he finds in his local male connections. As though Napoleon is not a sufficiently recent prototype for him, he compares himself to 'General Grant' (249) of American Civil War renown, mention of whose name not only suggests a triumphalist dimension to Dan's self-representation but also the thought of conflict on the home ground.

Dan's impact on the close-knit life of Shrule is the novel's main focus. But his efforts to make a difference in Lismahee are also noteworthy, though less for their success than for the town's reaction to them. The failure of everything he undertakes in public attains a rather simplistic consistency in terms of narrative interest, but it does underline the clash between two ways of life that Dan's homecoming precipitates. 'This country wants waking up . . . . Everyone is half asleep' (91) is his perception of his homeland, and whether or not Lismahee represents conditions in general, it is not a place that is prepared to change because Dan says it should. He has been away too long to count as a local, so his plans to quicken Lismahee's tempo and its well-entrenched practices no doubt strike the townspeople as opportunistic, even Bonapartist. Even if the natives believed in Dan's gospel of progress, they would still interpret it in their own way. And Dan himself seems oddly inexperienced in putting his revivalist aims to work, as though his main point is to give the appearance of possessing power and modern expertise. As a Chicago businessman, he seems strangely unfamiliar with commercial ventures, resulting in the failure of his boot factory. '[T]he chances of his taking an active part in local and even national politics' (144) make him 'the talk of the country' (ibid.). But he is not sufficiently in touch to articulate a political position. The local newspaper advises that '[c]ontesting a constituency in the Nationalist interest would be ill-advised' (158), and an alternative political home seems unlikely after an invitation to dine with the Marquis, the area's leading landlord, leaves an angry and humiliated Dan eating below stairs 'with a crowd of English menials' (253). Whether as an entrepreneur, an aspiring public representative, or an acceptable dinner guest, Dan is a misfit. Or perhaps he should be seen as a mere individual who, as somebody who has been out on his own, inevitably disturbs the sense of unity, or uniformity, that binds a community together in the seemingly eternal recurrence of its deprivations. Whatever the case, as everybody at home regards him, the terms in which Dan represents himself appear dubious, questionable, false.

What Dan can provide proves surplus to community requirements; to understate the case, 'old and new do not easily blend' (121). A neighbour considers him to be no more than 'a queer playboy' (123). And in time, he also finds that he is at odds with himself. 'Never did I know such a restless mortal' (113), Sarah remarks of one indication of the difficulty Dan experiences in adapting to a rhythm that is antithetical to that of metropolitan self-creation and self-advancement. At home, he encounters 'the great disturbance of himself, driving in like a tempest upon the peace of simple ways and thought and marring it' (121). And his attempts to instruct Phelim in American work habits fail to impress. 'Returned exiles of his stamp being rare in Ireland' (144), the local newspapers are intrigued by his presence, but, as the designation 'returned exile' indicates, Dan possesses a dual identity. Geographically speaking, he has returned, but he has arrived decked out in his American domicile's culture of change. Not only does Dan embody the desire to make a difference, or to see the difference that he has made to himself reflected in his place of origin, he also represents the successful realisation of the desire. Yet validation of his accomplishment where it would be most affirming remains at best problematical. Newspaper reports resolve the problem for him by claiming that 'under his

American exterior he keeps an Irish heart' (157). And indeed, the harsh outward marks of his exile, evident in such first impressions as his possession of 'an Irish face, materialized' (85), seem to soften: 'every day he's drawn, quite unconsciously, nearer the warm heart of his country. So it has always been, so may it ever be' (145). The facile piety of that hope is not what Dan's essential dissociation represents.

The exile's most substantial enactment of return is the purchase for his parents of Springfield, a spread of 120 acres. This acquisition gives Dan's dollars a local habitation and a name, and lends to the act of relocation the appearance of homecoming. Owning Springfield is intended to place Sarah and Felix on the same plane as their son, though that idea is contained less in the economic reality than in the existential one of uprooting and removal. The new property represents an effective exile from Shrule and from what that place connotes regarding Felix and Sarah's social status. The spatial enhancement that Dan provides belittles his parents by being too big for them. Now they, like their son, are misfits. In practical terms, a property like Springfield requires much more work than their previous homes, further calling into question the value of change: '[o]nce only the miseries of poverty, toil; now the cares of abundance and the slavery of it' (113). And going to Springfield also causes disunity in the family circle. Phelim refuses to leave where he is, declaring 'I've a kind of love for it' (126), a sentiment to which Dan's views of home, land, place and standing do not subscribe. In staying put, Phelim asserts 'a notion to be independent' (177), rejecting Dan's ideas of progress and social mobility. Emphasising the disruption of resettlement, Mary Troy accompanies the Ruddys to Springfield, abandoning the harmless fraternity of her closeness to Phelim. The latter is not merely attached to place. His affections also have a human face. Phelim may embody the cliché that home is where the heart is, but his simplicity and directness represent an integrity that Dan's restless doubleness denies him.

Though Phelim is convinced that the move to the big house will prove temporary, the rift it creates between him and Mary is 'something potent that mere understanding could not overcome' (152). Prior to Springfield, they were '[l]ike brother and sister . . . orphans both and best of good friends' (80). Sheltered and virginal, they seem made to replicate the way of life in which Felix and Sarah reared them: 'they knew only what lay within the narrow limits of their pastoral experience, [and] were strangely uninfluenced also by much that was in the depths of themselves, passions, emotions, impulses, lying dormant there' (79). Such latency is what Dan cannot help but dispel, having lost his own innocence and, as a consequence, being unable to disavow his egotism and his desires. His arousal of Mary is the most intimate, but also the least tenable, representation of both Dan's homecoming and his alienation. The thought of any kind of union between them seems the ultimate expression of a poor fit. For her part, 'what Mary saw clearest in Dan and disliked the most was his worldliness' (118). Yet she also finds herself susceptible to his sexuality. As for Dan, 'what claimed his attention chiefest was her innocence of mind' (131), the quality that his style of maleness seems most likely to devalue. To sustain such an attraction of opposites, both parties, either intentionally or unwittingly, must engage in at least some degree of false representation.

As a result of Dan's attentions, Mary must confront world, flesh and devil. And such is Dan's overbearing sense of purpose that innocent Mary reflects 'how like fate Dan was in his ways' (162). Not everything about him causes the same degree of duress, however; Mary acknowledges that the awakening of her sexual appetite feels 'just as if I was starving with the hunger' (238). And Sarah endorses such feelings – 'God never meant us to starve our hunger' (239). But it is not in sexual terms that Mary represents herself. Much more important to her is her Catholicism. That is what she possesses that Dan cannot supplant. She must remain loyal to the shaping influence that both pre-dates and must survive him. Dan, in one more sign that he inhabits the modern world, '[f]ull of pride in his manhood, or arrogance and self-will . . . had only contempt for all that she held most dear' (241–2). To him, Mary's unwavering adherence to her faith places her among 'these Irish who submitted and sat waiting and could not learn wisdom in the things of this world' (249). What the girl holds most dear Dan dismisses as a symptom of a paralysed country, a place where he cannot make his own mark. This difference between them is the insurmountable barrier to their marriage plans, for '[d]id not the Church say . . . that a want of union in faith was frequently attended with evil consequences, both material and spiritual?' (231). This failure of union – which is not caused by Sarah objecting to a mixed marriage on sectarian grounds but by a tenet of that to which Mary must remain true if she is to retain any sense of self – is the concluding panel of the novel's portrait of Dan as a misfit, a person without depth, a man who would override the loyalties that bind locals to their lives for his own essentially acquisitive ends. His courtship of Mary, instead of becoming the ultimate expression of his return home, is that return's crisis. Under great stress, Mary responds by becoming 'mistress of herself' (248). Instead of capitulating to Dan, she musters a declaration of no surrender.

An additional reason why Mary and Dan are a mismatch, however, is the former's view that '[t]his life is nothing' (239). That outlook may derive from her religion, but in any case it is plainly incompatible with Dan's need to be 'going out in the world again' (260). He quits Shrule, and in the aftermath of his 'sundering and enlightening' (268) presence, Mary looks forward to a restoration of 'that simpler earlier time of . . . innocence and friendship' (270) with Phelim. This outcome is a more fitting, a more unifying and consolidating form of return than Dan's has been. The spirit of the days before he reappeared – the spirit of fidelity, of long-suffering, of a relatedness that transcends differences – prevails; and Dan's attempts to change the way of life animated by that spirit reveals the outsider's potential for destructive disloyalty. It is only in his absence that Dan can be regarded fondly and tolerantly; though to all appearances 'it was almost as though he had never been' (265–6). In memory he becomes an 'idealised' (267) figure. Closeness and distance, home and world, communal and individual, modern and traditional: these are the central terms structuring *Dan the Dollar.* But the impossibility of reconciling those terms, of making a more comprehensive and complex unity from them, shows Dan to be an almost stereotypical embodiment of the exile's state of being between. His loyalties are not so much divided as opposed; and whatever his persona – whether Dan Ruddy or Dan the Dollar – he cannot avoid being conscious of how incomplete it is and thus how falsely it represents him.

# 1908

## Katherine Cecil Thurston, *The Fly on the Wheel*

*Katherine Cecil Thurston (1875–1911) was born in County Cork. Her father, Paul Madden, was a former mayor of Cork city. Her marriage to the English novelist Ernest Charles Temple Thurston in 1901 coincided with the beginning of her own writing career. Her first novel,* The Circle *(1903), was followed by the work that made her name,* John Chilcote, MP *(1904; published in America as* The Masquerader*), a runaway bestseller that her husband successfully adapted for the stage and which* *was also filmed. Other novels include* The Gambler *(1906), the first of her works to feature an Irish setting,* The Mystics *(1907) and* Max *(1910).*

*Until recently, Thurston had received little or no critical attention, and a complete study of her life and oeuvre is still awaited. Her works are fluently written, psychologically acute and reveal a keen eye to conflicts between social convention and modernistic individualism. Largely focusing on women's fate, Thurston is particularly noteworthy for her contribution to the history, sociology and aesthetic of the 'New Woman' phenomenon. Many of her plots deal with problems of self-representation – assumed identities, disguises and other forms of 'passing'. These venerable narrative strategies Thurston deploys with a view to probing the ostensibly stable frameworks of class and family, and of the male authority uncritically claimed to be their mainstay.*

Stephen Carey is a pillar of his community, no small accomplishment given the constraining duties and expectations of his Catholic middle-class, Waterford city milieu. The fact that he can be regarded as 'a type' (2) – that is, a representative citizen of that 'huge republic' (ibid.) that the middle class has become – is one reason for his high standing. But it is also clear that he possesses the characteristics that typify him to an exceptional, high-functioning degree, so much so that at first sight he may be viewed in a heroic light, 'so far as middle-class Irish life produces heroes' (ibid.). This designation is substantiated less by his professional activities as a solicitor than by the authority, uprightness and judgement that he exhibits in the domestic sphere. Having secured the family's fortunes and good name following the debacle of his late father's building speculations, Stephen is understandably entitled to be thought of as 'a man self-made' (ibid.), and perhaps it is an awareness of his feat of restoration that lends 'the faint savour of Orientalism so frequently to be found in his country and his class' (12) to the superior manner in which he treats his rather girlish and compliant wife, Daisy. In any event, he is undoubtedly 'the master spirit' (20) of the household – defender, director, arbiter and monitor.

Stephen's standing comes at a cost, however. In carrying out what he perceives to be his duty, he has made 'the conscious compromise with ambition that men of his country and of his class are daily and yearly driven to make' (35). This compromise consists in part of intellectual inhibition. 'Souse the country with modern thought' (105) may be what he advocates, and 'Spencer and Huxley, Haeckel and Kant' (106) may be the thinkers he recommends to secure that objective, but to act in the name of the modernity he espouses, to raise an individual voice in more morally testing contexts than that of the dinner party at which he makes his views known, would be to abandon his prominent place in the narrow local scheme of things. In doing so, Stephen would serve himself instead of serving what class and creed expect of him. Rather than accept responsibility for his intellectual interests, Stephen instead defers to their fatalistic dismissal by his friend and mentor, Father James Barron – a dismissal not only of modernism but of a modernising nationalism.

Repressing a taste for modern ideas and the social developments that they prefigure is not a very great challenge to somebody as apparently in command of himself as Stephen. When it comes to those facets of his inner life with which he is less consciously in touch – those that make up his emotional and sexual identity – stimulus proves more difficult to control. Thus, although his first meeting with twenty-year-old Isabel Costello ostensibly consists of no more than a dance and a chat, dancing with her leaves him 'tingling from contact with elemental things' (43), Isabel's 'admixture of southern blood' (48) contributing. And their talk takes them away from the party, a breach of the protocol of such closely scrutinised social gatherings that the glowing tip of Isabel's cigarette, one of the signatures of the New Woman, makes visible and intensifies. Racially, socially and in other ways, Isabel is different: 'As her body was built along gracious lines, so her mind had already flowered, where others lay folded in the bud' (ibid.). There is about her an aura of passion, daring and openness that, although it may be thought to represent a self-conscious feminism, is the hallmark of an essentialised Isabel, showing her to be a child of nature and, as such ,a vivid and threatening contrast to the locals and to the shibboleths that vigilantly nurture them. The elemental Isabel is free in ways that those for whom Stephen is the cynosure will never desire to be.

The threat that Isabel poses soon appears in the lovelorn figure of Stephen's younger brother, Frank. A medical student in Paris, Frank has lost his head to Isabel, whom he met when she briefly visited that city. Now Frank, believing himself to be engaged to Isabel, has broken off his studies to follow his heart. Such behaviour is the height of foolishness and irresponsibility in Stephen's eyes, an immature dereliction of Frank's obligation both to ensure the inviolability of the family name and to make something of himself in the world. The first of these duties is the more important. The power of gossip in the Carey circle has

already been made clear by Stephen's sister Mary, who is both its con-
summate disseminator and, because of her own excessively tentative
emotional engagement, its target. Stephen visits Isabel in the pokey
New Town (*sic*) house where she lives with her maiden aunt. (Stephen's
substantial home is in Lady Lane. The novel's attentive detailing of
domestic interiors is not only of forensic interest but also contributes to
its astute psychological and cultural charting of narrowness, limitation,
constraint and related aspects of the characters' inner lives.) Isabel is
persuaded by Stephen that she and Frank should part, and a crestfallen
Frank returns to Paris, though he does leave Isabel the inadvertent sou-
venir of 'a little phial containing half a dozen tabloids' (125) with which
he had thought to do away with himself should Isabel reject him.

One of the outcomes of Stephen's dutiful intervention is a repetition of the differences between him and Isabel. In response to her
telling her Aunt Theresa, 'You live in a little, little world, where if
people ever do feel anything, they're afraid to say so!' (81), Stephen
says that at her age he too saw his native city in those terms, but he has
come to accept that '[t]here's a big machine called expediency, and we
are its slaves . . . . It's only by pandering to it that we live' (82). Yet
there is evidently something in Stephen's decisive and masterful handling of the Frank affair that attracts Isabel. Moreover, she seems to
grasp intuitively that by complying with separation from Frank a space
will open in her life for Stephen. And when she proposes amity rather
than enmity between them, Stephen gratefully accepts; indeed, his first
sight of Isabel when she comes to make that proposal sparks in him
feelings of being a 'real man, unshackled by convention' (89).

Further, although Mary and Daisy Carey, in particular, find Isabel
less a breath of fresh air than a potentially tempestuous disturber of
their tightly wound circle, they are unable to exclude her from the
round of visits, dinners and similar rituals that represents and gives a
sense of purpose to their society, renews their class consciousness and
reinforces their shared moral attitudes. These occasions, together with
the well-regulated and repetitious performances that they sponsor, are
an efficient means of displaying the workings of what might be termed
the sublimated tribalism of the Careys and their friends. They also
reveal how that social system generates patterns of gossip, criticism and
judgement as a method of reiterating and protecting its putative
orthodoxies. To this system Isabel remains alien. A Catholic she may
be, 'but in her composition there was nothing of the ascetic' (65). A

bourgeoise she may be in social origin and education, but rather than the primness and propriety of hostesses whose emotional inertness is signified by their consuming interest in the local marriage market, Isabel is 'the most heedlessly spontaneous of beings' (94). The immutable bequest of her Spanish blood is one aspect of Isabel's makeup, but so also is her capacity for playing up to it, expressed by her out-spokenness, her indifference to standing out and to being considered unorthodox, her lack of vigilance and her lightheartedness. As she remarks to Aunt Theresa, 'I remember the nuns in Dublin used to talk about people having "qualms of conscience", but I never understood what it meant' (149). Isabel is committed to being a rebel; that is how she desires to represent herself. And Catholic middle-class Waterford seems committed to trying to contain somebody like her, if only to repudiate her rebelliousness and thereby reaffirm its own rectitude.

Local women's uneasy experience of intimacy and resistance intensi-fies when Isabel is invited to join Mary, Daisy and the children for their summer break in Kilmeaden. Here, 'in the air of homely dilapidation so racy of the soil' (216), city formality can be dispensed with. The natural surroundings, the fresh air, the relaxed vacation routine, the children at play, all make this setting an evocative backdrop for someone of Isabel's temperament – 'How splendid it is! . . . . How free it is!' (228), she remarks on the landscape. And in due course it is here that Mary, who believes that Isabel 'is different from the rest of us . . . [which] may be great harm' (190), begins to fear the worst about the girl and her brother, a fear that appears to be partly informed by Mary's reading of Tolstoy, Zola and what innocent Daisy calls 'those horrible foreign writers' (188). Some of the subject matter of those writers does not remain foreign, however; it unexpectedly finds a home for itself in Kilmeaden as relations between Stephen and Isabel ripen in the swel-tering summer heat. Stephen commutes to his office from the cottage in the car that he is so proud of, so that Isabel's availability is both limited and intensified. And even in the country it is impossible to escape the concerns of the marriage market, so that Isabel is exposed to almost daily reminders of how girls like herself are 'cruelly stereotyped' (223) by the confining socio-sexual roles assigned to them.

Soon enough the point is reached where Father Barron, also a house guest, favours Isabel with the fatherly attentions that he has so often provided Stephen. Once again, Isabel forthrightly criticises the life that Waterford has modelled for her, those of Daisy the wife and mother and of the various men that she has encountered, to whom Stephen, she declares, is a most noteworthy exception and, as such, deserving of a wider world. To this Father James replies with Aesop's fable of the fly and the wheel, the moral of which is that life moves at its own inscrutable pace – or rather that 'some great big power that knows what we don't know' (233) drives it. To attempt to accelerate its processes or arbitrarily to alter its arrangements, even when these seem pedestrian and underachieving, is to misapprehend the way of the world. Isabel, lacking the temperament to take the fable's point about orderly progress and who holds the whip hand, thinks the fable silly. But part of what it means is that Stephen is no less a personage for remaining in Waterford. And when Father Barron says, 'I'd give my life's blood to save him from harm' (ibid.), he is not only echoing Mary's intuition of Isabel's potential for damage, he is using language far removed from Aesop's understated homeliness. But here too, Isabel is deaf to what is being said.

The fable's terms – drive, pace, power – find alternative expression in a nocturnal excursion on which Stephen takes Isabel: 'a mad drive – mad as the thoughts that were racing through their minds' (259). Isabel has already been called a '[l]over of speed' (215), and their head-long run is graphically conveyed. They head westward, and in the darkness above Dungarvan their passion for each other declares itself, ratified not only when Stephen 'kissed her violently' (262) but anew when, ironically, he seems to repeat the sacrificial note in Father Barron's recent protective declaration by assuring Isabel, 'I'd go down to hell for you!' (ibid.). Passion sweeps all aside, and when Daisy, instructed by Mary, confronts Stephen, it appears that he is indeed prepared to abandon her for Isabel, an outcome made more likely when he rejects Father Barron's attempt to be his conscience on the Isabelesque grounds that 'even for me – the respectable citizen, the cut-and-dried lawyer – there's life to be lived; and, by God, do you think I'll refuse it?' (281). But Stephen is not able to continue for long being driven by his emotions, and when Isabel visits him in Lady Lane he feels 'maimed, mentally and physically; and with the shame of mutilation, his courage ebbed' (290). Far from experiencing the equivalent of this emasculation, Isabel is fired up – 'her blood was proving itself a riot of feeling' (299) – as she rages at Stephen's rejection.

Stephen returns to Kilmeaden and Daisy, and the house party prepares to celebrate Mary's long-awaited engagement. The weather breaks, and who emerges from the storm but a bedraggled Isabel, the very image of 'the poor gypsy' (190) that Father Barron thinks her to be. She has walked all the way from the city (a sharp contrast to the recent drive). Unwelcome, unwanted, unbecoming, Isabel is nevertheless most herself: 'There was no room in Isabel's mind for conventionality . . . . She was living now as her feelings prompted, undisciplined, primitive, careless of all comment' (304). And she has with her Frank's tabloids, with which she laces Stephen's drink. But before he can raise his glass, with characteristic impulsiveness Isabel takes the drink herself. As for Stephen, '[h]enceforth his way would lie along the common path' (313), a route that calls to mind that of the fly-resisting mule in Aesop's fable and which also raises questions about self-determination and independent-mindedness.

In Stephen Carey's situation it is possible to detect aspects of Joycean paralysis – 'Talk of rats in a trap!' (181) he exclaims in describing his limited life – and this is only one indication of how *The Fly on the Wheel* seems both a novel of its day and a work that anticipates the themes that will preoccupy later Irish novelists. Instead of focusing on issues with a collective interest – the national question, the land question, the role of the Church – this novel deals instead with marriage, intimacy, desire and related aspects of individual experience. These concerns are not new to the Irish novel, but Thurston gives them an unwonted significance as sources of meaning and as grounds of personal identity. It is in terms of their inner world, and its articulation in the flesh, that the characters of *The Fly on the Wheel* are represented. Public concerns of the day are not ignored – Daisy's enthusiastic brother Tom claims that the Gaelic League is 'going to make a nation of us' (118) – but for the most part this novel, in its treatment of the conflict between nature (Isabel) and nurture (Stephen), in its ironical subversion of an 'anticipated romance' (2) to critique conventional outlooks and expectations, and in the candour with which it addresses women's place and social destiny, makes it seem part of a different, perhaps Ibsenite, or more generally European, discursive world. This difference is reinforced by its modernistic overtones, expressed not only in Stephen's car and office telephone but in the emphasis on both Isabel's 'primitive [*sic*]' (53) aspects and on the existence of loneliness, tedium and spiritual hollowness even in the best regulated social circles. Modern inclinations and aspirations are stimulating and alluring, but they also threaten and are sources of anxiety, so that it becomes difficult for the characters to know if they can truly represent themselves outside the terms of their prescriptive contexts.

This doubt is crucial to the value and interest of *The Fly on the Wheel*'s new themes and perspectives, but such novelty does not entirely detach the work from the preoccupations of other Irish novels of its era. Like many of these – from *Luke Delmege* to *The Plough and the Cross* – this is a novel of crisis. And the crisis is sufficient to provoke rebellion. As in those works, the rebellion in *The Fly on the Wheel* is abortive, but it is no less significant on that account, nor does the fact that the rebellion is more *within* the characters than *against* an institution diminish it (in any case, the plot's institutional repercussions are by no means neglected). The ambition to represent oneself in terms of one's passions, one's uniqueness, one's unconstrained self – the self that is not merely a subject – may be considered youthful folly, but it is an aim that resonates revealingly with thoughts of independence, freedom and self-determination gaining currency both in the Irish novel and in its broader contexts.

# 1910

## W.P. Ryan, *The Plough and the Cross*

*William Patrick Ryan (1867–1942) was born near Templemore, County Tipperary. Although his first publication was the novel* The Heart of Tipperaray: A Romance of the Land League *(1893, with an introduction by William O'Brien), Ryan was a journalist by profession. He emigrated to London and, early in his career, there was Sir Charles Gavan Duffy's private secretary. Subsequently, he held a number of editorial positions in London and Dublin, and was active in both cities' literary and labour circles, and was also a member of the Gaelic League. This activity led to Ryan's documentation of cultural and social developments between the turn of the century and 1916. Relevant works include* The Irish Literary Revival: Its History, Pioneers and Possibilities *(1894, dealing in part with Ryan's connection with the path-breaking Southwark Irish Literary Club, and* The Labour Revolt and Larkinism *(1913). Other noteworthy works are* The Pope's Green Island *(1912) and* Irish Labour Movement from the Twenties to Our Own Day *(1919). The former responds to the role of the Church in the closure of* The Peasant, *a newspaper edited by Ryan based in Navan, County Meath. He revived the paper as* The Irish Peasant *and*

> Nation *and edited it in Dublin until it closed in 1910. The following*
> *year, Ryan returned to London, where he worked on the* Daily Herald.
>    *Ryan's other publications include the novel* Starlight through the
> Roof *(1895; published under the pseudonym Kevin Kennedy), a number*
> *of prose works that amplify his London experiences and his commitment*
> *to the cause of labour, and several volumes of poetry, much of it drawing*
> *on his relatively overlooked theosophical interests. Ryan also published*
> *under the names W.P. O'Ryan and Liam Ó Riain; he wrote a number of*
> *works in Irish. But perhaps his main work is as one of the outstanding*
> *Irish newspaper writers of his generation who not only made an impact*
> *on the English press but whose awareness of the cultural role of*
> *journalism helped to articulate and publicise independent and forward-*
> *looking thinking in a changing Ireland.*

'Within the four seas of the island the social and psychological conditions were various and divided. Several ages met and many modes and
nations jostled with one another unconsciously in Ireland' (338). The
embodiment of the resulting perplexities, antagonisms and ideals is
Fergus O'Hagan, social activist, advanced thinker and editor of the
radical Dublin newspaper *Fáinne an Lae*. In addition, he is a published
novelist, an accomplishment that implicitly places the novel form on the
same cultural footing as Fergus' other pursuits; and he has also worked
as a journalist in New York and London. In the latter city he worked for
Terence O'Connellan, a paper-thin caricature of T.P. O'Connor, the
leading Irish journalist of the day. (George Moore appears in *The Plough
and the Cross* as Geoffrey Mortimer, and Edward Martyn also has a cameo
role as the cardboard Mr Carton, notable for his 'profound pessimism'
(188).) Structurally a series of staged editorials, critical and reformist in
tone and focus, *The Plough and the Cross* is also an earnest representation
of the struggle for ideas in Ireland, depicting tensions between progressive and reactionary outlooks, clerical and lay apologists, rural and
urban values, as well as daily challenges regarded in the light of the
eternal verities enshrined in the visionary beliefs of 'that revolutionary
American woman' (226) Alice Lefanu, a theosophist. At the same time,
however, in addition to being a gauge of the contemporary intellectual
and cultural climate, the novel signals an impassioned desire for forward
movement, more open public discourse, a more liberal accommodation
of aspirations and ideals, and a greater sense of unity and commitment
in acting on a progressive agenda.

   Fergus' story moves through the difficulties arising from efforts to
satisfy that desire. These include problems of institutional resistance

and personal scepticism, of inadequate leadership and devitalised communities, of individual vulnerability and social anomie. Fuelled by purity of principle, Fergus confronts such issues with unremitting energy, despite the almost total futility of the results. Inevitably, crisis ensues, and though Fergus is restored largely through the uplifting example of Alice Lefanu and partly through his relationship with his elfin cousin Elsie O'Kennedy, the failure of his best intentions is something of a *j'accuse* to the forces of reaction. For although the novel's action is set in just two locations, Dublin and a place in County Meath called Baile na Boinne, *The Plough and the Cross* is concerned not with a local or parochial critique but with the creation and sustaining of an ideologically self-conscious, intellectually combative, independent Irish mentality. Such a departure is intended to overcome the fact that 'Ireland's worst disaster was that her mind had shrunk, that as a whole she had lost the heroic consciousness, that her inner life had grown weedy, pessimistic and vexatious' (344). In its treatment of remedial strategies and modernising thought, *The Plough and the Cross* is both diagnosis and symptom of this diminished consciousness.

While ideological embattlement and spiritual ardour contribute substantially to Fergus' eventual breakdown, so too does the more mundane fact that his efforts are spread over a very wide front. His life as an editor is demanding and thankless. Dublin is portrayed as degenerate, an evidently failed community where 'man has fallen from his highest nature . . . into savagery and spiritual and social inertia and chaos' (8). The likelihood of *Fáinne an Lae*'s message finding a receptive audience seems slim, as is tacitly acknowledged by Fergus' preoccupation with the quality of its contributors and with maintaining its position as 'the chief organ of a new movement' (2). And the challenges of advocating a dawn in a country that is said, with almost Joycean assurance, to be 'the world's most awful example of arrested development and inertia' (212), are not limited to concerns with reception and affiliation, as both Geoffrey Mortimer and Terence O'Connellan suggest. They both advise Fergus that his efforts are futile, and do so at such length and with such frequency that their meetings in the editorial office of *Fáinne an Lae* seem at times a sententious rehearsal of the 'Aeolus' episode of *Ulysses*. 'You are wasting your life by taking Ireland seriously' (20), Mortimer tells his friend. As for O'Connellan, the title of his publication, *Terence's Tittle Tattle*, hardly substantiates his reputation 'as a great journalistic leader of democracy'

(28), and his name as 'an expert on the gloomy side of destiny' (ibid.) is not exactly inspiring. Fergus respects these two men of letters, but he also regards them critically. Their cynicism and worldliness betray an indifference to leadership, and Fergus requires a father figure whose authority would vouch for the necessity of the new day that is the goal of his life's work. And perhaps father figures' absence creates the space that Alice Lefanu eventually occupies, a zone of faith and action in which Fergus can rededicate himself when he becomes 'a broken and incoherent personality intellectually' (340). To him, Alice Lefanu is the sole remaining embodiment of a way forward in thought and action, the link between what he has always sought and the severing of which has caused his temporary disintegration. She is the person who resembles the hero who is 'a world in himself, and has a creative effect on the racial mind' (278); and she also does not conform to gender stereotypes. Nor does Fergus, whose sexuality seems oddly unformed for somebody in his thirties.

The gap between Fergus and his two literary seniors is also notable for those abortive mentors' lack of national sentiment. O'Connellan, based in London and closely associated with the Irish Parliamentary Party, is too complacent an insider to rethink his commitments. His view that 'Young Ireland has a primitive and impossible idea of heroism and patriotism' (250) seems intended to belittle Fergus' efforts by implying that they lack his own sophistication and media savvy, though he proves not to be above manipulating a *Fáinne an Lae* article that strikes him as 'an amazing production for sheepish Ireland' (ibid.) to bolster his metropolitan standing. For him, '[a]ll talk about nationality is dry and barren' (31); and '[r]acial pride is only another illusion' (ibid.). Like Mortimer, O'Connellan is extremely negative regarding contemporary Irish culture, criticising the country for, of all things, being 'all but theatreless' (214), a comment that dismisses the Irish Literary Revival without rebuttal from Fergus. A merely literary revival is not what he has in mind.

London suits O'Connellan. Mortimer, on the other hand, finds the metropolis distasteful, fails to find a foothold there, and, rather than become an Anglophile, considers himself likely to go down in history as 'the literary undertaker of the British Empire' (243). But he is only interested in 'an Ireland of my own artistic consciousness' (20), a view that conflicts with Fergus' ethic of service, concern for the people and attachment to the country's cultural traditions, signified by his musical taste and his enthusiasm for ancient lore and legends. Clearly it helps to highlight Fergus' virtues and good faith by seeing him in the context of the two older nay-sayers. Their polished talk and intellectual nullity reinforce the drive for more forthright discourse, more inspirational ideas and a more self-actualising future. Such power and position as they possess merely represent Mortimer and O'Connellan in passé and reactionary terms.

The one subject on which Fergus, O'Connellan and Mortimer agree is the role of the Church in Irish life – or at least the role of the hierarchy. These father figures' uniquely repressive influence on national life makes them anathema to Fergus; and the Church's dilution of inner life in the name of its own spiritual values is the target that he most consistently attacks. One of O'Connellan's objections to the Church's role is that '[I]t is led and directed by sexless people' (32), a criticism that perhaps reflects a Parnellite perspective. And to Mortimer, 'Ireland as she really is' consists of 'a certain number of silly sheepfolds attached to a certain number of priests' houses' (23), a parody of the pastor and his flock. The Church is more interested in maintaining its own power than in the 'applied Christianity' (174) that Fergus and some local clergy wish to practise in Baile na Boinne, still less than in the spiritual advancement of the people at large. Rather than identify with national aspirations, '[t]he bishops and Rome hold Ireland for England' (80); and it is clear that, try as he will, Fergus is no match for 'an organization that spread fear and slept not' (339). Progressive young clergy in Maynooth are silenced; progressive diocesan clergy are dispersed; Fergus and his essential medium of self-representation, *Fáinne an Lae*, are isolated and banned. Such intensive hierarchical surveillance of the moral, spiritual and cultural order ensures that 'there's no Modernism in Ireland' (327). Under these conditions, Elsie O'Kennedy's question – 'Is not the spiritual life something immeasurably more important than ecclesiastical jurisprudence?' (63) – must wait indefinitely for an answer.

Nevertheless, Fergus maintains his critical opposition. If to him 'Dublin seems to exist chiefly for the humiliation of Irish idealists of all kinds' (58), he has an alternative milieu in the 'fairyland' (100) of Baile na Boinne. Here he represents himself in a manner reminiscent of the *narodniki* of nineteenth-century Russia. Himself a native of the rural south, Fergus endorses the proposed '"Garden City" scheme' (7), which people from his part of the country will inhabit. These 'new colonists . . . choice spirits and racy of the soil' (108) will not only form a community but will also 'begin the breaking up of the grass lands' (138). But reversion to tillage will not mean either an economy or a community solely based on agricultural production. That approach has no future. Fergus' own home place is 'dead as Knocknagow' (307); the new venture will not be allowed to go the same way. On the contrary, Milligan – who is funding the scheme – envisages a combination of farms and factories, with 'the concerns placed upon a co-operative basis' (139). In addition, the newcomers 'had been testing some of Kropotkin's theories with zeal and profit since Fergus had sent them *Field, Factories and Workshops*' (120). A new version of land reclamation now obtains, to which has been added modern modes of production, presumably adapted to local circumstances, though details of the latter are much scantier than elaborations of the ideas with which concrete conditions are expected to comply. A further modern element is added in the degree of informed consciousness that is being brought to bear on the project. The social experiment's deliberate and intentional character is one manifestation of that consciousness, and its prospect of unifying thought and action – 'tillage and thought are one' (279) – also appeals to Fergus. Indeed, it seems from his reproof of Mortimer – 'Must, the Parisian plough stop suddenly in the first furrow of the Untilled Field of Banba . . . [?]' (21) – that it is in Baile na Boinne and not at the editor's desk that new ground will be broken.

Awareness of what is being ventured is not restricted to Fergus or his students of Kropotkin. Milligan 'has been studying William Morris and the Kelmscott Press' (56), the latter with a view perhaps to a local arts-and-crafts initiative. More to the point, Milligan made his fortune from being the Church's stockbroker, and is acting now on the conviction that 'in one form or another I was bound to make restitution to the people' (138). The actual form that results is a model for a more equitable and innovative relationship between master and men. That arrangement in a County Meath location may also be taken as a rebuke to the hierarchy's plan to build a national cathedral on nearby Tara. Thus the eventual failure of the 'Garden City' project not only precipitates Fergus' crisis, it also demonstrates the difficulty of establishing institutional structures representing a more class-conscious and less oligarchical society. Even if Milligan is merely providing conscience money – and it would be inconsistent with Fergus' rejection of cynicism to suggest that this is the case – he establishes a venue where haves and have-nots are partners in each other's well-being, however prototypically. In the clerical imperium, however, no such economy, moral or otherwise, is evident. It may not be the cross, precisely, that is the plough's antagonist – Fergus continues to identify with 'Christ's appeal to divine fatherhood and human brotherhood' (359) – but it certainly does seem to be the crozier. And not only is the Church hostile to lay organisations (not just Baile na Boinne but also the Gaelic League), and to the collective energies that such organisations embody, it also treats private life repressively. 'It crushes romance and tenderness, or gives young people a false and poisonous notion of them' (242), as Fergus observes. Protesting such practices, as Elsie O'Kennedy does in her *Fáinne an Lae* article 'The Clergy Against Nature', though it brings the weight of episcopal authority down on the paper, also exemplifies representing oneself in terms of resistance and critique. Elsie may deny being 'a "revolted daughter" or a "new woman"' (259), but her outspoken views underline the significance of personal agency, emotional maturity and psychological awareness, all counterparts to the modernisation of the public sphere which Fergus advocates.

The material and intellectual cost of Fergus' rude awakening from the dream of community in the Boyne Valley, together with the suspension of *Fáinne an Lae*, leave him without a context in which to represent himself. The contemporary scene appears to have abandoned him, and the loss of his Dalkey home further reinforces his apparent outcast status. When first encountered, he is passing as an itinerant musician in Dublin's slums, complete with false beard. Now he cannot disguise his silence, his displacement, his déclassé standing; 'the end of a definite phase' (355) is at hand. But with Alice Lefanu's providential arrival, a different day dawns in the form of Raja Yoga combined with relief of the poor. Fergus immerses himself in both, enlightened by the possibility that 'the hitherto vague thing called theosophy contained a great deal of ideal Christianity' (351). Thus he is able to sublimate his experiences of a particularised, local *Kulturkampf* into the vision of 'Kingly Union' (208) – a translation of Raja Yoga – which emanates from and is represented by 'the international headquarters of Universal Brotherhood' (351), Point Loma, California.

His idealism renewed, and the integrity that it articulates ratified, Fergus once more finds himself intact. The effects of his defeats seem temporary; the commitments of his critique are transformed; his crisis passes. This capacity for intellectual realignment demonstrates a flexibility that had been missing hitherto. The 'great, quiet, ordered work' (367) headed by Alice Lefanu has supplanted what appeared to be revolutionary zeal. Readjusting and retreating in ways that recall Luke Delmege – to whose story and its contexts *The Plough and the Cross* is an intriguing, though probably unwitting, response – Fergus moves on from an explicit, and indeed conventional, rebel persona. He is more interested in representing himself in terms of inner peace than in those of ego and ardour, which were the hallmarks of good faith in his institutional conflicts and ideological assertiveness. In this triumph of his inner over his outer self, of his spiritual being over his social persona, in his recognition that '[o]ne had to crucify the lower self continually' (358), Fergus detours from the path onto which he had led his fellow-countrymen. His problems of self-representation persist, though now in ways that he either evades or cannot acknowledge, so that he ultimately seems out of step with the intersection of 'inner stress and . . . outer movement' (378) on which *The Plough and the Cross* is premised. In the larger picture, it remains unclear how Fergus' choice will equip him for what Elsie O'Kennedy foresees as 'probably a still more agitated Ireland before you' (373).

# Bibliographical Note

First editions appear in square brackets or where only one edition is noted. Other editions are those from which citations have been made.

*Castle Rackrent* [London: Joseph Johnson, 1800]; Edited with an Introduction by George Watson, Oxford: Oxford University Press, 1969

*Melmoth the Wanderer* [Edinburgh: Constable, 1820, 4 vols]; Edited by Althea Hayter, Harmondsworth: Penguin, 1977

*Charlton* [London: Baldwin, Cradock & Joy, 1823, 3 vols] http://tinyurl.gale-group.com.tinyurl/HzP30 Document number: Gale |GJGHTB066176233. Accessed 16 July 2014

*Memoirs of Captain Rock* [London: Longman, Hurst, Rees, Orme, Brown & Green, 1824]; Edited and Introduced by Emer Nolan; Annotations by Seamus Deane, Dublin: Field Day, 2008

*The Boyne Water* [London: Simkin & Marshall, 1826, 3 vols]; New York: Garland, 1979. 3 vols

*The O'Briens and the O'Flahertys* [London: Colburn, 1827, 4 vols]; Edited by Julia M. Wright, Peterborough, Ontario: Broadview, 2013

*The Collegians* [London: Saunders & Otley, 1829, 3 vols]; Belfast: Appletree, 1992

*Ireland: A Tale* [London: Charles Fox, 1832]; Boston: Bowles, 1833

*The Whiteboy* [London: Chapman & Hall, 1845]; New York: Garland, 1979. 2 vols

*The Black Prophet* [Belfast: Simms & M'Intyre, 1847]; Shannon: Irish University Press, 1972

*Memoirs of Barry Lyndon* [London: Bradbury & Evans, 1856]; Edited with an Introduction by Andrew Sanders, Oxford: Oxford University Press/The World's Classics, 1984

*Castle Richmond* [London: Chapman & Hall, 1860, 3 vols]; Edited with an Introduction by Mary Hamer, Oxford: Oxford University Press/The World's Classics, 1989

*The House by the Churchyard* [London: Tinsley, 1863, 3 vols]: Belfast: Appletree, 1992

*Laurence Bloomfield in Ireland* [London: Macmillan, 1864]; New York: AMS Press, 1972

*Luttrell of Arran* [London: Chapman & Hall, 1865]; London: Downey, 1898. 2 vols

*Knocknagow* [Dublin: Duffy, 1873]; Dublin: Gill & Macmillan, 1978

*Hogan, M.P.* [London: Henry King, 1876, 3 vols]; New York: Garland, 1979. 3 vols

*A Struggle for Fame* [London: Bentley, 1883, 3 vols]; http://babel.
    hathitrust.org/cgi/pt?id=uiuo.ark:/13960/t5n87vx0x;view=1up;seq=9.
    Accessed 15 September 2014

*A Mummer's Wife* [London: Vizetelly, 1885]; Edited by Anthony Patterson,
    Brighton: Victorian Secrets, 2011

*Marcella Grace* [London: Kegan Paul, 1886]; Edited with an Introduction by
    James H. Murphy, Dublin: Maunsel, 2001

*An Unsocial Socialist* [London: S. Sonnenschein, Lowery, 1887]; London:
    Virago, 1980

*When We Were Boys,* London: Longmans, Green, 1890

*The Picture of Dorian Gray* [London: Ward Lock, 1891]; Edited with an
    Introduction by Isobel Murray, Oxford: Oxford University Press/The
    World's Classics, 1981

*Grania* [London: Smith Elder, 1892, 2 vols]; Edited by Michael O'Flynn,
    Brighton: Victorian Secrets [2013]; revised edition, 2014

*The Real Charlotte* [London: Ward & Downey, 1894, 3 vols]; Edited by Virginia
    Beards, New Brunswick, NJ: Rutgers University Press, 1986

*Dracula* [London: Constable, 1897]; London: Penguin, 2003

*Luke Delmege* [London: Longmans, Green, 1901]; Chicago: Regnery, 1955

*Dan the Dollar,* Dublin: Maunsel, 1905

*The Fly on the Wheel* [Edinburgh: Blackwood, 1908]; London: Virago, 1987

*The Plough and the Cross,* Point Loma, California: Aryan Theosophical Press,
    1910

# Select Bibliography

## Individual Authors

### WILLIAM ALLINGHAM

Review of *Laurence Bloomfield in Ireland*, *Athenaeum*, 1903 (16 April 1864), pp. 537–38

Allingham, Helen and Dollie Radford (eds), *William Allingham: A Diary* (London: Macmillan, 1907)

——, (ed.), *Letters to William Allingham* (London: Longmans, Green, 1911)

Brown, Malcolm, 'Allingham's Ireland', *Irish University Review*, vol. 13, no. 1 (Spring 1983), pp. 7–13

Brown, Terence, *Northern Voices* (Dublin: Gill & Macmillan, 1975), pp. 42–54

Campbell, Matthew, 'Irish Poetry in the Union: William Allingham's *Laurence Bloomfield in Ireland*', *European Journal of English Studies*, vol. 3, no. 3 (1999), pp. 298–313

Cronin, Anthony, *Heritage Now: Irish Literature in the English Language* (Dingle: Brandon, 1982), pp. 61–8

Donaghy, J. Lyle, 'William Allingham', *Dublin Magazine*, vol. 20, no. 2 (July–September, 1945), pp. 34–8

Hewitt, John (ed.), *The Poems of William Allingham* (Dublin: Dolmen, 1967)

Hill, George Birkbeck (ed.), *The Letters of Dante Gabriel Rossetti to William Allingham, 1854–1870* (London: T. Fisher Unwin, 1897)

Howe, M.L., 'Robert Browning and William Allingham', *Studies in Philology*, vol. 31, no. 4 (1934), pp. 567–77

Hughes, Linda K., 'The Poetics of Empire and Resistance: William Allingham's *Laurence Bloomfield in Ireland*', *Victorian Poetry*, vol. 28, no. 2 (Summer 1990), pp. 103–17

Jeffares, A. Norman, 'Yeats, Allingham and the Western Fiction', *Canadian Journal of Irish Studies*, vol. 6, no. 2 (1980), pp. 2–17

Lasner, Mark Samuels, *William Allingham: A Bibliographical Study* (Philadelphia: Holmes, 1993)

MacDonough, Patrick, 'Laurence Bloomfield in Ireland', *Dublin Magazine*, vol. 25, no. 1 (January–March 1950), pp. 25–33

McMahon, Seán, 'The Boy from his Bedroom Window', *Éire-Ireland*, vol. 5, no. 2 (Summer 1970), pp. 142–53

Shields, Hugh, 'William Allingham and Folk Song', *Hermathena*, vol. 117 (July 1974), pp. 23–36

Warner, Alan, 'The Diary of William Allingham', *Dublin Magazine*, vol. 6, no. 2 (Summer 1967), pp. 20–8

_____, *William Allingham: An Introduction* (Dublin: Dolmen, 1971)

_____, 'Patricius Walker: Victorian Irishman on Foot', *Éire-Ireland*, vol. 8, no. 3 (Fall 1973), pp. 70–80

_____, *William Allingham* (Lewisburg, Pennsylvania: Bucknell University Press, 1975)

Welch, Robert, *Irish Poetry from Moore to Yeats* (Gerrards Cross: Colin Smythe, 1980), pp. 178–204

Wolff, Robert Lee, '*Laurence Bloomfield in Ireland* by William Allingham (1824–1889)', in *Laurence Bloomfield in Ireland* (New York: Garland, 1979), pp. v–xi

## JOHN BANIM

Carleton, William, 'The Late John Banim', *The Nation*, 23 September 1843

Corrigan, Karen P., '"Plain Life" Depicted in "Fiery Shorthand": Sociolinguistic Aspects of the Languages and Dialects of Scotland and Ulster as Portrayed in Scott's *Waverley* and Banim's *The Boyne Water*', *Scottish Language*, vol. 14 & 15 (1995/6), pp. 218–33

Dunne, Tom, 'An Insecure Voice: A Catholic Novelist in Support of Emancipation', in *Culture et Pratiques Politiques en France et en Irlande XVI–XVIII Siècle* (Paris: Centre de Recherches Historiques, 1989), pp. 213–33

Escarbelt, Bernard (ed.), *The Boyne Water* (Lille: Université de Lille III, 1976)

_____, 'Les Langues de *The Boyne Water*: Mémoire de l'Irlande', *Études Irlandais*, vol. 13, no. 1 (1988), pp. 27–40

Friedman, Barton R., 'Fabricating History; or, John Banim Refights the Boyne', *Éire-Ireland*, vol. 17, no. 1 (Spring 1982), pp. 39–56

Hawthorne, Mark D., *John and Michael Banim: A Study in the Early Development of the Anglo-Irish Novel* (Salzburg: Institut für Englische Sprache und Literatur, 1975)

Kilfeather, Siobhán, 'Ireland and Europe in 1825: Situating the Banims', in Colin Graham and Leon Litvack (eds), *Ireland and Europe in the Nineteenth Century* (Dublin: Four Courts Press, 2006), pp. 29–50

Maume, Patrick, 'Respectability against Ascendancy: The Banim Brothers and the Invention of the Irish Catholic Middle-Class Novel in the Age of O'Connell', in John Strachan and Alison O'Malley-Younger (eds), *Ireland: Revolution and Evolution* (Oxford: Peter Lang, 2010), pp. 80–93

Murphy, Willa, 'The Subaltern Can Whisper: Secrecy and Solidarity in the Fiction of John and Michael Banim', in Terence McDonough (ed.), *Was Ireland a Colony? Economy, Politics, Ideology and Culture in Nineteenth-century Ireland* (Dublin: Irish Academic Press, 2005), pp. 280–98

Murray, Patrick, *The Life of John Banim, the Irish Novelist* ([1857]; New York: Garland, 1978)

Nakamura, Tetsuo, '"Irish" Quests in Catholic-Oriented Novels of the 1820s and 1830s: The Banim Brothers and William Carleton', *Irish Studies*, vol. 26 (2011), pp. 38–51

Nolan, Emer, 'Banim and the Historical Novel', in Jacqueline Belanger (ed.), *The Irish Novel in the Nineteenth Century: Facts and Fictions* (Dublin: Four Courts Press, 2005), pp. 80–93

O'Connell, Helen, 'Reconciliation and Emancipation: The Banims and Carleton', in Julia M. Wright (ed.), *Companion to Irish Literature*, 2 vols (Oxford: Wiley-Blackwell, 2010), I, pp. 411–26

Tracy, Robert, 'Fiery Shorthand: The Banim Brothers at Work', in *The Unappeasable Host* (Dublin: University College Dublin Press, 1998), pp. 41–6

Wolff, Robert Lee, 'The Fiction of "The O'Hara Family"', in *The Boyne Water*, 3 vols (New York: Garland, 1978), I, pp. v–lii

### SHAN F. BULLOCK

Bullock, Shan F., 'An Irish Experiment', *Monthly Review*, vol. 22, no. 64 (January 1906), pp. 77–88

Foster, John Wilson, *Forces and Themes in Ulster Fiction* (Dublin: Gill & Macmillan, 1974), pp. 29–36

Graecen, Robert, 'Shan F. Bullock: Laureate of Lough Erne', *Éire-Ireland*, vol. 14, no. 4 (Winter 1979), pp. 109–24

Kiely, Benedict, 'Orange Lily in a Green Garden: Shan F. Bullock', in *A Raid into Dark Corners and Other Essays* (Cork: Cork University Press, 1999), pp. 215–31

Maume, Patrick, 'Ulstermen of Letters: The Unionism of Frank Frankfort Moore, Shan Bullock and St John Ervine', in Richard English and Graham Walker (eds), *Unionism in Modern Ireland: New Perspectives in Politics and Culture* (Basingstoke: Macmillan, 1996), pp. 63–80

____, 'The Margins of Subsistence: The Novels of Shan F. Bullock', *New Hibernia Review*, vol. 2, no. 4 (Winter 1998), pp. 133–46

____, 'The Papish Minister: Shan Bullock, John Haughton Steele, and the Portrayal of Nineteenth-Century Clergymen', in Leon Litvack and Glenn Hooper (eds), *Ireland in the Nineteenth Century: Regional Identity* (Dublin: Four Courts Press, 2000), pp. 108–22

### WILLIAM CARLETON

Boué, M. André, 'William Carleton and the Irish People', *Clogher Record*, vol. 6, no. 1 (1966), pp. 66–70

____, *William Carleton: Romancier Irlandais* (Paris: Publications de la Sorbonne, 1978)

Brand, Gordon (ed.), *William Carleton: The Authentic Voice* (Gerrards Cross: Colin Smythe, 2006)

Brown, Terence, 'The Death of William Carleton, 1869', *Hermathena*, vol. CX (January 1970), pp. 81–5

Buckley, Mary, 'Attitudes to Nationality in Four Nineteenth-Century Novelists: (2) William Carleton', *Journal of the Cork Historical and Archaeological Society*, vol. 78, no. 229 (1974), pp. 109–16

Casey, Daniel J., 'Three Roads Out of Clogher: A Study of Early Nineteenth-Century Ireland in *The Life of William Carleton*', *Clogher Record*, vol. 10, no. 3 (1981), pp. 392–404

Foster, John Wilson, *Forces and Themes in Ulster Fiction* (Dublin: Gill & Macmillan, 1974), pp. 1–20

Foster, R.F., 'Square-built Power and Fiery Shorthand: Yeats, Carleton and the Irish Nineteenth Century', in *The Irish Story: Telling Tales and Making It Up in Ireland* (London: Allen Lane, 2001), pp. 113–26

Harden, Elizabeth, 'William Carleton's Humor: The Whole of Everything', *Canadian Journal of Irish Studies*, vol. 19, no. 2 (1993), pp. 67–75

Hayley, Barbara, *A Bibliography of the Writings of William Carleton* (Gerrards Cross: Colin Smythe, 1986)

Holdridge, Jefferson, 'Dark Outlines, Grey Stone: Nature, Home and the Foreign in Lady Morgan's *The Wild Irish Girl* and William Carleton's *The Black Prophet*', in Christine Cusick (ed.), *Out of the Earth: Ecocritical Readings of Irish Texts* (Cork: Cork University Press, 2010), pp. 20–35

Kavanagh, Patrick, 'Preface', *The Autobiography of William Carleton* (London: MacGibbon & Kee, 1968), pp. 9–11 (Reprints vol. I of O'Donoghue, *infra*)

Kelleher, Margaret, *The Feminization of Famine* (Cork: Cork University Press, 1997), pp. 29–39

Kiberd, Declan, 'Confronting Famine: Carleton's Peasantry', in *Irish Classics* (London: Granta, 2000), pp. 265–86

Kiely, Benedict, *Poor Scholar* (London: Sheed & Ward, 1947)

King, Jason, 'Emigration and the Anglo-Irish Novel: William Carleton, "Home Sickness", and the Coherence of Gothic Conventions', *Canadian Journal of Irish Studies*, vol. 26–7, nos 1 & 2 (Fall 2000–Spring 2001), pp. 104–18

Krause, David, 'Carleton, Catholicism and the Comic Novel', *Irish University Review*, vol. 24, no. 2 (Autumn–Winter 1994), pp. 217–40

___, *William Carleton, the Novelist: His Carnival and Pastoral World of Tragicomedy* (Lanham, Maryland: University Press of America, 2000)

McCafferty, Kevin, 'William Carleton between Irish and English: Using Literary Dialect to Study Language Contact and Change', *Language and Literature*, vol. 14, no. 4 (2005), pp. 339–62

McHugh, Roger, 'William Carleton: A Portrait of the Artist as Propagandist', *Studies*, vol. 27, no. 105 (March 1938), pp. 47–62

Montague, John, 'William Carleton: The Fiery Gift', in *The Figure in the Cave and Other Essays* (Dublin: The Lilliput Press, 1989), pp. 78–85

Murphy, Maureen, 'Carleton and Columcille', *Carleton Newsletter*, vol. 2, no. 3 (1972), pp. 19–22

Murray, Patrick, 'Traits of the Irish Peasantry', *Edinburgh Review*, vol. 96, no. 196 (October 1852), pp. 384–403

O'Brien, George, 'Carleton and Education', *Rostrum*, vol. 2 (1984), pp. 109–17

___, 'The Walk of a Hundred Years: Kavanagh and Carleton', in Peter Kavanagh (ed.), *Patrick Kavanagh: Man and Poet* (Orono, Maine: National Poetry Foundation, 1986), pp. 351–7

O'Brien, Margaret, 'William Carleton: The Lough Derg Exile', in Paul Hyland and Neil Sammells (eds), *Irish Writing: Exile and Subversion* (London: Macmillan, 1991), pp. 82–97

O'Donoghue, D.J. (ed.), *The Life of William Carleton*, 2 vols (London: Downey, 1896)

Orel, Harold, 'William Carleton: Attitudes toward the English and Irish', in Wolfgang Zach and Heinz Kosok (eds), *Literary Interrelations: Ireland, England and the World*, 3 vols (Tübingen: Narr, 1987), III, pp. 85–93

Read, Charles A., 'William Carleton', in *The Cabinet of Irish Literature*, 3 vols (London: Blackie, 1880), III, pp. 213–31

Shaw, Rose, *Carleton Country* (Dublin: The Talbot Press, 1930)

Sullivan, Eileen A., *William Carleton* (Boston: Twayne, 1983)

Webb, Timothy, 'Introduction', in *The Black Prophet* (Shannon: Irish University Press, 1972), pp. v–xvii

Wolff, Robert Lee, *William Carleton, Irish Peasant Novelist: A Preface to His Fiction* (New York: Garland, 1980)

Yeats, W.B., 'William Carleton', in John P. Frayne (ed.), *Uncollected Prose by W.B. Yeats: First Reviews and Articles, 1886–1896* (London: Macmillan, 1970), pp. 141–6

___, 'Carleton as an Irish Historian', in John P. Frayne (ed.), *Uncollected Prose by W.B. Yeats: First Reviews and Articles, 1886–1896* (London: Macmillan, 1970), pp. 166–9

___, 'William Carleton', in John P. Frayne (ed.), *Uncollected Prose by W.B. Yeats: First Reviews and Articles, 1886–1896* (London: Macmillan, 1970), pp. 394–7

## MARIA EDGEWORTH

Anon, 'A Memoir of Maria Edgeworth, with a Selection from Her Letters', *Edinburgh Review*, vol. 126, no. 258 (October 1867), pp. 458–98

Altieri, Joanne, 'Style and Purpose in Maria Edgeworth's Fiction', *Nineteenth-Century Fiction*, vol. 23, no. 3 (December 1968), pp. 265–78

Barry, F.V. (ed.), *Maria Edgeworth: Chosen Letters* (London: Jonathan Cape, 1931)

Belanger, Jacqueline, 'Educating the Reading Public: British Critical Reception of Maria Edgeworth's Early Irish Writing', *Irish University Review*, vol. 28, no. 2 (Autumn 1998), pp. 240–55

Bilger, Audrey, *Laughing Feminism: Subversive Comedy in Frances Burney, Maria Edgeworth, and Jane Austen* (Detroit: Wayne State University Press, 1998)

Brooks, Gerry H., 'The Didacticism of Edgeworth's *Castle Rackrent*', *Studies in English Literature 1500–1900,* vol. 17, no. 4 (Autumn 1977), pp. 593–605

Buckley, Mary, 'Attitudes to Nationality in Four Nineteenth-Century Novelists: (1) Maria Edgeworth', *Journal of the Cork Historical and Archaeological Society*, vol. 78, no. 227 (1973), pp. 27–34

Butler, Harriet Jesse and Harold Edgeworth Butler (eds), *The Black Book of Edgeworthstown and Other Edgeworth Memories, 1585–1817* (London: Faber & Gwyer, 1927)

Butler, Marilyn, *Maria Edgeworth: A Literary Life* (Oxford: Clarendon Press, 1972)

____, 'Introduction', in *Castle Rackrent* and *Ennui* (London: Penguin, 1992), pp. 1–54

____, 'Edgeworth's Ireland: History, Popular Culture, and Secret Codes', *Novel*, vol. 34, no. 2 (Spring 2001), pp. 267–92

____, (general ed.), *The Works of Maria Edgeworth*, 12 vols (London: Pickering & Chatto, 2003)

Butler, R.F., 'Maria Edgeworth and Sir Walter Scott: Unpublished Letters, 1823', *Review of English Studies* (n.s.), vol. 9, no. 33 (1958), pp. 23–40

Cabajsky, Andrea, 'Reading Realism, Reception and the Changing Nation: *Castle Rackrent* and *Angéline de Montbrun*', *Canadian Journal of Irish Studies*, vol. 33, no. 1 (Spring 2007), pp. 67–74

Canavan, Bernard, 'The Edgeworths of Edgeworthstown: A Rediscovered Heritage', *History Workshop*, vol. 43 (Spring 1997), pp. 240–8

Clarke, Desmond, *The Ingenious Mr Edgeworth* (London: Oldbourne, 1965)

Clarke, Isabel, *Maria Edgeworth, Her Family and Friends* (London: Hutchinson, 1950)

Cochran, Kate, '"The Plain Round Tale of Faithful Thady": *Castle Rackrent* as Slave Narrative', *New Hibernia Review*, vol. 5, no. 4 (Winter 2001), pp. 57–72

Colgan, Maurice, 'After *Rackrent*: Ascendancy Nationalism in Maria Edgeworth's Later Irish Novels', in Heinz Kosok (ed.), *Studies in Anglo-Irish Literature* (Bonn: Bouvier, 1982), pp. 37–42

Colum, Padraic, 'Maria Edgeworth and Ivan Turgenev', *British Review*, vol. 11, no. 1 (July 1915), pp. 109–13

Coolidge, Bertha Slade, *Maria Edgeworth, 1767–1849: A Bibliographical Tribute* (London: Constable, 1937)

Corbett, Mary Jean, 'Another Tale to Tell: Postcolonial Theory and the Case of *Castle Rackrent*', *Criticism*, vol. 36, no. 3 (Summer 1994), pp. 383–400

Dunne, Tom, *Maria Edgeworth and the Colonial Mind* (Dublin: National University of Ireland, 1984)

____, '"A Gentleman's Estate Should Be a Moral School": Edgeworthstown in Fact and Fiction, 1760–1840', in Raymond Gillespie and Gerald Moran (eds), *Longford: Essays in County History* (Dublin: The Lilliput Press, 1991), pp. 95–122

Edgeworth, Richard Lovell, *Memoirs of Richard Lovell Edgeworth, Esq., Begun by Himself and Concluded by His Daughter Maria Edgeworth*, 2 vols (London: Hunter, 1820)

Edwards, Duane, 'The Narrator of *Castle Rackrent*', *South Atlantic Quarterly*, vol. 71, no. 1 (Winter 1970–1), pp. 124–9

Egenoff, Susan B., 'Maria Edgeworth in Blackface: *Castle Rackrent* and the Irish Rebellion of 1798', *ELH*, vol. 72, no. 4 (Winter 2005), pp. 845–69

Fierobe, Claude, 'The Peasantry in the Irish Novels of Maria Edgeworth', in Jacqueline Genet (ed.), *Rural Ireland, Real Ireland?* (Gerrards Cross: Colin Smythe, 1996), pp. 59–69

Friedman, Geraldine, 'Rereading 1798: Melancholy and Desire in the Construction of Edgeworth's Anglo-Irish Union', *European Romantic Review*, vol. 10, nos 1–4 (1999), pp. 175–92

Glover, Susan, 'Glossing the Unvarnished Tale: Contra-Dicting Possession in *Castle Rackrent*', *Studies in Philology*, vol. 99, no. 3 (Summer 2002), pp. 295–311

Hack, Daniel, 'Inter-Nationalism: *Castle Rackrent* and Anglo-Irish Union', *Novel*, vol. 29, no. 2 (Winter 1996), pp. 145–64

Harden, O. Elizabeth McWhorter, *Maria Edgeworth's Art of Prose Fiction* (The Hague: Mouton, 1971)

____, *Maria Edgeworth* (Boston: Twayne, 1984)

Hare, Augustus J.C., *The Life and Letters of Maria Edgeworth*, 2 vols (London: Arnold, 1894)

Häuserrmann, Hans Walter, *The Genovese Background: Studies of Shelley, Francis Danby, Maria Edgeworth, Ruskin, Meredith, and Joseph Conrad in Geneva, with hitherto unpublished letters* (London: Routledge & Kegan Paul, 1952)

Hawthorne, Mark D., *Doubt and Dogma in Maria Edgeworth* (Gainesville, Florida: University of Florida Press, 1967)

Hill, Constance, *Maria Edgeworth and Her Circle in the Days of Buonaparte and Bourbon* (London: John Lane, 1910)

Hollingsworth, Brian, *Maria Edgeworth's Irish Writing: Language, History, Politics* (New York: St Martin's Press, 1997)

Hurst, Michael, *Maria Edgeworth and the Public Scene: Intellect, Fine Feeling and Landlordism in the Age of Reform* (London: Macmillan, 1969)

Inglis-Jones, Elizabeth, *The Great Maria: A Portrait of Maria Edgeworth* (London: Faber & Faber, 1959)

Kaufman, Heidi and Chris Fauske (eds), *An Uncomfortable Authority: Maria Edgeworth and Her Contexts* (Newark, Delaware: University of Delaware Press, 2004)

Kelsall, Malcolm, 'Civilization, Savagery and Ireland: Maria Edgeworth's Tour in Connemara', *European Journal of English Studies*, vol. 6, no. 2 (2002), pp. 173–87

Kennedy, Eileen, 'Genesis of a Fiction: The Edgeworth–Turgenev Relationship', *English Language Notes*, vol. 6, no. 4 (June 1969), pp. 271–3

Kirkpatrick, Kathryn, '"Going to Law about that Jointure": Women and Property in *Castle Rackrent*', *Canadian Journal of Irish Studies*, vol. 22, no. 1 (July 1996), pp. 21–9

Kowaleski-Wallace, Elizabeth, *Their Father's Daughters: Hannah More, Maria Edgeworth and Patriarchal Complicity* (New York: Oxford University Press, 1991)

Lawless, Emily, *Maria Edgeworth* (London: Macmillan, 1904)

MacDonald, Edgar E. (ed.), *The Education of the Heart: The Correspondence of Rachel Mordecai Lazarus and Maria Edgeworth* (Chapel Hill, NC: University of North Carolina Press, 1977)

Maginn, William, 'Miss Edgeworth's Tales and Novels', *Fraser's Magazine*, vol. 6, no. 34 (November 1832), pp. 541–80

Maguire, W.A., 'Castle Nugent and *Castle Rackrent*: Fact and Fiction in Maria Edgeworth', *Eighteenth-Century Ireland*, vol. 11 (1996), pp. 146–59

McCormack, W.J., 'Setting and Ideology: With Reference to the Fiction of Maria Edgeworth', in Otto Rauchbauer (ed.), *Ancestral Voices: The Big House in Anglo-Irish Literature* (Dublin: The Lilliput Press, 1992), pp. 33–60

McHugh, Roger, 'Maria Edgeworth's Irish Novels', *Studies*, vol. 27, no. 108 (December 1938), pp. 556–70

Morin, Christina, 'Preferring Spinsterhood? Maria Edgeworth, *Castle Rackrent* and Ireland', *Eighteenth-Century Ireland*, vol. 23 (2008), pp. 36–54

Murphy, Sharon, *Maria Edgeworth and Romance* (Dublin: Four Courts Press, 2004)

Murphy, Willa, 'Maria Edgeworth and the Aesthetics of Secrecy', in Tadhg Foley and Seán Ryder (eds), *Ideology and Ireland in the Nineteenth Century* (Dublin: Four Courts Press, 1998), pp. 45–54

Myers, Mitzi, 'War Correspondence: Maria Edgeworth and the En-Gendering of Revolution, Rebellion, and Union', *Eighteenth-Century Life*, vol. 22, no. 3 (November 1998), pp. 74–91

Nash, Julie (ed.), *New Essays on Maria Edgeworth* (Aldershot: Ashgate, 2006)

____, *Servants and Paternalism in the Works of Maria Edgeworth and Elizabeth Gaskell* (Aldershot: Ashgate, 2007)

Newby, P.H., *Maria Edgeworth* (London: Arthur Barker, 1950)

Newcomer, James, *Maria Edgeworth, the Novelist, 1767–1849: A Bicentennial Study* (Forth Worth: Texas Christian University Press, 1967)

Ó Gallchoir, Clíona, *Maria Edgeworth: Women, Enlightenment and Nation* (Dublin: University College Dublin Press, 2005)

Oliver, Grace A., *A Study of Maria Edgeworth: With Notices of Her Father and Friends* (Boston: Williams, 1882)

O'Neill, Marie, 'Maria Edgeworth: Anglo-Irish Writer, 1768–1849', *Dublin Historical Record*, vol. 55, no. 2 (Autumn 2002), pp. 196–207

Owens, Cóilín (ed.), *Family Chronicles: Maria Edgeworth's* Castle Rackrent (Dublin: Wolfhound Press, 1987)

Pearson, Jacqueline, '"Arts of Appropriation": Language, Circulation, and Appropriation in the Work of Maria Edgeworth', *Yearbook of English Studies*, vol. 28 (1998), pp. 212–34

Saintsbury, George, 'Maria Edgeworth', *Macmillan's Magazine*, vol. 72, no. 429 (July 1895), pp. 161–70

Takakuwa, Haruko, 'Fictionalising a Family History in *Castle Rackrent*', *Journal of Irish Studies*, vol. 22 (2007), pp. 7–15

Topliss, Iain, 'Maria Edgeworth: The Novelist and the Union', in Oliver MacDonagh and W.F. Mandle (eds), *Ireland and Irish-Australia* (London: Croom Helm, 1986), pp. 270–84

Wohlgemut, Esther, 'Maria Edgeworth and the Question of National Identity', *Studies in English Literature, 1500–1900*, vol. 39, no. 4 (Autumn 1999), pp. 645–58

Žekulin, Nicholas G., 'Turgenev and Anglo-Irish Writers, I: Maria Edgeworth', *Canadian Slavic Papers*, vol. 25, no. 1 (March 1983), pp. 25–40

## JOHN GAMBLE

Review of *Charlton*, *Westminster Review*, vol. I, no. 1 (January 1824), pp. 278–9

Campbell, A.A., 'Dr John Gamble', *Irish Book-Lover*, vol. 1, no. 2 (September 1909), pp. 20–1

Dornan, Stephen, 'Scots in Two Early Ulster Novels', *Scots: Studies in Its Language and Literature*, vol. 21 (2013), pp. 171–82

Mac Suibhne, Breandán, 'Afterworld: The Gothic Travels of John Gamble (1770–1831)', *Field Day Review*, vol. 4 (2008), pp. 63–113

____, 'Editor's Introduction', in John Gamble, *Society and Manners in Early Nineteenth-Century Ireland* (Dublin: Field Day, 2011), pp. xv–lxxx

O'Brien, George, 'The First Ulster Author: John Gamble, 1770–1831', *Éire-Ireland*, vol. 21, no. 3 (Autumn 1986), pp. 131–41.

## GERALD GRIFFIN

'The Works of Gerald Griffin', *Dublin Review*, vol. 16, no. 32 (June 1844), pp. 281–307

Colum, Padraic, 'Introduction', in *The Collegians* (Dublin: Phoenix, 1918), pp. ix–xxii

Cronin, John, 'Gerald Griffin's Commonplace Book', *Éire-Ireland*, vol. 4, no. 3 (Winter 1969), pp. 22–37

____, 'A Selected List of Works Concerning Gerald Griffin', *Irish Booklore*, vol. 1, no. 2 (August 1971), pp. 150–6

____, *Gerald Griffin (1803–1840): A Critical Biography* (Cambridge: Cambridge University Press, 1978)

____, 'The Creative Dilemma of Gerald Griffin', *Canadian Journal of Irish Studies*, vol. 12, no. 2 (1986), pp. 105–18

____, 'Introduction', in *The Collegians* (Belfast: Appletree Press, 1992), pp. vii–x

Davie, Donald, 'Gerald Griffin's *The Collegians*', *Dublin Magazine* (n.s.), vol. 28, no. 2 (April–June 1953) pp. 23–31

Davis, Robert, *Gerald Griffin* (Boston: Twayne, 1980)

Dunne, Tom, 'Murder as Metaphor: Griffin's Portrayal of Ireland in the Year of

Catholic Emancipation', in Oliver MacDonagh and W.F. Mandle (eds), *Ireland and Irish-Australia* (London: Croom Helm, 1986), pp. 64–80

Eckley, Grace, 'Griffin's Irish Tragedy, *The Collegians* and Dreiser's *An American Tragedy*', *Éire 19*, vol. 1 (1977), pp. 39–45

———, 'The Fiction of Gerald Griffin', *Journal of Irish Literature*, vol. 7, no. 2 (1978), pp. 162–73

Fitzgerald, Richard, *Ellen Hanly; or The True History of the Colleen Bawn By One who Knew Her in Life, and Saw Her in Death* (Dublin: Moffat, 1868)

Gill, W.S., *Gerald Griffin: Poet, Novelist and Christian Brother* (Dublin: Gill, 1941)

Griffin, Daniel, *The Life of Gerald Griffin, by His Brother* ([1843]; New York: Garland, 1979)

Kavanagh, Rose, 'Gerald Griffin's Life and Poetry', *Irish Monthly*, vol. 28, no. 319 (1900), pp. 15–27

Kiely, Benedict, 'The Two Masks of Gerald Griffin', in *A Raid into Dark Corners and Other Essays* (Cork: Cork University Press, 1999), pp. 203–14

Mac Lysaght, William (with Sigerson Clifford), *Death Sails the Shannon: The Authentic Story of the Colleen Bawn* (Tralee: Kerryman, 1953)

Mannin, Ethel, *Two Studies in Integrity: Gerald Griffin and Rev. Francis Mahony ('Father Prout')* (London: Jarrolds, 1954)

Moynahan, Julian, 'Gerald Griffin and Charles Dickens', in Wolfgang Zack and Heinz Kosok (eds), *Literary Interrelations: Ireland, England and the World*, 3 vols (Tübingen: Narr, 1987), II, pp. 173–80

Murphy, Willa, 'Confessing Ireland: Gerald Griffin and the Secret of Emancipation', *Éire-Ireland*, vol. 48, no. 3 (2013), pp. 79–102

Tissot, Jacques, 'The Fantastic Vein in Gerald Griffin's Works', *Cahiers du Centre d'Etudes Irlandaises*, vol. 7 (1982), pp. 31–42

Tracy, Dominick, 'Squatting the Deserted Village: Idyllic Resistance in Griffin's *The Collegians*', in Jacqueline Belanger (ed.), *The Irish Novel in the Nineteenth Century: Facts and Fictions* (Dublin: Four Courts Press, 2005), pp. 94–109

Wolff, Robert Lee, 'The Fiction of Gerald Griffin (1803–1840)', in *The Collegians*, 3 vols (New York: Garland, 1979), I, pp. v–lxi

## ANNA MARIA HALL

Butler, W.A., 'Mrs. S.C. Hall', *Dublin University Magazine*, no. 16 (August 1840), pp. 146–9

Ferguson, Samuel, 'The Didactic Irish Novelists', *Dublin University Magazine*, vol. 26, no. 156 (December 1845), pp. 737–52

Hall, Samuel Carter, *Recollections of a Long Life* (London: Bentley, 1883)

Keane, Maureen, *Mrs S.C. Hall: A Literary Biography* (Gerrards Cross: Colin Smythe, 1997)

Maginn, William, 'Mrs. S.C. Hall', *Fraser's Magazine*, vol. 13, no. 78 (June 1836), pp. 718–20

Newcomer, James, 'Mrs Samuel Carter Hall and *The Whiteboy*', *Études Irlandaises*, vol. 8 (1983), pp. 113–19

____, 'Mr and Mrs S.C. Hall: Their Papers at Iowa', *Books at Iowa*, vol. 43 (1985), pp. 15–23

Sloan, Barry, 'Mrs Hall's Ireland', *Éire-Ireland*, vol. 19, no. 3 (Fall 1984), pp. 18–30

Wolff, Robert Lee, 'The Irish Fiction of Anna Maria Hall (1800–1881)', in *The Whiteboy*, 2 vols (New York: Garland, 1979), I, pp. v–xx

## MAY LAFFAN HARTLEY

'Literary Notices', *Dublin University Magazine*, vol. 88, no. 534 (August 1876), pp. 239–56

Kahn, Helena Kelleher, *Late Nineteenth-Century Ireland's Political and Religious Controversies in the Fiction of May Laffan Hartley* (Greensboro, NC: ELT Press, 2005)

Wolff, Robert Lee, 'May Laffan Hartley and Two Examples of her Irish Fiction', an introduction to *Hogan, M.P.,* 3 vols (New York: Garland, 1979), I, pp. v–x

## CHARLES KICKHAM

'Charles Kickham: A Sketch, with Some Letters', *Irish Monthly*, vol. 15, no. 171 (September 1887), pp. 483–98

Review of *Knocknagow, Irish Monthly*, vol. 7 (1879), pp. 554–5

Carpentier, Godeleine, *Charles Joseph Kickham Écrivain* (Paris: Université de Paris III, 1987)

____, 'The Peasantry in Kickham's Tales and Novels: An Epitome of the Writer's Realism, Idealism and Ideology', in Jacqueline Genet (ed.), *Rural Ireland, Real Ireland?* (Gerrards Cross: Colin Smythe, 1996), pp. 93–107

Comerford, R.V., *Charles J. Kickham: A Study in Irish Nationalism and Literature* (Dublin: Wolfhound Press, 1979)

Dalsimer, Adele M., '"Knocknagow Is No More", but When Was it?' in Toshi Furomoto et al. (eds), *International Aspects of Irish Literature* (Gerrards Cross: Colin Smythe, 1996), pp. 189–95

de Blacam, Aodh, 'The Valley near Slievenamon', *Irish Monthly*, vol. 70, no. 829 (July 1942), pp. 296–301

Healy, James J., *Life and Times of Charles J. Kickham* (Dublin: Duffy, 1915)

Kelly, Richard J., *Charles Joseph Kickham: Patriot and Poet. A Memoir* (Dublin: Duffy, 1914)

Kiely, Benedict, 'Charles Kickham and the Living Mountain', in *A Raid into Dark Corners and other essays* (Cork: Cork University Press, 1999), pp. 107–18

Murphy, William, *Charles J. Kickham: Patriot, Novelist, and Poet* (Dublin: Duffy, 1903)

Nealon, James D., 'Charles Kickham and *Knocknagow*', *Éire-Ireland*, vol. 23, no. 2 (Summer 1988), pp. 39–50

Ó Broin, Leon, 'A Charles J. Kickham Correspondence', *Studies*, vol. 63, no. 251 (Autumn 1974), pp. 251–8

O'Faoláin, Seán, '*Knocknagow* – Case History of an Irish Bestseller', *Irish Times*, 10 May 1941

O'Hegarty, P.S., 'Kickham's Novels', *Irish Book Lover*, vol. 26, no. 2 (September–October 1938), p. 41

Wolff, Robert Lee, '*Knocknagow* by Charles Joseph Kickham', an introduction to *Knocknagow* (New York: Garland, 1979), pp. v–xii

## EMILY LAWLESS

'A Great Irish Novelist': Review of *Grania*, *United Ireland* (April 1892)

Review of *Grania*, *Freeman's Journal* (13 May 1892)

Belanger, Jacqueline, 'The Desire of the West: The Aran Islands and Irish Identity in *Grania'*, in Leon Litvack and Glenn Hooper (eds), *Ireland in the Nineteenth Century: Regional Identity* (Dublin: Four Courts Press, 2000), pp. 95–107

Brewer, Betty Webb, 'She was Part of It', *Éire-Ireland*, vol. 18, no. 4 (Winter 1983), pp. 119–31

Cahalan, James M., 'Forging a Tradition: Emily Lawless and the Irish Literary Canon', *Colby Quarterly*, vol. 27, no. 1 (1991), pp. 27–39

Devlin-Glass, Frances, 'Engendering the Nation: Gender-Bending and Nationalism in Miles Franklin's *My Brilliant Career* and Emily Lawless's *Grania: The Story of an Island'*, *Australasian Journal of Irish Studies*, vol. 11 (2011), pp. 73–85

Edwards, Heather, 'The Irish New Woman and Emily Lawless's *Grania: The Story of an Island*: A Congenial Geography', *English Literature in Transition, 1880–1920*, vol. 51, no. 4 (2008), pp. 421–38

Grubgeld, Elizabeth, 'Emily Lawless's *Grania: The Story of an Island'*, *Éire-Ireland*, vol. 22, no. 3 (Autumn 1987), pp. 115–29

Hansson, Heidi, *Emily Lawless: Writing the Interspace* (Cork: Cork University Press, 2007)

Leeney, Cathy, 'The New Woman in a New Ireland? *Grania* after Naturalism', *Irish University Review*, vol. 34, no. 1 (Spring–Summer 2004), pp. 157–70

Matthews-Kane, Bridget, 'Emily Lawless's *Grania*: Making for the Open', *Colby Quarterly*, vol. 33, no. 3 (September 1997), pp. 223–35

Meaney, Gerardine, 'Decadence, Degeneration and Revolting Aesthetics: The Fiction of Emily Lawless and Katherine Cecil Thurston', *Colby Quarterly*, vol. 36, no. 2 (June 2000), pp. 157–75

O'Flynn, Michael, 'Introduction', in *Grania: The Story of an Island* (Brighton: Victorian Secrets, 2013), pp. 9–27

Oliphant, Margaret, Review of *Grania*, in 'The Old Saloon 26', *Blackwood's Magazine*, vol. 145, no. 924 (October 1892), pp. 591–6

O'Neill, Marie, 'Emily Lawless', *Dublin Historical Record*, vol. 48, no. 2 (Autumn 1995), pp. 125–41

Sichel, Edith, 'Emily Lawless', *The Nineteenth Century*, no. 76 (July 1914), pp. 80–100

Ward, Mrs Humphrey, Review of *Grania*, *New Review*, vol. 6, no. 35 (April 1892), pp. 399–407

Watson, Cresap S., 'The Date of Emily Lawless's *Grania*', *Notes and Queries*, no. 199 (March 1954), p. 129

Wolff, Robert Lee, 'The Irish Fiction of the Honourable Emily Lawless', in Lawless, *Traits and Confidences* (New York: Garland, 1979), pp. v–xv

Yeats, W.B., 'Irish National Literature, II: Contemporary Prose Writers – Mr O'Grady, Miss Lawless, Miss Barlow, Miss Hopper, and the Folklorists', in John P. Frayne (ed.), *Uncollected Prose Writings of W.B. Yeats,* I (London: Macmillan, 1970), pp. 366–73


## JOSEPH SHERIDAN LE FANU

Begnal, Michael, *Joseph Sheridan Le Fanu* (Lewisburg, Pennsylvania: Bucknell University Press, 1971)

Bowen, Elizabeth, 'Introduction', in *The House by the Churchyard* (London: Anthony Blond, 1968), pp. vii–xi

Brennan, Kevin, 'J. Sheridan Le Fanu, Chapelizod and the Dublin Connection', *Dublin Historical Record*, vol. 33, no. 4 (September 1980), pp. 122–33

Browne, Nelson, *Sheridan Le Fanu* (New York: Roy, 1951)

Byrne, Patrick F., 'Joseph Sheridan Le Fanu: A Centenary Memoir', *Dublin Historical Record*, vol. 26, no. 3 (June 1973), pp. 80–92

Crawford, Gary William, Jim Rockhill and Brian J. Showers (eds), *Reflections in a Glass Darkly: Essays on J. Sheridan Le Fanu* (New York: Hippocampus, 2011)

Custred, Glynn, 'Sheridan Le Fanu, the Supernatural and the Sounds of the Irish Countryman', *Neohelicon*, vol. 36, no. 1 (June 2009), pp. 215–36

Eldemann, Theo, 'The Unlucky Joseph Le Fanu', *Irish University Review,* vol. 20, no. 2 (Autumn/Winter 1991), pp. 3–24

Gates, David, '"A Dish of Village Chat": Narrative Technique in Sheridan Le Fanu's *The House by the Churchyard*', *Canadian Journal of Irish Studies*, vol. 10, no. 1 (1984), pp. 63–70

Haslam, Richard, 'Joseph Sheridan Le Fanu and the Fantastic Semantics of Ghost-Colonial Ireland', in Bruce Stewart (ed.), *That Other World: The Supernatural and Fantastic in Irish Literature and Its Contexts*, 2 vols (Gerrards Cross: Colin Smythe, 1998), I, pp. 268–86

Kilroy, Thomas, 'Introduction', in *The House by the Churchyard* (Belfast: Appletree Press, 1992), pp. xi–xiv

Langan, John, 'Through the Gates of Darkness: The Cosmopolitan Gothic of J. Sheridan Le Fanu and Bram Stoker', *Studies in the Fantastic*, vol. 1 (Summer 2008), pp. 59–70

Marsh, Stewart Ellis, *Wilkie Collins, Le Fanu and Others* (London: Constable, 1931)

McCormack, W.J., *Sheridan Le Fanu and Victorian Ireland* (Oxford: Clarendon Press, 1980)

_____, 'Mediating the Past: *The House by the Churchyard*', in *Dissolute Characters: Irish Literary History through Balzac, Sheridan Le Fanu, W.B. Yeats and Elizabeth Bowen* (Manchester: Manchester University Press, 1993), pp. 34–44

_____, '"When We Name Not": *The House by the Chuchyard*', in Christina Morin and Niall Gillespie (eds), *Irish Gothics* (Basingstoke: Palgrave Macmillan, 2014), pp. 147–67

McCorristine, Shane, 'Ghost Hands, Hands of Glory, and Manumission in the Fiction of Sheridan Le Fanu', *Irish Studies Review*, vol. 17, no. 3 (August 2009), pp. 275–95

Melada, Ivan, *Sheridan Le Fanu* (Boston: Twayne, 1987)

Sage, Victor, *Le Fanu's Gothic: The Rhetoric of Darkness* (Basingstoke: Palgrave Macmillan, 2004)

_____, 'Resurrecting the Regency: Horror and Eighteenth-Century Comedy in Le Fanu's Fiction', in Ruth Robbins and Julian Wolfreys (eds), *Victorian Gothic: Literary and Cultural Manifestations in the Nineteenth Century* (New York: Palgrave, 2000), pp. 12–30

_____, 'Irish Gothic: C.R. Maturin and J.S. Le Fanu', in David Punter (ed.), *A Companion to the Gothic* (Oxford: Blackwell, 2000), pp. 81–93

Stoddart, Helen, '"The Precautions of Nervous People are Infectious": Sheridan Le Fanu's Symptomatic Gothic', *Modern Language Review*, vol. 86, no. 1 (January 1991), pp. 19–34

Tracy, Robert, 'Sheridan Le Fanu and the Unmentionable', in *The Unappeasable Host* (Dublin: University College Dublin Press, 1998), pp. 57–72

Walton, James, *Vision and Vacancy: The Fictions of J.S. Le Fanu* (Dublin: University College Dublin Press, 2007)

Wegley, Mark, 'Unknown Fear: Joseph Sheridan Le Fanu and the Literary Fantastic', *Philological Review*, vol. 27, no. 2 (2001), pp. 59–77

Wolff, Robert Lee, 'The Irish Fiction of Joseph Sheridan Le Fanu (1814–73)', in *The House by the Churchyard*, 3 vols (New York: Garland, 1979), I, pp. v–xxv

Zuber, Devin P., 'Swedenborg and the Disintegration of Language in Sheridan Le Fanu's Sensation Fiction', in Kimberly Harrison and Richard Fantina (eds), *Victorian Sensations: Essays on a Scandalous Genre* (Columbus, Ohio: Ohio State University Press, 2006), pp. 78–84

## CHARLES LEVER

Bareham, Tony (ed.), *Charles Lever: New Evaluations* (Gerrards Cross: Colin Smythe, 1991)

Blake, Andrew, 'Charles Lever: Writing from the Outside In', in Neil McCaw (ed.), *Writing Irishness in Nineteenth-Century British Culture* (Aldershot: Ashgate, 2003), pp. 116–28

Boyce, George, 'Lever, the Landlords and the Union', *Anglistica Pisana*, vol. 4 (2007), pp. 53–68

Buckley, Mary, 'Attitudes to Nationality in Four Nineteenth-Century Novelists: (3) Charles Lever', *Journal of the Cork Historical and Archaeological Society*, vol. 80, no. 230 (1974), pp. 129–35

Bulwer-Lytton, Edward, 'The Works of Charles Lever', *Blackwood's Edinburgh Magazine*, vol. 91, no. 558 (April 1862), pp. 452–72

Downey, Edmund (ed.), *Charles Lever: His Life in His Letters*, 2 vols (Edinburgh: Blackwood, 1906)

Duffy, Charles Gavan, 'Mr. Lever's "Irish Novels"' [*The Nation*, 10 June 1843]; in Deane et al. (eds), *The Field Day Anthology of Irish Writing*, 3 vols (Derry: Field Day, 1991), I, pp. 1255–65

Fitzpatrick, W.J., *The Life of Charles Lever* (London: Ward, Lock, 1879; 1884, rev. ed.)

Haddesley, Stephen, *Charles Lever: The Lost Victorian* (Gerrards Cross: Colin Smythe, 2000)

Hoey, Frances Cashel, 'The Works of Charles Lever,' *Dublin Review*, vol. 18, no. 36 (April 1872), pp. 379–408

Jeffares, A. Norman, 'Yeats and the Wrong Lever', in Jeffares (ed.), *Yeats, Sligo and Ireland* (Gerrards Cross: Colin Smythe, 1980), pp. 98–111

____, 'Reading Lever', in *Images of Invention: Essays on Irish Writing* (Gerrards Cross: Colin Smythe, 1996), pp. 150–63

Kelsall, Malcolm, 'Writing Which Nation? *Luttrell of Arran* and the Romantic Invention of Ireland', in Gerald Carruthers and Alan Rawes (eds), *English Romanticism and the Celtic World* (Cambridge: Cambridge University Press, 2003), pp. 182–95

King, Jason, 'Emigration and the Irish Novel: Charles Lever, the Picaresque and the Emergence of the Irish Emigration Narrative Form', in Jacqueline Belanger (ed.), *The Irish Novel in the Nineteenth Century: Facts and Fictions* (Dublin: Four Courts Press, 2005), pp. 123–38

Livingston, Flora V. (ed.), *Charles Dickens's Letters to Charles Lever* (Cambridge, Massachusetts: Harvard University Press, 1933)

McHugh, Roger, 'Charles Lever', *Studies*, vol. 27, no. 106 (June 1938), pp. 247–60

Morash, Christopher, 'Reflecting Absent Interiors: The Big-House Novels of Charles Lever', in Otto Rauchbauer (ed.), *Ancestral Voices: The Big House in Anglo-Irish Literature* (Dublin: The Lilliput Press, 1992), pp. 61–76

Rix, Walter T., 'Charles Lever: The Irish Dimension of a Cosmopolitan', in Heinz Kosok (ed.), *Studies in Anglo-Irish Literature* (Bonn: Bouvier, 1982), pp. 54–64

Rolfe, Franklin P., 'Letters of Charles Lever to His Wife and Daughter', *Huntington Library Bulletin*, no. 10 (October 1936), pp. 149–84

Scott, J.A., 'A Group of New Novels', *Dublin University Magazine*, vol. 65, no. 387 (March 1865), pp. 339–51

Shaw, George Bernard, 'Preface', in *Major Barbara* (London: Constable, 1907)

Stark, Tom, 'Lever's Ireland: Fiction as Fact', *Anglistica Pisana*, vol. 4 (2007), pp. 69–82

Stevenson, Lionel, *Dr. Quicksilver* (London: Chapman & Hall, 1939)

Sutherland, John, 'Lever's Columns: A Novelist Who Contributed to Great Fiction Without Becoming Great', *Times Literary Supplement* (15 December 2006), p. 14

———, 'Charles Lever, W.M. Thackeray, Leo Tolstoy', *Anglistica Pisana*, vol. 4 (2007), pp. 37–46

Vann, J. Don, 'Dickens, Charles Lever and Mrs. Gaskell', *Victorian Periodicals Reviews*, vol. 22, no. 2 (Summer 1989), pp. 63–71

Weintraub, Stanley, 'Bernard Shaw, Charles Lever and *Immaturity*', *Bulletin (Shaw Society of America)*, vol. 2, no. 1 (January 1957), pp. 11–15

## HARRIET MARTINEAU

Ferguson, Samuel, 'Irish Storyists', *Dublin University Magazine*, vol. 4, no. 240 (September 1834), pp. 298–311

Hooper, Glenn (ed.), *Harriet Martineau: Letters from Ireland* (Dublin: Irish Academic Press, 2001)

Logan, Deborah Anna, *The Hour and the Woman: Harriet Martineau's 'Somewhat Remarkable' Life* (Dekalb, Illinois: Northern Illinois University Press, 2002)

———, (ed.), *Harriet Martineau and the Irish Question: Condition of Post-Famine Ireland* (Bethlehem, Pennsylvania: Lehigh University Press, 2012)

Oražem, Claudia, *Political Economy and Fiction in the Early Works of Harriet Martineau* (Frankfurt-am-Main: Lang, 1999)

Peterson, Linda H. (ed.), *Harriet Martineau, Autobiography* (Peterborough, Ontario: Broadview, 2007)

Ryall, Anka, 'Harriet Martineau and the Cause of the Irish Poor', in Jakob Lothe, Juan Christian Pellicer and Tore Rem (eds), *Literary Sinews: Essays in Honour of Bjorn Tysdahl* (Oslo: Novus, 2003), pp. 121–32

Sanders, Valerie, *Harriet Martineau: Selected Letters* (Oxford: Clarendon Press, 1990)

Spring-Rice, Thomas, Review of *Ireland: A Tale*, *Edinburgh Review*, vol. 57, no. 115 (April 1833), pp. 248–55

## CHARLES MATURIN

'Melmoth the Wanderer', *Edinburgh Review*, vol. 35, no. 70 (July 1821), pp. 353–62

'Maturin, *Melmoth the Wanderer*', *Quarterly Review*, vol. 24, no. 48 (January 1821), pp. 303–11

'Conversations of Maturin – No. 1', *New Monthly Magazine and Literary Journal*, vol. 19, no. 77 (May 1827), pp. 401–11

'Rev. Charles Robert Maturin', *The Irish Quarterly Review*, vol. 2, no. 5 (March 1852), pp. 141–70

Coughlan, Patricia, 'The Recycling of *Melmoth the Wanderer*: "A Very German Story"', in Wolfgang Zach and Heinz Kosok (eds), *Literary Interrelations: Ireland, England and the World*, 3 vols (Tübingen: Narr, 1987), II, pp. 181–91

Crampton, Hope, 'Melmoth in *La Comédie Humaine*', *Modern Language Review*, no. 61 (January 1966), pp. 42–50

Doyle, Laura, 'At World's Edge: Post/Coloniality, Charles Maturin, and the Gothic Wanderer', *Nineteenth-Century Literature*, vol. 65, no. 4 (2011), pp. 513–47

Eggenschwiler, David, '*Melmoth the Wanderer*: Gothic on Gothic', *Genre*, vol. 8, no. 2 (June 1975), pp. 165–81

Fierobe, Claude, 'L'univers Fantastique de *Melmoth the Wanderer*', in *La Raison et l'Imaginaire* (Paris: Didier, 1973), pp. 105–16

____, 'France in the Novels of Charles Robert Maturin', in Patrick Rafroidi, Guy Fehlmann and Maitiu Mac Conmara (eds), *France–Ireland Literary Relations* (Lille: Université de Lille III, 1974), pp. 119–31

____, *Charles Robert Maturin, 1780–1824: l'homme et l'oeuvre* (Lille: Université de Lille III, 1974)

Haslam, Richard, 'Maturin and the "Calvinist Sublime"', in Allan Lloyd Smith and Victor Sage (eds), *Gothick Origins and Innovations* (Amsterdam: Rodopi, 1994), pp. 44–56

Hennelly, Mark M., Jr., '*Melmoth the Wanderer* and Gothic Existentialism', *Studies in English Literature, 1500–1900*, vol. 21, no. 4 (Autumn 1981), pp. 665–79

Idman, Niilo, *Charles Robert Maturin: His Life and Works* (London: Constable, 1923)

Jeffares, A.N. and H.W. Piper, 'Maturin the Innovator', *Huntingdon Library Quarterly*, vol. 21, no. 3 (May 1958), pp. 261–84

Kiely, Robert, *The Romantic Novel in England* (Cambridge, Massachusetts: Harvard University Press, 1972), pp. 189–207

Kosok, Heinz, 'Charles Robert Maturin and Colonialism', in Mary Massoud (ed.), *Literary Inter-Relations: Ireland, Egypt, and the Far East* (Gerrards Cross: Colin Smythe, 1996), pp. 228–34

Kramer, Dale, *Charles Robert Maturin* (New York: Twayne, 1973)

Lew, Joseph W., '"Unprepared for Sudden Transformations": Identity and Politics in *Melmoth the Wanderer*', *Studies in the Novel*, vol. 26, no. 2 (Summer 1994), pp. 173–95

Lougy, Robert E., *Charles Robert Maturin* (Lewisburg, Pennsylvania: Bucknell University Press, 1975)

Null, Jack, 'Structure and Theme in *Melmoth the Wanderer*', *Papers on Language and Literature*, vol. 13, no. 2 (Spring 1977), pp. 136–47

Praz, Mario, 'The Shadow of the "Divine Marquis"', in *The Romantic Agony* ([1933]; New York: Meridian, 1956), pp. 93–186

Ragaz, Sharon, 'Maturin, Archibald Constable, and the Publication of *Melmoth the Wanderer*', *Review of English Studies,* vol. 57, no. 230 (2006), pp. 359–73

Ratchford, Fannie E. and William H. McCarthy, Jr., *The Correspondence of Sir Walter Scott and Charles Robert Maturin* (New York: Garland, 1980)

Sage, Victor, 'Diderot and Maturin: Enlightenment, Automata, and the Theatre of Terror', in Avril Horner (ed.), *European Gothic: A Spirited Exchange* (Manchester: Manchester University Press, 2002), pp. 55–70

Scott, Shirley, *Myths and Consciousness in the Novels of Charles Maturin* (New York: Arno, 1973)

Stott, G. St John, 'The Structure of *Melmoth the Wanderer*', *Études Irlandaises*, vol. 12, no. 1 (June 1987), pp. 41–52

Wilt, Judith, '"All about the Heart": The Material-Theology of Maturin's *Melmoth the Wanderer*', in J. Robert Barth (ed.), *The Fountain Light: Studies in Romanticism and Religion: In Honor of John L. Mahoney* (New York: Fordham University Press, 2002), pp. 256–73

## GEORGE MOORE

Review of *A Mummer's Wife*, *Saturday Review*, vol. 59, no. 1529 (14 February 1885), pp. 214–15

Bassett, Troy J., 'Circulating Morals: George Moore's Attack on Late-Victorian Literary Censorship', *Pacific Coast Philology*, vol. 40, no. 2 (2005), pp. 73–89

Blissett, William F., 'George Moore and Literary Wagnerism', *Comparative Literature*, vol. 13, no. 1 (1961), pp. 52–71

Brown, Malcolm, *George Moore: A Reconsideration* (Seattle: University of Washington Press, 1955)

Cave, Richard Allen, 'George Moore and His Irish Novels', in Augustine Martin (ed.), *The Genius of Irish Prose* (Cork: Mercier Press, 1984), pp. 22–31

____, *A Study of the Novels of George Moore* (Gerrards Cross: Colin Smythe, 1978)

Collet, Georges-Paul, *George Moore et la France* (Genève: Droz, 1957)

Colum, Padraic, 'George Moore', *Dubliner*, vol. 2, no. 2 (March 1962), pp. 49–55

Cordasco, Francesco, 'George Moore and Edouard Dujardin', *Modern Language Notes*, no. 62 (April 1947), pp. 244–51

Cunard, Nancy, *GM: Memories of George Moore* (London: Rupert Hart-Davis, 1936)

Dunleavy, Janet Egleson, *George Moore: The Artist's Vision, The Storyteller's Art* (Lewisburg, Pennsylvania: Bucknell University Press, 1973)

____, (ed.), *George Moore in Perspective* (Gerrards Cross: Colin Smythe, 1983)

Eglinton, John (ed.), *Letters of George Moore to Edouard Dujardin, 1886–1922* (New York: Crosby Gaige, 1929)

____, *Letters of George Moore* (Bournemouth: Sydenham, 1942)

Farrow, Anthony, *George Moore* (Boston: Twayne, 1978)

Ferguson, Walter D., *The Influence of Flaubert on George Moore* (Philadelphia: University of Pennsylvania Press, 1934)

Frazier, Adrian, *George Moore, 1852–1933* (New Haven, Connecticut: Yale University Press, 2000)

Frierson, William C., 'George Moore Compromised with the Victorians', *Trollopia*, no. I (March 1947), pp. 37–44

Furst, Lilian G., 'George Moore, Zola, and the Question of Influence', *Canadian Review of Comparative Literature/Revue Canadienne de Littérature Comparée*, vol. 1, no. 2 (1974), pp. 138–55

Gaspari, Fabienne, '"La peur du désir": *A Mummer's Wife* et *Esther Waters* de George Moore', *Cahiers victoriens et édouardiens*, vol. 67 (2008), pp. 253–67

Gerber, Helmut E. (ed.), 'George Moore: An Annotated Bibliography of Writings About Him', *English Literature in Transition, 1880–1920*, vol. 2, nos 1 & 2 (1951), pp. 1–91

____, 'George Moore: From Pure Poetry to Pure Criticism', *Journal of Aesthetics and Art Criticism*, no. 25 (Spring 1967), pp 281–91

____, (ed.), *George Moore on Parnassus: Letters (1900–1933)* (Newark, Delaware: University of Delaware Press, 1988)

Grubgeld, Elizabeth, *George Moore and the Autogenous Self: The Autobiography and Fiction* (Syracuse, NY: Syracuse University Press, 1994)

Heilmann, Ann, 'The Sublime and Satanic North: The Potteries in George Moore's *A Mummer's Wife* (1885) and Arnold Bennett's *Anna of the Five Towns* (1902)', in Katherine Cockin (ed.), *The Literary North* (Basingstoke: Palgrave Macmillan, 2012), pp. 56–72

Henn, T.R., 'George Moore', in *Last Essays* (Gerrards Cross: Colin Smythe, 1976), pp. 173–90

Heywood, C., 'Flaubert, Miss Braddon and George Moore', *Comparative Literature*, vol. 12, no. 2 (Spring 1960), pp. 151–8

Hone, Joseph M., *The Life of George Moore* (London: Gollancz, 1936)

____, *The Moores of Moore Hall* (London: Cape, 1939)

Hough, Graham, 'George Moore and the Novel', *Review of English Literature*, no. 1 (January 1960), pp. 35–44

____, 'George Moore and the Nineties', in Richard Ellmann (ed.), *Edwardians and Late Victorians* (New York: English Institute/Columbia University Press, 1960), pp. 1–27

Hughes, Douglas A. (ed.), *The Man of Wax: Critical Essays on George Moore* (New York: New York University Press, 1971)

Huguet, Christine and Fabienne Dabrigeon-Garcier (eds), *George Moore: Across Borders* (Amsterdam: Rodopi, 2013)

Jernigan, Jay, 'The Bibliographical and Textual Complexities of George Moore's *A Mummer's Wife*', *Bulletin of the New York Public Library*, vol. 74, no. 6 (June 1970), pp. 396–410

King, Carla, 'Introduction', in *Parnell and His Island* (Dublin: University College Dublin Press, 2004), pp. vii–xxvii

Lernout, Geert, 'George Moore: Wagnerian and Symbolist', *Cahiers du Centre d'Etudes Irlandaises,* vol. 5 (1980), pp. 55–69

Masters, Joellen, '"A Great Part to Play": Gender, Genre, and Literary Fame in George Moore's *A Mummer's Wife'*, *Victorian Literature and Culture,* vol. 29, no. 2 (2001), pp. 285–301

Mitchell, Judith, 'Fictional Worlds in George Moore's *A Mummer's Wife'*, *English Studies,* vol. 67, no. 1 (1986), pp. 345–54

___, 'Naturalism in George Moore's *A Mummer's Wife',* in Barbara Harman and Susan Meyer (eds), *The New Nineteenth Century: Feminist Readings of Underread Victorian Fiction* (New York: Garland, 1996), pp. 159–79

Mitchell, Susan L., *George Moore* (New York: Dodd, Mead, 1916)

Montague, Conor and Adrian Frazier (eds), *George Moore: Dublin, Paris, Hollywood* (Dublin: Irish Academic Press, 2012)

Montague, John, 'George Moore: The Tyranny of Memory', in *The Figure in the Cave and Other Essays* (Dublin: The Lilliput Press, 1989), pp. 86–97

Nejdefors-Frisk, Sonja, *George Moore's Naturalistic Prose* (Upsala: Upsala Irish Studies, 1952)

Noël, Jean C., 'George Moore et Mallarmé', *Revue de Littérature Comparée',* no. 32 (July 1958), pp. 363–76

___, *George Moore: l'homme et l'œuvre (1852–1933)* (Paris: Didier, 1966)

Owens, Graham (ed.), *George Moore's Mind and Art* (Edinburgh: Oliver & Boyd, 1968)

Patterson, Anthony, 'Introduction', in *A Mummer's Wife* (Brighton: Victorian Secrets, 2011), pp. 7–15

Pierce, Mary (ed.), *George Moore: Artistic Visions and Literary Worlds* (Newcastle-upon-Tyne: Cambridge Scholars, 2006)

Roberts, Jane, 'George Moore: A Wild Goose's Portrait of His Country', *Irish University Review,* vol. 22, no. 2 (Autumn–Winter 1992), pp. 305–18

Shields, Agnes, 'Religion as Trope in the Naturalistic Novels of George Moore: *A Mummer's Wife, A Drama in Muslin,* and *Esther Waters',* *Excavatio,* vol. 18, nos 1–2 (2003), pp. 363–71

Steward, S.M., 'J.-K. Huysmans and George Moore', *Romantic Review,* no. 25 (July–September 1934), pp. 197–206

Ure, Peter, 'George Moore as Historian of Consciences', in Maynard Mack and Ian Gregor (eds), *Imagined Worlds: Essays on Some English Novels and Novelists in Honour of John Butt* (London: Methuen, 1968), pp. 257–76

Ward, Patrick, *Exile, Emigration and Irish Writing* (Dublin: Irish Academic Press, 2002), pp. 182–231

Welch, Robert, 'George Moore: "The Law of Change is the Law of Life"', in *Changing States: Transformations in Modern Irish Writing* (London: Routledge, 1993), pp. 35–54

Wolfe, Humbert, *George Moore* (London: Butterworth, 1933)

Woolf, Virginia, 'George Moore', in *The Death of the Moth* (London: Hogarth Press, 1942), pp. 156–61

THOMAS MOORE

Review of *Memoirs of Captain Rock*, *Westminster Review*, vol. 1, no. 2 (April 1824), pp. 492–504

Review of *Memoirs of Captain Rock*, *Monthly Review,* 2nd series, no. 106 (January 1825), pp. 85–94

Brown, Terence, 'Thomas Moore: A Reputation', in *Ireland's Literature: Selected Essays* (Dublin: The Lilliput Press, 1988), pp. 14–28

de Paor, Liam, 'Tom Moore and Modern Ireland', in *Landscapes with Figures* (Dublin: Four Courts Press, 1998), pp. 68–80

Eagleton, Terry, 'The Masochism of Thomas Moore', in *Crazy Jane and the Bishop* (Notre Dame, Indiana: University of Notre Dame Press/Field Day, 1998), pp. 140–57

Gibbons, Luke, 'Between Captain Rock and a Hard Place: Art and Agrarian Insurgency', in Tadhg Foley and Seán Ryder (eds), *Ideology and Ireland in the Nineteenth Century* (Dublin: Four Courts Press, 1998), pp. 23–44

Jones, Catherine A., '"Our Partial Attachments": Tom Moore and 1798', *Eighteenth-Century Ireland*, vol. 13 (1998), pp. 24–43

Jones, Howard Mumford, *The Harp that Once: A Chronicle of the Life of Thomas Moore* (New York: Holt, 1937)

Jordan, Hoover, *Bolt Upright: The Life of Thomas Moore* (Salzburg: Salzburg Studies in English Literature, 1975)

Mahony, Sylvester, 'The Rogueries of Tom Moore', *Fraser's Magazine*, vol. 10, no. 56 (August 1834), pp. 194–210

Moore, Jane, 'Thomas Moore as Irish Satirist', in David Duff and Catherine Jones (eds), *Scotland, Ireland, and the Romantic Aesthetic* (Lewisburg, Pennsylvania: Bucknell University Press, 2007), pp. 152–71

Moore, Thomas, 'To-day in Ireland', *Edinburgh Review*, vol. 43, no. 86 (February 1826), pp. 356–72

Nolan, Emer, 'Irish Melodies and Discordant Politics: Thomas Moore's *Memoirs of Captain Rock* (1824)', *Field Day Review*, vol. 2 (2006), pp. 40–53

Ó Casaide, Seamus, 'Thomas Moore and Robert Emmet', *Irish Book-Lover*, vol. 22, no. 1 (February 1935), pp. 8–9

O'Sullivan, Mortimer, *Captain Rock Detected* (London: Cadell, 1824)

O'Sullivan, Patrick, 'A Literary Difficulty in Explaining Ireland: Tom Moore and Captain Rock', in Roger Swift and Sheridan Gilley (eds), *The Irish in Britain, 1815–1939* (London: Pinter, 1989), pp. 239–74

Rafroidi, Patrick, 'Thomas Moore: Towards a Reassessment?', in Michael Kenneally (ed.), *Irish Literature and Culture* (Gerrards Cross: Colin Smythe, 1992), pp. 55–62

Smith, Sydney, Review of *Memoirs of Captain Rock*, *Edinburgh Review*, vol. 41, no. 81 (October 1824), pp. 143–53

Stockley, W.F.P., 'Moore and Ireland', in *Essays in Irish Biography* (Cork: Cork University Press, 1933), pp. 1–34

Strong, L.A.G., *The Minstrel Boy: A Portrait of Tom Moore* (London: Hodder & Stoughton, 1937)

Wright, Julia, '"The Same Dull Round Over Again": Colonial History in Moore's *Memoirs of Captain Rock*', *European Romantic Review*, vol. 14, no. 2 (2003), pp. 239–49

## Lady Morgan

'The Late Lady Morgan and Her Autobiography', *Fraser's Magazine*, vol. 67, no. 398 (February 1863), pp. 172–91

Atkinson, Colin B. and Jo Atkinson, 'Sydney Owenson, Lady Morgan: Irish Patriot and First Professional Woman Writer', *Éire-Ireland*, vol. 15, no. 2 (Summer 1980), pp. 60–90

Belanger, Jacqueline, *Critical Responses: Sydney Owenson, Lady Morgan* (Bethesda, Maryland: Academia, 2007)

Botkin, Frances R., 'Performing Irishness: Sydney Owenson, Lady Morgan, and the "Doubt of Identity"', *Interactions: Aegean Journal of English and American Studies*, vol. 16, no. 2 (2007), pp. 41–54

Brihault, Jean, 'Lady Morgan, Mother of the Irish Historical Novel?', *Études Irlandaises*, vol. 18, no. 1 (1993), pp. 29–37

——, 'Lady Morgan: Deep Furrows', in Jacqueline Genet (ed.), *Rural Ireland, Real Ireland?* (Gerrards Cross: Colin Smythe, 1996), pp. 71–81

Campbell, Mary, *Lady Morgan: The Life and Times of Sydney Owenson* (London: Pandora, 1988)

——, 'Introduction', in *The O'Briens and the O'Flahertys* (London: Pandora, 1988)

Dixon, W.H. (ed.), *Lady Morgan's Memoirs: Autobiography, Diaries and Correspondence*, 2 vols (London: W.H. Allen, 1862; rev. ed., 1863)

Donovan, Julie, *Lady Morgan and the Politics of Style* (Bethesda, Maryland: Academica, 2009)

Dunne, Eamonn, '"She Sang Beyond the Genius of the Sea": Sydney Owenson's Topographical Ethics', *Nordic Irish Studies*, vol. 8 (2009), pp. 1–15

Dunne, Tom, 'Fiction as "the Best History of Nations": Lady Morgan's Irish Novels', in *The Writer as Witness: Literature as Historical Evidence* (Cork: Cork University Press, 1987), pp. 133–59

Egenolf, Susan, 'Lady Morgan (Sydney Owenson) and the Politics of Romanticism', in Jim Kelly (ed.), *Ireland and Romanticism: Publics, Nations and Scenes of Cultural Production* (Basingstoke: Palgrave Macmillan, 2011), pp. 109–21

Ferris, Ina, 'Narrating Cultural Encounter: Lady Morgan and the Irish National Tale', *Nineteenth-Century Literature*, vol. 51, no. 3 (1996), pp. 287–303

Fitzpatrick, W.J., *Lady Morgan: Her Career, Literary and Personal, with a Glimpse at her Friends, and a Word to her Calumniators* (London: Skeet, 1860)

Haslam, Richard, 'Lady Morgan's Novels from 1806–1833 [*sic*]: Cultural Aesthetics and National Identity', *Éire-Ireland*, vol. 22, no. 4 (Winter 1987), pp. 11–25

Ingelbein, Raphael, 'Paradoxes of National Liberation: Lady Morgan, O'Connellism, and the Belgian Revolution', *Éire-Ireland*, vol. 42, no. 3 (Autumn 2007), pp. 104–25

Kelly, Gary, 'Gender and Memory in Post-Revolutionary Women's Writing', in Matthew Campbell, Jacqueline M. Labbe and Sally Shuttleworth (eds), *Memory and Memorials, 1789–1914: Literary and Cultural Perspectives* (London: Routledge, 2000), pp. 119–31

Kucich, Greg, 'Lady Morgan, Women's Cosmopolitan History, and Virtual Travel', *Prose Studies*, vol. 31, no. 2 (2009), pp. 151–9

Lew, Joseph W., 'Sidney Owenson and the Fate of Empire', *Keats–Shelley Journal*, vol. 39 (1990), pp. 39–65

Maume, Patrick, 'Father Boyce, Lady Morgan and Sir Walter Scott: A Study in Intertextuality and Catholic Polemics', in James H. Murphy (ed.), *Evangelicals and Catholics in Nineteenth-Century Ireland* (Dublin: Four Courts Press: 2005), pp. 165–78

Newcomer, James, *Lady Morgan the Novelist* (Lewisburg, Pennsylvania: Bucknell University Press, 1990)

Ross, Bianca, 'Of Prejudice and Predilection: Lady Morgan and Her "Annals of St. Grellan"', *Eighteenth-Century Ireland*, vol. 9 (1994), pp. 99–113

Spender, Dale, 'Lady Morgan and Political Fiction', in Spender, *Mothers of the Novel: 100 Good Women Writers Before Jane Austen* (London: Pandora, 1986), pp. 301–14

Takakuwa, Haruko, '"Wild Irish" Heroines: Sydney Owenson's National Tales of the 1810s', *Journal of Irish Studies*, vol. 26 (2011), pp. 24–37

Tessone, Natasha, 'Displaying Ireland: Sydney Owenson and the Politics of Spectacular Antiquarianism', *Éire-Ireland*, vol. 37, nos 3–4 (Fall/Winter 2002), pp. 169–86

Thuente, Mary Helen, 'Lady Morgan's Beavoin O'Flaherty: Ancient Irish Goddess and Enlightenment Cosmopolitan', *New Hibernia Review*, vol. 16, no. 2 (Summer 2012), pp. 33–53

Wolff, Robert Lee, 'The Irish Novels of Sydney Owenson, lady Morgan (1776–1859)', in *The O'Briens and the O'Flahertys*, 4 vols (New York: Garland, 1979), 1, pp. v–xxix

Wright, Julia M, '"The Nation Begins to Form": Competing Nationalisms in Morgan's *The O'Briens and the O'Flahertys*', *English Literary History*, vol. 66, no. 4 (Winter 1999), pp. 939–63

_____, 'National Erotics and Political Theory in Morgan's *The O'Briens and the O'Flahertys*', *European Romantic Review*, vol. 15, no. 2 (2004), pp. 229–41

_____, 'Introduction', in *The O'Briens and the O'Flahertys* (Peterborough, Ontario: Broadview, 2013), pp. 9–29

## ROSA MULHOLLAND

Cahill, Susan, 'Making Space for the Irish Girl: Rosa Mulholland and Irish Girls in Fiction at the Turn of the Century', in Kristine Moruzi and Michelle J. Smith (eds), *Colonial Girlhood in Literature, Culture and History, 1840–1950* (Basingstoke: Palgrave Macmillan, 2014), pp. 167–79

Crone, John S., 'Obituary of Rosa Mulholland', *Irish Book Lover*, vol. 13, nos 1 & 2 (August–September 1921), pp. 21–22

Gilbert, Rosa Mulholland, 'The Late Father Matthew Russell, SJ: An Anniversary Sketch', *Irish Monthly*, no. 41 (September 1913), pp. 465–75

Hansson, Heidi, 'From Reformer to Sufferer: The Returning Exile in Rosa Mulholland's Fiction', in Michael Böss, Irene Gilsenan Nordin and Britta Olinder (eds), *Re-Mapping Exile: Realities and Metaphors in Irish Literature and History* (Aarhus: Aarhus University Press, 2005), pp. 89–106

Mulholland, Rosa, 'Wanted: An Irish Novelist', *Irish Monthly*, no. 19 (July 1891), pp. 368–73

Murphy, James H., 'Rosa Mulholland, W.P. Ryan and Irish Catholic Fiction at the Time of the Anglo-Irish Revival', in Joep Leerssen, A.H. van der Weel and Bart Westerweel (eds), *Forging in the Smithy: National Identity and Representation in Anglo-Irish Literature* (Amsterdam: Rodopi, 1995), pp. 219–28

____, 'Introduction', in *Marcella Grace* (Dublin: Maunsel, 2001), pp. 1–16

## WILLIAM O'BRIEN

MacDonagh, Michael, *The Life of William O'Brien* (London: Benn, 1928)

Maume, Patrick, 'In the Fenians' Wake: Ireland's Nineteenth-Century Crises and their Representation in the Sentimental Rhetoric of William O'Brien MP and Canon Sheehan', *Bullán*, vol. 4, no. 1 (Autumn 1998), pp. 59–80

Murphy, James H., 'William O'Brien's *When We Were Boys*: A New Voice from Old Conventions', *Irish University Review*, vol. 22, no. 2 (Autumn/Winter 1992), pp. 298–304

O'Brien, Joseph V., *William O'Brien and the Course of Irish Politics, 1881–1918* (Berkeley, California: University of California Press, 1976)

Warwick-Haller, Sally E., *William O'Brien and the Irish Land War* (Dublin: Irish Academic Press, 1991)

Wolff, Robert Lee, '*When We Were Boys* by William O'Brien (1852–1928)', in *When We Were Boys* (New York: Garland, 1979), pp. v–xiii

## CHARLOTTE RIDDELL

Review of *A Struggle for Fame*, *Saturday Review*, vol. 56, no. 1,451 (18 August 1883), pp. 216–17

Blathwayt, Raymond, 'A Chat with Mrs. J.H. Riddell', *Pall Mall Gazette* (18 February 1890)

Bleiler, E.F., 'Mrs. Riddell, Mid-Victorian Ghosts, and Christmas Annuals', *The Collected Ghost Stories of Mrs. J.H. Riddell* (New York: Dover, 1977), pp. v–xxvi

Clarke, John Stock, '*Home*: A Lost Victorian Periodical', *Victorian Periodicals Review*, vol. 25, no. 2 (Summer 1992), pp. 85–8

Henry, Nancy, 'Charlotte Riddell: Novelist of "The City"', in Lana J. Dally and Jill Rappoport (eds), *Economic Women: Essays in Desire and Dispossession in Nineteenth-Century British Culture* (Columbus Ohio: Ohio State University Press, 2013), pp. 193–205

Kelleher, Margaret, 'Charlotte Riddell's *A Struggle for Fame*: The Field of Women's Literary Production', *Colby Quarterly*, vol. 36, no. 2 (June 2000), pp. 116–31

Peterson, Linda H., 'Charlotte Riddell's *A Struggle for Fame*: Myths of Authorship, Facts of the Market', *Women's Writing*, vol. 11, no. 1 (2004), pp. 99–116

Riddell, Mrs J.H., 'Literature as a Profession', *Illustrated Review*, vol. 2, no. 132 (July 1874), pp. 6–7

Srebrnik, Patricia Thomas, 'Mrs. Riddell and the Reviewers: A Case Study in Victorian Popular Fiction', *Women's Studies*, vol. 23, no. 1 (1994), pp. 69–84

Wolff, Robert Lee. 'Two Irish Novels by Mrs. J.H. Riddell', in *Maxwell Drewitt*, 3 vols (New York: Garland, 1979), I, pp. v–ix

www.charlotteriddell.co.uk (accessed 5 June 2014)

## W.P. RYAN

McDonald, Walter, *Reminiscences of a Maynooth Professor* (Cork: Mercier Press, 1967)

Murphy, Niall, '"Social Sinn Féin and Hard Labour": The Journalism of W.P. Ryan and Jim Larkin, 1907–14', *Irish Studies Review*, vol. 22, no. 1 (January 2014), pp. 43–52

O'Hegarty, P.S., 'Obituary of W.P. Ryan', *Dublin Magazine* (N.S.), vol. 28, no. 3 (July–September 1942), pp. 72–3

Ryan, W.P., 'John Mitchel and Young Ireland, Parts 1 and 2', *New Ireland Review*, no. 4 (January–February 1896), pp. 288–97, 341–51

Sheehy-Skeffington, Francis, Review of W.P. Ryan, *The Pope's Green Island*, *Irish Review*, no. 2 (June 1912), pp. 222–4

van de Kamp, Peter, 'Whose Revival? Yeats and the Southwark Irish Literary Club', in Peter Liebregts and Peter van de Kamp (eds), *Tumult of Images* (Amsterdam: Rodopi, 1995), pp. 157–82

## GEORGE BERNARD SHAW

'Novels of the Week: *An Unsocial Socialist*', *Atheneaum*, no. 3,097 (5 March 1887), p. 318

Archer, Peter, 'Shaw and the Irish Question', *SHAW: The Annual of Bernard Shaw Studies*, vol. 11 (1991), pp. 119–29

Bissell, Claude T., 'The Novels of George Bernard Shaw', *University of Toronto Quarterly*, vol. 17, no. 1 (October 1947), pp. 38–51

Chesterton, G.K. *George Bernard Shaw* ([1910]; New York: Hill & Wang, 1956)

Dietrich, Richard F., 'Shaw and Yeats: Two Irishmen Divided by a Common Language', *SHAW: The Annual of Bernard Shaw Studies*, vol. 15 (1995), pp. 65–84

____, *Bernard Shaw's Novels: Portraits of the Artist as Man and Superman* (Gainesville, Florida: University Press of Florida, 1996)

Gahan, Peter, 'John Bull's Other War: Bernard Shaw and the Anglo-Irish War, 1918–1921', *SHAW: The Annual of Bernard Shaw Studies*, vol. 28 (2008), pp. 209–38

____, 'Bernard Shaw and the Irish Literary Tradition', *SHAW: The Annual of Bernard Shaw Studies*, vol. 30 (2010), pp. 1–26

____, 'Dégringolade and Derision in Dublin City', *SHAW: The Annual of Bernard Shaw Studies*, vol. 32 (2012), pp. 39–58

Gibbs, A.M. (ed.), *Shaw: Interviews and Recollections* (Iowa City: University of Iowa Press, 1990)

Glicksberg, Charles I., 'Shaw the Novelist', *Prairie Schooner*, vol. 25, no. 1 (Spring 1951), pp. 1–9

Greene, David H. and Dan H. Laurence (eds), *Bernard Shaw: The Matter with Ireland* (London: Rupert Hart-Davis, 1962)

Grene, Nicholas, 'Shaw in Ireland: Visitor or Returning Exile?', *SHAW: The Annual of Bernard Shaw Studies*, vol. 5 (1985), pp. 45–62

Haddad, Rosalie Rahal, *Bernard Shaw's Novels: His Drama of Ideas in Embryo* (Trier: Wissenschaftlicher Verlag, 2004)

Harris, Nathaniel, *The Shaws: The Family of George Bernard Shaw* (London: Dent, 1977)

Henderson, Archibald, 'Shaw's Novels: And Why They Failed', *Shaw Bulletin*, no. 1 (May 1955), pp. 11–18

Hogan, Robert, 'The Novels of Bernard Shaw', *English Literature in Transition, 1880–1920*, vol. 8, no. 2 (1965), pp. 63–114

Holroyd, Michael, 'G.B.S. and Ireland', *Sewanee Review*, vol. 84, no. 1 (Winter 1976), pp. 37–55

____, 'Introduction', in *An Unsocial Socialist* (London: Virago, 1980), n.p.

____, *Bernard Shaw, Volume I, 1856–1898: The Search for Love* (London: Chatto & Windus, 1988)

____, *Bernard Shaw, Volume II, 1898–1918: The Pursuit of Power* (London: Chatto & Windus, 1989)

____, *Bernard Shaw, Volume III, 1918–1951: The Lure of Fantasy* (London: Chatto & Windus, 1991)

____, 'Bernard Shaw the Immature Novelist', *Irish University Review*, vol. 30, no. 2 (Autumn/Winter 2000), pp. 209–19

Irvine, William, 'Bernard Shaw's Early Novels', *Trollopian*, vol. 2, no. 1 (1947), pp. 27–42

Mercier, Vivian, 'Shaw and the Anglo-Irish Comedy of Manners', *New Edinburgh Review*, vol. 28 (March 1975), pp. 22–4

____, 'Bernard Shaw: Irish International', in Mercier, *Modern Irish Literature: Sources and Founders* (Oxford: Clarendon Press, 1994), pp. 110–56

Merriman, Victor, 'Bernard Shaw in Contemporary Irish Studies: "Passé and Contemptible"?', *SHAW: The Annual of Bernard Shaw Studies*, vol. 30 (2010), pp. 216–35

O'Flaherty, Gearóid, 'George Bernard Shaw and Ireland', in Shaun Richards (ed.), *Cambridge Companion to Twentieth-Century Irish Drama* (Cambridge: Cambridge University Press, 2004), pp. 122–35

O'Leary, Philip, 'Lost Tribesman or Prodigal Son? George Bernard Shaw and the Gaelic Movement', *Éire-Ireland*, vol. 29, no. 2 (Summer 1994), pp. 51–64

Ritschel, Nelson O'Ceallaigh, *Shaw, Synge, Connolly, and Socialist Provocation* (Gainesville, Florida: University Press of Florida, 2011)

Rossett, B.C., *Shaw of Dublin: The Formative Years* (University Park, Pennsylvania: Pennsylvania State University Press, 1964)

Ryan, Kiernan, 'Citizens of Centuries to Come: The Ruling-Class Rebel in Socialist Fiction', in H. Gustave Klaus (ed.), *The Rise of Socialist Fiction, 1880–1914* (Brighton: Harvester, 1987), pp. 6–27

Shaw, George Bernard, *Sixteen Self Sketches* (London: Constable, 1949)

____, 'The Roger Casement Trial', *Massachusetts Review*, vol. 5, no. 2 (Winter 1964), pp. 311–14

____, 'Mr. Bernard Shaw's Works of Fiction: Reviewed by Himself', in Dan H. Laurence (ed.), *Selected Non-Dramatic Writings of Bernard Shaw* (Boston: Houghton Mifflin, 1965), pp. 309–14

____, 'Shaw's Advice to Irishmen', *SHAW: The Annual of Bernard Shaw Studies*, vol. 18 (1998), pp. 63–6

Sidnell, M.J., 'Hic and Ille: Shaw and Yeats', in Robert Driscoll (ed.), *Theatre and Nationalism in Twentieth-Century Ireland* (Toronto: University of Toronto Press, 1971), pp. 156–7

Sypher, Eileen, *Wisps of Violence: Producing Public and Private Politics in the Turn-of-the-Century British Novel* (London: Verso, 1993), pp. 69–85

Turner, Tramble T., 'Bernard Shaw's "Eternal" Irish Concern', *Éire-Ireland*, vol. 21, no. 2 (Summer 1986), pp. 57–69

Weintraub, Stanley, 'Bernard Shaw, Charles Lever and *Immaturity*', *Bulletin of the Shaw Society of America*, vol. 2, no. 1 (January 1957), pp. 11–15

____, 'The Embryo Playwright in Bernard Shaw's Early Novels', *Texas Studies in Literature and Language*, vol. 1, no. 3 (Autumn 1959), pp. 327–55

____, *Shaw: An Autobiography, 1856–98* (London: Max Reinhardt, 1970)

____, 'The Making of an Irish Patriot: Bernard Shaw, 1914–1916', *Éire-Ireland*, vol. 5, no. 4 (Winter 1970), pp. 9–27

____, '"The Hibernian School": Oscar Wilde and Bernard Shaw', *SHAW: The Annual of Bernard Shaw Studies*, vol. 13 (1993), pp. 25–49

____, 'Bernard Shaw's Other Irelands', *English Literature in Transition (1880–1920)*, vol. 42, no. 4 (1999), pp. 433–42

____, 'Shaw in "Sallust's House"', *SHAW: The Annual of Bernard Shaw Studies* vol. 33, 1 (2013), pp. 153–9

P.A. SHEEHAN

'Concerning the Author of *Luke Delmege*', *Irish Monthly*, vol. 30, no. 354 (1902), pp. 661–9

'Luke Delmege', *Edinburgh Review*, vol. 196, no. 401 (July 1902), pp. 120–38

Barry, Michael, *By Pen and Pulpit: The Life and Times of the Author Canon Sheehan* (Fermoy: Saturn Books, 1990)

Boyle, Francis, *Canon Sheehan: A Sketch of His Life and Works* (New York: Kennedy, 1927)

Braybrooke, Patrick, 'Canon Sheehan: Irish Priest and Novelist', in *Some Victorian and Georgian Catholics: Their Art and Outlook* (London: Burns, Oates & Washbourne, 1932), pp. 103–33

Brown, Terence, 'Canon Sheehan and the Catholic Intellectual', in Robert Welch and Suheil Bushrui (eds), *Literature and the Art of Creation: Essays and Poems in Honour of A. Norman Jeffares* (Gerrards Cross: Colin Smythe, 1988), pp. 7–17

Burton, David H. (ed.), *The Holmes–Sheehan Correspondence: Letters of Justice Oliver Wendell Holmes, Jr. and Canon Patrick Augustine Sheehan* (Port Washington, NY: Kennikat, 1976)

____, 'The Friendship of Justice Holmes and Canon Sheehan', *Harvard Library Bulletin*, vol. 25, no. 2 (1977), pp. 155–69

Candy, Catherine, 'Canon Sheehan: The Conflicts of the Priest-Author', in R.V. Comerford, Mary Cullen, Jacqueline R. Hill and Colm Lennon (eds), *Religion, Conflict and Coexistence in Ireland: Essays Presented to Monsignor Patrick J. Corish* (Dublin: Gill & Macmillan, 1990), pp. 252–77

____, *Priestly Fictions: Popular Irish Novelists of the Early Twentieth Century. Patrick A. Sheehan, Joseph Guinan, Gerald O'Donovan* (Dublin: Wolfhound Press, 1995)

Clifford, Brendan, *Canon Sheehan: A Turbulent Priest* (Millstreet: Aubane Historical Society, 2008)

Colclough, John D., 'Canon Sheehan: A Reminiscence and an Appreciation', *Studies*, vol. 6, no. 22 (June 1917), pp. 275–88

Coleman, Anthony, 'Priest as Artist: The Dilemma of Canon Sheehan', *Studies*, vol. 58, no. 229 (Spring 1969), pp. 30–41

Collie, D.M., 'The Nineteenth-Century Novel, A Postscript: The Case for Canon Sheehan', *Linenhall Review*, vol. 10, no. 3 (Winter 1993), p. 8

Cronin, John, 'Luke Delmege', in *The Anglo-Irish Novel: Volume II, 1900–1940* (Belfast: Appletree Press, 1990), pp. 22–9

Fleishmann, Ruth, 'Catholicism in the Culture of the New Ireland: Canon

Sheehan and Daniel Corkery', in Robert Welch (ed.), *Irish Writers and Religion* (Gerrards Cross: Colin Smythe, 1992), pp. 89–104

____, 'Knowledge of the World as the Forbidden Fruit: Canon Sheehan and Joyce on the *Sacrificium Intellectus*', in Donald E. Morse, Csilla Bertha and István Pálffy (eds), *A Small Nation's Contribution to the World: Essays on Anglo-Irish Literature and Language* (Gerrards Cross: Colin Smythe, 1993), pp. 127–37

____, *Catholic Nationalism in the Irish Revival: A Study of Canon Sheehan, 1852–1913* (Basingstoke: Macmillan, 1997)

Garvin, Tom, 'The Quiet Tragedy of Canon Sheehan', *Studies*, vol. 98, no. 390 (Summer 2009), pp. 159–68

Gaughan, J. Anthony, *Doneraile* (Dublin: Kamac, 1970)

Gilley, Sheridan, 'Canon Patrick Augustine Sheehan: Priest and Novelist', in Peter Clarke and Charlotte Methuen (eds), *The Church and Literature* (Woodbridge, Suffolk: Boydell, 2012), pp. 397–422

Hennig, John, 'A Note on Canon Sheehan's Interest in German Literature', *Modern Language Review*, vol. 49, no. 3 (July 1954), pp. 352–5

Heuser, Herman J., *Canon Sheehan of Doneraile: The Story of an Irish Parish Priest as Told Chiefly by Himself . . .* (New York: Longmans, Green, 1917)

Horgan, John J., 'Canon Sheehan: A Memory and an Appreciation', *Irish Monthly*, no. 42 (January 1914), pp. 1–12

Kiely, Benedict, 'Canon Sheehan: The Reluctant Novelist', in *A Raid into Dark Corners* (Cork: Cork University Press, 1999), pp. 181–91

Linehan, M.P., *Canon Sheehan of Doneraile: Priest, Novelist, Man of Letters* (Dublin: Talbot Press, 1952)

MacGowan, Kenneth, *Patrick Augustine Sheehan* (Dublin: Catholic Truth Society of Ireland, 1963)

MacManus, Francis, 'The Fate of Canon Sheehan', *The Bell*, no. 15 (November 1947), pp. 6–27

McBride, Lawrence W., 'A Literary Life of a Socially and Politically Engaged Priest: Canon Patrick Augustine Sheehan (1852–1913)', in Gerard Moran (ed.), *Radical Irish Priests, 1660–1970* (Dublin: Four Courts Press, 1998), pp. 131–48

Michael, Father, 'Twilight and Dawn', *Capuchin Annual* (1942), pp. 263–302

O'Brien, James (ed.), *The Collected Letters of Canon Sheehan of Doneraile, 1883–1913* (Wells: Smenos, 2013)

O'Brien, William and Sophie R., 'Memories of Canon Sheehan', *Studies*, vol. 19, no. 75 (September 1930), pp. 492–8

O'Faoláin, Seán, 'Almost a Great Novelist?' *Commonweal*, no. 23 (10 January 1936), pp. 293–6

O'Leary, Don, 'Faith, Nature and Science in the Works of Canon Sheehan', *New Hibernia Review*, vol. 17, no. 2 (Summer 2013), pp. 119–35

O'Neill, George, 'A Relic of Canon Sheehan', *Studies*, vol. 6, no. 23 (September 1917), pp. 385–97

Pelly, Cornelia, 'An Hour with Canon Sheehan', *Irish Monthly*, vol. 36, no. 426 (December 1908), pp. 489–93

Stockley, W.F.P., 'Canon Sheehan and His People', in *Essays in Irish Biography* (Cork: Cork University Press, 1933), pp. 93–130

## SOMERVILLE AND ROSS

Review of *The Real Charlotte*, *Athenaeum*, no. 3,476 (9 June 1894), p. 738

Beards, Virginia, 'Introduction', in *The Real Charlotte* (New Brunswick, NJ: Rutgers University Press, 1986), pp. xi–xx

Bence-Jones, Mark, 'The Real Somerville and Ross', *Cork Review* (1993), pp. 26–8

Coghill, Sir Patrick, 'Somerville and Ross', *Hermathena*, vol. 79 (May 1952), pp. 47–50

Collis, Maurice, *Somerville and Ross: A Biography* (London: Faber, 1968)

Cowman, Roz, 'Lost Time: The Smell and Taste of Castle T', in Éibhear Walshe (ed.), *Sex, Nation and Dissent in Irish Writing* (Cork: Cork University Press, 1997), pp. 87–102

Cronin, Anthony, 'Somerville and Ross: Women Fighting Back', in *Heritage Now: Irish Literature in the English Language* (Dingle: Brandon, 1982), pp. 75–86

Cronin, John (ed.), *Somerville and Ross: A Symposium* (Belfast: Institute of Irish Studies, 1969)

——, *Somerville and Ross* (Lewisburg, Pennsylvania: Bucknell University Press, 1972)

——, '"An Ideal of Art": The Assertion of Realities in the Fiction of Somerville and Ross', *Canadian Journal of Irish Studies*, vol. 11, no. 1 (1985), pp. 3–19

Cummins, Geraldine, *Dr E. Œ Somerville: A Biography* (New York: British Book Centre, 1953)

Ehnenn, Jill R., *Women's Literary Collaboration, Queerness, and Late-Victorian Culture* (Aldershot: Ashgate, 2008), pp. 145–82

Fehlmann, Guy, 'L'Irlande Dispatue de Somerville et Ross', *Langues Modernes*, no. 2 (March 1967), pp. 57–62

——, 'Somerville and Ross and France', in Patrick Rafroidi, Guy Fehlmann and Matiu Mac Conmara (eds), *France–Ireland: Literary Relations* (Paris: Éditions Universitaires, 1974), pp. 153–63

Flanagan, Thomas, 'The Big House of Ross-Drishane', *Kenyon Review*, vol. 28, no. 1 (January 1966), pp. 54–78

Greene, Nicole Pepinster, 'Dialect and Social Identity in *The Real Charlotte*', *New Hibernia Review*, vol. 4, no. 1 (Spring 2000), pp. 122–37

Hall, Wayne, 'Landscape as Frame in *The Real Charlotte*', *New Hibernia Review*, vol. 3, no. 3 (Autumn 1999), pp. 96–115

Imhof, Rüdiger, 'Somerville and Ross: *The Real Charlotte* and *The Big House of Inver*', in Otto Rauchbauer (ed.), *Ancestral Voices: The Big House in Anglo-Irish Literature* (Dublin: The Lilliput Press, 1992), pp. 95–107

Lewis, Gifford, *The World of the Irish R.M.* (Harmondsworth: Penguin, 1985)

____, (ed.), *The Selected Letters of Somerville and Ross* (London: Faber & Faber, 1989)

____, *Edith Somerville* (Dublin: Four Courts Press, 2005)

MacCarthy, B.G., 'E. Œ. Somerville and Martin Ross', *Studies*, vol. 34, no. 134 (June 1945), pp. 183–94

McClellan, Ann, 'Dialect, Gender and Colonialism in *The Real Charlotte*', *Études Irlandaises*, vol. 31, no. 1 (2006), pp. 69–86

McMahon, Seán, 'John Bull's Other Island: A Consideration of *The Real Charlotte* by Somerville and Ross', *Éire-Ireland*, vol. 3, no. 4 (Winter 1968), pp. 119–35

McNamara, Donald, '*The Real Charlotte*: The Exclusive Myth of Somerville and Ross', *Proceedings of the Harvard Celtic Colloquium*, nos 26/27 (2006/2007), pp. 356–69

Powell, Violet, *The Irish Cousins: The Books and Background of Somerville and Ross* (London: Heinemann, 1970)

Robinson, Hilary, *Somerville and Ross: A Critical Appreciation* (Dublin: Gill & Macmillan, 1980)

Ryan, Angela, 'Tragic Heroines and Wise Women in the Novels of Somerville and Ross', *Estudios Irlandeses* (2005), pp. 117–26

Somerville, Edith, *Irish Memories* (London: Longmans, Green, 1917)

____, and Boyle Townshend Somerville, *Records of the Somerville Family of Castlehaven and Drishane from 1174 to 1940* (Cork: Guy, 1940)

Stevens, Julie Anne, *The Irish Scene in Somerville and Ross* (Dublin: Irish Academic Press, 2006)

Tóibín, Colm, 'Foreword', in Somerville and Ross, *The Real Charlotte* (London: Capuchin Classics, 2011), pp. 7–12

Walshe, Éibhear, 'Protestant Perspectives on Ireland: *John Bull's Other Island* and *The Real Charlotte*', *SHAW: The Annual of Bernard Shaw Studies*, vol. 30, no. 1 (2010), pp. 63–74

Watson, Cresap S., 'Realism, Determinism, and Symmetry in *The Real Charlotte*', *Hermathena*, vol. 84 (November 1954), pp. 26–44

## BRAM STOKER

Bentley, C.F., 'The Monster in the Bedroom: Sexual Symbolism in Bram Stoker's *Dracula*', *Literature and Psychology*, vol. 22, no. 1 (1972), pp. 27–34

Cranny-Francis, Anne, 'Sexual Politics and Political Repression in Bram Stoker's *Dracula*', in Clive Bloom, Brian Docherty, Jane Gibb and Keith Shand (eds), *Nineteenth-Century Suspense: From Poe to Conan Doyle* (New York: St Martin's Press, 1988), pp. 64–79

FitzGerald, Mary, 'Mina's Disclosure: Bram Stoker's *Dracula*', in Toni O'Brien Johnson and David Cairns (eds), *Gender in Irish Writing* (Milton Keynes: Open University Press, 1991), pp. 40–5

Gibson, Matthew, *Dracula and the Eastern Question: British and French Vampire*

*Narratives of the Nineteenth-Century Near East* (Basingstoke: Palgrave Macmillan, 2006)

Glover, David, '"Dark Enough fur Any Man": Bram Stoker's Sexual Ethnology and the Question of Irish Nationalism', in Roman de la Campa, E. Ann Kaplan and Michael Sprinker (eds), *Late Imperial Culture* (London: Verso, 1995), pp. 53–71

——, *Vampires, Mummies, and Liberals: Bram Stoker and the Politics of Popular Fiction* (Durham, NC: Duke University Press, 1996)

Goss, Sarah, 'Dracula and the Spectre of Famine', in George Cusack and Sarah Goss (eds), *Hungry Words: Images of Famine in the Irish Canon* (Dublin: Irish Academic Press, 2005), pp. 77–107

Halberstam, Judith, 'Technologies of Monstrosity: Bram Stoker's *Dracula*', *Victorian Studies*, vol. 36, no. 3 (Spring 1993), pp. 333–52

Howes, Marjorie, 'The Mediation of the Feminine: Bisexuality, Homoerotic Desire, and Self-Expression in Bram Stoker's *Dracula*', *Texas Studies in Language and Literature*, vol. 30, no. 1 (Spring 1988), pp. 104–19

Ingelbein, Raphäel, 'Gothic Genealogies: *Dracula*, *Bowen's Court*, and Anglo-Irish Psychology', *ELH*, vol. 70, no. 4 (Winter 2003), pp. 1089–1105

Killeen, Jarlath (ed.), *Bram Stoker: Centenary Essays* (Dublin: Four Courts Press, 2014)

Kreisel, Deanna K., 'Demand and Desire in *Dracula*', in Lana J. Dally and Jill Rappoport (eds), *Economic Women: Essays in Desire and Dispossession in Nineteenth-Century British Culture* (Columbus, Ohio: Ohio State University Press, 2013), pp. 110–26

Maloy, Kelli, 'Deconstructing Ireland: Identity, Theory, Culture/Dracula's Crypt: Bram Stoker, Irishness, and the Question of Blood', *College Literature*, vol. 30, no. 4 (Fall 2003), pp. 167–73

Morash, Chris, '"Ever under Some Unnatural Condition": Bram Stoker and the Colonial Fantastic', in Brian Cosgrove (ed.), *Literature and the Supernatural* (Dublin: Columba Press, 1995), pp. 95–119

Murray, Paul, *From the Shadow of Dracula: A Life of Bram Stoker* (London: Cape, 2004)

Spencer, Kathleen L., 'Purity and Danger: *Dracula*, the Urban Gothic, and the Late Victorian Degeneracy Crisis', *ELH*, vol. 59, no. 1 (Spring 1992), pp. 197–225

Stewart, Bruce, 'Bram Stoker's *Dracula*: Possessed by the Spirit of the Nation?' *Irish University Review*, vol. 29, no. 2 (Autumn–Winter 1999), pp. 238–55

Valente, Joseph, '"Double Born": Bram Stoker and the Metrocolonial Gothic', *Modern Fiction Studies*, vol. 46, no. 3 (Fall 2000), pp. 632–45

Warwick, Alexandra, 'Vampires and the Empire: Fears and Fictions of the 1890s', in Sally Ledger and Scott McCracken (eds), *Cultural Politics at the Fin de Siècle* (Cambridge: Cambridge University Press, 1995), pp. 202–20

Wasson, Richard, 'The Politics of *Dracula*', *English Literature in Transition, 1880–1920*, vol. 9, no. 1 (1966), pp. 24–7

### W.M. THACKERAY

Brewer, Kenneth L., Jr., 'Colonial Discourse and William Makepeace Thackeray's *Irish Sketch Book*', *Papers on Language & Literature*, vol. 29, no. 3 (1993), pp. 259–83

Clarke, Micael [sic] M., 'Thackeray's *Barry Lyndon*: An Irony against Misogynists', *Texas Studies in Literature and Language*, vol. 29, no. 3 (Fall 1987), pp. 261–77

Colby, Robert A., 'Barry Lyndon and the Irish Hero', *Nineteenth-Century Fiction*, vol. 21, no. 2 (September 1966), pp. 109–30

____, *Thackeray's Canvass of Humanity: An Author and His Public* (Columbus: Ohio State University Press, 1979), pp. 201–27

Collins, Philip, *Thackeray: Interviews and Recollections,* 2 vols (London: Macmillan, 1983)

Connelly, Joseph F., 'Transparent Poses: *Castle Rackrent* and *The Memoirs of Barry Lyndon*', *Éire-Ireland*, vol. 14, no. 2 (Summer 1979), pp. 37–43

Douglas, Dennis, 'Thackeray and the Uses of History', *Yearbook of English Studies*, vol. 5 (1975), pp. 164–77

Fletcher, Robert P., '"Proving a Thing Even While You Contradict It": Fictions, Beliefs and Legitimation in *The Memoirs of Barry Lyndon, Esq.*', *Studies in the Novel*, vol. 27, no. 4 (Winter 1995), pp. 493–514

Harden, Edgar F. (ed.), *The Luck of Barry Lyndon: A Romance of the Last Century* (Ann Arbor: University of Michigan Press, 1999)

Klotz, Günther, 'Thackeray's Ireland: Image and Attitude in *The Irish Sketchbook* and *Barry Lyndon*', in Wolfgang Zach and Heinz Kosok (eds), *Literary Interrelations: Ireland, England and the World*, 3 vols (Tübingen: Narr, 1987), III, pp. 85–93

MacCarthy, B.G., 'Thackeray in Ireland', *Studies*, vol. 40, no. 157 (March 1951), pp. 55–68

McAuliffe, John, 'Taking the Sting Out of the Traveller's Tale: Thackeray's *Irish Sketchbook*', *Irish Studies Review*, vol. 9, no. 1 (2001), pp. 25–40

McCarthy, Terence, 'Chronological Inconsistencies in *Barry Lyndon*', *English Language Notes*, vol. 21, no. 2 (1983), pp. 29–37

Nolan, Edward F., 'The Death of Bryan Lyndon: An Analogue in *Gone with the Wind*', *Nineteenth-Century Fiction*, vol. 8, no. 3 (December, 1953), pp. 225–8

O'Neill-Debrabant, Mary, '"No Pen or Pencil Can Describe . . .": The Challenge of Representation in Thackeray's *Irish Sketch-Book*', *Interface: Image, Text, Language*, vol. 29 (2010), pp. 195–205

Parker, David, 'Thackeray's *Barry Lyndon*', *Ariel*, vol. 6, no. 4 (Winter 1975), pp. 68–80

Ray, Gordon N. (ed.), *The Letters and Private Papers of William Makepeace Thackeray*, 4 vols (Cambridge, Massachusetts: Harvard University Press, 1945–6)

____, *The Buried Life: A Study of the Relation between Thackeray's Fiction and his Personal History* (London: Oxford University Press, 1952)

____, *William Makepeace Thackeray: The Uses of Adversity, 1811–1846* (London: Oxford University Press, 1955)

____, *William Makepeace Thackeray: The Age of Wisdom, 1848–1863* (London: Oxford University Press, 1958)

Rosdeitcher, Elizabeth, 'Empires at Stake: Gambling and the Economic Unconscious in Thackeray', *Genre*, vol. 29, no. 4 (1996), pp. 407–28

Sanders, Andrew, 'Introduction', in *The Memoirs of Barry Lyndon, Esq.* (Oxford: Oxford University Press/The World's Classics, 1984), pp. vii–xxii

Tierney, Michael, 'Ireland in the Seven Years' War', *Studies,* vol. 32, no. 126 (1943), pp. 175–85

Tillotson, Geoffrey and Donald Hawes (eds), *Thackeray: The Critical Heritage* (London: Routledge & Kegan Paul, 1968)

Trollope, Anthony, *Thackeray* (London: Macmillan, 1879)

Watson, John, 'Thackeray's Composite Characters: Autobiography and "True History" in *Barry Lyndon*', *AUMLA: Journal of the Australian Universities Language and Literature Association*, vol. 87 (1997), pp. 25–42

## KATHERINE CECIL THURSTON

'A Note on How Mrs. Thurston Wrote Her Books', *Irish Book Lover*, vol. 3, no. 73 (December 1911)

Copeland, Caroline, 'An Oasis in a Desert: The Transatlantic Publishing Success of Katherine Cecil Thurston', *Journal of the Edinburgh Bibliographical Society*, vol. 2 (2007), pp. 23–41

Madden-Simpson, Janet, 'Afterword', in *The Fly on the Wheel* (London: Virago, 1987), pp. 329–44

## ANTHONY TROLLOPE

'*Castle Richmond*', *New Quarterly Review*, vol. 9, no. 34 (1860), pp. 199–201

'The Novels of Anthony Trollope', *Dublin Review*, vol. 9, no. 2 (1883), pp. 314–34

Bigelow, Gordon, 'Trollope and Ireland', in Carolyn Dever and Lisa Niles (eds), *The Cambridge Companion to Anthony Trollope* (Cambridge: Cambridge University Press, 2011), pp. 196–209

Byrne, P.F., 'Anthony Trollope and Ireland', *Dublin Historical Review*, vol. 45, no. 2 (1992), pp. 126–8

Cronin, John, 'Trollope and the Matter of Ireland', in Tony Bareham (ed.), *Anthony Trollope* (Totowa, NJ: Barnes & Noble, 1980), pp. 13–35

Delaney, Frank, 'Trollope and Ireland', *Trollopiana*, vol. 11 (1990), pp. 8–18

Donovan, Robert A., 'Trollope's Prentice Work', *Modern Philology*, vol. 53, no. 3 (February 1956), pp. 179–86

Dougherty, Jane Elizabeth, 'The Angel in the House: The Act of Union and Anthony Trollope's Irish Hero', *Victorian Literature and Culture*, vol. 32, no. 1 (2004), pp. 133–45

Dunleavy, Janet Egleson, 'Introduction', in *Castle Richmond* (New York: Arno, 1981), n.p.

——, 'Trollope and Ireland', in John Halperin (ed.), *Trollope Centenary Essays* (New York: St Martin's Press, 1982), pp. 53–69

Edwards, Owen Dudley, 'Anthony Trollope, the Irish Writer', *Nineteenth-Century Fiction*, vol. 38, no. 1 (June 1983), pp. 1–42

Faulkner, Karen, 'Anthony Trollope's Apprenticeship', *Nineteenth-Century Fiction*, vol. 38, no. 2 (September 1983), pp. 161–88

Glendinning, Victoria, *Trollope* (London: Hutchinson, 1992)

Hall, N. John (ed.), *The Letters of Anthony Trollope,* 2 vols (Stanford: Stanford University Press, 1983)

——, *Trollope: A Biography* (Oxford: Oxford University Press, 1991)

Hamer, Mary 'Introduction', in *Castle Richmond* (Oxford: Oxford University Press/World's Classics, 1989), pp. vii–xxii

Hastings, Max, 'Introduction', in *Castle Richmond* (London: Trollope Society, 1994), pp. vii–xvi

Hennedy, Hugh L., 'Love and Famine, Family and Country in Trollope's *Castle Richmond*', *Éire-Ireland*, vol. 7, no. 4 (Winter 1972), pp. 49–66

Hynes, John, 'Anthony Trollope and the "Irish Question", *Études Irlandais*, vol. 8 (1983), pp. 212–28

——, 'Anthony Trollope's Creative "Culture-Shock"', *Éire-Ireland*, vol. 21, no. 3 (Fall 1986), pp. 124–31

Johnston, Conor, 'Parsons, Priests, and Politics: Anthony Trollope's Irish Clergy', *Éire-Ireland*, vol. 25, no. 1 (Spring 1990), pp. 80–97

Kelleher, Margaret, 'Anthony Trollope's *Castle Richmond*: A "Horrid Novel"?' *Irish University Review*, vol. 25, no. 2 (1995), pp. 242–62

Knelman, Judith, 'Anthony Trollope, English Journalist and Novelist, Writing About the Famine in Ireland', *Éire-Ireland*, vol. 23, no. 3 (Fall 1988), pp. 57–67

McCourt, John, 'Trollope's Adulterous Irish-English Texts', *Neohelicon,* vol. 40, no. 1 (2013), pp. 169–82

Moore, W.S., 'Trollope and Ireland', *Irish Monthly*, vol. 56, no. 656 (1928), pp. 74–9

Mullen, Richard, with James Munson, *The Penguin Companion to Trollope* (London: Penguin Books, 1996)

Nardin, Jane, '*Castle Richmond,* the Famine, and the Critics', *Cahiers Victoriens et Édouardiens*, no. 58 (October 2003), pp. 81–90

Smalley, Donald (ed.), *Trollope: The Critical Heritage* (London: Routledge & Kegan Paul, 1969)

Terry, R.C. (ed.), *Trollope: Interviews and Recollections* (Basingstoke: Macmillan, 1987)

Tingay, Lance O., 'The Reception of Trollope's First Novel', *Nineteenth-Century Fiction*, vol. 6, no. 3 (December 1951), pp. 195–200

Tracy, Robert, '"The Unnatural Ruin": Trollope and Nineteenth-Century Irish Fiction', *Nineteenth-Century Fiction*, vol. 37, no. 3 (December 1982), pp. 358–82

Trollope, Anthony, *An Autobiography* (Edinburgh: Blackwood, 1883)

Wittig, E.W., 'Trollope's Irish Fiction', *Éire-Ireland*, vol. 9, no. 3 (1974), pp. 97–118

## OSCAR WILDE

Byrne, Patrick, *The Wildes of Merrion Square* (London: Staples Press, 1953)

Coakley, Davis, *Oscar Wilde: The Importance of Being Irish* (Dublin: Town House, 1994)

Ellmann, Richard (ed.), *The Artist as Critic: Critical Writings of Oscar Wilde* (New York: Random House, 1969)

____, *Oscar Wilde* (London: Hamish Hamilton, 1987)

Frankel, Nicholas (ed.), 'General Introduction', 'Textual Introduction', in *The Picture of Dorian Gray: An Annotated, Uncensored Edition* (Cambridge, Massachusetts: The Belknap Press of Harvard University Press, 2011), pp. 1–37; 38–64

Haslam, Richard, '"Melmoth" (OW): Gothic Modes in *The Picture of Dorian Gray*', *Irish Studies Review*, vol. 12, no. 3 (2004), pp. 303–14

____, 'The Hermeneutic Hazards of Hibernicizing Oscar Wilde's *The Picture of Dorian Gray*', *English Literature in Transition, 1880–1920*, vol. 57, no. 1 (2014), pp. 37–58

Killeen, Jarlath, *The Faiths of Oscar Wilde: Catholicism, Folklore and Ireland* (Basingstoke: Palgrave, 2005)

Mason, Stuart, *Oscar Wilde: Art and Morality. A Defence of* The Picture of Dorian Gray (London: Jacobs, 1908)

Milbank, Alison, 'Sacrificial Exchange and the Gothic Double in *Melmoth the Wanderer* and *The Picture of Dorian Gray*', in Victoria Morgan and Clare Williams (eds), *Shaping Belief: Culture, Politics and Religion in Nineteenth-Century Writing* (Liverpool: Liverpool University Press, 2008), pp. 113–28

Mullen, Patrick R., *The Poor Bugger's Tool: Irish Modernism, Queer Labour, and Postcolonial History* (New York: Oxford University Press, 2012), pp. 22–46

O'Connor, Maureen, '*The Picture of Dorian Gray* as Irish National Tale', in Neil McCaw (ed.), *Writing Irishness in Nineteenth-Century British Culture* (Aldershot: Ashgate, 2003), pp. 194–209

Pater, Walter, 'A Novel by Mr. Oscar Wilde', *Bookman* (November 1891), pp. 59–60

Pine, Richard, *The Thief of Reason: Oscar Wilde and Modern Ireland* (Dublin: Gill & Macmillan, 1995)

Pyle, Fitzroy, 'Wilde and His Early Critics', *Hermathena*, vol. 113 (July 1972), pp. 49–53

Sammells, Neil, 'Oscar Wilde: Quite Another Thing', in Paul Hyland and Neil Sammells (eds), *Irish Writing: Exile and Subversion* (London: Macmillan, 1991), pp. 116–25

Sandelescu, George C. (ed.), *Rediscovering Oscar Wilde* (Gerrards Cross: Colin Smythe, 1994)

van de Kamp, Peter and Patrick Leahy, 'Notes on Oscar Wilde's Socialism', *Crane Bag*, vol. 7, no. 1 (1983), pp. 141–50

Waldron, Martin, 'Oscar Wilde: His Life, His Irish Affiliation, and Glimpses of his Religious Beliefs', *Éire-Ireland*, vol. 24, no. 2 (Summer 1989), pp. 11–26

Walshe, Éibhear, 'A Wilde Irish Rebel: Queerness versus Nationalism in Irish Imaginative Presentations of Wilde', *Canadian Journal of Irish Studies*, vol. 36, no. 1 (Spring 2010), pp. 45–67

——, *Oscar's Shadow: Wilde, Homosexuality and Modern Ireland* (Cork: Cork University Press, 2011)

White, Terence de Vere, *The Parents of Oscar Wilde* (London: Hodder & Stoughton, 1967)

## General Studies

Anon, 'Writers on Irish Character', *Dublin University Magazine*, no. 1 (January 1833), pp. 31–41

Backus, Margot Gayle, *The Gothic Family Romance: Heterosexuality, Child Sacrifice and the Anglo-Irish Colonial Order* (Durham, NC: Duke University Press, 1999)

Baker, Ernest A., 'The Irish Novelists', in *The History of the English Novel: The Age of Dickens and Thackeray* (London: H.F. & G. Witherby, 1936), pp. 11–61

Barfoot, C.C. and Theo D'haen (eds), *The Clash of Ireland: Literary Contrasts and Connections* (Amsterdam: Rodopi, 1989)

Beckett, J.C., 'The Irish Writer and His Public in the Nineteenth Century', *Yearbook of English Studies*, vol. 11 (1981), pp. 102–16

Belanger, Jacqueline (ed.), *The Irish Novel in the Nineteenth Century: Facts and Fictions* (Dublin: Four Courts Press, 2005)

Bernstein, Stephen, 'Form and Ideology in the Gothic Novel', *Essays in Literature*, vol. 18, no. 2 (1991), pp. 151–65

Berol, Laura M., 'The Anglo-Irish Threat in Thackeray's and Trollope's Writings of the 1840s', *Victorian Literature and Culture*, vol. 32, no. 1 (2004), pp. 103–16

——, 'Irish Prisoners and the Indictment of British Rule in the Writings of William Makepeace Thackeray and Anthony Trollope', in Jan Alber and Frank Lauterback (eds), *Stones of Law, Bricks of Shame: Narrating Imprisonment in the Victorian Age* (Toronto: University of Toronto Press, 2009), pp. 112–33

Bolster, R., 'French Romanticism and the Ireland Myth', *Hermathena*, vol. 99 (October 1964), pp. 42–8

Boltwood, Scott, '"The Ineffaceable Curse of Cain": Race, Miscegenation and the Victorian Staging of Irishness', *Victorian Literature and Culture*, vol. 29, no. 2 (2001), pp. 383–96

Bostrom, Irene, 'The Novel and Catholic Emancipation', *Studies in Romanticism*, vol. 2, no. 3 (Spring 1963), pp. 155–76

Bourke, Angela, Siobhán Kilfeather, Maria Luddy, Margaret Mac Curtain, Gerardine Meaney, Máirín Ní Dhonnchadha, Mary O'Dowd and Clair Wills (eds), *The Field Day Anthology of Irish Writing*, vols 4–5 (Cork: Cork University Press/Field Day, 2002)

Bowen, Elizabeth, *Collected Impressions* (London: Longmans, Green, 1950)

Boyce, D. George and Alan O'Day (eds), *Ireland in Transition, 1867–1921* (London: Routledge, 2004)

Boyd, Andrew, 'Fat Hogs and Hungry Men: Thackeray, de Tocqueville and Cobbett in Ireland', *Seanchas Ardmhaca*, vol. 19, no. 2 (2003), pp. 197–205

Boyd, Ernest A., *Appreciations and Depreciations: Irish Literary Studies* (New York: John Lane, 1918)

Brittaine, George, *Recollections of Hyacinth O'Gara* (Dublin: Richard Moore Tims, 1829)

Brown, Malcolm, *The Politics of Irish Literature: From Thomas Davis to W.B. Yeats* (London: Allen & Unwin, 1972)

____, *Sir Samuel Ferguson* (Lewisburg, Pennsylvania: Bucknell University Press, 1973)

Brown, Ray, William John Roscelli and Richard Loftus (eds), *The Celtic Cross* (Lafayette, Indiana: Purdue University Press, 1973)

Brown, Stephen J., SJ, 'Irish Historical Fiction', *Studies*, vol. 4, no. 15 (September 1915), pp. 441–53

____, 'Irish Historical Fiction II – Chiefly Concerning Gaps', *Studies*, vol. 5, no. 17 (March 1916), pp. 82–95

____, *Ireland in Fiction: A Guide to Irish Novels* (Dublin: Maunsel, 1919)

____, 'Novels of the National Idea', *Irish Monthly*, vol. 48, no. 563 (May 1920), pp. 254–62

Brown, Terence, 'Saxon and Celt: The Stereotypes', in Wolfgang Zach and Heinz Kosok (eds), *Literary Interrelations: Ireland, England and the World*, 3 vols (Tübingen: Narr, 1987), III, pp. 1–9

____, (ed.), *Celticism* (Amsterdam: Rodopi, 1996)

____, 'The Edwardian Condition of Ireland', in Brian Cliff and Nicholas Grene (eds), *Synge and Edwardian Ireland* (Oxford: Oxford University Press, 2012), pp. 9–20

Brown, Thomas N., 'Nationalism and the Irish Peasant, 1800–1848', *Review of Politics*, vol. 15, no. 4 (October 1953), pp. 403–45

Burgess, Miranda J., 'Violent Translations: Allegory, Gender, and Cultural

Nationalism in Ireland, 1796–1806', *Modern Language Quarterly*, vol. 59, no. 1 (March 1998), pp. 33–70

Butler, W.A., 'Irish Female Writers: Lady Blessington and Maria Edgeworth', *Dublin University Magazine*, no. 3 (April 1834), pp. 431–46

Cahalan, James M., *Great Hatred, Little Room: The Irish Historical Novel* (Syracuse, NY: Syracuse University Press, 1983)

____, *The Irish Novel* (Dublin: Gill & Macmillan, 1988)

____, *Double Visions: Women and Men in Modern and Contemporary Irish Fiction* (Syracuse, NY: Syracuse University Press, 1999), pp. 41–7

Campbell, Matthew, 'Victorian Ireland?', *Journal of Victorian Culture*, vol. 10, no. 2 (2005), pp. 197–303

Carlyle, Thomas, *Reminiscences of My Irish Journey in 1849* (London: Sampson Low, 1882)

Carruthers, Gerard and Alan Rawes (eds), *English Romanticism and the Celtic World* (Cambridge: Cambridge University Press, 2003)

Casey, Daniel J. and Robert E. Rhodes (eds), *Views of the Irish Peasantry, 1800–1916* (Hamden, Connecticut: Archon Books, 1977)

Cashman, Ray, 'The Heroic Outlaw in Irish Folklore and Popular Literature', *Folklore*, vol. 111, no. 2 (October 2000), pp. 191–215

Clare, David, 'Wilde, Shaw, and Somerville and Ross: Irish Revivalists, Irish Britons, or Both?' *Irish Studies Review*, vol. 22, no. 1 (2014), pp. 1–13

Colgan, Maurice, 'Young Ireland: Literature and Nationalism', in Francis Barker et al. (eds), *1848: The Sociology of Literature* (Colchester: University of Essex, 1979), pp. 47–52

____, 'Exotics or Provincials? Anglo-Irish Writers and the English Problem', in Wolfgang Zach and Heinz Kosok (eds), *Literary Interrelations: Ireland, England and the World,* 3 vols (Tübingen: Narr, 1987), III, pp. 35–40

Connell, Kenneth, *Irish Peasant Society* (Oxford: Clarendon Press, 1968)

Connolly, Claire, 'Irish Romanticism, 1800–1830', in Margaret Kelleher and Philip O'Leary (eds), *The Cambridge History of Irish Literature,* 2 vols (Cambridge: Cambridge University Press, 2006), I, pp. 407–48

____, 'Ugly Criticism: Union and Division in Irish Literature', *Field Day Review*, vol. 4 (2008), pp. 114–31

____, *A Cultural History of the Irish Novel, 1790–1829* (Cambridge: Cambridge University Press, 2012)

Corbett, Mary Jean, *Allegories of Union in Irish and English Writing, 1790–1870: Politics, History and the Family from Edgeworth to Arnold* (Cambridge: Cambridge University Press, 2000)

Corkery, Daniel, *Synge and Anglo-Irish Literature* ([1931]; Cork: Mercier Press, 1966)

Corporaal, Marguérite, Christopher Cusack and Lindsay Janssen (eds), *Recollecting Hunger: An Anthology. Cultural Memories of the Great Famine in Irish and British Fiction, 1847–1920* (Dublin: Irish Academic Press, 2012)

Coughlan, Patricia and Tina O'Toole (eds), *Irish Literature: Feminist Perspectives* (Dublin: Carysfort Press, 2008)

Croker, Thomas Crofton, *Researches in the South of Ireland: Illustrative of the Scenery, Architectural Remains, and the Manners and Superstitions of the Peasantry; With an Appendix Containing a Private Narrative of the Rebellion of 1798* (London: John Murray, 1824)

Cronin, John, *The Anglo-Irish Novel, Volume I: The Nineteenth Century* (Belfast: Appletree Press, 1980)

____, 'The Nineteenth Century: A Retrospect', in Augustine Martin (ed.), *The Genius of Irish Prose* (Cork: Mercier Press, 1984), pp. 10–21

Curtis, L.P., Jr., *Anglo-Saxons and Celts* (Bridgeport, Connecticut: University of Bridgeport, 1968)

____, *Apes and Angels* (Newton Abbot: David & Charles, 1971)

Davie, Donald, *The Heyday of Sir Walter Scott* (London: Routledge, 1961)

Deane, Seamus, 'National Character and National Audience: Race, Crowds and Readers', in Michael Allen and Angela Wilcox (eds), *Critical Approaches to Anglo-Irish Literature* (Gerrards Cross: Colin Smythe, 1989), pp. 40–52

____, 'The Production of Cultural Space in Irish Writing', *boundary 2*, vol. 21, no. 2 (Autumn 1994), pp. 117–44

____, *Strange Country: Modernity and Nationhood in Irish Writing since 1790* (Oxford: Clarendon Press, 1997)

de Beaumont, Gustave, *Ireland: Social, Political, and Religious* ([1839]; Cambridge, Massachusetts: Harvard University Press, 2006)

de Bovet, Marie Anne, *Three Months' Tour in Ireland* (London: Chapman & Hall, 1891)

de Tocqueville, Alexis, *Alexis de Tocqueville's Journey in Ireland, July–August, 1835* (Washington, DC: Catholic University of America Press, 1990)

D'hoker, Elke, Raphaël Ingelbien and Hedwig Schwall (eds), *Irish Women Writers: New Critical Perspectives* (New York: Peter Lang, 2010)

Donnelly, Brian, 'Inventing a Voice: Irish Fiction from 1800', *The Harp*, vol. 15 (2000), pp. 65–74

Donnelly, James S., 'Pastorini and Captain Rock: Millenarianism and Sectarianism in the Rockite Movement of 1821–4', in Samuel Clark and James S. Donnelly (eds), *Irish Peasants: Violence and Political Unrest, 1780–1914* (Madison, Wisconsin: University of Wisconsin Press, 1983), pp. 102–39

____, *Captain Rock: The Irish Agrarian Rebellion of 1821–1824* (Madison, Wisconsin: University of Wisconsin Press, 2009)

Douglas, Aileen, '"Whom Gentler Stars Unite": Fiction and Union in the Irish Novel', *Irish University Review*, vol. 41, no. 1 (Spring 2011), pp. 183–95

Dowling, P.J., *The Hedgeschools of Ireland* ([1935]; Cork: Mercier Press, 1968)

Dunne, Tom, 'Haunted by History: Irish Romantic Writing, 1800–1850', in Roy Porter and Mikuláš Teich (eds), *Romanticism in National Context* (Cambridge: Cambridge University Press, 1988), pp. 68–91

Eagleton, Terry, *Heathcliff and the Great Hunger* (London: Verso, 1995)

____, *Scholars and Rebels in Nineteenth-Century Ireland* (Oxford: Blackwell, 1999)

Earls, Brian, 'Supernatural Legends in Nineteenth-Century Irish Writing', *Béaloideas*, vols 60/61 (1992/3), pp. 93–141

Ervine, St John, *Some Impressions of My Elders* (London: Allen and Unwin, 1923)

Faragó, Borbála and Moynagh Sullivan (eds), *Facing the Other: Interdisciplinary Studies on Race, Gender and Social Justice in Ireland* (Newcastle upon Tyne: Cambridge Scholars, 2008)

Fegan, Melissa, *Literature and the Irish Famine, 1845–1919* (Oxford: Oxford University Press, 2002)

Ferguson, Samuel, 'A Dialogue between the Head and Heart of an Irish Protestant', *Dublin University Magazine*, vol. 2, no. 11 (November 1833), pp. 586–93

Ferris, Ina, 'Writing on the Border: The National Tale, Female Writing, and the Public Sphere', in Tilottama Rajan and Julia M. Wright (eds), *Romanticism, History and the Possibilities of Genre: Re-Forming Literature, 1789–1837* (Cambridge: Cambridge University Press, 1998), pp. 86–106

____, *The Romantic National Tale and the Question of Ireland* (Cambridge: Cambridge University Press, 2002)

____, 'The Irish Novel, 1800–1829', in Richard Maxwell and Katie Trumpener (eds), *The Cambridge Companion to Fiction in the Romantic Period* (Cambridge: Cambridge University Press, 2008), pp. 235–49

Fierobe, Claude, 'The Big House and the Fantastic: From Architecture to Literature', in Bruce Stewart (ed.), *That Other World: The Supernatural and Fantastic in Irish Literature and its Contexts,* 2 vols (Gerrards Cross: Colin Smythe, 1998), I, pp. 256–65

Flanagan, Thomas, *The Irish Novelists, 1800–1850* (New York: Columbia University Press, 1959)

____, 'Literature in English, 1800–91', in W.E. Vaughan (ed.), *A New History of Ireland, V: Ireland Under the Union, I, 1801–1870* (Oxford: Clarendon Press, 1989), pp. 483–552

Fogarty, Anne, 'Irish Women Novelists, 1800–1940', *Colby Quarterly*, vol. 36, no. 2 (June 2000), pp. 81–5

Foley, Tadhg and Seán Ryder (eds), *Ideology and Ireland in the Nineteenth Century* (Dublin: Four Courts Press, 1998)

Foster, John Wilson, *Forces and Themes in Ulster Fiction* (Dublin: Gill & Macmillan, 1974)

____, (ed.), *The Cambridge Companion to the Irish Novel* (Cambridge: Cambridge University Press, 2006)

____, *Irish Novels, 1890–1940: New Bearings in Culture and Fiction* (Oxford: Oxford University Press, 2008)

Foster, R.F., *Paddy and Mr. Punch* (London: Allen Lane, 1993), pp. 262–80

____, *The Irish Story: Telling Tales and Making It Up in Ireland* (London: Allen Lane, 2001), pp. 113–26

Foster, Sally, 'Irish Wrong: Samuel Lover and the Stage Irishman', *Éire-Ireland*, vol. 13, no. 4 (Winter 1978), pp. 34–44

Franklin, Caroline, 'Romantic Patriotism as Feminist Critique of Empire: Helen Maria Williams, Sydney Owenson and Germaine de Staël', in Sarah Knott and Barbara Taylor (eds), *Women, Gender and Enlightenment* (Basingstoke: Palgrave Macmillan, 2005), pp. 51–64

Frehner, Ruth, *The Colonizer's Daughters: Gender in the Anglo-Irish Big House Novel* (Tübingen: Franacke, 1999)

Frierson, William C., 'The English Controversy over Realism in Fiction, 1885–1895', *PMLA*, vol. 43, no. 2 (June 1928), pp. 533–50

Gahan, Peter, 'Introduction: Bernard Shaw and the Irish Literary Tradition', *SHAW: The Annual of Bernard Shaw Studies*, vol. 30 (2010), pp. 1–26

Garvin, Tom, 'Priests and Patriots: Irish Separatism and Fear of the Modern, 1890–1914', *Irish Historical Studies*, vol. 25, no. 97 (May 1986), pp. 67–81

Geary, Lawrence and Margaret Kelleher (eds), *Nineteenth-Century Ireland: A Guide to Recent Research* (Dublin: University College Dublin Press, 2005)

Genet, Jacqueline, *The Big House: Reality and Representation* (Dingle: Brandon, 1991)

Gibbons, Luke, *Gaelic Gothic: Race, Colonization and Irish Culture* (Dublin: Arlen House, 2004)

____, 'Romantic Ireland, 1750–1845', in James Chandler (ed.), *The Cambridge History of English Romantic Literature* (Cambridge: Cambridge University Press, 2009), pp. 182–203

Gilmartin, Sophie, *Ancestry and Narrative in Nineteenth-Century British Literature: Blood Relations from Edgeworth to Hardy* (Cambridge: Cambridge University Press, 1998)

Gray, Peter (ed.), *Victoria's Ireland? Irishness and Britishness, 1837–1901* (Dublin: Four Courts Press, 2004)

Guinness, Selina '"Protestant Magic" Reappraised: Evangelism, Dissent and Theosophy', *Irish University Review*, vol. 33, no. 1 (Spring–Summer 2003), pp. 14–27

Gwynn, Stephen, *Irish Books and Irish People* (Dublin: Talbot Press, n.d. [1919])

____, *Irish Literature and Drama in the English Language: A Short History* (London: Nelson, 1936)

Hall, Wayne E., *Dialogues in the Margin: A Study of the 'Dublin University Magazine'* (Gerrards Cross: Colin Smythe, 2000)

Hand, Derek, *The Irish Novel* (Cambridge: Cambridge University Press, 2011)

Hansson, Heidi (ed.), *New Contexts: Re-Framing Nineteenth-Century Irish Women's Prose* (Cork: Cork University Press, 2008)

Harmon, Maurice, 'Aspects of the Peasantry in Anglo-Irish Literature from 1800 to 1916', *Studia Hibernica*, vol. 15 (1975), pp. 105–27

Harvey, Alison, 'Irish Aestheticism in Fin-de-Siècle Women's Writing: Art, Realism, and the Nation', *Modernism/Modernity*, vol. 21, no. 3 (September 2014), pp. 805–26

Haslam, Richard, '"Broad Farce and Thrilling Tragedy": Mangan's Fiction and Irish Gothic', *Éire-Ireland*, vol. 41, nos 3 & 4 (Fall/Winter 2006), pp. 215–44

____, 'Irish Gothic', in Catherine Spooner and Emma McEvoy (eds), *Routledge Companion to Gothic* (London: Routledge, 2007), pp. 83–94

Hayley, Barbara, '"The Eerishers are Marchin": British Critical Receptions of Nineteenth-Century Anglo-Irish Fiction', in Wolfgang Zach and Heinz Kosok (eds), *Literary Interrelations: Ireland, England and the World,* 3 vols (Tübingen: Narr, 1987), I, pp. 39–50

____, and Enda McKay (eds), *Three Hundred Years of Irish Periodicals* (Dublin: Association of Irish Learned Journals, 1987)

____, 'Religion and Society in Nineteenth-Century Fiction', in Robert Welch (ed.), *Irish Writers and Religion* (Gerrards Cross: Colin Smythe, 1992), pp. 32–42

Hennig, John, 'Jean Paul and Ireland', *Modern Language Review*, vol. 40, no. 3 (July 1945), pp. 190–96

____, 'The Brothers Grimm and Thomas Crofton Croker', *Modern Language Review*, vol. 41 (1946), pp. 44–54

____, 'Contes Irlandais', *Modern Language Review*, vol. 42, no. 2 (April 1947), pp. 237–42

____, 'Dickens and Ireland', *Irish Monthly*, vol. 75, no. 888 (June 1947), pp. 248–55

Hirsch, Edward, 'The Imaginary Irish Peasant', *PMLA*, vol. 106, no. 5 (October 1991), pp. 1116–33

Hogan, Patrick Colm, 'Ireland, Colonialism and the Fancy of Difference: A Tale', *College Literature*, vol. 23, no. 3 (October 1996), pp. 178–88

Hooper, Glenn, 'The Wasteland: Writing and Resettlement in Post-Famine Ireland', *Canadian Journal of Irish Studies*, vol. 23, no. 2 (December 1997), pp. 55–76

____, *Travel Writing and Ireland, 1760–1860: Culture, History, Politics* (Basingstoke: Palgrave Macmillan, 2005)

____, 'The Isles/Ireland: The Wilder Shores', in Peter Hulme and Tim Youngs (eds), *The Cambridge Companion to Travel Writing* (Cambridge: Cambridge University Press, 2002), pp. 174–90

____, and Úna Ní Bhroiméil, 'Introduction', in Glenn Hooper and Úna Ní Bhroiméil (eds), *Land and Landscape in Nineteenth-Century Ireland* (Dublin: Four Courts Press, 2008), pp. 9–12

Huber, Werner, 'Irish Novels in a German Court Library in the Early Nineteenth Century', in Toshi Furamoto et al. (eds), *International Aspects of Irish Literature* (Gerrards Cross: Colin Smythe, 1996), pp. 37–44

Hutchinson, John, *The Dynamics of Cultural Nationalism: The Gaelic Revival and the Creation of the Irish Nation State* (London: Allen & Unwin, 1987)

Hutton, Clare, '"The Promise of Literature in the Coming Days": The Best Hundred Irish Books Controversy of 1886', *Victorian Literature and Culture*, vol. 39, no. 2 (2011), pp. 581–92

Ingelbien, Raphael, 'Elizabeth Gaskell's "The Poor Clare" and the Irish Famine', *Irish University Review*, vol. 40, no. 2 (2010), pp. 1–19

Inglis, Henry D., *Ireland in 1834: A Journey throughout Ireland during the Spring, Summer, and Autumn of 1834* (London: Whittaker, 1835)

Johansen, Ib, 'Shadows in a Black Mirror: Reflections on the Irish Fantastic from Sheridan Le Fanu to John Banville', *Nordic Irish Studies*, vol. 1 (2002), pp. 51–61

Johnson, Alan, 'The Ghost of the Irish Famine in J.G. Farrell's *The Siege of Krishnapur*', *The Journal of Commonwealth Literature*, vol. 46, no. 2 (June 2011), pp. 275–92

Johnston, John I.D., 'Hedge Schools of Tyrone and Monaghan', *Clogher Record*, vol. 7, no. 1 (1969), pp. 34–55

Kelleher, Margaret, 'Irish Famine in Literature', in Cathal Póirtéir (ed.), *The Great Irish Famine* (Cork: Mercier Press, 1995), pp. 232–47

____, *The Feminization of Famine: Expressions of the Inexpressible?* (Cork: Cork University Press, 1997)

____, and James H. Murphy (eds), *Gender Perspectives in Nineteenth-Century Ireland: Public and Private Spheres* (Dublin: Irish Academic Press, 1997)

____, 'Introduction: Women's Fiction, 1845–1900', in Angela Bourke et al. (eds), *Field Day Anthology of Irish Writing* (Cork University Press/Field Day, 2002), vol. 5, pp. 924–30

____, and Philip O'Leary (eds), *The Cambridge History of Irish Literature,* 2 vols (Cambridge: Cambridge University Press, 2006)

____, 'Prose Writing and Drama in English, 1830–1890', in Margaret Kelleher and Philip O'Leary (eds), *The Cambridge History of Irish Literature*, 2 vols (Cambridge: Cambridge University Press, 2006), I, pp. 449–99

____, 'Writing Irish Women's Literary History', *Irish Studies Review*, vol. 9, no. 1 (April 2001), pp. 5–14

Kelly, Jim (ed.), *Ireland and Romanticism: Publics, Nations and Scenes of Cultural Production* (Basingstoke: Palgrave Macmillan, 2011)

Kelly, John S., 'The Fall of Parnell and the Rise of Irish Literature: An Investigation', *Anglo-Irish Studies*, vol. 2 (1976), pp. 1–23

Kelsall, Malcolm, *Literary Representations of the Irish Country House: Civilization and Savagery under the Union* (Basingstoke: Palgrave Macmillan, 2003)

Kenny, Kevin (ed.), *Ireland and the British Empire* (Oxford: Oxford University Press, 2004)

Keogh, Dáire and Kevin Whelan (eds), *Acts of Union: The Courses, Contexts and Consequences of the Act of Union* (Dublin: Four Courts Press, 2001)

Kiberd, Declan, *Inventing Ireland* (London: Cape, 1995)

____, *Irish Classics* (London: Granta, 2000)

Kickham, Lisbeth, *Protestant Women Novelists and Irish Society, 1879–1922* (Lund: Lund University Press, 2004)

Kilfeather, Siobhán, 'Sex and Sensation in the Nineteenth-Century Novel', in Claire Connolly (ed.), *Theorizing Ireland* (Basingstoke: Palgrave Macmillan, 2003), pp. 105–13

____, 'Terrific Register: The Gothicization of Atrocity in Irish Romanticism', *boundary 2*, vol. 31, no. 1 (Spring 2004), pp. 49–71

Killeen, Jarlath, *Gothic Ireland: Horror and the Irish Anglican Imagination in the Long Eighteenth Century* (Dublin: Four Courts Press, 2005)

____, *The Emergence of Irish Gothic: History, Origins, Theories* (Edinburgh: Edinburgh University Press, 2014)

Kinzer, Bruce L., *England's Disgrace? J.S. Mill and the Irish Question* (Toronto: University of Toronto Press, 2001)

Kirkpatrick, Kathryn (ed.), *Border Crossings: Irish Women Writers and National Identities* (Tuscaloosa: University of Alabama Press, 2000)

Kosok, Heinz, 'Anthologies of Anglo-Irish Literature, 1772–1986', *Irish University Review*, vol. 18, no. 2 (Autumn 1988), pp. 251–62

Krans, Horatio Sheafe, *Irish Life in Irish Fiction* (New York: Columbia University Press, 1903)

Kreilkamp, Vera, *The Anglo-Irish Novel and the Big House* (Syracuse: Syracuse University Press, 1998)

____, 'Fiction and Empire: The Irish Novel', in Kevin Kenny (ed.), *Ireland and the British Empire* (Oxford: Oxford University Press, 2004), pp. 123–53

Lane, Denny, 'The Irish Accent in English Literature', *Irish Monthly*, vol. 21, no. 237 (March 1893), pp. 151–6

Lane, Pádraig G., 'The Irish Agricultural Labourer in Folklore and Fiction', *Saothar*, vol. 28 (2003), pp. 79–89

____, 'Mapping the Money Lenders: Pre-Famine Dublin of Fiction', *Dublin Historical Record*, vol. 62, no. 1 (Spring 2009), pp. 98–102

Leary, Patrick, '*Fraser's Magazine* and the Literary Life, 1830–1847', *Victorian Periodicals Review*, vol. 27, no. 6 (Summer 1994), pp. 105–26

Leerssen, Joep, 'On the Treatment of Irishness in Romantic Anglo-Irish Fiction', *Irish University Review*, vol. 20, no. 2 (Autumn 1990), pp. 251–63

____, 'Fiction Poetics and Cultural Stereotype in Scott, Morgan, and Maturin', *Modern Language Review*, vol. 86, no. 2 (April 1991), pp. 273–84

____, A.H. van der Weel and Bart Westerweel (eds), *Forging in the Smithy: National Identity and Representation in Anglo-Irish Literary History* (Amsterdam: Rodopi, 1995)

____, *Remembrance and Imagination: Patterns in the Historical and Literary Representation of Ireland in the Nineteenth Century* (Cork: Cork University Press/Field Day, 1996)

Le Fanu, W.R., *Seventy Years of Irish Life* (London: Arnold, n.d.)

Lengel, Edward G., *The Irish through British Eyes: Perceptions of Ireland in the Famine Era* (Westport, Connecticut: Praeger, 2002)

Lister, T.H., 'Some Novels of Military and Naval Life', *Edinburgh Review*, no. 52 (August 1830), pp. 119–38

____, 'Novels Descriptive of Irish Life', *Edinburgh Review*, no. 52 (January 1831), pp. 410–31

Litvack, Leon and Colin Graham (eds), *Ireland and Europe in the Nineteenth Century* (Dublin: Four Courts Press, 2006)

Lloyd, David, *Nationalism and Minority Literature: James Clarence Mangan and the Emergence of Irish Cultural Nationalism* (Berkeley, California: University of California Press, 1987)

____, *Anomalous States: Irish Writing and the Post-Colonial Moment* (Dublin: The Lilliput Press, 1993)

Loeber, Rolf and Magda, with Anne Mullen Burnham, *Guide to Irish Fiction, 1650–1900* (Dublin: Four Courts Press, 2006)

Lozes, Jean, 'Aspects du Fantastiques Anglo-Irlandais chez Charles Robert Maturin, Gerald Griffin, William Carleton et Sheridan Le Fanu', *Littératures*, vol. 26 (1992), pp. 25–40

Lubbers, Klaus, 'Author and Audience in the Early Nineteenth Century', in Peter Connolly (ed.), *Literature and the Changing Ireland* (Gerrards Cross: Colin Smythe, 1982), pp. 25–36

____, 'Emancipatory Women in Late Nineteenth-Century Anglo-Irish Fiction: A Note on the Emergence of a Motif', *Canadian Journal of Irish Studies*, vol. 12, no. 1 (June 1986), pp. 53–58

____, 'Continuity and Change in Irish Fiction: The Case of the Big-House Novel', in Otto Rauchbauer (ed.), *Ancestral Voices: The Big House in Anglo-Irish Literature* (Dublin: The Lilliput Press, 1992), pp. 17–29

Lukács, Georg, *Studies in European Realism* (London: Hillway, 1950)

____, *The Historical Novel* (Harmondsworth: Peregrine, 1969)

____, *Writer and Critic* (London: Merlin Press, 1978)

Lyons, F.S.L., *Ireland Since the Famine* (London: Fontana, 1973, rev. ed.)

____, *Culture and Anarchy in Ireland, 1890–1939* (Oxford: Clarendon Press, 1979)

____, and R.A.J. Hawkins (eds), *Ireland under the Union: Varieties of Tensions. Essays in Honour of T.W. Moody* (Oxford: Clarendon Press, 1980)

Mac Curtain, Margaret, 'Pre-Famine Peasantry in Ireland: Definition and Theme', *Irish University Review*, no. 4 (Autumn 1974), pp. 188–98

MacDonagh, Oliver, *The Nineteenth-Century Novel and Irish Social History* (Dublin: National University of Ireland, 1970)

____, *Ireland: The Union and Its Aftermath* (London: Allen & Unwin, 1977)

____, *States of Mind* (London: Allen & Unwin, 1983)

MacDonagh, Thomas, *Literature in Ireland* (Dublin: The Talbot Press, 1916)

MacDowell, R.B. (ed.), *Social Life in Ireland, 1800–1845* (Cork: Mercier Press, 1963)

MacGrath, Kevin M., 'Writers in the *Nation*, 1842–5', *Irish Historical Studies*, vol. 6, no. 23 (Spring 1948), pp. 189–223

Maciuliwicz, Joanna, 'Dialogic Encounter of Cultures in *Castle Rackrent* and *The Absentee* by Maria Edgeworth and in *The Wild Irish Girl* by Lady Morgan', in Liliana Sikorska (ed.), *Ironies of Art/Tragedies of Life* (Frankfurt: Peter Lang, 2005), pp. 27–40

Madden-Simpson, Janet, 'Haunted Houses: The Image of the Anglo-Irish in Anglo-Irish Literature', in Wolfgang Zach and Heinz Kosok (eds), *Literary Interrelations: Ireland, England and the World*, 3 vols (Tübingen: Narr, 1987), III, pp. 41–6

Marcus, Philip, *Yeats and the Beginning of the Irish Renaissance* (Ithaca, NY: Cornell University Press, 1970)

Markey, Anne, 'The Discovery of Irish Folklore', *New Hibernia Review*, vol. 10, no. 4 (Winter 2006), pp. 21–43

Maume, Patrick, *The Long Gestation: Irish Nationalist Life, 1891–1918* (Dublin: Gill & Macmillan, 1999)

____, 'A Pastoral Vision: The Novels of Canon Joseph Guinan', *New Hibernia Review*, vol. 9, no. 4 (Winter 2005), pp. 79–98

Maurer, Sara L., *The Dispossessed State: Narratives of Ownership in Nineteenth-Century Britain and Ireland* (Baltimore: Johns Hopkins University Press, 2012)

McAteer, Michael, 'A Troubled Union: Representations of Eastern Europe in Nineteenth-Century Irish Protestant Literature', in Barbara Korte, Eva Ulricke Pirker and Sissy Helff (eds), *Facing the East in the West: Images of Eastern Europe in British Literature, Film and Culture* (Amsterdam: Rodopi, 2010), pp. 205–18

McCarthy, B.G., 'Irish Regional Novelists of the Early Nineteenth Century', *Dublin Magazine* (n.s.), vol. 21, no. 3 (July–September 1946 ), pp. 28–37

McCaw, Neil (ed.), *Writing Irishness in Nineteenth-Century British Culture* (Aldershot: Ashgate, 2003)

McKenna, Brian, *Irish Literature, 1800–1875: A Guide to Information Sources* (Detroit: Gale, 1978)

McNulty, Eugene, 'From *The Wild Irish Girl* to *A Royal Democrat*: Remembering the Future in the 1890s', *Canadian Journal of Irish Studies*, vol. 30, no. 1 (Spring 2004), pp. 32–40

Meaney, Gerardine, 'Identity and Opposition: Women's Writing, 1890–1960', in Angela Bourke et al. (eds), *Field Day Anthology of Irish Writing*, vol. 5 (Cork: Cork University Press/Field Day, 2002), pp. 976–80

____, *Gender, Ireland and Cultural Change: Race, Sex and Nation* (New York: Routledge, 2010)

Mercier, Vivian, *The Irish Comic Tradition* (Oxford: Oxford University Press, 1969)

____, 'English Readers: Three Historical "Moments"', in Okifumi Komesu and Masaru Sekine (eds), *Irish Writers and Politics* (Gerrards Cross: Colin Smythe, 1990), pp. 3–35

____, *Modern Irish Literature: Sources and Founders* (Oxford: Clarendon Press, 1994)

____, 'Literature in English, 1891–1921', in R.V. Comerford (ed.), *A New History of Ireland, Vol. VI: Ireland under the Union, II, 1870–1921* (Oxford: Clarendon Press, 1996), pp. 357–81

Moody, T.W., 'Thomas Davis and the Irish Nation', *Hermathena*, no. 103 (Autumn 1966), pp. 5–31

Moore, Lisa L., 'Acts of Union: Sexuality and Nationalism, Romance and Realism in the Irish National Tale', *Cultural Critique*, no. 44 (Winter 2000), pp. 113–44

Morash, Chris, *Writing the Irish Famine* (Oxford: Oxford University Press, 1995)

____, 'Literature, Memory, Atrocity', in Chris Morash and Richard Hayes (eds), *'Fearful Realities': New Perspectives on the Irish Famine* (Dublin: Irish Academic Press, 1996), pp. 110–18

Mossman, Mark, *Disability, Representation and the Body in Irish Writing, 1800–1922* (Basingstoke: Palgrave Macmillan, 2009)

Moynahan, Julian, *Anglo-Irish: The Literary Imagination in a Hyphenated Culture* (Princeton NJ: Princeton University Press, 1995)

M.R., 'Irish Writers of the Nineteenth Century', *Irish Monthly*, vol. 27, no. 314 (August 1899), pp. 423–6

Murphy, James H., *Catholic Fiction and Social Reality in Ireland, 1873–1922* (Westport, Connecticut: Greenwood, 1997)

____, *Abject Loyalty: Nationalism and Monarchy during the Reign of Queen Victoria* (Cork: Cork University Press, 2001)

____, *Ireland: A Social, Cultural and Literary History, 1791–1891* (Dublin: Four Courts Press, 2003)

____, 'Canonicity: The Literature of Nineteenth-Century Ireland', *New Hibernia Review*, vol. 7, no. 2 (Summer 2003), pp. 45–54

____, (ed.), *Evangelicals and Catholics in Nineteenth-Century Ireland* (Dublin: Four Courts Press, 2005)

____, 'Catholics and Fiction During the Union, 1801–1922', in John Wilson Foster (ed.), *Cambridge Companion to the Irish Novel* (Cambridge: Cambridge University Press, 2006), pp. 97–112

____, *Irish Novelists and the Victorian Age* (Oxford: Oxford University Press, 2011)

____, (ed.), *The Irish Book in English, 1800–1890* (Oxford: Oxford University Press, 2011)

____, 'Daniel O'Connell and the Catholic Lawyer in Irish Victorian Fiction', *New Hibernian Review*, vol. 17, no. 3 (Autumn 2013), pp. 119–26

Nakamura, Tetsuko, 'The Big House as a Problematic Space in Irish Fiction', *Journal of Irish Studies*, vol. 22 (2007), pp. 3–6

Nash, John (ed.), *James Joyce in the Nineteenth Century* (Cambridge: Cambridge University Press, 2013)

Nicholson, Asenath, *Ireland's Welcome to the Stranger* (London: Gilpin, 1847)

____, *Annals of the Famine in Ireland* (New York: French, 1851)

Nolan, Emer, *Catholic Emancipations: Irish Fiction from Thomas Moore to James Joyce* (Syracuse: Syracuse University Press, 2007)

Noonan, J.D., 'The Library of Thomas Davis', *Irish Book-Lover*, vol. 5, no. 3 (1913), pp. 37–41

Norris, Claire, 'The Big House: Space, Place and Identity in Irish Fiction', *New Hibernia Review*, vol. 8, no. 1 (Spring 2004), pp. 107–21

Nowlan, K.B., 'Agrarian Unrest in Ireland, 1800–1845', *University Review*, vol. 11, no. 6 (1959), pp. 7–16

Nugent, Joseph, 'The Sword and the Prayerbook: Ideals of Authentic Irish Manliness', *Victorian Studies*, vol. 50, no. 4 (Summer 2008), pp. 587–613

O'Brien, George. 'The Fictional Irishman, 1665–1850', *Studies*, vol. 66, no. 264 (Winter 1977), pp. 319–29

O'Brien, Peggy, *Writing Lough Derg: From William Carleton to Seamus Heaney* (Syracuse: Syracuse University Press, 2006)

O'Connell, Helen, 'Improved English: And the Silence of Irish', *Canadian Journal of Irish Studies,* vol. 30, no. 1 (Spring 2004), pp. 13–20

____, *Ireland and the Fiction of Improvement* (Oxford: Oxford University Press, 2006)

____, '"A Raking Pot of Tea": Consumption and Excess in Early Nineteenth-Century Ireland', *Literature and History*, vol. 21, no. 2 (Autumn 2012), pp. 32–47

O'Conor, Norreys Jephson, *Changing Ireland: Literary Backgrounds to the Irish Free State, 1889–1922* (Cambridge, Massachusetts: Harvard University Press, 1924)

Ó Corráin, Donnchadh and Tomás O'Riordan (eds), *Ireland, 1815–1870: Emancipation, Famine and Religion* (Dublin: Four Courts Press, 2011)

O'Dwyer, Riana, 'Introduction: Women's Narratives, 1800–1840', in Angela Bourke et al. (eds), *Field Day Anthology of Irish Writing*, vol. 5 (Cork: Cork University Press/Field Day, 2002), pp. 833–48

O'Faoláin, Seán, *King of the Beggars* ([1938]; Dublin: Figgis, 1970)

O'Farrell, Patrick, 'Whose Reality? The Irish Famine in History and Literature', *Historical Studies,* vol. 20, no. 78 (1982), pp. 1–13

Ó Gráda, Cormac, 'Literary Sources and Irish Economic History', *Studies*, vol. 80, no. 319 (Autumn 1991), pp. 290–9

Ó hÓgáin, Daithí, 'Folklore and Literature: 1700–1850', in Mary Daly and David Dickson (eds), *The Origins of Popular Culture and Literacy in Ireland: Language Change and Educational Development, 1700–1920* (Dublin: University College and Trinity College, 1990), pp. 1–14

O'Keefe, Declan, 'A Beacon in the Twilight: Matthew Russell, SJ and the *Irish Monthly*', *Studies,* vol. 99, no. 394 (Summer 2010), pp. 169–79

O'Leary, John, *How Irishmen Should Feel* (Dublin: Cahill, 1886)

O'Neill, Patrick, 'The Reception of German Literature in Ireland, 1750–1850', Part I, *Studia Hibernica*, vol. 16 (1976), pp. 122–39

——, 'The Reception of German Literature in Ireland, 1750–1850', Part II, *Studia Hibernica*, vols 17–18 (1977–8), pp. 91–106

——, 'Image and Reception: The German Fortunes of Maria Edgeworth, Lady Morgan, Thomas Moore, and Charles Maturin', *Canadian Journal of Irish Studies*, vol. 6, no. 1 (1980), pp. 36–49

O'Reilly, Vincent, 'Books from the Libraries of Wolfe Tone and William Sampson', *The Recorder*, vol. 2 (1924), pp. 5–15

Ó Síocháin, Séamas, *Social Thought on Ireland in the Nineteenth Century* (Dublin: University College Dublin Press, 2009)

O'Sullivan, Samuel, 'Modern Reformation in Ireland', *Blackwood's Magazine*, no. 26 (July 1829), pp. 84–96

——, 'Past and Present State of Literature in Ireland', *Dublin University Magazine*, no. 9 (March 1837), pp. 365–76

O'Toole, Tina, *The Irish New Woman* (Basingstoke: Palgrave Macmillan, 2013)

Ó Tuama, Seán, 'Stability and Ambivalence: Aspects of the Sense of Place and Religion in Irish Literature', in Joseph Lee (ed.), *Ireland: Towards a Sense of Place* (Cork: Cork University Press, 1985), pp. 21–33

Ó Tuathaigh, Gearóid, *Ireland Before the Famine* (Dublin: Gill & Macmillan, 1972)

Otway, Caesar, *Sketches in Ireland* (Dublin: Curry, 1828)

Rafroidi, Patrick, 'The Uses of Irish Myth in the Nineteenth Century', *Studies*, vol. 62, nos 247 & 248 (Autumn/Winter 1973), pp. 251–61

——, *Irish Literature in English: The Romantic Period (1789–1850)*, 2 vols (Gerrards Cross: Colin Smythe, 1980)

Rauchbauer, Otto, 'The Big House and Irish History: An Introductory Sketch', in Rauchbauer (ed.), *The Big House in Anglo-Irish Literature* (Dublin: The Lilliput Press, 1992), pp. 1–15

——, 'The Fluidity of Fact: The Big House, People's Perspective, and Folklore into Art', *Fabula*, vol. 40, nos 3–4 (January 1999), pp. 222–58

Regan, Stephen, 'The Celtic Spirit in Literature: Renan, Arnold, Wilde and Yeats', in Alan Marshall and Neil Sammells (eds), *Irish Encounters: Poetry, Politics and Prose since 1880* (Bath: Sulis Press, 1998), pp. 28–39

Reilly, Eileen, 'Rebel, Muse, and Spouse: The Female in '98 Fiction', *Éire-Ireland*, vol. 34, no. 2 (Summer 1999), pp. 135–54

Riordan, Maurice, 'Matthew Arnold and the Irish Revival', in Wolfgang Zach and Heinz Kosok (eds), *Literary Interrelations: Ireland, England and the World*, 3 vols (Tübingen: Narr, 1987), III, pp. 145–52

Ryle, Martin H., *Journeys in Ireland: Literary Travellers, Rural Landscapes, Cultural Relations* (Aldershot: Ashgate, 1999)

Sadleir, Michael, *Dublin University Magazine: Its History, Contents and Bibliography* (Dublin: Bibliographical Society of Ireland, 1938)

——, *XIXth Century Fiction: A Bibliographical Record*, 2 vols (London: Constable, 1951)

Sheeran, P.F., 'Some Aspects of Anglo-Irish Literature from Swift to Joyce', *Yearbook of English Studies*, vol. 13 (1983), pp. 97–115

Sloan, Barry, *The Pioneers of Anglo-Irish Fiction, 1800–1850* (Gerrards Cross: Colin Smythe, 1986)

Smart, Robert A. and Michael Hutcheson, '"Negative History" and Irish Gothic Literature: Persistence and Politics', *Anglophonia*, vol. 15 (2004), pp. 105–18

Smith, Angèle, 'Landscapes of Power in Nineteenth-Century Ireland', *Archaeological Dialogues*, vol. 5, no. 1 (1998), pp. 69–84

Smith, James M. (ed.), *Two Irish National Tales* (Boston: Houghton Mifflin, 2005)

Spence, Joseph, '"The Great Angelic Sin": The Faust Legend in Irish Literature, 1820–1900', *Bullán*, vol. 1, no. 2 (Autumn 1994), pp. 47–58

____, 'Allegories for a Protestant Nation: Irish Tory Historical Fiction, 1820–1850', *Religion and Literature*, vol. 28, nos 2/3 (Summer–Autumn 1996), pp. 59–78

Standlee, Whitney, *Erin's 'Revolting Daughters' and Britannia: The Fiction of Diasporic Irish Women in Britain, 1890–1916* (Liverpool: Liverpool University Press, 2011)

Stewart, Bruce, 'Anthologising Ireland: "Irish Literature" (1904) and Its Contexts', *Irish Review*, vol. 15 (Winter 1998), pp. 105–26

____, (ed.), *That Other World: The Supernatural and Fantastic in Irish Literature and its Contexts,* 2 vols (Gerrards Cross: Colin Smythe, 1998)

____, (ed.), *Hearts and Minds: Irish Culture and Society under the Act of Union* (Gerrards Cross: Colin Smythe, 2002)

Thuente, Mary Helen, 'Foreword', in W.B. Yeats (ed.), *Representative Irish Tales* (Gerrards Cross: Colin Smythe, 1979), pp. 7–20

____, 'Violence in Pre-Famine Ireland: The Testimony of Irish Folklore and Fiction', *Irish University Review*, vol. 15, no. 2 (Autumn 1985), pp. 129–47

____, 'The Literary Significance of the United Irishmen', in Michael Kenneally (ed.), *Irish Literature and Culture* (Gerrards Cross: Colin Smythe, 1992), pp. 35–54

____, *The Harp Re-Strung: The United Irishmen and the Rise of Irish Literary Nationalism* (Syracuse, NY: Syracuse University Press, 1994)

Tracy, Robert, 'Undead, Unburied: Anglo-Ireland and the Predatory Past', *LIT: Literature, Interpretation, Theory*, vol. 10, no. 1 (1999), pp. 13–33

____, '"The Cracked Looking-glass of a Servant": Inventing the Colonial Novel', in Shlomith Rimmon-Kennan, Leona Toker and Shuli Barzilai (eds), *Rereading Texts/Rethinking Critical Presuppositions: Essays in Honour of H.M. Daleski* (Frankfurt-am-Main: Peter Lang, 1997), pp. 197–212

Vance, Norman, 'Celts, Carthaginians, and Constitutions: Anglo-Irish Literary Relations, 1780–1820', *Irish Historical Studies*, vol. 22, no. 86 (March 1981), pp. 216–38

____, *Irish Literature: A Social History* (Oxford: Blackwell, 1990)

____, 'The Problems of Unionist Literature: Macauley, Froude and Lawless', in D. George Boyce and Alan O'Day (eds), *Defenders of the Union: A Survey of British and Irish Unionism Since 1801* (London: Routledge, 2001), pp. 176–87

Waters, Maureen, *The Comic Irishman* (Albany, New York: State University of New York Press, 1984)

Webb, Timothy, 'A "Great Theatre of Outrage and Disorder": Figuring Ireland in the *Edinburgh Review,* 1802–29', in Massimiliano Demata and Duncan Wu (eds), *British Romanticism and the* Edinburgh Review: *Bicentennial Essays* (Basingstoke: Palgrave Macmillan, 2002), pp. 58–81

Weekes, Ann Owens, *Irish Women Writers: An Uncharted Tradition* (Lexington, Kentucky: University Press of Kentucky, 1990)

Whelan, Kevin, 'Reading the Ruins: The Presence of Absence in the Irish Landscape', in Howard B. Clarke, Jacinta Prunty and Mark Hennessy (eds), *Surveying Ireland's Past: Multidisciplinary Essays in Honour of Anngret Simms* (Dublin: Geography, 2004), pp. 297–328

White, Terence de Vere, *The Road of Excess* (Dublin: Browne & Nolan, n.d.)

____, *The Parents of Oscar Wilde* (London: Hodder & Stoughton, 1967)

Williams, T. Desmond (ed.), *Secret Societies in Ireland* (Dublin: Gill & Macmillan, 1973)

Williams, William H.A. 'Into the West: Landscape and Imperial Imagination in Connemara, 1820–1870', *New Hibernia Review*, vol. 2, no. 1 (Spring 1998), pp. 69–90

Wohlgemut, Esther, '"What Do You Do with That at Home?": The Cosmopolitan Heroine and the National Tale', *European Romantic Review*, vol. 13, no. 2 (2002), pp. 191–7

Wolffe, John, *God and Greater Britain: Religion and National Life in Britain and Ireland, 1843–1945* (London: Routledge, 1994)

Wright, Julia M., *Ireland, India and Nationalism in Nineteenth-Century Literature* (Cambridge: Cambridge University Press, 2007)

____, (ed.), *Irish Literature, 1750–1900* (Oxford: Wiley-Blackwell, 2008)

____, 'Atlantic Exile and the Stateless Citizen in Irish Romanticism', *Wordsworth Circle*, vol. 40, no. 1 (2009), pp. 36–44

____, *Representing the National Landscape in Irish Romanticism* (Syracuse, NY: Syracuse University Press, 2014)

Yeats, W.B., 'The De-Anglicizing of Ireland', in John P. Frayne (ed.), *Uncollected Prose by W.B. Yeats: First Reviews and Articles, 1886–1896* (London: Macmillan, 1970), pp. 254–6

____, 'Nationality and Literature', in John P. Frayne (ed.), *Uncollected Prose by W.B. Yeats: First Reviews and Articles, 1886–1896* (London: Macmillan, 1970), pp. 266–75

____, 'Irish National Literature, I: From Callanan to Carleton', in John P. Frayne (ed.), *Uncollected Prose by W.B. Yeats: First Reviews and Articles, 1886–1896* (London: Macmillan, 1970), pp. 359–64

___, 'Irish National Literature, II: Contemporary Prose Writers', in John P. Frayne (ed.), *Uncollected Prose by W.B. Yeats: First Reviews and Articles, 1886–1896* (London: Macmillan, 1970), pp. 366–73

___, 'Irish National Literature, IV: A List of the Best Irish Books', in John P. Frayne (ed.), *Uncollected Prose by W.B. Yeats: First Reviews and Articles, 1886–1896* (London: Macmillan, 1970), pp. 382–7

___, *Explorations* (New York: Collier, 1973)

___, (ed.), *Representative Irish Tales* (Gerrards Cross: Colin Smythe, 1979)

___, *Prefaces and Introductions* (William H. O'Donnell, ed.) (New York: Macmillan, 1989)

___, *Letters to the New Island* (George Bornstein and Hugh Witemeyer, eds) (New York: Macmillan, 1989)

# Index